GRADE 4

Learn at Home

Reading, Language Skills,
Spelling, Math,
Science, Social Studies

School Specialty.
Publishing

Copyright © 2008 School Specialty Publishing. Published by American Education Publishing™, an imprint of School Specialty Publishing, a member of the School Specialty Family.

Send all inquiries to:
School Specialty Publishing
8720 Orion Place
Columbus, OH 43240-2111

ISBN 0-7696-8374-6

1 2 3 4 5 6 7 8 9 10 COU 13 12 11 10 09 08

Table of Contents

Welcome!

Congratulations on your decision to educate your child at home! Perhaps you are a bit nervous or overwhelmed by the task ahead of you. The *Learn at Home* curriculum will give you the resources and guidance you need to provide your child with the best fourth-grade education possible. This book is only a guide, however. You are encouraged to supplement your child's fourth-grade curriculum with other books, activities and resources that suit your situation and your child's interests.

Create an inviting learning environment for your child. It should be comfortable and attractive, yet a place in which your child can work without distractions. Your child's work area should include a desk or table for him/her, a chalkboard or dry-erase board, an easel, appropriate writing and art materials, a cozy area for reading (perhaps with pillows or a bean bag chair), a bulletin board for displaying work and shelves for books and storage. Collect blocks or other building toys, old magazines and a variety of small manipulatives for various activities. Hang a clock and a calendar in the room as well.

The Learn at Home Series

The Learn at Home series is an easy-to-use line of resource guides for parents who have chosen to teach their children at home. The series covers grades K through 6, one volume per grade level. Each book in the series is organized the same. An introductory section called **Background Information and Supporting Activities** provides general information and activity ideas for each area of the curriculum. This section is then followed by 36 weeks of instruction in six curricular areas. At the fourth-grade level, these areas include Reading, Language Skills, Spelling, Math, Science and Social Studies.

Each of the 36 weeks is then further divided into three sections: **Lesson Plans**, **Teaching Suggestions and Activities** and **Activity Sheets**. Each week's **Lesson Plans** include lessons and activity suggestions for all six curricular areas. Though divided into separate areas of the curriculum, many of these activities are actually cross-curricular in nature. The lesson plans are brief, but further explanations are often provided in the next section, **Teaching Suggestions and Activities**. This section generally contains background information, detailed directions for activities mentioned in the lesson plans, as well as a variety of suggestions for related activities and extensions. **Activity Sheets** round out each week's materials. These sheets are grouped by subject and arranged in the order in which they appear in the lesson plans. **Activity Sheets** are referred to by name and page number and are highlighted by **bold** print throughout this book. **Answer Keys** are provided for your convenience.

Background Information and Supporting Activities

Language, spelling and reading skills are all closely related. It is difficult—and often undesirable—to isolate these skills completely, given their inter-relatedness. Therefore, the lessons and activity suggestions in these three sections may often overlap.

 ## LANGUAGE SKILLS

The primary focus of the language skills curriculum of this book will be on handwriting, grammar and writing skills. Special attention is given to the writing process, which your child will learn and put into practice each week.

▶ HANDWRITING

Each weekly lesson plan includes suggestions for teaching and practicing handwriting. You may want to purchase alphabet desk tape or an alphabet chart to hang on the wall for your child's reference. These items can be found at most parent/teacher stores. Since there is more than one style of cursive handwriting, you should choose the one that is compatible with the printing style taught at younger grades. *See* **Let's Write!** (p. 20) as a guide to forming the letters of a traditional cursive handwriting style.

▶ GRAMMAR

Each week's lesson plan also provides activities for teaching grammar skills that will improve your child's ability to read and write. Listed below are the language skills typically taught in the fourth grade. You may wish to supplement your lesson plans with additional activities that focus on these skills.

Parts of speech: nouns (common and proper, singular and plural, subject nouns)
verbs (action and helping, correct verb forms)
adverbs and adjectives
prepositions
interjections

Dictionary skills: alphabetical order
guide words
abbreviations

Sentences: complete sentences
punctuation and capitalization
kinds of sentences (declarative, imperative, interrogative, exclamatory)
writing paragraphs
writing letters (friendly letters, business letters)

▶ WRITING

Each week's language lesson includes suggestions for engaging your child in meaningful writing activities. You may wish to use a writing lesson as an opportunity to stress a newly learned grammatical skill. While the focus of some writing activities will be correctness, others will encourage fluency. The writing lesson will usually be introduced on Monday so your child has all week to work through the writing process. Your child may not wish to take every story through the entire writing process. This will allow him/her to spend more than a week on selected stories or articles that have the most promise.

▶ THE WRITING PROCESS

Devote at least 30 minutes of each day to writing, whether it is creative writing or writing in other areas of the curriculum. The process of writing generally includes the steps listed below. These steps are not necessarily part of a linear sequence but rather a cycle.

Prewriting: Prewriting activities help prepare your child for a writing activity. They engage the child and get him/her thinking. Typical prewriting activities include brainstorming, reading literature, discussing a topic, going on a field trip, observing art, listening to music and webbing a topic.

Writing: Writing, or composing, is the rough draft stage of the writing process. Encourage your child to get all his/her ideas on a topic down on paper. At this stage, the emphasis is on fluency rather than accuracy—do not worry about mistakes. Always have your child date the drafts and save them in a writing folder.

Revision: First, have your child read the piece aloud to him/herself. Ask him/her to analyze whether the piece is fluent, interesting and stays on the topic. Then, have the child read the rough draft to one or more other people. Listeners can provide specific feedback about word choice, fluency, clarity and interest. Have your child make changes to the rough draft, making additions or deletions based on the comments offered. Questions to guide revision: *Is the main idea clear? Should anything be added or deleted? Do the words say what was intended? Should the sentence order be changed?*

Proofreading: You and your child proofread the revised piece for proper spelling, capitalization and grammar.

Publishing: Your child copies the corrected proof in an appropriate format. He/she may add illustrations. The piece is now ready to be shared with others.

There are plenty of interesting activities that will engage your child in writing. For instance, ask your child to keep a diary or a journal (personal or on a specific topic, such as science). Offer suggested writing topics only occasionally—let your child write about anything. You might also wish to have your child write and send a personal note each week to a parent, grandparent, other relative or friend. The note could include a description of what the child learned that week. Finally, have your child write stories or captions based on photos mounted on sheets of writing paper. Ask him/her to write about the picture. Provide photos on a regular basis. Keep the accumulated pictures and writing in a three-ring binder.

You may also want to establish a writing center for your child. Provide materials and topics for writing.

a. Place pictures in a folder marked "Story Starter Pictures." Ask your child to choose a picture, then write about it. Use pictures from magazines and ads, as well as family photographs. Continually update the file.

b. Keep a changing supply of books in the writing center. The books may be nonfiction, to motivate your child to write a report about an interesting topic, or children's literature to spark creative ideas for a fantastic, make-believe story.

c. Provide examples of a variety of poems (limericks, haiku, quatrains, free verse) from works of well-liked poets. Have your child use one of the poems as a model and write an original poem.

d. Introduce your child to the following eight types of writing: autobiography, biography, essay, fiction, interview, report (event, trip, how to). Write each category of writing on an index card. On the back of each card, copy the outlines shown on the next page. Encourage your child to use these cards as guides when writing.

Finally, create a quarterly literary magazine for publishing your child's best poems, stories, articles and essays. Each week, ask your child to select a written piece to save for the magazine. When there is a large collection, edit and arrange the pieces to form an interesting magazine. Your child may want to supplement the pieces with pictures, creative ads, puzzles, riddles and editorials. Send copies to relatives and friends.

5

Autobiography

I. Facts about yourself
   A. Name
   B. Age and date of birth
   C. Place of birth
II. Family
   A. Family members
   B. Something you want to
      tell about your family
III. An interesting event in your life
   A. Description of the event
   B. Feelings about the event
IV. Opinions
   A. Likes and dislikes
   B. Something you especially
      enjoy doing
   C. Hobbies

Biography

I. Identification
   A. Name of the subject of
      the biography
   B. Reasons for choosing this
      particular person
II. Factual information
   A. Date of birth (and death)
   B. Place of birth
   C. Family information
III. What makes this person famous?
IV. Things to know about the
    person
   A. An important event
   B. Hobbies and interests
   C. Likes and dislikes

Essay

I. What is the topic?
II. What is your opinion about
    the topic?
   A. Positive
   B. Negative
III. Explanation of why you feel
     this way
IV. Changes
   A. Would you make changes?
   B. What would you change and
      how would you go about
      making the changes?
   C. Why?

Fiction

I. Introduction
   A. Name the main characters
   B. Describe the characters
   C. Describe the setting
II. Plot development—beginning
   A. What happened first?
   B. Introduce problem or conflict
III. Plot development—middle
   A. List the main events
   B. How did the situation
      develop?
IV. Plot development—end
   A. How did the story end?
   B. Cover the events leading to
      the solution of the problem
   C. Conclusion

Interview

I. Identification
   A. Name of interviewee
   B. Job or occupation of
      the interviewee
II. Job description
   A. Responsibilities
   B. Best aspects of job
III. Personal information
   A. Hobbies
   B. Favorite things: books,
      TV shows, movies, foods,
      places to visit, etc.
IV. Opinions on various subjects

Report (Event)

I. Introduction
   A. What was the event?
   B. Where did it take place?
   C. When did it take place?
II. Involvement
   A. Who witnessed this event?
   B. How were you involved?
III. Description
   A. What happened first?
   B. What happened next?
   C. How did it end?
   D. What are the lasting
      consequences of this event?
IV. Reaction
   A. How do you feel about it?
   B. What is your opinion?

Report (Trip)

I. Introduction
   A. Where did you go?
   B. When did you go and for
      how long?
   C. How did you get there?
   D. With whom did you go?
   E. Why did you go?
II. Explanation
   A. What did you do?
   B. What did you see?
III. Opinions
   A. What was the best part of
      the trip? the worst?
   B. What was the most unusual
      thing that happened?
   C. Do you recommend the trip?

Report (How to…)

I. Identification
   A. What are the directions for?
   B. What will be the final
      product or outcome?
II. Materials
   A. What materials are needed?
   B. Where can you get these
      materials?
III. Directions
   *List and number specific
   directions, step by step*
IV. Value of project
   A. Why did you choose this
      project?
   B. How can it be used?

SPELLING

▶ SPELLING LISTS

Each weekly lesson plan contains a list of fifteen or sixteen vocabulary words for your child to learn. Review weeks are the only exceptions—spelling lists for Weeks 9, 18, 27 and 36 are generated by you and your child based on words from previous weeks' lists that need to be reviewed. The best method for teaching spelling is to test first, allow your child to study the misspelled words, then test again. Therefore, Monday's lesson is always a pretest. Ask your child to correct his/her own test under your direction. During the week, he/she should study and practice only the misspelled words. This will make the assignments for the week more meaningful. Adding personalized words to the list will make the assignments even more meaningful to your child. After he/she has taken the pretest, determine how many personalized words you can add to his/her study list. Take words from other areas of the curriculum and from your child's own writing.

▶ BUILDING SPELLING SKILLS

Repeating spelling words during the week will help your child memorize words for a test, but it will not help him/her retain the words for the long term. The most effective technique for retaining accurate spelling is to use the words in context. Each week, engage your child in a writing activity using the spelling words. Steady exposure to words through reading also improves spelling ability.

Teach your child the following study method: *Look at the word and say it to yourself. Then, close your eyes. Try to envision the word as you spell it to yourself. Check to see if you were right. (If not, start over.) Cover up the word and try to write it. Check to see if you were right. (If not, start over.) Repeat two more times.* Also use study activities that involve visual, auditory and kinesthetic modalities. Engaging the child's many different intelligences will help him/her retain information. Consider using music, physical activity and art for practicing words.

▶ WORD BANK

Provide your child with a stack of index cards and a file box for maintaining a word bank throughout the year. Have the child record spelling words (one word per card) and file them alphabetically. Add words from the spelling lists each Friday. Add misspelled words that are found in his/her writing and challenging words from other curricular areas.

▶ WEEKLY SPELLING PLAN

Follow the schedule below for each week's spelling lessons.

Monday

- Give a pretest of the word list. Read the word, use it in a sentence and read the word again.

- Have your child correct his/her own pretest. Read the word aloud and spell it as the child touches each letter. Ask your child to make a checkmark next to each word that is spelled correctly and circle each word that is misspelled. After you have gone through the list, have your child write each misspelled word correctly next to the incorrect spelling. These words will comprise the study list for the week.

- Add words to the list from your child's written work or from other curriculum areas. Keep the list at sixteen or fewer words. Have your child copy the study list twice: once for him/herself and a second time for your records.

- Discuss any spelling rules that apply to the words in the list.

Tuesday–Thursday

- Have your child spend 10 to 15 minutes each day studying the spelling words. Engage him/her in activities that are motivating and meaningful. Choose a variety of activities that reinforce the concepts and methods mentioned above. You will find activity suggestions in the lesson plans, as well as on pages 7 and 8.

Friday

- Administer a final test of the words studied this week. Add a few words from previous lists to the final test to assess whether your child has retained the correct spelling. Do not tell your child in advance which review words you will add to the final test.

- Correct the test. Any misspelled words should be noted and added to future study lists.

▶ SPELLING ACTIVITIES

The following list of activities can be used with or adapted to just about any word list. Use a variety of activities in your teaching to keep your child challenged and motivated. (Unless otherwise noted, activity directions are written for your child.)

1. Alphabetize the list of words.

2. Write original sentences using all the words on the list.

3. Categorize the words by parts of speech.

4. Write a story using the spelling words. Then, underline the spelling words.

5. Look up each word in the dictionary. Copy some dictionary information in the word bank.

6. Write words that rhyme with the spelling words.

7. Make up a mnemonic device to help remember a difficult spelling.
   Example: geography—George Elliott's old grandmother rode a pig home yesterday.

8. *Parent:* Write sentences on the chalkboard using the spelling words. Erase the spelling words in each sentence. *Child:* Read the sentences and write in the missing words, spelled correctly.

9. Type each spelling word three times on a typewriter or computer.

10. **Stamp pad spelling:** You will need a stamp pad, a pencil with a new eraser and unlined paper. Choose a spelling word. Say the word. Write the word in large letters on your paper. Press your pencil eraser onto the stamp pad. Print dots with your eraser, tracing each letter. Read and spell the completed word. Repeat for each spelling word.

11. **Clap-tap spelling:** Choose a spelling word. Say the word. Look at the word and decide which letters are consonants. Clap when you say these letters. Decide which letters are vowels. Tap on your knee when you say these letters. Spell out the word, clapping for each consonant and tapping for each vowel. Say the word again. Repeat three times with the same word. Repeat the activity with other spelling words.

12. **Colored vowels:** You will need a pencil, paper and crayons (colored pencils or markers will also work). Choose a spelling word. Say the word and write it in pencil on your paper. Look at the word and decide which letters are vowels. Using one crayon, trace each vowel in the word. Repeat for each spelling word.

13. **Decorate it:** You will need drawing paper, a pencil and crayons (colored pencils or markers will also work). Choose a spelling word. Write it neatly at the top and bottom of the paper. In the center of the paper, write the word in large letters. You may write it fancy, doodle it, decorate it or use the letters to make a picture. Repeat for each word.

14. **Silly Sybil Game:** The object of this game is to acquire the syllables needed to form spelling words. *Preparation:* On index cards, write all the syllables from the spelling words, one syllable per card. On one card, draw a picture of Silly Sybil (any silly female face). *Play:* Deal the cards evenly among the players. Players look at the cards in their hands. If they have syllables that combine to form a spelling word, they lay them out for their opponents to see and check. The first player takes a card from any opponent's hand. If it combines with syllables in his/her own hand to form a word, the player lays the word down for his/her opponents to check. Players take turns choosing a card from an opponent's hand, attempting to acquire syllables to form spelling words. Play continues until all the words have been formed. Players count the number of cards they have that form words. Each card is worth one point. The player who has Silly Sybil adds five points to his/her score. The player with the highest score wins.

15. **Charades:** Act out spelling words for others to guess. To act out a word, first indicate the number of syllables in the word by holding up that number of fingers and tapping that number of times on the inside of your arm. The word may be acted out by syllables or as a whole. If the word is acted out by syllables, indicate which syllable by holding up that number of fingers and tapping the arm again.

16. **Add a letter:** *Parent:* Assign each letter of the alphabet a numerical value. *Child:* Choose a spelling word. Write the word neatly in large letters. Under each letter, write the assigned value. Add the values and write the sum of the word. Repeat for each spelling word.

17. **Guide words:** You will need a dictionary, a pencil and lined paper. Write your spelling words on lined paper. Look up a spelling word in the dictionary. Write the guide words from the top of the dictionary page on the line following the spelling word. Repeat for the rest of the week's spelling words.

18. **Word shapes:** You will need grid paper, a crayon and a pencil. Choose a spelling word. Write the word in the squares of the grid paper. Each letter should take up one or two squares of the grid. For example, a lowercase *a* will fill one box and a lowercase *h* will fill two boxes. Trace the boxes of the finished word. On a separate sheet of grid paper, color an identical shape. Repeat for each spelling word. Cut the grid paper around the words and word shapes. Match each word with the appropriate word shape. *See* diagram A below.

19. **Acrostic:** Choose a spelling word. Write it vertically on a sheet of paper. Underline each letter. Look at the first letter. Think of words that begin with this letter. Choose one of the words to begin a sentence. Look at the next letter. Think of words that begin with this letter. Choose one of the words to continue the sentence you began with the first letter. Continue with each letter of the word until you have written a silly sentence. Repeat for each of your spelling words.

Example: inside—<u>i</u>f
                    <u>n</u>o one
                    <u>s</u>ays
                    <u>i</u>ce cream
                    <u>d</u>on't
                    <u>e</u>at

A.   eight

20. **Spelling stairs:** You will need grid paper and a pencil. Choose a spelling word. Say the word. Write the first letter of the spelling word in a box on the first line. On the second line, directly below the first letter, write the first and second letters of the word in two boxes. Write the first, second and third letters of the word in three boxes on the third line. Write the first, second, third and fourth letters of the word in four boxes on the fourth line. Continue until the full word is written. You have made a staircase out of this word. Count how many steps make up this staircase and write the number at the top of the steps. Repeat the procedure to make steps out of the rest of the words.

21. **Texture writing:** "Write" words in a pan containing sand or salt.

22. **Clay:** Roll a ball of modeling clay in the palms of your hands. Flatten the ball on a paper plate. Write a spelling word on the smooth clay with your pencil. Erase the word with your finger. Write the rest of your words in the same manner. Alternative: Roll the dough into small, thin "snakes." Use these to form assigned words in cursive.

23. **Fine print:** Look through newspapers for current spelling words. Highlight or cut out the words.

READING

Teach reading through books that fit your child's abilities and interests. Use a basal reader or a variety of books from a bookstore or library. You will find a book suggestion in each week's lesson plan. The suggested books are age-appropriate and of the highest quality, but you are also encouraged to choose other literature that may better suit your child's interests and abilities. Reading a wide variety of literature, including fantasy, adventure, biography and poetry, is highly recommended. There is so much great literature for children available today. Find the latest titles and instill the joy of reading in your child.

▶ SILENT READING AND READING ALOUD

Set aside 15 to 30 minutes each day for your child to read silently. Let him/her choose which book to read. Silent reading time should be a time to read for pleasure. Do not evaluate your child at this time. On the other hand, do not avoid talking about the book. Read books aloud to your child that are at a higher level than his/her independent reading level. This will spark interest in various topics and motivate him/her to improve. Read-aloud time is very special and can continue even after your child is reading independently. Some parents continue reading aloud well into the middle school years. For more on this subject, see *The Read-Aloud Handbook* by Jim Trelease. You may also want to use this time to do some recreational reading, as well.

▶ READING SKILLS

Teach your child a variety of reading skills. Skills necessary for successful reading and general learning include:

- critical analysis
- following directions
- vocabulary building
- classification
- listening comprehension

Skills that build a child's comprehension ability include:

- recognizing the main idea
- character analysis
- recalling details
- similarities and differences
- identifying the problem
- sequencing

Skills that build a child's interpretive ability include:

- recognizing fact and opinion
- drawing conclusions
- evaluating
- interpreting facts
- critical thinking
- determining cause and effect
- predicting outcomes

Many of these reading skills have already been introduced in the earlier grades. Mastery of these skills will help your child become a strategic, independent reader. When you notice yourself using one of these skills in your own reading, call attention to it. Talk about how you used the skill.

▶ WEEKLY READING PLAN

In general, follow these three steps when reading a text. Note that not all steps apply to each book.

1. **Introduce the book.** Before reading, make a copy of **Story Organizer** (p. 101) from Week 8. Write several vocabulary words on the activity sheet and discuss their meanings. Then, ask your child to complete the page up to "Setting." Activate your child's prior knowledge by relating the story to his/her own experience. Clarify the purpose in reading this story, if applicable.

2. **Read the book**. Have your child write definitions of vocabulary words as he/she reads and keep them in a word bank. Have the child monitor his/her own comprehension by asking him/herself questions. *Does the book make sense?* Reread any confusing passages. Look back through pages already read to check understanding. Have your child make inferences about what has happened and predictions about what might happen next. If reading nonfiction, ask your child to take notes. Encourage your child to consult a knowledgeable person when he/she is unsure of a word or meaning.

3. **Follow up with skills or projects**. After finishing the book, have your child complete the **Story Organizer** (p. 101). Teach your child a specific skill. Look for examples in the book. Have your child reread parts of the selection for more information. Plan a project that involves thinking more deeply about the story content. Have your child evaluate a certain aspect of the book (theme, character or event).

▶ MORE READING SUGGESTIONS

Reading conference—Hold a reading conference with your child two or more times during the reading of a book (number of times depends on the length of the book). Ask questions to assess your child's comprehension and challenge him/her to look for more information. Asking your child to predict the next event will involve him/her more deeply in the text.

Reading Journal—Have your child maintain a Reading Journal in which he/she writes the names of the books read along with personal reflections on characters or events. You may also assign questions for him/her to answer in the Journal—some questions are provided in the lesson plans. The best questions will ask your child to express an opinion about an event, recommend that a character act in a certain way, criticize a decision by the author or debate an issue presented in the book.

Read a variety of literature—Read literature such as fantasy, fables, mystery, adventure, nonfiction, biography, poems, short stories and picture books. Picture books often have sophisticated vocabulary and themes. Because they are short, they make great books for teaching a specific reading skill.

Read for enjoyment—Show your enthusiasm for reading. There is a direct correlation between a child's success in reading and positive experiences with books, which you model.

Choose appropriate books—There is no such thing as a fourth-grade level book. Each child is unique in his/her reading interests and abilities. You can determine if a book is appropriate by having your child read a short passage. Evaluate your child's fluency, understanding and interest in the book.

- If your child breezes through the reading with no hesitancy, the book is probably at his/her *independent reading level*. At the independent level, the child should recognize about 95% of the words in a passage and be able to answer 85% of the comprehension questions.

- If your child struggles with five or more words on a single page, the book is too hard. Struggling through this book could make the child dislike reading. Do not choose books at your child's frustration level.

- Choose a book at the child's *instructional level* when you read together. At this level, the child should recognize 85–90% of the words and be able to answer 75% of the comprehension questions.

▶ SUGGESTED BOOKS AND AUTHORS

Children at the fourth-grade level often enjoy authors such as Judy Blume, Beverly Cleary, Roald Dahl, Marguerite Henry and Laura Ingalls Wilder. The partial list of books below is arranged alphabetically by title and is meant to get you started in your search for quality books for your child.

Arabian Nights: Three Tales retold and illustrated by Deborah Nourse Lattimore
Arthur and the Sword retold and illustrated by Robert Sabuda

11

A Barrel of Laughs, a Vale of Tears by Jules Feiffer
Beatrix Potter: The Story of the Creator of Peter Rabbit by Elizabeth Buchan
The Boy Who Lived With the Bears and Other Iroquois Stories by Joseph Bruchac
A Child's Anthology of Poetry edited by Elizabeth Hauge Sword with Victoria Flournoy McCarthy
The Enormous Egg by Oliver Butterworth
Falling Up by Shel Silverstein (poetry)
From the Mixed-Up Files of Mrs. Basil E. Frankweiler by E.L. Konigsburg
The Golden Hoard: Myths and Legends of the World by Geraldine McCaughrean
Helen Keller: From Tragedy to Triumph by Katharine E. Wilkie
In the Year of the Boar and Jackie Robinson by Bette Bao Lord
The Indian in the Cupboard by Lynne Reid Banks
The Island of the Blue Dolphins by Scott O'Dell
The Legend of Sleepy Hollow by Washington Irving
The Lion, the Witch and the Wardrobe by C.S. Lewis
Minty: A Story of Young Harriet Tubman by Alan Schroeder
Mr. Popper's Penguins by Richard and Florence Atwater
Mrs. Frisby and the Rats of NIMH by Robert C. O'Brien
Myths and Legends From Around the World by Sandy Shepherd
Oh, the Places He Went: A Story about Dr. Seuss–Theodor Seuss Geisel by Maryann N. Weidt
The Owl and the Pussy-Cat and Other Nonsense Poems by Edward Lear
Owl in the Cedar Tree by Natachee Scott Momaday
The Oxford Book of Story Poems compiled by Michael Harrison and Christopher Stuart-Clark
The Secret Garden by Frances Hodgson Burnett
The Sign of the Beaver by Elizabeth George Speare
Sounder by William H. Armstrong
The Story of the Lewis and Clark Expedition by R. Conrad Stein
What Made Them Great series of biographies published by Silver Burdett
The Wind in the Willows by Kenneth Grahame

Character 1   Character 2

Venn diagram

▶ IDEAS FOR BOOK PROJECTS

After reading a book, engage your child in an activity that requires imagination and creativity, as well as an understanding of the story just read. Have him/her:

- design and create a diorama
- write a poem about a character
- retell a poem in story form
- write a sequel
- write a critique of a book
- illustrate a favorite scene
- write a new ending
- make a filmstrip of the events
- prepare and perform a puppet show

- rewrite a scene from a book in play form
- compare two characters using a Venn diagram (*See* above)
- illustrate a fable and write out the moral
- write three questions to ask the subject of a biography
- design and create a commercial to sell the book
- list things a character might say in given situations
- draw a comic strip with characters from a book
- write a sensational news story about an event in a book
- build a mobile representing attributes of a character

▶ TEACHING A THEMATIC UNIT

A thematic unit is a way of organizing lessons from more than one subject area around one theme. For example, if you are reading a novel about the American West, design math story problems related to that theme. In science, you could set up experiments by growing different plants in sand. In social studies, you could study the geography of the west. In spelling, add words from the novel or theme-related vocabulary to the spelling list. Teaching thematically takes imagination and planning, but the lessons can be more meaningful to the child if they are taught in an interesting context.

▶ READING INCENTIVES

Reading can be its own reward, but sometimes a child needs a little more encouragement. Choose an incentive that fits your child's interests and your own philosophy.

Build a library—As your child completes a book, ask him/her to add it to a personal library poster. At the end of the year, the shelves will be filled with titles and the child's ratings of quality. Offer additional incentives based on personal goals: reward the child with special time together after reading a given number of books, have a book party when one bookshelf is full or go on a field trip after your child reads a book from each genre. **Directions:** Start with a 12" x 18" sheet of construction paper. Turn the paper so the 12" sides are at the top and bottom. Divide the paper into three "shelves" that are 6" apart, as shown. Cut several construction paper rectangles (1–2" x 6") to resemble the spines of books (vary the widths). When the child completes a book, have him/her write the title on a "spine" and attach stars to indicate the book's quality rating (design the rating system together). Then, have your child glue the "book" on the "bookshelf."

Set a reading goal—Choose a theme that appeals to your child. Design a bulletin board display around the theme. For each book your child reads, add something to the display. When the display is full, your child will earn a reward related to the theme. **Example:** Ice cream—Put a cone at the bottom of the display. For each book read, the child gets to add a scoop of ice cream. Write a book title on each scoop. When the scoops reach the top, reward your child with a sundae.

MATH

▶ GETTING STARTED

Mathematical literacy is the ability to think mathematically in a variety of real-life situations and to interpret and use mathematical references. Math is much more than mastering a set of basic computation skills. Basic skills are to math as spelling is to writing: They are the tools with which we explore, test and explain. A good teacher will provide a child with an understanding of basic math skills, as well as the applications of these skills. Such applications include designing and interpreting graphs, discovering patterns, measuring, comparing and problem solving.

▶ QUARTERLY RECORD OF PROGRESS

When children are held responsible for their own learning, they are often more motivated. They are also more likely to value their education. You can make your child responsible for his/her own progress by having him/her maintain a record of progress each quarter. On a sheet of graph paper, have your child plot the name of the skill or assignment, the date and a score (from 0 to 100). Set a standard of excellence, such as 90%, that your child should strive to attain. Provide opportunities for your child to improve low scores, whether it be repeating an assignment after further instruction or completing a related assignment.

Assignment Title

Scores: 100 90 80 70 60 50 40 30 20 10 0

Date of Assignment

▶ PROBLEM-SOLVING JOURNAL

Every two or three days, give your child a new problem to solve. You may wish to purchase books of story problems and puzzlers for this purpose. Post each problem on the chalkboard or on a bulletin board. Set aside time and materials for your child to solve the problem. Ask your child to copy the problem and write the solution in a Problem-Solving Journal. A challenging problem may require your child to draw a picture, create a model, look for patterns, think creatively or solve computations in unusual ways.

▶ MATHEMATICAL CONNECTIONS

Mathematical thinking often occurs outside of math class. Help your child realize the importance of math in real-life situations and that math can be fun. Read the *I Hate Mathematics!* book and other books by Marilyn Burns for activity ideas. Here are some ways to apply math to other areas of the curriculum:

Creative Writing—Ask your child to complete this sentence starter: "Arithmetic is. . . ." Then, read the poem, "Arithmetic," by Carl Sandburg. Compare your child's insights with those of Sandburg. Have your child illustrate a concept from Sandburg's poem or one of his/her own thoughts.

Game—Play a game to practice a new math skill. Provide instructions for a game or let your child design a new game. Here are two simple dice games to try:

  a. Choose an operation for the game (addition, subtraction, multiplication or division). Roll two dice and apply the chosen operation.

  b. Roll three dice and arrange them to form a 3-digit number. Write the number on lined paper. Roll the three dice again and arrange them to form a number smaller than the first. Write the second 3-digit number on the lined paper. Subtract the smaller number from the larger number.

Poetry—Read a poem that contains a number in its title, such as "Forty Performing Bananas" by Jack Prelutsky (found in *For Laughing Out Loud: Poems To Tickle Your Funny Bone*, collected by Jack Prelutsky). Have your child look for and read more poems whose titles contain numbers. Then, challenge him/her to write an original poem with a number in the title.

Reading—Many common sayings contain numbers. You can find famous sayings and quotations in *The Concise Oxford Book of Proverbs* and *Poor Richard's Almanac*. Have your child illustrate a saying in a silly or literal way. **Examples:** One picture is worth a thousand words. Two wrongs don't make a right.

Spelling—Include new math words in weekly spelling lists.

SCIENCE

▶ THE SCIENCE LEARNING CYCLE

Teach your child the steps involved in scientific investigation. Listed below are the basic steps.

  1. A science lesson may begin with a question that sparks the curiosity of your child. **Example:** *I wonder what will happen if I leave this half-eaten apple on the counter.* Encourage your child to venture a hypothesis.

  2. Follow up the question with an exploration involving experimentation, observation, play, debate and other methods of inquiry. Encourage your child to use descriptive language, measure when appropriate and keep a log of observations.

3. The next step in the cycle involves proposing explanations and solutions for the initial question. The explanation may prove or disprove the earlier hypothesis. This is a time of writing, talking and evaluating. After this step, your child may need to return to the second step of the cycle to explore the topic further.

4. Applying the knowledge to your child's world makes the event more meaningful. *Where have you seen this happen before? How will the results of this experiment affect your actions in the future? Will you act or proceed any differently?* This fourth step may also spark new questions that begin the cycle again. Do not worry if you don't have answers to all your child's questions. The Science Learning Cycle promotes exploration and encourages your child to construct his/her own knowledge based on experience. The more experience you provide, the clearer and more accurate your child's understanding will be. If your child presses you for an answer, respond with "Let's find out," "What do you think?" or "Where have you seen something like that?" Your child will not always be satisfied. Keep in mind, however, that your vocabulary-filled answers may not necessarily provide a satisfactory answer either. Science is a process of wonder and discovery. Keep the wonder alive. A good scientist asks a lot of questions!

▶ SPECIAL SCIENTIST

Feature a different "Special Scientist" for each 9-week period of the school year. Provide information about the scientist and his/her work. Make a large paper frame and decorative border for the bulletin board. Near the top of the frame, write the name of the scientist and display his/her picture. (Copy a picture from an encyclopedia or other resource.) List some facts about the scientist and his/her accomplishments within the frame. Supply resource books about the scientist and his/her field of expertise. Invite your child to read and write about the scientist. Some suggestions for "Special Scientist" include Wernher von Braun, Nicolaus Copernicus, Marie and Pierre Curie, Albert Einstein, Robert H. Goddard, Gregor Mendel, Maria Mitchell, Lise Meitner and Louis Pasteur.

SOCIAL STUDIES

At the fourth-grade level, the social studies curriculum should expand a child's knowledge of explorers and exploration, Native Americans, the states and the Middle Ages. Use the lessons and activities provided and expand on the concepts as they pertain to your experience and to your child's interests.

▶ CURRENT EVENTS

Encourage your child to read about current events in the newspapers, watch local and national news and listen to NPR (National Public Radio). Discuss news events with your child daily. Listen to his/her interpretation of current events. Help your child gather the necessary information to make careful judgments.

▶ SOCIAL STUDIES CENTER

Establish an area in your home as a social studies center. Gather books, maps, a globe, an atlas, pictures, charts and encyclopedias that relate to the topics you and your child will be studying. Refer to these resources often during your course of study, adding new resources as necessary.

	Language Skills	Spelling	Reading
Monday	Brainstorm writing topics together. Have your child keep a list of ideas in his/her writing folder for future reference. Have your child choose one writing topic and make a plan for writing (an outline or topic web). Have him/her begin work on a rough draft and continue working on the story this week. *See* **The Writing Process** (p. 5).	Pretest your child on these spelling words. ache bathroom manage admit camera navy animal flap plane April grateful radish bacon happiness waste Have your child correct the pretest, add personalized words and make two copies of this week's study list.	**Compound Words** Review compound words. Generate a list of compound words and write them on the chalkboard. Have your child read each word, define it and tell what two words were combined to create the compound word. *See* Reading, Week 1, number 1. Cover one half of a compound word with an index card. Have your child add an alternate word to form a new compound word.
Tuesday	Have your child write one row of each capital letter A–I in cursive. Have him/her circle the best letter in each row. Make a copy of **Let's Write!** (p. 20) for your child. Encourage him/her to use this sheet as a reference for handwriting activities over the next several weeks.	Have your child write each of this week's spelling words correctly in a sentence.	Introduce *The Boxcar Children* by Gertrude Chandler Warner. Have your child imagine life for four orphaned children who do not want to live with a grandfather they have never met. Read chapters 1–3.
Wednesday	**Nouns:** Begin a review of nouns. Ask your child to define a noun. Have him/her underline all the nouns in his/her story (*see* Monday's lesson). Ask your child to identify and capitalize all the proper nouns in his/her story. Have your child complete **Common and Proper Nouns** (p. 21).	Have your child complete **A Is for Apple** (p. 24).	Read chapters 4–6 of *The Boxcar Children*. Ask your child for a brief summary of the story thus far. Ask questions to determine whether he/she comprehends the reading.
Thursday	Review the rules for possessive nouns. Give your child a list of singular and plural nouns. Ask him/her to make each noun possessive. *See* Language Skills, number 1. For variety in this week's writing draft, have your child try alternating nouns and pronouns, when appropriate. Have your child complete **Forming Plural Nouns** (p. 22).	Help your child study this week's spelling words with a game of "Charades." Take turns with your child acting out the words.	Have your child read chapter 7 of *The Boxcar Children*. Discuss how the boxcar children are faring on their own. Ask: *Are the children acting responsibly? Are there any things they will not be able to do on their own?* Have your child illustrate compound words with two pictures. **Example:** a foot and a ball for the word *football*. Do one word per page. Staple finished pages together to create a book.
Friday	Review the rules for forming plural nouns. Introduce subject and object pronouns. Explain that a pronoun may take the place of a noun in a sentence. Give your child several sentences from *The Boxcar Children*. Have him/her rewrite them using pronouns wherever possible. Have your child complete **I, We; Me, Us** (p. 23).	Give your child the final spelling test. Have your child record the pretest and final test words in his/her word bank.	Discuss main idea. Read chapters 8–10 of *The Boxcar Children*. Ask your child to jot down the main idea of each chapter as he/she reads today. Have your child complete **Camp Rules** (p. 25) to reinforce the concept.

Math	Science	Social Studies
Place-Value Write a number, such as 1,865. Ask your child to tell the value of a given digit. **Example:** *What is the value of the 6? (60)* Repeat this exercise with other 4-digit numbers until your child seems comfortable with the concept. You may want to include place-value vocabulary in this week's spelling list: *ones, tens, hundreds* and *thousands*.	**Force** Ask your child to recall watching construction workers or machinery. Ask: *How did the people or machines move objects in opposition to gravity? How do tools make moving objects easier?* Have your child formulate an explanation as to why things move. Compare his/her explanation with this one: *Motion is caused by a force acting upon an object.* A force may be in the form of a push or pull and may cause a change in speed or direction.	**Early Explorers** Discuss the broad meaning of *exploration*. *See* Social Studies, Week 1, number 1. Give your child the following story starter: *If I were an explorer, I would _____, because....* Be sure your child includes details of the voyage as well as some illustrations.
Draw a place-value chart that shows the first six places. *See* Math, Week 1, number 1. Make a list of fifteen to twenty 6-digit numbers. Have your child name the value of a given digit in each number. See examples below: 823,107 (3,000) 525,762 (700) 210,618 (8) 169,632 (30) Show your child how to count using the place-value chart. *See* Math, Week 1, number 2.	Read about Sir Isaac Newton and his discoveries about gravity. Drop unbreakable objects of various sizes and have your child observe how they move. Add other forces and ask your child to predict how the movement will change. *See* Science, Week 1, number 1.	Introduce the well-known ancient explorers (before the 1300s). Gather information from the library on the Vikings, Zhang Qian, Marco Polo and Alexander the Great. Discuss their various achievements. Help your child create a chart showing the explorers, their countries of origin, where they explored, the years they explored and other relevant information. Post the chart for reference.
Teach your child where to place commas in numbers greater than 1,000. Read several 4-digit numbers together out loud. Make a list of several scrambled number words, such as four thousands, three ones, one hundred, six tens, two ten thousands. Use a place-value chart to show how to put the numbers in the proper order. Let your child try to unscramble the other numbers on the list.	Ask your child to hypothesize how to measure the amount of force it takes to move an object. Collect several objects varying in size and weight. Have your child arrange the objects according to how much force it will take to move them. Then, measure each object to see if the order was correct using a spring scale if possible. Alternately, weigh the objects using ounces, pounds or grams. A greater force is required to move heavier objects.	Help your child draw a map to show what lands the ancient explorers had covered by the 1300s. Use the *World Book Encyclopedia* and other books and resources as a guide.
Teach your child to name the number that is 10 greater than a given number. **Example:** The number 10 greater than 250 is 260. Continue the lesson with variations of this exercise, finding the number that is 10 less, 100 greater and 100 less than a given number.	Friction is a force that acts against or *resists* motion. Ask your child to name some sources of friction, such as brakes, carpeting and rough surfaces. Roll a variety of objects over a smooth surface, then over a carpeted or rough surface. Ask your child to explain how and why the objects act differently on the two surfaces.	Have your child research the routes of the early explorers and trace them on a world map. Ask him/her to trace each journey with a different color and create a key for the map.
Give your child a set of 3 digits. Ask him/her to arrange the numerals to form six 3-digit numbers. Repeat with other sets of 3 digits. **Example:** 2, 5, 1 251, 215, 521, 512, 125, 152 Have your child order each set of 3-digit numbers from least to greatest. **Example:** 125, 152, 215, 251, 512, 521.	Explore the concept of inertia. *See* Science, Week 1, number 2. Ask: *What happens in a car when you hit the brakes suddenly? Why does your body continue to move forward?* Discuss other instances when an object tends to continue what it is already doing. Encourage your child to design experiments that will demonstrate the force of inertia.	Help your child choose an explorer to research. Have him/her write a biography of the explorer, including details of his/her most famous discoveries and interesting facts about his/her life. Have your child include a drawing of the explorer, paying careful attention to the hair and clothing styles of the time.

Learn at Home, Grade 4

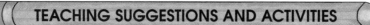

TEACHING SUGGESTIONS AND ACTIVITIES

LANGUAGE SKILLS (Nouns)

BACKGROUND

Possessive pronouns—*my, your, his, her, its, our, their*—show ownership but do not use an apostrophe.
Subject pronouns—*I, we, they, he, she, it*—do the action.
Object pronouns—*me, us, them, him, her, it*—have action being done to them (not by them).

▶ 1. Write the paragraph below on the chalkboard. Have your child underline each possessive pronoun and circle what is possessed.

There are many kinds of sharks, and their sizes vary greatly. Their lengths can range from 6 inches to over 40 feet long. Our fear of sharks is based on occasional attacks on human beings. Many a fisherman has had his catch eaten by sharks. A shark doesn't have any bones in its body. Its skeleton is quite different from your skeleton which is made of bones. Its skeleton is made of cartilage.

READING (Compound Words)

▶ 1. Copy the grid at the right for your child and review how to read the coordinates on a grid. **Example:** the word *her* is at (B, 2). Tell your child to find compound words by combining words on the grid. Have him/her write the compound word as well as the locations of both words that form the compound word. **Example:** (C, 2) and (E, 6) = toothpaste. Use the words listed here or substitute vocabulary from *The Boxcar Children*.

	A	B	C	D	E
1	light	foot	class	house	some
2	birth	her	tooth	snow	base
3	thing	man	side	him	day
4	room	one	work	out	bare
5	boat	roar	every	in	ball
6	self	time	no	mail	paste
7	stairs	to	shop	mate	up

MATH (Place-Value)

▶ 1. Learning place value will help your child conceptualize large numbers and will lead to greater understanding of addition, subtraction, multiplication and division. Each digit of a number is given a place value. This distinguishes a 4 from a 40. Use models to teach the concept of tens, ones and hundreds, then lead your child to generalize the pattern for larger numbers.

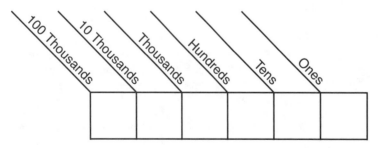

Place-Value Chart

Learn at Home, Grade 4

2. Demonstrate how to count a handful of manipulatives (such as buttons, toothpicks or dry beans) using the place-value board:

    a. Count the objects by ones in the ones place on the place-value board. When you reach 10, put the ten objects in a paper cup and slide the cup to the tens place. Count that as 1 ten. It is important for your child to see 10 as a unit. Continue counting the remaining objects, naming the number of tens and ones (12 should be read as 1 ten, 2 ones).

    b. When the handful of objects has been counted, have your child use number cards to name the total. **Example:** If there are four sets in the tens place, place the 4 card on the tens place.

    c. Have your child recount the objects by ones, away from the place-value board, confirming that 4 tens, 6 ones is the same as 46. Even if it seems unnecessary, have your child recount to solidify the concept at least once. Continue this habit of recounting until your child is reluctant, because the number is obvious to him/her.

SCIENCE (Force)

1. *Gravity* is a force in the form of a pull. Gravity pulls objects to the ground. But more than one force may act on an object at once. Try dropping a light object in front of a fan to observe the two forces at work. Gravity pulls the object down while the fan pushes the falling object sideways. Try dropping a heavier object into a bowl of water. Water may act as resistance to the force of gravity. Observe the difference when you drop the same object through the air.

2. The tendency of an object to continue what it is doing is referred to as *inertia*. An object that is standing still tends to stay still until force is applied to get it moving. An object that is moving tends to continue moving until force is applied to stop it. Heavier objects have more inertia than lighter objects. Picture how difficult it is to get a heavy object to move. It takes much more energy to get a car rolling than a bicycle. Faster moving objects have more inertia than slower moving objects.

SOCIAL STUDIES (Early Explorers)

BACKGROUND

The names of the earliest explorers are not known. They left no written records of who they were or where they traveled. They roamed the land thousands of years ago, moving from one place to another in search of food. These groups of people eventually settled where the land and climate best suited their needs. Motivations for later exploration were not so basic as the need for food or shelter. Rulers of the ancient world sent explorers on expeditions in pursuit of their desires. They longed to expand their lands. They wanted to develop trade routes, find treasures, build empires and cultivate new settlements. Many of the famous explorers were sent off for these reasons. Often curious people who loved adventure, they obtained their funding by pursuing the dreams of their rulers.

1. Discuss what it means to explore. Exploration includes any investigation of the unknown. Brainstorm possible reasons for exploration. *What sort of unknowns might be explored?* Talk about the scientific processes that might be used in any exploration (trial and error, investigation, gathering information, discovery, etc.). What characteristics might an explorer possess? Ask if your child would like to be an explorer. Why or why not?

Let's Write!

Trace each letter, then **write** it on your own.

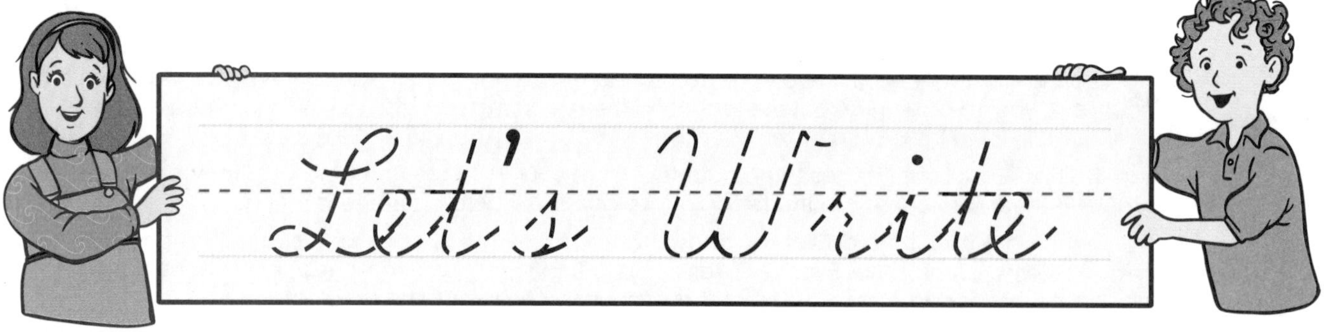

Let's Write

Aa   Bb   Cc

Dd   Ee   Ff

Gg   Hh   Ii

Jj   Kk   Ll

Mm   Nn   Oo

Pp   Qq   Rr

Ss   Tt   Uu

Vv   Ww   Xx

Yy   Zz

Common and Proper Nouns

A **common noun** names any person, place or thing.
A **proper noun** names a specific person, place or thing.
A proper noun always begins with a capital letter.

Example: boy, state (common nouns)
            Peter, Georgia (proper nouns)

Underline the nouns in the sentences.

1. Bobby was wondering what the weather would be on Friday.
2. The boys and girls from Lang School were planning a picnic.
3. Bobby asked his teacher, Mr. Lewis, how the class could find out.
4. The teacher suggested that the children call a local newspaper, *The Bugle*.
5. Ms. Canyon, the editor, read the forecast to Eddie.
6. Rain was predicted for the day of their picnic.
7. Their town, Grand Forks, also had a radio station.
8. When Rick called the number, he was disappointed.
9. The weatherman, George Lee, said that rain was possible.
10. The children were delighted when the sun came out on Friday.

Now, **write** each noun you have underlined in the correct category below.
Do not use any words more than once.

Common Nouns

1. _____
2. _____
3. _____
4. _____
5. _____
6. _____
7. _____
8. _____
9. _____
10. _____
11. _____
12. _____
13. _____
14. _____
15. _____
16. _____
17. _____

Proper Nouns

1. _____
2. _____
3. _____
4. _____
5. _____
6. _____
7. _____
8. _____
9. _____
10. _____

21

Forming Plural Nouns

Most **singular nouns** can be made into **plural nouns** by following one of these rules.

Rules	Examples
1. Add **s** to most nouns.	elephant, elephant**s**
2. If the noun ends in **s**, **sh**, **ch** or **x**, add **es**.	box, box**es**
3. If the noun ends in **y** with a consonant before it, change the **y** to **i** and add **es**.	fly, fl**ies**
4. If the noun ends in **y** with a vowel before it, add **s**.	monkey, monkey**s**
5. To some nouns ending in **f**, add **s**.	chief, chief**s**
6. To some nouns ending in **f** or **fe**, change the **f** to **v** and add **es**.	knife, kni**ves** thief, thie**ves**
7. Some nouns stay the same for singular and plural.	sheep, **sheep**
8. Some nouns have an irregular plural.	goose, **geese**

Change each singular noun to plural. Write the number of the rule you used. Use a dictionary when needed.

Singular	Plural	Rule #	Singular	Plural	Rule #
1. chimney			11. woman		
2. class			12. bus		
3. wolf			13. judge		
4. deer			14. shelf		
5. story			15. chair		
6. elf			16. beach		
7. tooth			17. tax		
8. brush			18. lady		
9. attorney			19. roof		
10. mouse			20. penny		

Learn at Home, Grade 4

I, We; Me, Us

I and **we** are **subject pronouns**. **Me** and **us** are **object pronouns**.

Examples:

Mark and **I** are on our way to the park.
    (subject pronoun)

We just love to launch rockets!
    (subject pronoun)

Will Sara come with **me**?
    (object pronoun)

Please feel welcome to join **us**.
    (object pronoun)

Choose the correct pronoun for each sentence from those in parentheses. **Write** it in the blank.

1. _____ plan to launch rockets at the park on Saturday.
   (we, us)

2. Monica bought _____ a two-stage rocket.
                (I, me)

3. Bill and _____ both brought fresh batteries for the rocket launcher.
      (I, me)

4. Curt plans to build _____ a rocket.
           (we, us)

5. Gwen wants _____ to attend the rocket safety course.
       (I, me)

6. _____ always like to paint the fins a bright color.
  (I, me)

7. Tom wants Michele and _____ to chase after his rocket when it lands.
        (I, me)

8. Heather wants _____ to go to the launching site.
       (we, us)

9. Carolyn and _____ just bought a model rocket with a payload section.
     (I, me)

10. Jim will be showing _____ his model rocket.
       (we, us)

11. David taught _____ all the same safety rules.
     (I, me)

A Is for Apple

ache
admit
animal
April
bacon
bathroom
camera
flap
grateful
happiness
manage
navy
plane
radish
waste

Write the spelling words that contain a **short a** that sounds like the **a** in **apple**.

_____ _____

_____ _____

_____ _____

_____ _____

List all the spelling words that contain a **long a** that sounds like the **a** in **cake**.

_____ _____

_____ _____

_____ _____

_____

Use the spelling words to complete the word search. The words are written vertically, horizontally and diagonally.

```
T F I U H F C B K Q G H E N P N
M X G O A X J K I W G T I U R M
O C S B P J I P R E J T D P V R
C Q A I P M W L P H M F C F J Z
E E Y Y I N U A H W T L L N A V
B C V Y N F Y D C E W V L B X L
W A S T E L B O A T A D X S M H
N M C T S S A B L K A V J J U X
I E A O S R T O A U B P U J E M
G R T K N I H E P G O T E G U R
G A E A M U R R R M S A A C H E
D F K D U Y O B I D L N U U O A
A W A B V M O X L R A D I S H N
G L N C U Z M X E M N Y F Z A H
H U V I Z K U K J U I S E L T E
K S Y K Q R H T Q W M N T V W L
M D T B H T C R F L A P T I F K
L C L N A V Q H R L L D Z Y A J
S B N T D J K M P C U I I E H A
```

24

Camp Rules

Donald, Arnold and Jack are at Camp Explore-It-All this week. They think camp is a lot of fun. They have also learned from their instructors that there are some very important rules all campers must obey so that everyone has a good time.

All campers must take swimming tests to see what depth of water they can swim in safely. Donald and Jack pass the advanced test and can swim in the deep water. Arnold, however, only passes the intermediate test. He is supposed to stay in the area where the water is waist deep. When it is time to swim, Arnold decides to sneak into advanced with Donald and Jack. After all, he has been swimming in deep water for three years. No way is he going to stay in the shallow water with the babies.

Donald and Jack don't think Arnold should come into the deep water, but they can't tell him anything. So the boys jump into the water and start swimming and playing. Fifteen minutes later, Arnold is yelling, "Help!" He swims out too far and is too tired to make it back in. The lifeguard jumps in and pulls him out. Everyone stops to see what is happening. Arnold feels very foolish.

Check:
The main idea of this story is
- ☐ Arnold ends up feeling foolish.
- ☐ All campers take swimming tests.
- ☐ You can learn a lot from instructors.
- ☐ Camp is fun.
- ☐ Rules are made for good reasons.
- ☐ Rules are made to be broken.

Underline:
Arnold got himself into a(n) _____ situation.
　　　　amusing　　funny　　dangerous　　ambiguous

Circle:
Arnold thought the guys in the shallow area were (bullies/babies). However, he should have (stayed with them/gone to the advanced area).

Write:
What lesson do you think Arnold learned? _____

_____

What do you think the other campers learned? _____

_____

Language Skills	Spelling	Reading

Monday

Adjectives/Articles
Discuss how the use of descriptive words can improve writing. Then, have your child write a descriptive article using adjectives and colorful language, such as metaphors and similes. Encourage him/her to use all or several of the senses in writing the article. Topic ideas: hiking in the woods, baking chocolate chip cookies, visiting a water treatment plant. Have your child work on a rough draft.

Pretest your child on these spelling words.

bedtime	elegant	meteor
being	female	rectangle
beverage	jelly	recycle
cedar	lemon	secret
decoy	medicine	skeleton

Have your child correct the pretest, add personalized words and make two copies of this week's study list.

Contractions/Possessives
Before reading further, ask your child what he/she thinks the boxcar children would do if one of them were to become ill. Read chapters 11 and 12 of *The Boxcar Children*.

Tuesday

Review the correct formation of the cursive capital letters J–R. Have your child practice handwriting. Have your child write one row of each capital letter J–R. Let him/her circle the best letter in each row.

Have your child use each of this week's spelling words correctly in a sentence.

Read the final chapter of *The Boxcar Children*. Have your child create a model of the boxcar based on descriptions from the book. Use an empty shoe box for the frame of the boxcar. Then, collect items or use modeling clay to make the items inside.

Wednesday

Adjectives modify nouns by describing what kind, how many or which one. With your child, brainstorm a list of adjectives. Keep them on a chart for easy reference. Show your child how to make a dull sentence more exciting by adding adjectives. *See* Language Skills, Week 2, number 1.

Have your child complete **Easy Does It** (p. 31).

Locate a passage from *The Boxcar Children* or another book that contains several contractions. Have your child identify the contractions and name the two words that name the contraction. *See* Reading, Week 2, number 1 for more practice. Have your child write a summary of *The Boxcar Children* in his/her Reading Journal, along with a review of the book.

Thursday

Teach your child how to form and to use comparative adjectives. Explain how to add *er* when comparing two things and *est* when comparing three or more. Review the rules for spelling changes, as explained at the top of the activity sheet (p. 30). Have your child complete **How Adjectives Compare** (p. 30).

Have your child write a short story using as many of this week's words as possible.

Introduce *Matthew Jackson Meets the Wall* by Patricia Reilly Giff. Have your child imagine what it would be like to leave a neighborhood where he/she had several good friends and move to a new state. Ask: *How would he/she feel? What would he/she miss the most? the least?* Read chapter 1 of *Matthew Jackson Meets the Wall*.

Friday

Show your child how to form proper adjectives and to use the articles *a, an* and *the* correctly. *See* Language Skills, Week 2. Write out a paragraph from *Matthew Jackson Meets the Wall* or make up your own. Omit all the articles and have your child fill them in. Have your child continue work on his/her article from Monday; remind your child to include adjectives in the article to make it more interesting.

Give your child the final spelling test. Have your child record the pretest and final test words in his/her word bank.

Review the proper use of apostrophes. Write several possessive nouns and contractions on index cards. Have your child sort the cards into two categories: possessives and contractions. Emphasize the distinction between *its* (possessive) and *it's* (contraction), using sample sentences to illustrate the difference. *See* Reading, Week 2, number 2. Read chapters 2–4 of *Matthew Jackson*. Have your child make a list of story events so far.

Math	Science	Social Studies
Show your child where to add the millions place on the place-value chart from last week. Teach comma placement and how to read a 7-digit number aloud. Have your child complete **Place Value** (p. 32).	Each time force is applied to an object, work is being done. Work can be as simple as lifting a pencil. Guide your child in analyzing the force that makes an object move. Have your child make a chart to record the specific motion (or work) and the force that caused the movement. **Examples:** lift a pencil—fingers/arm muscles drop a ball—gravity	Continue to study the early explorers. Assign your child to read one or more books of historical fiction on early explorers. Have him/her illustrate the main idea of each chapter with a picture. Create a picture book on the subject by stapling together the chapter illustrations, each one labeled with a chapter title or number.
Give your child two numbers. Have him/her write a greater than (>) or less than (<) symbol between them. Ask how he/she knew which number was greater or less than the other. Have him/her practice with a variety of numbers including numbers with different amounts of digits. **Examples:** 2,164 1,164 36 125 58,001 5,631	**Simple Machines:** Introduce the six *simple machines:* lever, pulley, wedge, wheel, screw and inclined plane. Have your child give examples of each. *See* Science, Week 2, number 1, for an illustration and description of each type of machine.	Discuss the life of an explorer. Then, have your child imagine him/herself aboard an explorer's ship. Have him/her write five Social Studies Journal entries as a crew member on the ship describing conditions on board the ship, the type of work that must be done, the crew member's feelings and other personal information.
Teach your child to use a zero to hold a place that contains no numeral. Make a list of scrambled numbers as on Wednesday, Week 1, but omit one number place. **Example:** nine tens, six thousands and three ones. Here, the hundreds place is missing. Have your child write out the number, putting a 0 in the hundreds place to show that it is empty (6,093).	All simple machines require a force (effort) to do work. The effort moves an object (resistance). Study tools and kitchen utensils. Encourage your child to classify each according to type of simple machine and identify the effort required to use the tool and the resistance commonly moved by the tool. **Example:** can opener—wedge and lever. The effort is a push that separates metal from metal to create a triangle-shaped hole in the can.	Help your child prepare a slide show about the life of a particular explorer. Go to a photo lab to obtain slides mounted with clear film. You can also buy a roll of 35mm black and white film and have it developed as slides without taking any pictures or exposing the film. Have your child begin planning the slide show by sketching twenty-four frames on scratch paper.
Rounding: Introduce rounding to the nearest ten. Have your child answer questions like these: *Is the number 37 closer to 30 or 40? If I have $147 in the bank, about how much money do I have? See* Math, Week 2, number 1.	Machines often make work easier by reducing the effort required. For example, a hammer moves a nail into wood with much less effort than a hand could move the nail. Have your child brainstorm machines that help people move heavy objects.	Once your child has finished the sketches, he/she can begin coloring the slides. Use fine point pens and markers. Be sure to number the slides to keep them in order. Your child should also write a script to go along with the slides.
Teach your child to round large numbers to the nearest hundred or thousand. *See* Math, Week 2, number 2. Have your child complete **The First State** (p. 33).	Some simple machines reduce effort by increasing distance. Sit on a teeter-totter with your child. Have him/her move backward and forward to determine which way requires less effort to lift you. He/she will quickly discover that moving away from you makes the work easier. Encourage him/her to explore other machines that work on this same principle. *See* Science, Week 2, number 2.	Present the slide show to friends or family. Have your child narrate the show.

TEACHING SUGGESTIONS AND ACTIVITIES

LANGUAGE SKILLS (Adjectives/Articles)

BACKGROUND

A *proper noun* names a specific person, place or thing and is always capitalized. A proper adjective is made from a proper noun. It, too, is always capitalized.
Examples: English language, French bread, Alaskan pipeline, Chinese food, American car

A, an and *the* are articles. *A* is used before words that start with a consonant sound. *An* is used before words that start with a vowel sound. *The* is more specific than *a* or *an* and can be used before a singular or plural noun regardless of its beginning letter or sound.

▶ 1. Write the following groups of words and sentences on the chalkboard. Have your child circle the three adjectives in each group and add them to the sentence.

a.	beautiful	happily	c.	gray	four
	blue	twenty		eat	powerful

        a.   beautiful   happily   c.   gray   four
           blue   twenty   eat   powerful
           The fish darted through the water.   The elephants trudged along the path.

        b.   two   tall   d.   quickly   scaly
           little   run   green   striped
           The monkeys swung through the trees.   A snake slithered through the grass.

READING (Contractions/Possessives)

▶ 1. Copy the following paragraph for your child to read. Ask him/her to identify each contraction and add apostrophes in the proper places.

Ryan wasnt sure what to give his sister for her birthday. He didnt have a lot of money, but he wanted to get her something shed like. Last year hed given her a stuffed animal. Ryan decided to ask his mother for ideas. "Why dont you buy her a new book?" she suggested. "Thats a great idea," said Ryan. "Shell like that."

▶ 2. Teach your child to place the apostrophe appropriately to show singular and plural possessives. Write the following phrases, leaving out the apostrophes, and have your child write the apostrophes in the correct places.

a dog's tail	Annette's glasses	California's coastline	Charles's coat
two houses' windows	one man's shoe	each flower's petals	the clock's battery

MATH (Rounding)

▶ 1. Your child will see a reason for rounding a number to the nearest ten if you teach the skill of rounding through estimation. Provide opportunities for your child to estimate numbers. When you are in a crowded room, ask, "How many people do you think are here?" Put a large number of items in a jar for your child to estimate. When adding two numbers, it is helpful to round to determine if your answer is reasonable. For example, "If I add 26 + 13 and get the answer 39, I can check my answer by rounding 26 to 30 and 13 to 10. I know my answer should be somewhere around 40."

▶ 2. For rounding large numbers, ask your child to what hundred or thousand the given number is closer. With a number up to 249, your child should round down to 200. Round up to 300 for 250 or above. Create a number line like the one below.

Choose a random number. Have your child tell to which hundred the given number is closer. Make a number line from 1,000 to 20,000 (intervals of 1,000) and have your child round a number to the nearest thousand.

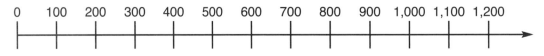

SCIENCE (Simple Machines)

▶ 1. There are six types of simple machines. They are pictured and described below.

Lever—This type of machine helps to move things with less force. A hammer can be used as a kind of lever.

Pulley—Pulleys can be used to lift loads more easily. A pulley can be used to hoist a flag or pail.

Wedge—Wedges help cut or split things. An ax is an example of a wedge.

Wheel—Wheels (as on a wagon or car) can be used to move things easily from one place to another.

Screw—Screws are typically used to hold things together.

Inclined Plane—This type of simple machine can be used to move things from a lower place to a higher place and vice versa. A ramp up to a building is an example of an inclined plane.

▶ 2. Levers, inclined planes and pulleys work on the principle that increased distance (length of lever, plane or pulley rope) makes work easier. Have your child try to shovel a load of dirt holding the handle near the load (the resistance) and then again, holding the handle far from the load. Next, have your child try to lift a heavy box straight up to a shelf, then slide it up a long ramp to the shelf. Compare ways to climb a steep hill: straight up or zig-zag. Compare the work required to turn on a faucet with a large handle to one with a small handle.

How Adjectives Compare

There are certain spelling rules to follow when **adjectives** are used to compare people, places or things.

1. To many adjectives, simply add **er** or **est** to the end.

   fast   fast**er**   fast**est**

2. When an adjective ends with a consonant preceded by a single vowel, double the final consonant and add **er** or **est**.

   fat   fatt**er**   fatt**est**

3. When an adjective ends in an **e**, drop the final **e** and add **er** or **est**.

   brave   brav**er**   brav**est**

4. If an adjective ends in a **y** preceded by a consonant, change the **y** to **i** and add **er** or **est**.

   heavy   heav**ier**   heav**iest**

Complete the chart below using the spelling rules you have learned. **Write** the number of the rule you used.

Adjective	Add **er**	Add **est**	Rule
1. weak	weaker	weakest	1
2. kind			
3. easy			
4. clear			
5. close			
6. noisy			
7. large			
8. red			
9. pretty			
10. hungry			
11. big			
12. happy			
13. wet			
14. cute			
15. plain			
16. busy			
17. loud			
18. strong			
19. fresh			
20. hot			

Learn at Home, Grade 4

Easy Does It

Use spelling words containing the **short e** sound to **fill in** the blanks.

bedtime
being
beverage
cedar
decoy
elegant
female
jelly
lemon
medicine
meteor
rectangle
recycle
secret
skeleton

1. A _____ is sour.

2. The new living room carpet was stained by grape

_____ and a spilled _____ .

3. For your sore throat, you can take _____

before _____ .

4. The body's bony frame is called a _____.

5. A queen would probably be _____ .

6. A _____ has four sides.

Use spelling words containing a **long e** sound to **fill in** the blanks.

1. In the night sky, a _____ could be seen near the Big Dipper.

2. It is no _____ that the _____ star of the movie is quite ill.

3. Our neighbor is _____ thoughtful of the environment because he tries to _____ things like newspaper, aluminum cans and plastic milk jugs.

4. For his birthday, Dad received a _____ to use when he goes duck hunting.

5. The storm damaged a large _____ tree in our yard.

Place Value

1 , 2 3 4 , 5 6 7

millions
hundred thousands
ten thousands
thousands
hundreds
tens
ones

1. The number 8,672,019 has:

_____ thousands   _____ ten   _____ hundred thousands

_____ millions   _____ ones   _____ ten thousands

_____ hundreds

2. What number has

    6 ones   3 millions   9 tens

    7 hundreds   4 ten thousands   8 thousands

    5 hundred thousands

The number is _____.

3. The number 6,792,510 has:

_____ ten thousands   _____ millions   _____ hundreds

_____ ones   _____ thousands   _____ ten

_____ hundred thousands

4. What number has

    5 millions   3 tens   6 thousands

    1 hundred   8 ten thousands   4 ones

    0 hundred thousands

The number is _____.

The First State

What state is known as the first state? Follow the directions below to find out.

1. If 31,842 rounded to the nearest thousand is 31,000, put an A above number 2.
2. If 62 rounded to the nearest ten is 60, put an E above number 2 .
3. If 4,234 rounded to the nearest hundred is 4,200, put an R above number 7.
4. If 677 rounded to the nearest hundred is 600, put an L above number 3.
5. If 344 rounded to the nearest ten is 350, put an E above number 5.

**Peach Blossom
State Flower**

**Blue Hen Chicken
State Bird**

6. If 5,599 rounded to the nearest thousand is 6,000, put an A above number 4.
7. If 1,549 rounded to the nearest hundred is 1,500, put an A above number 6.
8. If 885 rounded to the nearest hundred is 800, put a W above number 2.
9. If 521 rounded to the nearest ten is 520, put an E above number 8.
10. If 74 rounded to the nearest ten is 80, put an R above number 6.

11. If 3,291 rounded to the nearest thousand is 3,000, put an L above number 3.
12. If 248 rounded to the nearest hundred is 300, put an R above number 4.
13. If 615 rounded to the nearest ten is 620, put a D above number 1.
14. If 188 rounded to the nearest ten is 200, put a W above number 1.
15. If 6,817 rounded to the nearest thousand is 7,000, put a W above number 5.

**Fort Christina—site of the first
state's first permanent settlement.
Built by the Swedes and Finns.**

___ ___ ___ ___ ___ ___ ___ ___
 1   2   3   4   5   6   7   8

33

	Language Skills	Spelling	Reading
Monday	Teach your child how to recognize the elements of a news story: *who, what, when, where, why* and *how*. Clip short articles from a newspaper or news magazine and have your child identify the elements in each. Have your child write a news story—including all six elements—about a recent event that affected his/her family or neighborhood. Have him/her write an outline and rough draft today.	Pretest your child on these spelling words. blindfold imagine rifle cinnamon island silence dentist minus skid giant pirate spinach history principal whine Have your child correct the pretest, add personalized words and make two copies of this week's study list.	**Punctuation** Review ending punctuation. Copy several sentences from a book, leaving off the end punctuation. Include a variety of sentences, such as questions, commands, statements and exclamations. Have your child add the ending punctuation. Reteach if necessary. Read chapters 5 and 6 of *Matthew Jackson Meets the Wall*. Have your child write about the children Matthew has encountered.
Tuesday	Review the correct formation of the cursive capital letters S–Z. Have your child practice handwriting. Have your child write one row of each capital letter S–Z. Let him/her circle the best letter in each row.	Have your child use each of this week's spelling words correctly in a sentence.	Review the use of punctuation marks with quotations. Gather some examples from *Matthew Jackson Meets the Wall* or from other books. *See* Reading, Week 3, number 1. Read chapters 7 and 8 of *Matthew Jackson*. Have your child imagine that he/she is a friend of Matthew's and write Matthew a letter telling him how he should deal with the wall.
Wednesday	**Verb Types:** Teach your child the three types of verbs: *action, linking* and *helping*. Also introduce the concept of a verb phrase. *See* Language Skills, Week 3. Give your child a choice of twelve action verbs. Have him/her choose eight and write a sentence using each, underlining the verb. Have your child complete **Helping Verbs** (p. 38).	Have your child complete **I Can Do This** (p. 41).	Have your child add punctuation to quotations. *See* Reading, Week 3, number 2. Read the final chapters of *Matthew Jackson Meets the Wall*. Have your child recall details from the story that describe the type of person Matthew is. What adjectives would he/she use to describe Matthew? List them on the chalkboard. Then, have your child write an argument for or against the "new" Matthew's behavior.
Thursday	Review *past, present* and *future* tenses of verbs. Read your child's news article together to make sure all the verbs are written in the same tense. *See* Language Skills, Week 3. Have your child complete **Verb Tenses** (p. 39).	Have your child create a mnemonic phrase to help him/her spell some of the more difficult words. *See* **Spelling Activities,** number 7, page 8.	Discuss the proper use of capital letters. *See* Reading, Week 3, number 3. Read the first chapter of *Pippi Longstocking* by Astrid Lindgren. Have your child write a paragraph describing Pippi's appearance and her lifestyle. If there is time, have your child create a likeness of Pippi using colored construction paper. Display Pippi and the paragraph about her somewhere in the room.
Friday	Teach your child about *irregular verbs* (verbs that change spelling in the past tense). Have him/her form the past tense of these irregular verbs: catch, choose, do, draw, drink, drive, eat, know and take. Have your child complete **Irregular Verbs** (p. 40).	Give your child the final spelling test. Have your child record the pretest and final test words in his/her word bank.	Review proper use of the comma. *See* Reading, Week 3, number 4. Read chapters 2 and 3 of *Pippi Longstocking*. Have your child make a sequential list of Pippi's activities for 2 days.

Learn at Home, Grade 4

Math	Science	Social Studies
Addition Introduce 2-digit addition with a copy of the **Hundred Chart** (p. 42). Give your child a sample problem, such as 31 + 27 = ___. Starting at the number 31, have him/her trace down two rows (adding 2 tens) and over seven columns (adding 7 ones). Your child's finger should land on the correct answer: 58. Repeat with other problems. Then, challenge your child to write his/her own addition problems using the chart.	**Compound Machines** *Compound machines* are made of two or more simple machines. **Example:** a pair of scissors is made from two levers and two wedges. Review the six types of simple machines. Analyze a variety of tools, kitchen utensils, cleaning materials and garden equipment with your child. Ask him/her to identify the simple machines that comprise each of these compound machines.	Introduce the well-known European explorers of the 1400 and 1500s. Discuss some of the forces behind European exploration at that time and what these explorers hoped to find or achieve. Help your child create a chart showing the explorers, their countries of origin, where they explored, the years they explored and other relevant information. *See* Social Studies, Week 3.
Following the same procedure as yesterday's lesson, teach your child to solve 2-digit problems with regrouping. When adding ones on the chart, your child must continue to the next row of numbers. **Example:** 36 + 19 = ___. He/she will begin at 36 on the chart, move down one row to 46, then to the right nine spaces (four over to 50, then continuing another five spaces on the next line) to 55.	Study a bicycle. Have your child draw a detailed diagram of his/her bicycle. Then, ask him/her to label the simple machines that form the bike.	Portuguese explorers aggressively sought an eastern sea route to Asia and a route around the southern tip of Africa. Read about the journey of Bartolomeu Dias. Have your child trace the journey of Dias to the Cape of Good Hope.
Use colored paper squares as manipulatives for adding 3- and 4-digit numbers. Have your child model and solve problems without regrouping. *See* Math, Week 3, numbers 1 and 2. **Examples:** 1,268 315 2,274 + 4,721 + 640 + 6,023	Study the movement of gears. Discuss everyday objects that contain gears. Ask your child to name some. Have him/her observe and draw models of gears. Explain how gears of different sizes operate together to make work easier. Have your child design a new compound machine made up of at least three different simple machines. Have him/her illustrate and name the invention, then explain how it works.	What kind of person sponsors explorers? Read with your child about Henry the Navigator. Have your child draw a cartoon strip of Henry the Navigator interacting with an explorer and include dialogue balloons.
Review addition with regrouping. Give your child an addition problem. Have him/her build the two numbers using the colored squares from Wednesday's lesson. When your child joins the squares in one "place," he/she may need to trade ten squares of one color for a single square of the next color. Help your child construct problems several times before giving him/her independent work.	Read about how the Egyptians built the pyramids without machinery. Have your child draw a picture of a simple machine being used in the construction of the pyramids. Then, have him/her write a brief explanation of how the pyramids were built.	Have your child imagine that he/she is one of the European explorers (choose one). Have him/her send a written message back to the sponsor telling about the crew's discovery. Encourage your child to imagine how that explorer felt and to capture the spirit of the occasion in his/her message.
Teach your child how to complete an addition box (*see* below) by adding vertically and horizontally to fill in the blank squares. The shaded box in the bottom right-hand corner holds the sum of the third row. This is also the sum of the third column *and* the sum of the original four numbers. Have your child complete **Batter Up!** (p. 43). | 427	611	
319	582	
				Visit a nearby factory with large machinery. Observe the many identifiable simple machines that combine to make the large machines.	Scramble the letters of five explorers' names. Have your child unscramble each of the five names and write a sentence for each telling about his most famous accomplishment.

TEACHING SUGGESTIONS AND ACTIVITIES

LANGUAGE SKILLS (Verb Types)

BACKGROUND

If you ask your child what a verb is, he/she will most likely respond, "an action word." Teach him/her that there are two additional kinds of verbs: linking verbs and helping verbs.

- Action verbs: *sing, write, play, think, draw*
  An action verb shows the action of the subject.

- Linking verbs: *am, is, are, was, were*
  A linking verb does not show action. It links the subject with a noun or adjective in the predicate of the sentence. When a linking verb is followed by a predicate noun, the noun renames the subject.

  Example: *Harry is a teacher.*

When a linking verb is followed by a predicate adjective, the adjective describes the subject. **Example:** *Harry is confident.*

- Helping verbs: *am, is, are, was, were, have, has*
  A helping verb is part of a verb phrase. It comes before the main verb.

  Examples: *Tim has practiced hard. Jean is working at night.*

(Irregular Past-Tense Verbs)

To form the past tense of regular verbs, add *ed.*

boil, boiled   walk, walked   miss, missed   show, showed

There are several exceptions:

- When a verb ends with a consonant preceded by a single vowel, double the final consonant before adding *ed.*

  Examples: tip, tipped   fan, fanned

- When a verb ends in an *e*, drop the *e* and add *ed.*

  Examples: race, raced   hike, hiked

- When a verb ends in *y*, change the *y* to *i* and add *ed.*

  Examples: fry, fried   apply, applied

READING (Punctuation)

▶ 1. Practice reading dialogue with your child. Choose a conversational dialogue from a book. Let your child pick a role and you take the other. Read the dialogue as actual conversation, reading only the words within quotation marks.

▶ 2. Give your child a passage of dialogue, omitting all punctuation. Let him/her edit the passage by adding all necessary punctuation. Reading the passage aloud may help him/her determine where it is needed.

▶ 3. Review the proper use of capital letters. Have your child find examples of each application.

- beginning of a sentence
- first word inside quotation marks
- days of the week, months of the year
- some abbreviations and titles (Mr., U.S.)
- important historical events (World War II)
- holidays (Independence Day)

- first letter in each line of poetry
- proper nouns
- important documents (the Bill of Rights)
- key landmarks and buildings (the White House)
- words in a title (except prepositions and articles)

4. Have your child find examples of commas being used in the following ways:

    In a series: Karl had cereal, toast and orange juice for breakfast.
    In a compound sentence joined by *and, but* or *or*: Jen made dinner, and Lee washed the dishes. I want to buy the shirt, but I don't have enough money.
    In a quotation: "I'll be there at 7:00," said Kim. (or) Kim said, "I'll be there at 7:00."

MATH (Addition)

1. Create a place-value board and manipulatives for adding large numbers. Choose four different colors of construction paper. Cut out eighteen small squares (2" x 2") of each color. Designate one color for the ones place, a second color for the tens, a third for the hundreds and a fourth for the thousands. Divide a 9" x 12" sheet of construction paper into four columns and label the columns as shown below.

Thousands	Hundreds	Tens	Ones

Sample
$$4,216 + 1,352$$

2. Use the colored squares to model an addition problem (see the example above right). Have your child "build" the first number of the equation by placing the appropriate number of colored squares in each place on the place-value board. Then, have your child "build" the second number of the equation below the first, adding the squares in each place as well as writing the total.

SOCIAL STUDIES (Early Explorers)

BACKGROUND

Marco Polo's tales of riches and adventure in the Far East spurred others to explore the areas. Wealthy Europeans sought to buy jewels, spices and silks from the eastern world. Unfortunately, in the 1400s, Turkish Muslims controlled the main overland trade routes between Europe and the East and charged high prices for passage. European traders were determined to find sea routes to the East. The "great age of European discovery" began with a quest to find a route to the "Indies," yet resulted in much more.

European explorers of the 1400 and 1500s included:

Vasco Núñez de Balboa
Sebastian Cabot
Pedro Álvares Cabral
Jacques Cartier
Christopher Columbus
Francisco Vásquez de Coronado
Hernando Cortés

Bartholomeu Dias
Sir Frances Drake
Sir Martin Frobisher
Vasco da Gama
Ferdinand Magellan
Amerigo Vespucci

Helping Verbs

A **verb phrase** is a verb that has more than one word. It is made up of a **main verb** plus one or more **helping verbs**.

Example: verb phrase

Tim **has practiced** hard.

helping verb   main verb

These words are often used as helping verbs with the main verb.

am, is, are, was, were, have, has

Underline the helping verbs and **circle** the main verbs in the sentences below.

1. The instructor has taught science for several years.
2. The concert pianist was practicing before the performance.
3. Researchers are attempting to find a cure for the disease.
4. The architect has drawn detailed blueprints.
5. The scientist has researched the project carefully.
6. Several patients were waiting in the doctor's office.
7. During his lifetime, the artist has painted many beautiful pictures.
8. A touchdown was scored by the quarterback.
9. The ship's captain is giving orders to the first mate.
10. The clown has performed for many years.
11. The tailor was hemming the man's trousers.
12. The construction workers have finished with the project.
13. The secretary was typing the letters yesterday.
14. Lawyers have passed difficult state examinations.
15. A cab driver has transported many passengers by the end of the day.

Verb Tenses

A **present-tense** verb shows action that is happening now. A **past-tense** verb shows action that happened earlier. A **future-tense** verb shows action that will take place in the future.

Examples: The clockmaker **repairs** the clock. (present)
The clockmaker **repaired** the clock. (past)
The clockmaker **will repair** the clock. (future)

Write these verbs using the tenses shown in parentheses.

	try	**walk**	**work**
(present)	Tom _____	Karen _____	They _____
(past)	Tom _____	Karen _____	They _____
(future)	Tom _____	Karen _____	They _____

Write the correct verb in each blank below.

1. time (future)   5. tell (present)   9. help (past)
2. chart (present)   6. reset (future)   10. invent (past)
3. trickle (past)   7. dine (present)   11. operate (future)
4. use (past)   8. move (future)

1. John ____**will time**____ the runners in the race.

2. A calendar _____ the days of each month.

3. Sand _____ through the hourglass.

4. People _____ the hourglass before clocks were invented.

5. A pendulum _____ time by Earth's rotation.

6. John _____ his watch when changing time zones.

7. He _____ at 8:00 every evening during the week.

8. Martha _____ the hands of the clock.

9. In the distant past, the Sun and the Moon _____ man tell time.

10. The Egyptians _____ the solar calendar.

11. Timepieces 100 years from now _____ differently.

39

Irregular Verbs

Verbs that do not add **ed** to form the past tense are called **irregular verbs**.
The spelling of these verbs changes.

Examples:

present	past	present	past
begin, begins	**began**	do, does	**did**
break, breaks	**broke**	eat, eats	**ate**

Write the past tense of each irregular verb below.

1. Samuel almost _____ (fall) when he kicked a rock in the path.

2. Diana made sure she _____ (take) a canteen on her hike.

3. David _____ (run) over to a shady tree for a quick break.

4. Jimmy _____ (break) off a long piece of grass to put in his mouth
   while he was walking.

5. Eva _____ (know) the path along the river very well.

6. The clouds _____ (begin) to sprinkle raindrops on the hikers.

7. Kathy _____ (throw) a small piece of bread to the birds.

8. Everyone _____ (eat) a very nutritious meal after a long adventure.

9. We all _____ (sleep) very well that night.

Many irregular verbs have a different past-tense ending when the helping
verbs **have** and **has** are used.

Examples: Steven **has worn** special hiking shoes today.
           Marlene and I **have known** about this trail for years.

Circle the correct irregular verb below.

1. Peter has (flew, flown) down to join us for the adventure.

2. Mark has (saw, seen) a lot of animals on the hike today.

3. Andy and Mike have (went, gone) on this trail before.

4. Bill has (took, taken) extra precautions to make sure no cacti prick his legs.

5. Heather has (ate, eaten) all the snacks her mom packed for her.

Learn at Home, Grade 4

I Can Do This

Complete the crossword puzzle.

blindfold
cinnamon
dentist
giant
history
imagine
island
minus
pirate
principal
rifle
silence
skid
spinach
whine

Across
1. green, leafy vegetable
3. think about
6. covering for eyes
10. noiseless
12. land surrounded by water
13. robber on the seas
14. less

Down
1. slide
2. brown spice
4. head of a school
5. a study of the past
7. one who fixes teeth
8. gun
9. complain
11. very large person

Learn at Home, Grade 4

Hundred Chart

1	2	3	4	5	6	7	8	9	10
11	12	13	14	15	16	17	18	19	20
21	22	23	24	25	26	27	28	29	30
31	32	33	34	35	36	37	38	39	40
41	42	43	44	45	46	47	48	49	50
51	52	53	54	55	56	57	58	59	60
61	62	63	64	65	66	67	68	69	70
71	72	73	74	75	76	77	78	79	80
81	82	83	84	85	86	87	88	89	90
91	92	93	94	95	96	97	98	99	100

Batter Up!

Complete each addition box.

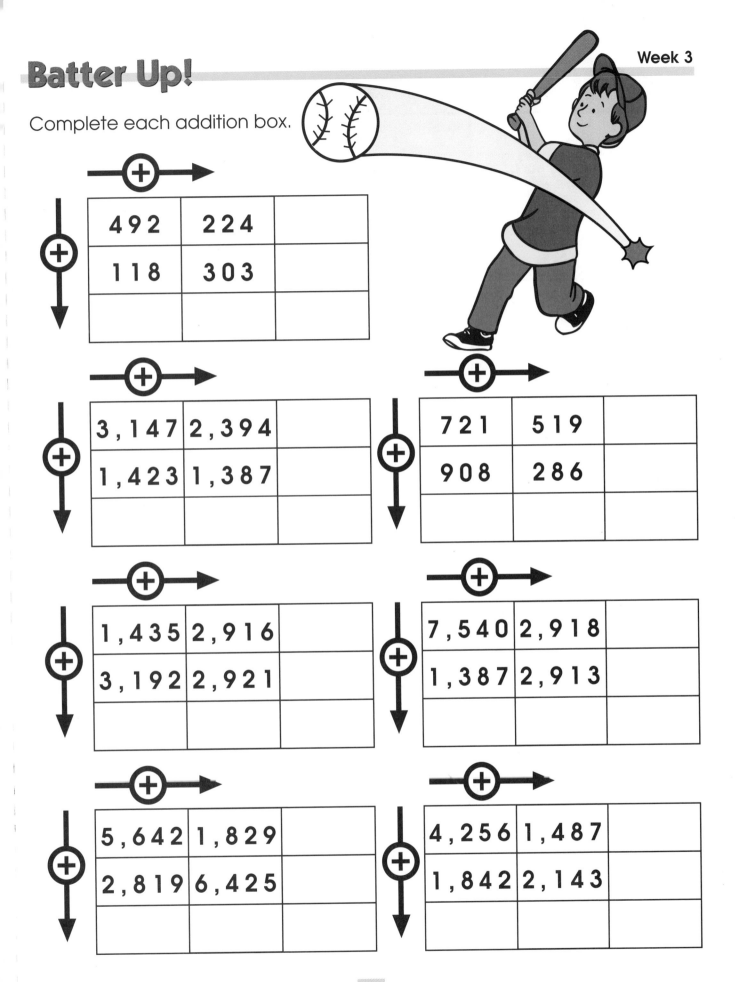

+ →		
492	224	
118	303	

+ →		
3,147	2,394	
1,423	1,387	

+ →		
721	519	
908	286	

+ →		
1,435	2,916	
3,192	2,921	

+ →		
7,540	2,918	
1,387	2,913	

+ →		
5,642	1,829	
2,819	6,425	

+ →		
4,256	1,487	
1,842	2,143	

43

Language Skills	Spelling	Reading

Monday

Dreams can be a source for interesting writing assignments. Have your child recall a recent dream. Discuss the content of the dream and help your child fill in the missing parts. Help him/her start writing about the dream by creating a topic sentence. Have your child write a rough draft about a recent dream and include descriptive language.

Pretest your child on these spelling words.

auto	doctor	object
bobbin	elbow	poetry
bony	frozen	solemn
closet	hotel	solve
cobra	knot	total

Have your child correct the pretest, add personalized words and make two copies of this week's study list.

Prefixes and Suffixes
Read words that contain prefixes and discuss the meaning of each prefix. Recognizing prefixes will help your child decode unfamiliar words. *See* Reading, Week 4. Read chapters 4 and 5 of *Pippi Longstocking*. Ask your child if he/she would like to have a friend like Pippi and why. Have your child respond in his/her Reading Journal.

Tuesday

Review the correct formation of the cursive lower-case letters a–i. Have your child practice handwriting, writing one row of each lower-case letter a–i. Let him/her circle the best letter in each row.

Have your child use each of this week's spelling words correctly in a sentence.

Teach your child to identify common suffixes. Discuss the rules of spelling that apply when adding a suffix. *See* Reading, Week 4, numbers 1 and 2. Read chapters 6 and 7 of *Pippi Longstocking*. Ask your child what he/she would recommend to Pippi at the circus and if her behavior was appropriate. Have your child write a response in his/her Reading Journal.

Wednesday

Adverbs: Teach your child to recognize and use *adverbs*. Whereas adjectives modify nouns, adverbs modify verbs. Adverbs tell how (slowly), when (yesterday) or where (outside) something is done. *See* Language Skills, Week 4, number 1. Find the adjectives in your child's dream story. Help him/her add adverbs, if appropriate. Have your child complete **That's How It's Done** (p. 48).

Have your child complete **Often-Used O's** (p. 50).

Read chapters 8 and 9 of *Pippi Longstocking*. Pose the following questions for your child to address in his/her Reading Journal: *Do you think Pippi was trying to trick the burglars? Did Pippi intend to disrupt the coffee party? Explain your answers.* Have your child complete **Break It Up!** (p. 51).

Thursday

Comparative Words: Teach the comparative forms of adverbs. Like adjectives, adverbs show comparison when given the endings *er* or *est*. **Examples:** The plane flew high*er* than the balloon. The jet flew high*est* of all. You can also show comparison by placing the word *more, most, less* or *least* before an adverb. *See* Language Skills, Week 4, numbers 2 and 3.

Have your child group the spelling words by parts of speech: noun, adjective, verb.

Teach your child to use context clues when he/she comes to an unfamiliar word in a book. Copy a paragraph from a book at your child's reading level. Replace every fifteenth word with a blank. Have your child try to fill in the blanks by thinking logically and looking at context clues. He/she should use this same strategy to define unfamiliar words in a text. Finish reading *Pippi Longstocking*.

Friday

People sometimes confuse adverbs and adjectives. Write several adjective/noun and adverb/verb pairs (i.e., red car, quietly spoke) on the chalkboard. Have your child circle the adjectives in red and the adverbs in blue. Review the rules for using the words *good, well, sure, surely, real* and *really*. Have your child complete **Misused Words** (p. 49).

Give your child the final spelling test. Have your child record the pretest and final test words in his/her word bank.

Have your child compose a poem or song about Pippi or draw a comic strip that tells about an adventure she might have next.

Math	Science	Social Studies
Model for your child how to align numbers for column addition. *See* Math, Week 4, number 1. Choose equations that do not require regrouping for your child to complete independently. Have your child add the numbers column by column to solve each equation, using manipulatives as needed.	**Solar System** Begin to fill out a KWHL chart. *See* Science, Week 4, number 1. Use the information gained from this activity to guide your planning and motivate your child. Discover what he/she already knows, any misconceptions he/she may have and his/her specific interests. Introduce pertinent solar system vocabulary into spelling lessons over the next few weeks.	Take your child to a nearby library (or work with resources you have at home). Guide your child in finding resources where he/she can find the origins of the name "America." On a map, trace the routes of Amerigo Vespucci. Compare them to the routes of earlier explorers. Ask: *How do they differ? What did Vespucci hope to accomplish in his travels?*
Give your child several column addition problems with regrouping, using colored squares to help with the regrouping. Solve some problems together before assigning independent work. Have your child add columns of numbers with regrouping. Remind him/her to keep the columns straight.	Go to the library with your child and gather books related to the solar system. Find books that focus on topics of special interest to your child. Bring these books back to the house and set up a resource center for his/her study of the solar system.	With your child, read about the travels of Hernando Cortés. *See* Social Studies, Week 4, number 1. Discuss the meaning of conquest. The Aztec capital of Tenochtitlán was destroyed when Cortés conquered the city. Mexico City now sits atop the ruins. Discuss whether Cortés acted appropriately.
Design story problems involving several 2-, 3- or 4-digit numbers. *See* Math, Week 4, number 2. Have your child solve the problems. Discuss the clue words that indicate addition and ask what other words might signal addition. Have your child write and solve an addition story problem using at least four 2-, 3- or 4-digit numbers.	Discuss the definition of solar system and pose the question, *What is the Sun? See* Science, Week 4, number 2. Introduce your child to the contributions of Copernicus and Galileo and discuss their impact on modern astronomy. Ask your child: *How were these scientists regarded by their contemporaries?*	Discuss ways that Cortés and Montezuma might have avoided the fighting and destruction. How might they have compromised? Have your child make puppets and act out an imaginary dialogue between the two leaders.
Subtraction: Show your child how to subtract 2-digit numbers using the **Hundred Chart** (p. 42). Use only problems without regrouping for now. Review how the chart was used for addition, then introduce subtraction. Starting at the first number, your child will trace UP a certain number of rows (to subtract tens), then LEFT a certain number of columns (to subtract ones). *See* Math, Week 4, number 3.	Teach your child the names of the planets. Use a model of the solar system to show the relative distance of each planet from the Sun. Have your child complete **Keeping the Order** (p. 52).	Read about Ferdinand Magellan and Sir Frances Drake. Discuss why these explorers wanted to sail around the world and what obstacles they faced. Have your child trace the routes of Magellan and Drake on a globe or world map, then imagine that he/she, too, will sail around the world. Ask what route he/she would take and where the voyage would begin and end. *See* Social Studies, Week 4, number 2.
Following the same procedure as Thursday's lesson, show your child how to solve 2-digit subtraction problems with regrouping. When subtracting ones on the chart, your child must continue to the previous row of numbers, moving right to left.	Using your library resources and the information found on the activity sheets (pgs. 52 and 53), have your child research and write some facts about each planet. Play "Planet Match." *See* directions and game cards on **Planet Match** (p. 53).	Have your child plan an imaginary voyage to an "unknown" place. Planning should include reasons for exploration, expected length of the trip, supplies needed, mode of transportation, predicted discoveries and plans upon returning home. Have your child write about the voyage and include at least one illustration.

Learn at Home, Grade 4

TEACHING SUGGESTIONS AND ACTIVITIES

LANGUAGE SKILLS (Adverbs and Comparative Words)

▶ 1. Write the following adverbs on the chalkboard and have your child indicate whether the adverb tells when, where or how.

easily	today	below	busily	fast	here	carefully
there	thirstily	downhill	slowly	lately	away	perfectly
inside	noisily	yearly	neatly	after	early	annually

▶ 2. Have your child complete each sentence below with a comparative adverb.

George ran <u>fast</u>.
Marcy ran _____ than George.
Chris ran _____ of all.

Generate other groups of sentences similar to these for your child to complete.

▶ 3. Write the following sentences on the chalkboard. Have your child write *more, most, less* or *least* before each adverb to complete the sentence. Answers may vary.

Andrew flies to Dallas ____ frequently than Roberto.
Veronique flies to Dallas ____ often of all.
Phyllis drives her race car _____ skillfully than Eric.
David races _____ expertly of all.
Aaron uses his boat _____ often than Timothy.

READING (Prefixes and Suffixes)

BACKGROUND

A *prefix* is a word element added to the beginning of a word that modifies the word's meaning.

antibiotic (against)
bicycle (two)
cofounder / **com**pact / **con**text (together/with)
defrost (undo)
disapprove (not)
export (out)
foretell (before)
insignificant (lacking)
misdeed (wrong/bad)

preterm (before)
propose (for/in favor of)
return (again)
submarine (under)
supermarket (over)
transatlantic (across)
tripod (three)
undesirable (not)

▶ 1. A *suffix* is a word element added to the end of a word that modifies the word's meaning. Read the following words with your child and help him/her identify the suffixes.

visi**ble**	like**ly**	height**en**	avail**able**	imita**tion**
hand**ful**	sing**er**	redd**en**	happi**ness**	disappoint**ment**
rela**tion**	blu**ish**	quartz**ite**	mother**hood**	

▶ 2. Discuss some rules about adding suffixes.

  a. When adding a suffix that begins with a vowel, double the final consonant after a short vowel.

  b. Drop the final *e* when adding a suffix that begins with a vowel.

  c. Change *y* to *i* before adding a suffix.

46

MATH (Addition and Subtraction)

▶ 1. On the chalkboard, write four 2-, 3- or 4-digit numbers. Have your child write the numbers in a column to prepare for addition, lining up the ones, tens, hundreds and thousands. Guide your child until he/she is writing the numbers correctly in a column. If your child has difficulty writing the numbers in a column, provide graph paper and have him/her write one digit in each box.

▶ 2. Read the following problem to your child: *The basketball team scored 10 points in the first quarter, 12 in the second, 28 in the third and 19 in the fourth. How many points did the team score in all?*
Have your child determine the operation (addition) and write the numbers in a column to solve. Create and dictate other story problems with topics meaningful to your child.

▶ 3. Challenge your child to write several 2-digit subtraction problems using the **Hundred Chart** (p. 42). Allow him/her to choose the numbers and trace with his/her finger on the chart to determine the answer. You could allow your child to check his/her work with a calculator.

```
  3 1 2
    2 4
  5 4 1
+ 1 0 1 0
```

SCIENCE (Solar System)

▶ 1. Make a KWHL chart. Divide a large sheet of butcher paper into four columns. Label the columns: *What I Know, What I Want to Know, How I Will Get the Information* and *What I Learned.* Use the questions below to get your child thinking about the solar system. Have him/her list facts and thoughts under the first three columns. Save the final column for the end of the unit. **Sample questions:** What planets are in our solar system? What makes each one unique? What has been in the news lately concerning our solar system? What are meteorites? What is the name of our galaxy? What are stars? What constellations have you seen? How do Earth and the Moon move? Why is Pluto considered a dwarf planet?

▶ 2. The Sun is the center of our solar system. The solar system consists of the Sun and all the objects that travel around it, including the nine planets, moons, asteroids, meteoroids, comets and other drifting particles. Each is held in place by gravity. The solar system is shaped like a disk and is only a small part of the Milky Way galaxy. The Sun is a star. It gives off energy that benefits all the planets. Gather resource books about the solar system. Obtain a model and posters of the solar system. There are many fascinating areas of study related to the solar system. Encourage your child to explore the provided resources.

SOCIAL STUDIES (Early Explorers)

▶ 1. Cortés was sent to Mexico to find gold and claim the land. The Aztec emperor Montezuma welcomed Cortés warmly. The Aztecs thought he was a god. Imagine how the Aztecs felt when Cortés imprisoned Montezuma and ruled the empire himself. Within 3 years, Cortés had conquered all of central Mexico. Discuss Cortés's behavior toward the Aztecs.

▶ 2. Discuss recent adventurers' attempts at sailing around the world. Ask: *How do today's voyages differ from those of Magellan and Drake? In what ways are they similar?*

That's How It's Done

Adverbs answer the questions **when**, **where** and **how**. The adverbs in the sentences below answer **how**. **Underline** the adverbs in each sentence. Then, **circle** the verb it describes. The first one is done for you.

1. The two boys <u>solemnly</u> (shook) hands.
2. Chip looked down incredulously at the fallen shingle which landed softly at this feet.
3. "I don't salvage," remarked Rudy calmly when his counselor glared at him.
4. "Rudy," whispered Mike warningly. Chip was glaring in his direction.
5. The door opened and Mr. Warden emerged, smartly dressed in a white tennis outfit.
6. "Harold, you have no soul," explained Rudy pleasantly.
7. "Why do you immediately assume that I'm guilty?" asked Rudy in a hurt tone.
8. "I'd rather go back to arts and crafts," nodded Mike sheepishly.
9. "Tomorrow," Rudy said thoughtfully as they carefully daubed pale blue paint onto their creation, "we'll go earlier."
10. Arms flailing wildly, Chip rushed anxiously toward his cabin.
11. "Let's just walk directly away from the lake," declared Rudy.

Write four sentences of your own containing adverbs. **Underline** the adverbs and **circle** the verbs that are described.

1. _____

_____

2. _____

_____

3. _____

_____

4. _____

_____

Learn at Home, Grade 4

Misused Words

Sometimes people have difficulty using **good**, **well**, **sure**, **surely**, **real** and **really** correctly. This chart may help you.

Adjectives	Adverbs
Good is an adjective when it describes a noun. 　That was a **good** dinner.	**Good** is never used as an adverb.
Well is an adjective when it means in good health or having a good appearance. 　She looks **well**.	**Well** is an adverb when it is used to tell that something is done capably or effectively. 　She writes **well**.
Sure is an adjective when it modifies a noun. 　A robin is a **sure** sign of spring.	**Surely** is an adverb. 　He **surely** wants a job.
Real is an adjective that means genuine or true. 　That was a **real** diamond.	**Really** is an adverb. 　Mary **really** played a good game.

Use the chart to help you choose the correct word from those in parentheses. **Write** it in the blank.

1. You did a very _____ job of writing your book report. (good, well)

2. The detective in the story used his skills _____ . (good, well)

3. He _____ solved the case before anyone else did. (sure, surely)

4. I _____ want to read that book now. (real, really)

5. Did it take you long to decide who the _____ criminal was?

   (real, really)

6. Although the butler looked _____ and healthy, he died. (well, good)

7. Detective Rains read the clues _____ as he worked on the case. (good, well)

8. You will _____ get a good grade on that report. (surely, sure)

9. You had to _____ work hard to get those good grades. (real, really)

Often-Used O's

auto	bobbin	bony
closet	cobra	doctor
elbow	frozen	hotel
knot	object	poetry
solemn	solve	total

Put a check to the left of the words in the list that have a **short o** sound as in **hot**. Put a star to the right of the words in the list that have a **long o** sound as in **open**.

Write a spelling word to answer each question.

1. What's another word for "sum"? __ __ __ [ ] __

2. Which word names a snake? [ ] __ __ __ __

3. Which word describes ice cream? __ __ __ __ [ ] __

4. Where might you stay on a vacation? [ ] __ __ __ __

5. Where is thread kept? __ __ __ __ [ ] __

6. What can be tied in a rope? [ ] __ __ __

7. What happens when you find a solution? __ __ [ ] __ __

8. What word means serious? __ __ __ __ [ ] __

9. What's between the wrist and the shoulder? __ __ __ [ ] __

10. Which word describes rhyming verse? [ ] __ __ __ __ __

11. Where do clothes hang? __ __ [ ] __ __

12. Who helps those who are sick? __ __ __ [ ] __

13. Which word means "car"? __ [ ] __ __

14. Which word describes a skeleton? __ __ __ [ ]

Match the boxed letter from each line to the numbered lines below to answer the riddle. *Where can you always find a lost object?*

__ __   __ __ __   __ __ __ __
5 8   12 4 3   7 1 11 12

__ __ __ __ __   __ __ __   __ __ __ __!
10 7 1 2 3   14 9 13   7 9 9 6

Break It Up!

For each word given below, **write** the root word and the prefix and/or suffix. Remember, some root words' spellings have been changed before adding suffixes. Not all words will have a prefix and a suffix.

Word	Prefix	Root Word	Suffix
resourceful			
accomplishment			
numbness			
convincing			
merciless			
sturdiest			
disobeying			
unmistakable			
disinfecting			
disclaimed			
reopening			
inventive			
restless			
precaution			
imitating			

Keeping the Order

Nine planets orbit the Sun. These planets are arranged in order according to their distance from the Sun.

Number the planets below in order with number one being the planet closest to the Sun. Use the mean (average) distances in miles to help you.

_____Venus — 67,200,000   _____Neptune — 2,794,000,000

_____Mercury — 36,000,000   _____Uranus —1,783,100,000

_____Earth — 92,900,000   _____Jupiter — 483,300,000

_____Mars —141,500,000   _____Saturn — 886,200,000

To help you remember the order of the planets, **write** a sentence, using the first letter of each planet. Order them from the planet closest to the Sun to the one farthest from it. **Note: Write** the planets in order on the lines below, then **write** down some words on each line that begin with the first letter of that planet.

Your sentence:_____

_____

_____

_____

_____

_____

_____

_____

Planet Match

1. Make several copies of the game card.
2. **Cut out** the fact cards and place them facedown.
3. You and your partner should each have a game card.
4. With your partner, take turns flipping over one card and matching it with the correct planet on your game card.
5. The first person to get 3 in a row, up and down, across or diagonally is the winner.
6. Use a science book to make additional cards.

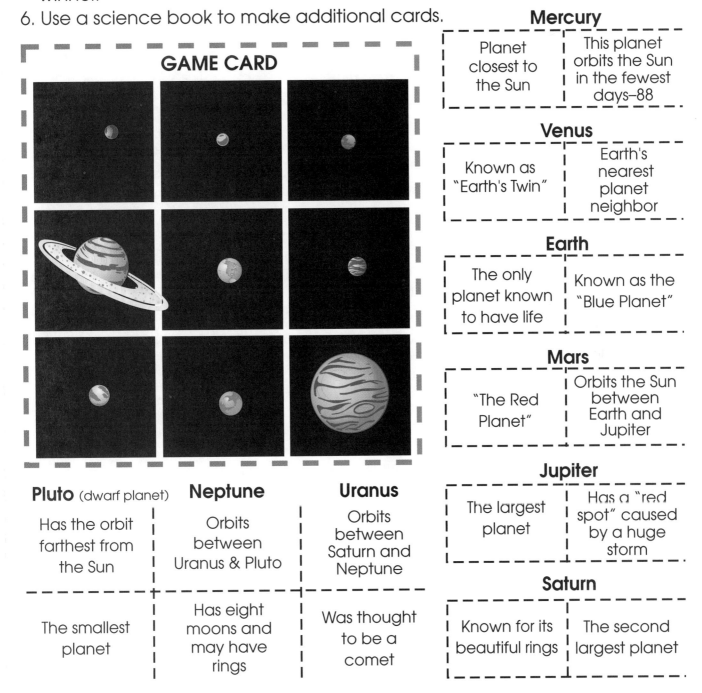

GAME CARD

Mercury

| Planet closest to the Sun | This planet orbits the Sun in the fewest days–88 |

Venus

| Known as "Earth's Twin" | Earth's nearest planet neighbor |

Earth

| The only planet known to have life | Known as the "Blue Planet" |

Mars

| "The Red Planet" | Orbits the Sun between Earth and Jupiter |

Jupiter

| The largest planet | Has a "red spot" caused by a huge storm |

Saturn

| Known for its beautiful rings | The second largest planet |

Pluto (dwarf planet) | **Neptune** | **Uranus**

| Has the orbit farthest from the Sun | Orbits between Uranus & Pluto | Orbits between Saturn and Neptune |
| The smallest planet | Has eight moons and may have rings | Was thought to be a comet |

	Language Skills	Spelling	Reading
Monday	Guide your child in writing a book report on a book he/she has read recently. Ask him/her to make an outline before writing the rough draft. Have him/her work on the report for the rest of the week.	Pretest your child on these spelling words. amuse customer Jupiter bubble duty number budding humor sundown budge hungry summer computer husky usual Have your child correct the pretest, add personalized words and make two copies of this week's study list.	**Dictionary Skills** Introduce *A Grain of Rice* by Helena Clare Pittman by asking your child to imagine how a peasant might win the hand of a princess in marriage. Have your child read to find out who the characters are and what the problem is. Review dictionary skills. *See* Reading, Week 5, number 1. Have your child complete **Watch for Grandpa's Watch** (p. 60).
Tuesday	Review the correct formation of the cursive lower-case letters j–r. Have your child practice handwriting, writing one row of each lower-case letter j–r. Let him/her circle the best letter in each row.	Have your child use each of this week's spelling words correctly in a sentence.	Discuss the pages read so far in *A Grain of Rice*. Ask: *What is Pong Lo like? Why does he work so hard? Describe the princess's feelings.* Help your child make a mosaic with rice. Put 1 tbsp. rubbing alcohol, 2–3 drops of food coloring and 1 cup of uncooked rice in a resealable plastic bag. Shake until coated. Spread on newspaper to dry. Make several colors. Have your child glue rice onto heavy paper to make a design or scene.
Wednesday	**Prepositions:** Introduce *prepositions*. Teach your child to recognize prepositional phrases in sentences. *See* Language Skills, Week 5. Have your child skim through *A Grain of Rice* and point out any prepositional phrases (such as *of Rice*).	Have your child complete **You Can Spell Us** (p. 59).	Discuss your child's reading so far in *A Grain of Rice*. Questions: *What was the princess's problem? Why did Pong Lo ask that the emperor tell the princess the potion was from him? Why do you think the emperor had the grains of rice delivered in such fancy containers?* Review alphabetical order to the second and third letter. Have your child complete **The Imperial Alphabet** (p. 61).
Thursday	Help your child practice forming prepositional phrases that describe location. Place a small object somewhere in the room and have your child describe where it is—e.g., "The ball is on the chair." Repeat, setting the object in different positions within the room. Vary the activity by calling out a location and asking your child to place the object in the appropriate place. Then, let your child call out locations for you.	Have your child write a poem (serious or silly, free verse or rhyming) using as many of the spelling words as possible.	Read the paragraphs found in Reading, Week 5, number 2 aloud to your child. Let him/her choose one of the scenes to draw in detail. Repeat the paragraph several times as your child draws. Stress any details that he/she may have overlooked.
Friday	Once your child has completed the activity sheet, have him/her to go back through the sentences and underline all the prepositional phrases. Have your child complete **Tennis Anyone?** (p. 58).	Give your child the final spelling test. Have your child record the pretest and final test words in his/her word bank.	After your child has completed *A Grain of Rice*, have him/her write about the story in the Reading Journal. Questions to get him/her started: *How did the peasant finally win the hand of the princess? What kind of person is the princess? How is this book like a fairy tale? What were the long-term effects of the marriage?* Have your child complete **A Clever Crossword** (62).

Learn at Home, Grade 4

Math	Science	Social Studies
Use the colored paper squares or other manipulatives to model subtracting 3-digit numbers without regrouping. Have your child model and solve problems using manipulatives and a place-value board. **Examples:** 647 926 245 　　　　 − 402 − 124 − 231	Have your child use **Our Solar System** (p. 64) and resources gathered from the library to fill in the chart.	Introduce the well-known explorers of North America. *See* Social Studies, Week 5, for a list of explorers. Help your child create a chart showing the explorers, their countries of origin, where they explored, the years they explored and other relevant information.
Review subtraction with regrouping. Have your child build the first number with the colored squares, then remove the amount indicated by the second number. He/she may need to trade (or regroup) one square of the next color for ten of the needed color in order to have enough squares in a given place. Help your child construct problems several times before assigning independent work.	Have your child do further research on Galileo. Then, ask him/her to write a short newspaper article. Have your child complete a headline, reporting Galileo's claims. Your child should imagine that he/she is writing at the time Galileo was alive. How were Galileo's claims generally received?	Discuss the different reasons that explorers were commissioned. Compare the expedition of Cortés to Mexico with the expedition of Champlain and Nicolet. *See* Social Studies, Week 5, number 1. Have your child describe his/her feelings about the way Jolliet and Marquette interacted with the people living in the area of their travels.
Allow your child to use manipulatives to help, as needed. Have your child complete **Jungle Math** (p. 63).	Help your child make a model of the solar system. This will take several days. *See* Science, Week 5, number 1.	Read about Christopher Columbus with your child. Have him/her gather and write down Columbus's biographical data (i.e., where he was born, who his parents were, where he went to school, etc.), then make a list of events that outline his attempts to explore the globe.
Write an addition problem with a missing addend, such as 231 + ____ = 680. Have your child propose how to find the missing addend. Allow your child to test his/her proposals. The best method may be through subtraction (680 − 231), but let him/her discover that on his/her own. Give your child ten addition problems with missing addends to solve independently.	Have your child continue working on the model of the solar system.	Read about Henry Hudson. Hudson was hired by trading companies to find better trade routes. Hudson Bay, Hudson Strait and the Hudson River are all named after this explorer. Have your child imagine that he/she has just discovered an unknown place or geographical feature. What would he/she most like to discover and how would he/she want it to be named?
Create story problems involving 2-, 3- or 4-digit subtraction equations. Have your child solve the problems. Discuss clue words that indicate subtraction (compare, difference, more than, less than, how many left). *See* Math, Week 5, number 1. Have your child write and solve a subtraction story problem using 2-, 3- or 4-digit numbers.	Have your child finish the model of the solar system and display it for future reference. Invite friends and family over to see the finished product. Have your child complete **Who Am I in the Solar System?** (p. 65).	Read a book of historical fiction about the journey of Lewis and Clark across the western U.S. Have your child keep a journal (much like Lewis and Clark themselves did) as he/she reads, jotting down main ideas and particularly interesting facts.

Learn at Home, Grade 4

TEACHING SUGGESTIONS AND ACTIVITIES

LANGUAGE SKILLS (Prepositions)

BACKGROUND

A *preposition* connects words in a sentence and it may tell how, when or where. A preposition and its object form a *prepositional phrase.*

Examples: *through* the deep dark forest *behind* the huge oak tree
toward the western horizon *under* the prickly cactus

Some prepositions are *above, across, after, along, at, before, behind, below, between, by, down, during, for, from, in, inside, into, near, of, on, since, through, to, toward, under, until, with.*

READING (Dictionary Skills)

▷ 1. Review dictionary skills.

    a. Explain how to use each of the following elements of a dictionary: *guide words, entry words, pronunciation, syllable notation, part of speech* and *definitions.* Look up words that have more than one definition. Point out when different definitions come from different parts of speech. For example, the word *spring* can be a noun or a verb.

    b. Write a list of words unfamiliar to your child. Have him/her look up each word, pronounce it and copy its pronunciation.

    c. Write a list of words using dictionary pronunciations and diacritical marks. Have your child read each word phonetically, identify the word and write its correct spelling.

▷ 2. Read the following paragraphs to your child. Let him/her choose one to draw in detail.

    a. The emperor sat on a golden throne. The huge chair was taller than any man and carved with dragons and snakes. Multicolored jewels were embedded in the gold. The emperor wore a royal blue and gold robe. His hat resembled a blue graduation cap with several strands of multicolored beads hanging from the brim. His shoes were black. He held a paper scroll in both hands.

    b. The princess was beautiful. Her long black hair was braided into several sections. A pink butterfly hair clip was fastened off to one side. She had black, almond-shaped eyes and rosy cheeks. Her flowered pink, green and yellow silk gown was tied with a green sash. Pink slippers adorned her feet. She carried a pink fan decorated with Chinese nature scenes.

MATH (Subtraction)

▷ 1. Read the following examples to your child. Ask him/her to listen carefully. What key words signal subtraction? Have your child solve the problems.

    a. There were 690 invitations sent to the families of Wilson School to ask them to come to the Health Fair. If 575 families came, how many did not come?

    b. There are 1,235 ants in Jason's ant farm and 905 in Rebecca's. How many more ants are there in Jason's farm than there are in Rebecca's?

    c. What is the difference in height between the Empire State Building at 1,250 feet and the Sears Tower at 1,454 feet?

    d. Colin has 109 freckles on his nose. Kelly has 142. How many fewer freckles does Colin have than Kelly?

SCIENCE (Solar System)

▶ 1. Create a two-dimensional model of the solar system with your child. Use colored construction paper or white poster board and colored pencils to make the planets. Provide pictures of the planets so your child can try to match the appearance of each. Refer to the chart below for specific dimensions and colors. Glue the finished planets in the proper sequence onto a large sheet of chart paper.

PLANET	DIAMETER	COLOR	DISTANCE FROM SUN
Mercury	$^1/_8$ "	red	$1^3/_4$ "
Venus	$^1/_4$ "	green	$3^1/_2$ "
Earth	$^1/_4$ "	green and blue	$4^3/_4$ "
Mars	$^1/_8$ "	pink	7 "
Jupiter	$2^1/_2$ "	gray with orange stripes	2'
Saturn	$2^1/_4$ "	gray with 1 blue ring, 1 brown ring	3' 8 "
Uranus	1 "	light green, 1 blue ring	7' 5 "
Neptune	1 "	greenish blue	11' 8 "

In order to accommodate the great size of the solar system, this model uses two different scales. The distance from the Sun in the model described here is based on a scale of 1 inch = approx. 20,000,000 miles. The size of the planets is based on a scale of 1 inch = approx. 33,000 miles. It would be impractical to show the planets at the same scale used for distance from the Sun—even the largest planets would be barely visible. Even at this reduced scale, the size of the Sun is immense. If you have the space and materials, create a model of the Sun as well. The Sun should be approximately 26 inches in diameter and yellow in color.

SOCIAL STUDIES (Early Explorers)

BACKGROUND
Famous explorers of North America include:

Samuel de Champlain	Meriwether Lewis
William Clark	Sir Alexander Mackenzie
John Charles Frémont	Jacques Marquette
Henry Hudson	Jean Nicolet
Louis Jolliet	Zebulon Pike
Sieur de La Salle	Jedediah Strong Smith

1. The French were some of the earliest explorers of North America. They learned about the land from the fur traders and Native Americans. Have your child read about Samuel de Champlain and Jean Nicolet. How did these explorers interact with Native Americans?

▶

Learn at Home, Grade 4

Tennis Anyone?

Jack and Ron are playing tennis.

1. It is a very hot day. **Draw** a yellow sun in the sky above the shortest tree.
2. Use red to mark the thermometer up to **93** degrees.
3. Jack is on the right side of the net. **Color** his shirt yellow and his shorts blue with a green stripe.
4. **Color** Ron's shorts the color of Jack's stripe. **Color** his shirt the color of Jack's shorts.
5. Ron has just hit the ball. It is in the air, but it has not gone over the net yet. Use yellow to **draw** the ball.
6. Jack dropped his racket. Use brown to **draw** the racket.
7. **Count** all the balls on the ground. **Add** your age to that number. **Write** the total in the top of the tallest tree.
8. On the trunk of the middle tree, **write** the names of three other sports which use balls.
9. Between the shortest tree and the middle tree, **write** three words that you can make from the letters in the word *tennis*.

You Can Spell Us

Circle the spelling words that contain the **short u** sound as in **cup**. Use your calculator to find the point value of each word that contains the **long u** sound as in **use**.

Assign a number to each letter in the alphabet.

(A = 1, B = 2, C = 3, and so forth)

a ___	
b ___	
c ___	
d ___	
e ___	
f ___	
g ___	
h ___	
i ___	
j ___	
k ___	
l ___	
m ___	
n ___	
o ___	
p ___	
q ___	
r ___	
s ___	
t ___	
u ___	
v ___	
w ___	
x ___	
y ___	
z ___	

amuse

bubble

budding

budge

computer

customer

duty

humor

hungry

husky

Jupiter

number

sundown

summer

usual

SUMMER COMPUTER SALE

Best Buys on Jupiter!

Example: music = 13 + 21 + 19 + 9 + 3 = 65

_____ = _____

_____ = _____

_____ = _____

_____ = _____

_____ = _____

_____ = _____

Which word has the greatest point value? _____

Which has the least? _____

Now, find the point value of your own words. _____

_____ _____ _____

Learn at Home, Grade 4

Watch for Grandpa's Watch

Each "watch" in the title of this activity sheet has a different meaning. One means "to look for," and the other means "a timepiece." **Write** two meanings for the words below.

	Meaning 1	**Meaning 2**
1. spring		
2. run		
3. ruler		
4. duck		
5. suit		
6. cold		
7. fall		
8. tire		
9. rose		
10. face		
11. train		
12. play		
13. foot		
14. pen		
15. box		
16. fly		
17. seal		
18. bowl		
19. ride		
20. line		

The Imperial Alphabet

Number each group of words to show alphabetical order.

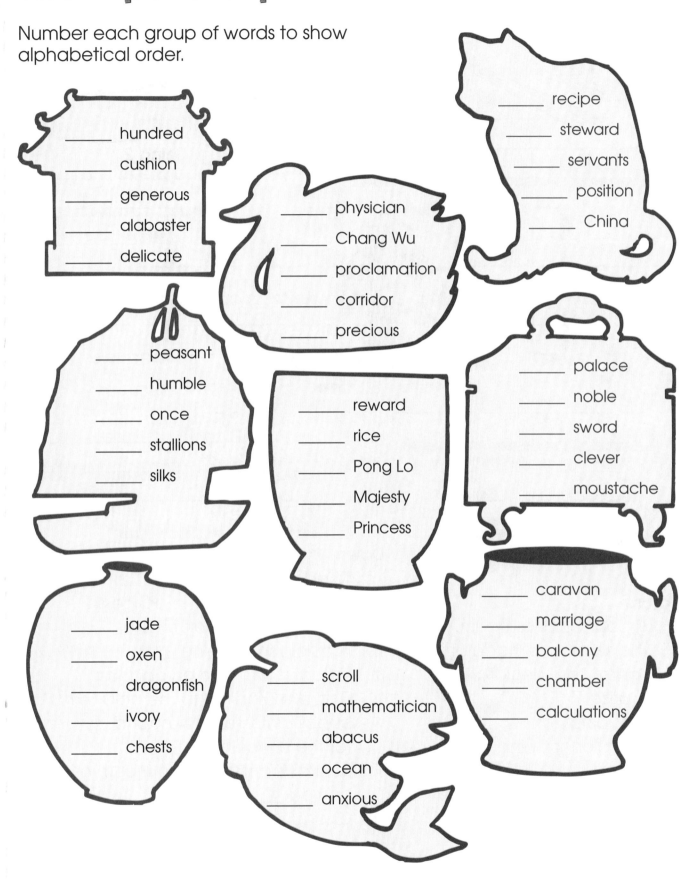

_____ hundred
_____ cushion
_____ generous
_____ alabaster
_____ delicate

_____ physician
_____ Chang Wu
_____ proclamation
_____ corridor
_____ precious

_____ recipe
_____ steward
_____ servants
_____ position
_____ China

_____ peasant
_____ humble
_____ once
_____ stallions
_____ silks

_____ reward
_____ rice
_____ Pong Lo
_____ Majesty
_____ Princess

_____ palace
_____ noble
_____ sword
_____ clever
_____ moustache

_____ jade
_____ oxen
_____ dragonfish
_____ ivory
_____ chests

_____ scroll
_____ mathematician
_____ abacus
_____ ocean
_____ anxious

_____ caravan
_____ marriage
_____ balcony
_____ chamber
_____ calculations

Learn at Home, Grade 4

A Clever Crossword

Across

2. A poor Chinese countryman
4. The swan was made of it
6. An Imperial declaration
9. A prize
12. Wedding
13. The ruler of China
14. Sadness
16. The emperor's facial hair
17. Palace workers
19. The author's last name
20. The princess's name

Down

1. To address the emperor: "Your_____."
2. Wanted to marry the princess
3. Counting beads on rods
5. A quick, sharp mind
7. He calculated on an abacus
8. They were called to the palace in hopes of finding a husband for the princess
10. 32 grains arrived in the mouth of a carved _____
11. Chang Wu's country
15. A long line of one hundred elephants
18. A grain of _____.

Jungle Math

Across

2. 517
   − 228
   _____

3. 428
   − 249
   _____

4. 562
   − 274
   _____

5. 924
   − 348
   _____

6. 923
   − 346
   _____

7. 535
   − 248
   _____

8. 857
   − 389
   _____

9. 561
   − 247
   _____

11. 845
   − 599
   _____

13. 325
   − 186
   _____

14. 356
   − 168
   _____

6. 921
   − 346
   _____

Down

1. 421
   − 342
   _____

2. 627
   − 348
   _____

3. 362
   − 194
   _____

4. 582
   − 346
   _____

5. 824
   − 247
   _____

7. 926
   − 718
   _____

8. 721
   − 240
   _____

10. 768
   − 292
   _____

12. 826
   − 337
   _____

13. 247
   − 129
   _____

Learn at Home, Grade 4

Our Solar System

Thousands of small rocky bodies, called asteroids or minor planets, orbit the Sun in a wide belt between Mars and Jupiter. They vary in size from that of a car to a small moonlike sphere 500 miles in diameter.

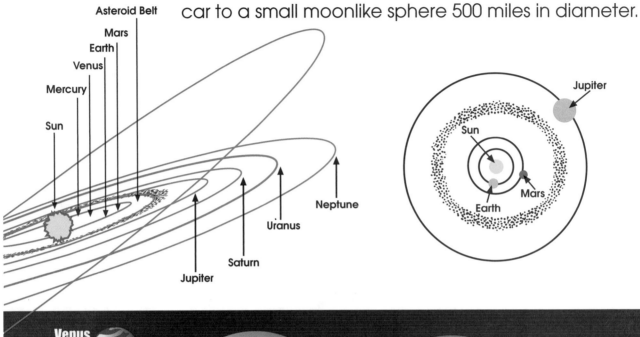

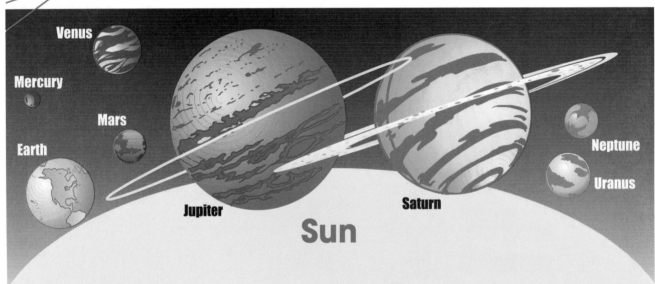

	MERCURY	VENUS	EARTH	MARS	JUPITER	SATURN	URANUS	NEPTUNE
DIAMETER								
AVERAGE DISTANCE FROM THE SUN								
REVOLUTION								
ROTATION								
KNOWN SATELLITES								

64

Who Am I in the Solar System?

The solar system contains many different objects that travel around the Sun. Use the information from **Our Solar System** (p. 64) and other sources to explore the solar system and solve the following "Who Am I?" riddles.

1. I am the largest planet. _____

2. I am the planet best known for my rings. _____

3. I am the planet known for my "Great Red Spot." _____

4. I am considered a dwarf planet, along with Ceres and Eris. _____

5. I am the planet closest to the Sun. _____

6. I am known as the "Red Planet." _____

7. Voyager 2 discovered new moons and rings around me._____

8. In 2006, the International Astronomical Union re-classified me as a dwarf planet. _____

9. I am the planet closest in size to the Earth. _____

10. I am the planet with the shortest rotation time. _____

11. My moon, Titan, is larger than the planet Mercury. _____

12. My rotation time is the most similar to Earth's. _____

13. I am the planet with the most natural satellites. _____

14. My buddies and I form a belt between Mars and Jupiter. _____

15. I am the largest object in the solar system. _____

16. I am the brightest planet in the sky. _____

17. I am the only planet known to support life. _____

18. I am the planet that orbits the Sun "on my side." _____

19. I am known as "Earth's Twin." _____

20. I am the brightest object in the sky. _____

21. I am the most distant planet that can be seen with the unaided eye. _____

	Language Skills	Spelling	Reading
Monday	Give your child a blank sheet of lined paper to write a letter to a friend or relative. Stress the correct format. Have your child revise and edit the letter over the next few days before sending it. Review the elements of a friendly letter. Use **Friendly Letter** (p. 70) as a guide and as practice for your child.	Pretest your child on these spelling words. already envy library balcony February reply country greedy satisfy deny hydrant skyline early hymn syllable Have your child correct the pretest, add personalized words and make two copies of this week's study list.	Teach your child about *homophones*. Compare *homographs* to *homonyms*. *See* Reading, Week 6. Have your child complete **Homophone Hype** (p. 72).
Tuesday	Review the correct formation of the cursive lower-case letters s–z. Have your child practice handwriting. Have your child write one row of each lower-case letter s–z. Let him/her circle the best letter in each row.	Have your child use each of this week's spelling words correctly in a sentence.	Introduce *Tales of a Fourth Grade Nothing* by Judy Blume by asking your child what it is like (or what he/she thinks it is like) to have a three-year-old brother. Read chapters 1 and 2 of *Tales of a Fourth Grade Nothing*.
Wednesday	**Conjunctions:** Introduce conjunctions. A *conjunction* is a word used to join other words or phrases. The most common conjunctions are *and, but, for, nor* and *or*. Write several sample sentences containing conjunctions on the chalkboard. *See* Language Skills, Week 6, numbers 1 and 2.	Have your child complete **The Y's Have It** (p. 71).	Read chapters 3 and 4 of *Tales of a Fourth Grade Nothing*. Motivate your child to write in the Reading Journal about his/her reaction to Fudge. Discuss some of the problems that Fudge causes. Ask how Fudge's behavior affects Peter. Have your child complete a copy of **Order in the Story!** (p. 73).
Thursday	Teach your child to recognize and use interjections. *Interjections* usually express strong feelings. They either stand alone followed by an exclamation point or they are separated from the rest of a sentence by commas or dashes. Have your child look through *Tales of a Fourth Grade Nothing* for interjections. Discuss what words or phrases are interjections and how they are punctuated.	Scramble the letters in each spelling word. Have your child unscramble them and write out each word correctly.	Read chapters 5 and 6 of *Tales of a Fourth Grade Nothing*. *See* Reading, Week 6, number 1.
Friday	Listen to commercials on the radio and television. Advertisers use interjections to create strong feelings for their products. Discuss interjections you hear. Ask your child to suggest how they convince the consumer to buy a particular product. Have your child write a radio or TV advertisement for an imaginary product. Ask him/her to include some interjections in the sales copy.	Give your child the final spelling test. Have your child record the pretest and final test words in his/her word bank.	Read chapters 7 and 8 of *Tales of a Fourth Grade Nothing*. Discuss the purposes of different types of print (books, newspapers, magazines, ads). Introduce the concepts of *persuasion, entertainment* and *information* as they relate to print. Have your child complete **What's the Point?** (p. 74).

Learn at Home, Grade 4

Math	Science	Social Studies
Multiplication Assess your child's knowledge of multiplication facts. Use flash cards for extra practice and encourage your child to memorize math facts. Use multiplication to count windows on large buildings. *See* Math, Week 6, number 1. Have your child complete **Multiplying 2 to 12** (p. 75).	**Seasons** Discuss what makes the Earth unique among the planets. Ask: *What are some of the things that make life on Earth possible? How does the composition of the Earth and its atmosphere differ from other planets?* Discuss NASA's findings that life may have existed in some form on Mars billions of years ago. Discuss what the significance of such a find would be.	Compare the Lewis and Clark expedition with the explorations of Jolliet and Marquette. On a map, have your child draw the route each party took. Compare the accomplishments of each expedition. Ask: *What were the hardships, modes of transportation, necessary supplies and time lines for the two expeditions?*
Work with your child to create a multiplication table that can be reused. *See* Math, Week 6, number 2. Place the multiplication flash cards on the table and have your child look for patterns and strategies for learning the math facts.	Using your library resources or textbooks, read about the spinning Earth and the Earth's rotation around the Sun. Demonstrate the movement with a flashlight and ball or piece of fruit. Explain that the Earth rotates on its axis once every 24 hours, while at the same time orbiting around the Sun once every year. Have your child complete **Spinning Top** and **Lo-o-o-o-ong Trip** (pgs. 77 and 78).	Describe America's early settlements to your child. Help him/her find the location on a map. Ask your child to describe what life may have been like for the early European settlers. Provide both textual and visual resources for your child to examine. Have your child write one or two paragraphs describing life in America's early settlements.
Use a collection of manipulatives, such as marbles, beans or pennies. Place a different number of objects in each of several bags or boxes. (Use numbers that have multiple factors, like 18, 24 and 32.) Have your child count the items in each bag and divide them into as many different equal sets as possible (18 = 2 sets of 9, 3 sets of 6, 6 sets of 3, 9 sets of 2). Then, have him/her write multiplication facts based on these sets.	Help your child make a simple sundial to observe the movement of the Earth. The position of the Sun in relation to the Earth casts a rotating shadow off the sundial. *See* Science, Week 6, number 1.	Discuss the effects of exploration on the native people and the environment. What impact might explorers have on an area? Have your child write a proposal for "low-impact exploration." He/she should explain how an explorer can travel to an area, achieve his/her goals and not have a negative impact on the land or people already living there.
Tape a number line (0–144) to the chalkboard. Teach your child how to use the number line as an aid in multiplication. Give your child a problem: 4 x ____ = 20. Starting at 0, have your child use a piece of chalk to jump by fours to 20. How many jumps did it take? (5). Thus, 4 x 5 = 20. Repeat with other problems, practicing up to 12 x 12. *See* Math, Week 6, number 3.	Using the library resources and textbooks, read about the seasons and their relationship to the tilt of the Earth. Demonstrate the changes with a flashlight and a ball or piece of fruit. *See* Science, Week 6.	Read about Sir Alexander Mackenzie, David Thompson and Samuel Hearne, three Canadian explorers. Mackenzie's expedition involved tracing waterways, looking for a river system that crossed the continent to the Pacific Ocean. Have your child draw and label the routes of these Canadian explorers on a map of Canada.
Children retain more when given the opportunity to teach. Provide your child with a list of challenging math facts and ask him/her to teach you strategies for solving each one. Have your child complete **Multiplication** (p. 76).	Use the diagram on the activity sheet to illustrate the difference in seasons between the Northern Hemisphere and the Southern Hemisphere. Explain that, when it is summer in the U.S., it is winter in Australia, and vice versa. Have your child complete **Leaning Into Summer** (p. 79).	Help your child construct a time line of the explorers studied so far. Are there any other explorers who traveled at the same time?

Learn at Home, Grade 4

TEACHING SUGGESTIONS AND ACTIVITIES

LANGUAGE SKILLS (Conjunctions)

▶ 1. Generate several sentences, omitting the conjunctions. Have your child choose the conjunction that best fits each sentence.

Examples: My friend _____ I went to a movie yesterday.
I wanted some popcorn, _____ I didn't have enough money.

▶ 2. Write several sentence starters ending with conjunctions. Have your child complete the sentences.

Examples: My brother is twelve, and . . . .   The girls went fishing, but . . . .
We will go to the game by bus or . . . .   It was snowing, and . . . .
Ellen worked all day on a report, but . . . .   They had to win or . . . .

If there is time, have your child develop one of the sentences into a short story.

READING (Story Analysis)

BACKGROUND

Homophones are words that are identical in pronunciation but different in spelling and meaning.

Example: pear/pair, rain/reign

Homographs are identical in spelling but different in meaning and sometimes pronunciation.

Examples: pan (*n*. cooking vessel/*v*. put down), sole (*n*. a kind of fish/*n*. bottom of foot or shoe), wound (*n*. a sore/*v*. wrapped something around)

Homonyms are pronounced the same and often spelled the same but have different meanings.

Examples: March (month)/march (steady walk), chord (as in music)/chord (as in geometry)

▶ 1. On the chalkboard, make a chart with three columns: *before*, *during* and *after*. Give your child the list of events below. Ask him/her to decide if each event would have happened before, during or after Fudge's party. Have your child write each sentence in the appropriate column of the chart.

Events

1. Buy the paper cups.
2. Sam didn't want to go home.
3. Mother snapped pictures.
4. Set the table.
5. Buy napkins and plates.
6. Mother took two aspirin.
7. Peter blew up balloons.
8. Invite the guests.
9. A neighbor complained of noise.
10. Jennie bit Grandma.
11. Grandma lit candles.
12. The children meet Dribble.
13. Fudge opened presents.
14. Ralph threw up.
15. Father came home.
16. They put on party hats.
17. Ralph's mother came to get him.
18. Mother put Jennie's wet pants in a plastic bag.

MATH (Multiplication)

▶ 1. Introduce multiplication.

a. Read *The Giraffe and the Pelly and Me*, written by Roald Dahl, as an introduction to a window counting activity. This story is about some exceptional animals that have a window-washing business.

b. After reading the story, use multiplication to count windows in a large building. Locate a tall building nearby or use a photograph of one for this activity. Have your child count the number of windows across and the number of windows down on one side of the building. Then, multiply to find how many windows are on the one side. Repeat with other number combinations.

c. **Extension:** Have your child figure out what he/she would charge (based on a per window charge) to wash all the windows of a building.

▶ 2. Start with a large square of butcher paper (3 feet by 3 feet). Divide the square into ten rows and ten columns, forming one hundred boxes. Write the numbers 1–10 along the top and along the left side of the grid (one number per row or column). Cut one hundred squares of construction paper (same size as the boxes). Have your child call out the intersecting numbers for each box of the table while you write an equation on each construction paper square and the answer on the back. To use the table, have your child scramble all the cards and one-by-one place them on the correct boxes of the table. Discuss the patterns that appear as well as the commutative property (3 x 4 is equal to 4 x 3).

▶ 3. Challenge your child with this variation on the number line activity. Have your child jump to a given number in a specific number of jumps: "Jump to 63 in 9 jumps." Then, ask what each interval was. Have your child write the multiplication problem. Repeat with other numbers.

SCIENCE (Seasons)

BACKGROUND

The seasons change because the tilt of the Earth causes different amounts of sunlight throughout the year. When the North Pole is tilted towards the Sun, it is summer in the Northern Hemisphere. The angle of the Sun is more direct in the Northern Hemisphere at this time, producing maximum sunlight. When the North Pole tilts away from the Sun, the rays of the Sun are less direct and it is winter in the Northern Hemisphere.

▶ 1. A sundial may be as simple as a stick standing upright in the ground. Draw a circle in a sandy location and place a stick vertically in the center. Determine north with a compass and place a small stone on the circle in that direction. That mark will also indicate 12:00 on the sundial. Based on the 12:00 mark, place stones to indicate the other hours on the clock face. Notice where the shadow of the stick falls on the circle. That should match the time on your watch. If you find that the sundial is an hour off, it may be a result of Daylight Savings Time. Your child may be interested in making a more complex or permanent sundial. If that is the case, check your local library for books on the subject.

Friendly Letter

A friendly letter is a casual letter between family or friends. A friendly letter can express your own personality. It can be written for a special reason or just for fun.

Write a friendly letter to a "friend" in another city. Invite the friend to visit you sometime during the summer. Follow these guidelines:

A. Write your address and the date.
B. Write a greeting (**Example**: Dear _____,).
C. Write three paragraphs.
   First: pleasant greeting and invitation
   Second: details about the visit
   Third: summarize your excitement about the visit
D. Closing (**Example**: Your friend,).
E. Your signature

Learn at Home, Grade 4

The Y's Have It

Put a check to the left of each spelling word that has a **y** sound like the **long e** in **bee**.

Put a star to the right of each word that has a **y** sound like the **long i** in **ice**.

Write the two words that do not have a mark.

_____   _____

What vowel sound do they have? _____

_____ already _____   _____ greedy _____
_____ balcony _____   _____ hydrant _____
_____ country _____   _____ hymn _____
_____ deny _____   _____ library _____
_____ early _____   _____ reply _____
_____ envy _____   _____ satisfy _____
_____ February   _____ skyline _____
                           _____ syllable _____

Answer each question.

1. Which word has the most syllables? _____
2. Which word has only one syllable? _____
3. Which word is a compound word? _____
4. Which word is an antonym for "late"? _____
5. Which word is a synonym for "jealousy"? _____
6. Which word is a geographic region? _____
7. Which word is a home for books? _____
8. Which word is capitalized? _____
9. Which word denotes life-saving equipment? _____
10. Which word rhymes with "needy"? _____

Homophone Hype

 **= b**

For each word given below, list the homophones in the spaces provided. Find and **circle** the homophone in the word search. Then, **write** a sentence using the given word and at least one homophone.

```
G S B R I D L E W O J M
E H R Q M N S L H G V A
G N I L A X H E A R W N
D R D W I C R N F A S E
R M A I N E Q I S Z K R
V G L Y W N F S C E N T
N D I N S T L L K H N S
R U U O N P W E I G H T
D E W S P C H D L V E Y
O F A I S L E I L B R L
R L Y O M S Y E R G T A
```

1. Here _____

   Sentence: _____

2. Bridle _____

   Sentence: _____

3. I'll _____   _____

   Sentence: _____

4. Graze (Hint: plural forms of a color) _____   _____

   Sentence: _____

5. Main _____   _____

   Sentence: _____

6. Whey _____   _____

   Sentence: _____

7. Dew _____   _____

   Sentence: _____

8. Scent _____   _____

   Sentence: _____

72

Order in the Story!

Number the rocks in story order. **Cut out** each large rock and **glue** it in order on another sheet of paper to make a rock pyramid like the one shown here. After making the pyramid, draw in the details of Central Park that are described.

Peter and Jimmy Fargo take a walk through Central Park. They want to play secret agent on their favorite rocks. The day is nice and sunny.

Fudge falls off the jungle gym while pretending to fly like the pigeons. Sheila and the boys had not been watching him. They were all busy playing "cooties."

Sheila offers to watch Fudge for Mrs. Hatcher. Mrs. Hatcher is unsure at first but remembers that the oven is not yet turned on. She tells Peter and Jimmy to help Sheila and that she will be right back.

Peter's mother apologizes to him later that evening. When she first returned to the playground, she had been very angry at Peter but not at Sheila who was in charge.

Sheila, a girl in the boys' class, is already on the rocks when Peter and Jimmy arrive. The boys are very upset that she took their favorite rock so they yell at her to leave.

Mrs. Hatcher and Fudge come tearing down the path toward the rocks. Fudge is chasing pigeons and running way ahead of his mother.

73

What's the Point?

Write the correct purpose of each sentence on the line provided.

Persuade

Entertain

Inform

1. Exercise and maintain a good diet and you won't become overweight.

   _____

2. Dad yelled at Timmy, "Don't ride that Toddle-Bike in the street!"

   _____

3. "You ate the broccoli and left all the cookies," cried Mother.

   _____

4. The advertiser uses cute kindergarteners in his ads to sell products.

   _____

5. The Toddle-Bike was just voted the best new toy vehicle for 1999.

   _____

6. "I saw the new Julie on TV and I just had to have it," said Katy.

   _____

7. Keep current on homework assignments and you'll be less frustrated at school.

   _____

8. "My fingers are numb after only four hours of video games," complained Brad.

   _____

9. Toddle-Bikes are so fun your children will be entertained for hours.

   _____

10. Fast food and video game advertisers target their ads toward the Saturday morning television audience.

    _____

11. There are many more vitamins in vegetables than there are in hamburgers.

    _____

12. "Toddle-Bikes will change your life," promised the television announcer.

    _____

13. Eat more fruits and vegetables for a healthier, stronger body.

    _____

14. Two out of every three teenagers eat fast food more than twice a week.

    _____

15. Avoid a steady routine of TV-watching and video games to stay alert.

    _____

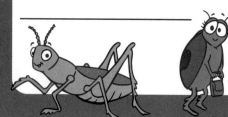

74

Multiplying 2 to 12

Multiplication is simply a quick way to add!

Example: 3 x 6

1. The first factor tells how many groups there are. There are 3 groups.
2. The second factor tells how many are in each group. There are 6 in each group.

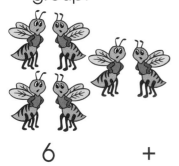   +   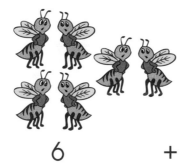   +   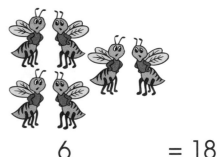   = 18

6   +   6   +   6   = 18

3 groups of 6 equal 18.

3 x 6 = 18

Some helpful hints to remember when multiplying:

- When you multiply by 0, the product is always 0. **Example:** 0 x 7 = 0
- When you multiply by 1, the product is always the factor being multiplied. **Example:** 1 x 12 = 12
- When multiplying by 2, double the factor other than 2. **Example:** 2 x 4 = 8
- The order doesn't matter when multiplying. **Example:** 5 x 3 = 15, 3 x 5 = 15
- When you multiply by 9, the digits in the product add up to 9 (until 9 x 11). **Example:** 7 x 9 = 63, 6 + 3 = 9
- When you multiply by 10, multiply by 1 and add 0 to the product. **Example:** 10 x 3 = 30
- When you multiply by 11, double the factor you are multiplying by (until 10). **Example:** 11 x 8 = 88

Multiply:

2	3	4	2	5	10	7	8
x 9	x 8	x 9	x 11	x 9	x 5	x 6	x 8

11	9	8			
x 12	x 7	x 5	8 x 5 = ____	10 x 10 = ____	4 x 8 = ____

5 x 5 = ____   3 x 6 = ____   7 x 8 = ____

Multiplication

5
x 5

5
x 3

2   2
x 9   x 5

7   5
x 8   x 7

9   9
x 7   x 9

6   8
x 6   x 5

8   8
x 9   x 8

9   6
x 5   x 5

6   9
x 7   x 8

8
x 3

6
x 3

6   9
x 4   x 7

7   6
x 7   x 9

7   5
x 6   x 4

8   8
x 4   x 7

4   4
x 4   x 9

3   6
x 9   x 8

7   7
x 9   x 3

3
x 8

4
x 7

8
x 6

Learn at Home, Grade 4

Spinning Top

Whir-r-r-ling! Matt's top is spinning very fast. Just like Matt's top, the Earth is also spinning. The Earth spins around an imaginary line that is drawn from the North **Pole** to the South Pole through the center of the Earth. This line is called Earth's **axis**. Instead of using the word "spin," though we say that the Earth **rotates** on its axis. The Earth rotates **one** time every 24 hours. The part of the Earth facing the sun experiences **day**. The side that is away from the sun's light experiences **night**.

Draw a line from each picture of Matt to the correct picture of the Earth.

Matt lives here.

Matt lives here.

Use some of the words in **bold** above to fill in the puzzle.

1. The part of the Earth not facing the Sun experiences _____.
2. Earth's axis goes from the North to the South _____.
3. The Earth spins.
4. Number of times the Earth rotates in 24 hours.
5. Imaginary line on which the Earth rotates.

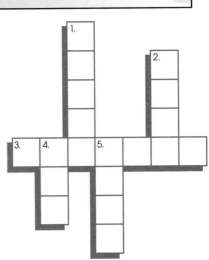

Lo-o-o-o-ong Trip

What is the longest trip you have ever taken? Was it 100 miles? 500 miles? Maybe it was more than 1,000 miles. You probably didn't know it, but last year you traveled 620 million miles.

The Earth travels in a path around the Sun called its **orbit**. Earth's orbit is almost 620 million miles. It takes 1 year, or 365 days, for the Earth to orbit or **revolve** around the Sun.

Look at the picture of Earth's orbit. It is not a perfect circle. It is a shape called an **ellipse**.

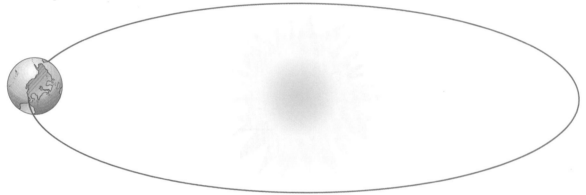

1. How long does it take for the Earth to revolve around the Sun?
   _____

2. How many times has the Earth revolved around the Sun since you were born? _____

3. How many miles has the Earth traveled in orbit since you were born?
   _____

4. **Draw** an **X** on Earth's orbit to show where it will be in 6 months.

Experiment: To draw an ellipse, place two straight pins about 3 inches apart in a piece of cardboard. Tie the ends of a 10 inch piece of string to the pins. Place your pencil inside the string. Keeping the string tight, draw an ellipse.

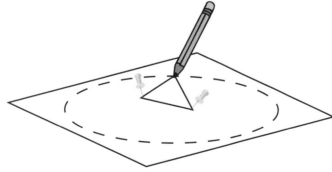

Make four different ellipses by changing the length of the string and the distance between the pins. How do the ellipses change?

Learn at Home, Grade 4

Leaning Into Summer

Why isn't it summer all year long?

The seasons change because the Earth is tilted like the Leaning Tower of Pisa. As the Earth orbits the Sun, it stays tilted in the same direction in space.

Let's look at the seasons in the Northern Hemisphere. When the North Pole is tilted toward the Sun, the days become warmer and longer. It is summer. Six months later, the North Pole tilts away from the Sun. The days become cooler and shorter. It is winter.

Label the Northern Hemisphere's seasons on the chart below. **Write** a make-believe weather forecast for each season. Each forecast should show what the weather is like in your region for that season.

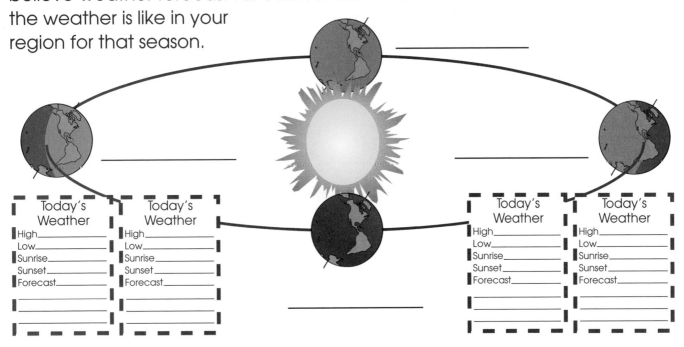

Today's Weather

High_____
Low_____
Sunrise_____
Sunset_____
Forecast_____
_____
_____
_____

Today's Weather

High_____
Low_____
Sunrise_____
Sunset_____
Forecast_____
_____
_____
_____

Today's Weather

High_____
Low_____
Sunrise_____
Sunset_____
Forecast_____
_____
_____
_____

Today's Weather

High_____
Low_____
Sunrise_____
Sunset_____
Forecast_____
_____
_____
_____

Learn at Home, Grade 4

Language Skills	Spelling	Reading
Monday Review the term *autobiography* with your child. Use **Autobiography** (p. 84) as a guide. Have your child complete the activity sheet as a warm-up, then ask him/her to work on a rough draft of his/her autobiography.	Pretest your child on these spelling words. afraid delay prey aide failure refrain bay great remain break maize stain chain payment waist Have your child correct the pretest, add personalized words and make two copies of this week's study list.	Have your child finish reading *Tales of a Fourth Grade Nothing*. Teach your child to recognize the main idea of a paragraph. Have your child complete **It's Major** (p. 87).
Tuesday **Figurative Language:** For handwriting practice, have your child write (copy) several figures of speech in his/her best cursive writing. *See* Language Skills, Week 7, number 1 for a list of some common figures of speech. Ask your child if he/she has heard of any other figures of speech. Write those down as well. Have your child select three figures of speech and explain their figurative meanings in writing.	Have your child use each of this week's spelling words correctly in a sentence.	**Synonyms and Antonyms:** Review the definition of a *synonym*. Show your child how to use a thesaurus. Have him/her look up a word and find a synonym. Have your child use the original word in a sentence, then replace it with the synonym. Which is more precise? Repeat with other words. *See* Reading, Week 7, number 1.
Wednesday Teach your child to recognize and use *figures of speech* to make his/her writing more interesting. Have your child write several sentences using figurative language. **Example:** *Kurt's mouth was on fire.* Then, have your child draw a literal interpretation of each sentence. Have your child complete **Figures of Speech** (p. 85).	Have your child complete **A's Are Back** (p. 86).	Teach your child about antonyms. An *antonym* is a word that means the opposite of another word. Write the following words on the chalkboard: *descended, impatient, indignant, mournful, resentful, retreated, scornful, swiftly.* Use each word in a sentence for your child. Have him/her replace the word in each sentence with an antonym. Have your child complete **Synonyms and Antonyms** (p. 88).
Thursday Discuss *personification. See* Language Skills, Week 7, number 2. Have your child brainstorm ten nouns (inanimate objects) and ten adjectives (human characteristics). Ask him/her to combine one adjective with one noun and write a sentence, bringing the words to life. Repeat until all the words have been used. Read several poems to your child. Ask him/her to jot down any figures of speech. Discuss the impact of these words on the poem's imagery.	Write each spelling word on an index card. Mix up the cards, then have your child arrange them alphabetically.	Have your child read and write antonyms. Write fifteen words and their antonyms on index cards (one word per card). Shuffle the cards, then have your child match the antonym pairs. Next, let him/her choose five pairs of antonyms and write a sentence for each word. *See* Reading, Week 7, number 2.
Friday Discuss *hyperbole*. Have your child write several sentences using hyperbole to describe him/herself or to tell about something he/she has done. Have your child choose one or more of these sentences to include in his/her autobiography. Read a tall tale. Discuss the use of hyperbole and figurative language in the story. Have your child cite some examples.	Give your child the final spelling test. Have your child record the pretest and final test words in his/her word bank.	*The Whipping Boy* by Sid Fleischman won the Newbery Medal in 1987. Read the jacket and look at the pictures. Have your child predict what the book is about, based on these clues. Briefly describe a situation: e.g., *Matt just turned four. He has chocolate all over his face and he looks sheepish.* Have your child draw a conclusion. Repeat with other situations. Then, let your child do the describing.

Learn at Home, Grade 4

Math	Science	Social Studies
Show your child how to multiply a 2-digit number by a 1-digit number (24 x 2) without regrouping. Read the problem aloud. Have your child write it out as shown below. Demonstrate the order for multiplying the digits. Guide your child as needed through other problems. **Example:** 24 x 2 Have your child complete **Multiplication** (p. 89).	**The Moon** Discuss the Moon with your child. Use library resources to learn facts about the Moon that interest your child. Have him/her read about the Moon in several sources. Discuss the size of the Moon, its orbit around the Earth, its source of light, its phases and its connection to tides here on Earth.	Introduce the explorers from 1700 to 1900. *See* Social Studies, Week 7. Help your child create a chart showing the explorers, their countries of origin, where they explored, the years they explored and other relevant information.
Teach multiplication with regrouping. Use the colored squares and place-value board introduced in Week 3. *See* Math, Week 7, number 1. Have your child complete **Regrouping** (p. 90).	Study the phases of the Moon. Help your child make a "Moon phase" box, following the directions in Science, Week 7, number 1. Then, have your child complete the response card about the Moon phases. *See* Science, Week 7, number 2. If the sky is relatively clear, have your child observe the Moon tonight. Ask him/her to write down any questions or observations to discuss tomorrow.	Help your child find the origin of the famous quote, "Dr. Livingston, I presume." Take this opportunity to explore the reference section of the library with your child. Show him/her that there is much more than just dictionaries and encyclopedias there. Guide your child to books on quotations.
Teach your child to multiply a 3-digit number by a 1-digit number. Provide him/her with several practice problems, both with and without regrouping. Have your child complete **Space Math** (p. 91).	Help your child complete a copy of **Moon's "Faces"** (p. 92).	With your child, discuss why Sir Richard Francis Burton and John Hanning Speke might have been looking for the source of the White Nile River. What did they eventually discover?
Teach your child how to multiply when there is a zero present. Reiterate that zero multiplied by any number is still zero. Work through a sample problem, such as 206 x 4, using colored squares and the place-value board. Provide guided practice for your child with ten to twelve multiplication problems involving zero.	Discuss Moon lore—e.g., the man in the Moon and the Moon being made of cheese. Where did these stories originate? Help your child find out. Have your child start his/her own version of a Moon log following the instructions in **Moon Logs** (p. 93).	Discuss the exploration of the South Pole. In 1911, Roald Amundsen and Robert Scott each led expeditions to reach the South Pole. Have your child read to discover: *Which party arrived first and how far ahead of the second group? What happened to the Scott party?* Ask your child why he/she thinks the two parties raced to the South Pole. Have him/her name at least two possible reasons.
Present an alternate approach to multiplication. Teach multiplication of tens and ones separately before combining. *See* Math, Week 7, number 2. Give your child several space-related word problems. Ask him/her to solve them using this alternate approach.	Conditions on the surface of the Moon are very calm. The U.S. flags that stand there should stay in place for millions of years. Have your child imagine that he/she is responsible for placing a time capsule on the Moon. Ask what he/she would include in the capsule for future visitors to find. Have your child explain his/her choices.	Read about the controversy over who made it to the North Pole first. Have your child write a paragraph about how airplane travel changed the nature of explorations to the poles. See if your library has any films or videos on pole exploration. Watch it with your child.

TEACHING SUGGESTIONS AND ACTIVITIES

LANGUAGE SKILLS (Figurative Language)

BACKGROUND

Personification lends human characteristics to inanimate objects.

Examples: The old tree moaned during the wind storm.
Yellow sunflowers danced in the Kansas Sun.
The music from the merry-go-round beckoned us to the fair.

Hyperbole is a great exaggeration.

Examples: Jack can throw a ball a mile.
The scout leader had to tell the boys a hundred times not to climb the rocks.

A *simile* compares two unlike things, using the words *like* or *as*.

Example: John is as happy as a lark with his new skates.

A *metaphor* states that one thing is another.

Example: The Sun is a red ball.

▶ 1. Write several of these figures of speech on the chalkboard for your child to copy neatly.

Beauty is only skin deep.	Half a loaf is better than none.
Birds of a feather flock together.	A bird in the hand is worth two in the bush.
Look before you leap.	Into everyone's life some rain must fall.
Too many cooks spoil the broth.	If at first you don't succeed, try, try again.
The early bird catches the worm.	Don't put all your eggs in one basket.
Don't count your chickens before they hatch.	Two heads are better than one.
He who hesitates is lost.	Waste not, want not.
You can lead a horse to water,	Laugh and the world laughs with you;
but you can't make it drink.	cry and you cry alone.

▶ 2. Discuss the use of personification in the examples above. Ask: *What words give the inanimate objects human characteristics? How does personification improve the sentences?*

READING (Synonyms and Antonyms)

▶ 1. Using a black marker, write bold words (entries) from a thesaurus on index cards. Using a red marker, write synonyms for these bold words on another set of cards. Some words will have more than one synonym. Write each word on a separate card. Lay out the original cards. Have your child place the synonyms under each original word.

▶ 2. Use these antonym pairs or others for Thursday's activity.

approve — deny	exit — enter	liquid — solid
modern — ancient	destroy — construct	bright — dreary
cowardly — brave	conform — rebel	clean — soiled
honest — corrupt	fresh — stale	hide — revel
educated — ignorant	generous — greedy	general — specific

MATH (Multiplication)

▷ 1. Using the colored squares and the place-value board, have your child build the first number in the multiplication problem 26 x 3. Ask him/her to explain the meaning of "x 3." Then, have your child build the first number two more times. Count the number of squares in the ones place (18) and guide him/her through the process of trading ten squares for one of the next color. Write the 1 (ten) above the tens place on the written equation. Count the total and show your child how to write the answer correctly. Provide plenty of guided practice as he/she gains confidence in multiplying a 2-digit number by a 1-digit number, with and without the help of the manipulatives.

▷ 2. Have your child read the first number in the equation 436 x 4, as 400 + 30 + 6. Have him/her multiply each number by 4 and add the products to get the sum. Then, multiply the numbers in the traditional way. The zeros are place holders that help you put the numbers into the correct columns. Repeat this activity several times.

SCIENCE (The Moon)

▷ 1. Help your child make a "Moon phase" box. Begin by cutting an opening at one end of a shoe box large enough for a flashlight. Cut a 1" viewing hole on all four sides of the box. Hang a ping-pong ball from the lid of the box. Using a long needle and heavy thread, knot the end of the thread and push the needle through one side of the ping-pong ball and out through the opposite side. Push the needle up through the lid of the box. Put a brad (paper fastener) into the lid near where the needle entered. Tie the thread around the brad so that the ball hangs into the box about an inch and a half. Put the lid back on the box, and number the sides of the box 1, 2, 3 and 4.

▷ 2. Look through the different viewing holes. Tell your child to think of him/herself as an observer on Earth. The flashlight acts as the Sun while the ball simulates the Moon. Have your child describe the view from each position and record the phases of the Moon on the response card at the right.

RESPONSE CARD

Position	1	2	3	4
Phase				

Explain what conditions would be like when the moon is full. _____
_____
_____

SOCIAL STUDIES (Explorers)

BACKGROUND

From the late 1700s to the early 1900s, explorers set out to find new lands, map unfamiliar places and gather scientific data. The locations listed below were still largely a mystery to Europeans and Americans until the following men were sent out to explore.

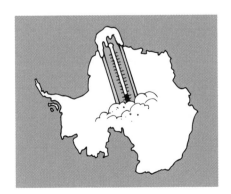

South Pacific Ocean	James Cook
River Systems in Africa	David Livingston
	Sir Henry Stanley
Arctic	Vilhjalmur Stefansson
	Richard E. Byrd
	Sir John Franklin
	Robert E. Peary
Antarctica	Roald Amundsen
	Sir Vivian Fuchs
	Robert Scott
	Charles Wilkes

Autobiography

An **autobiography** is a written account of your life.
Use the outline to fill in information about your life.

I. **My Early Years**
    A. Birthdate _____
        Place _____
    B. Favorite activities _____
    _____
    C. Family members _____
    _____
    D. Things I learned _____
    E. First school _____

II. **My Present**
    A. School _____ Grade _____
    B. Friends _____
    C. Favorite subjects _____
    D. Sports or hobbies _____
    E. Family fun _____

III. **My Future**
    A. Junior and senior high school _____
    B. College _____
    C. Ambitions _____
    D. Places I would like to see _____
    E. Things I would like to accomplish _____
    _____

Use the information in the outline to write an autobiography. **Write** a
paragraph about your **past**, **present** and **future**. _____

_____

_____

_____

_____

Finish your autobiography on another sheet of paper.

Figures of Speech

A **figure of speech** can make a sentence more interesting.
Here are four popular kinds of figures of speech:

Personification—gives human characteristics to things. **Example**: The Sun touched us with its warm fingers.

Hyperbole—a great exaggeration. **Example**: She's the happiest person in the universe.

Simile—compares two unlike things, using **like** or **as**. **Example**: He is hungry as a horse.

Metaphor—suggests a comparison of two unlike things. **Example**: The vacant field was a desert.

Underline each figure of speech. **Write** the type on each line.

1. The wind howled as the storm grew closer. _____
2. The little lady nibbled at her lunch like a bird. _____
3. Sarah's little sister was a doll in her new clothes. _____
4. The camp leader said he would never sleep again. _____
5. The banana cream pie was heaven. _____
6. We were as busy as bees all day long. _____
7. His patience just flew out the window. _____
8. He said that his life was an open book. _____
9. The newlyweds were as happy as two lovebirds. _____
10. The heavy fog crept slowly into shore. _____
11. The champion wrestler is as strong as an ox. _____
12. The twins were angels for helping their mom. _____
13. I am so full that I never want to eat again. _____
14. Sometimes my memory is a blank tape. _____

Write four sentences that contain a figure of speech.

1. (personification) _____
2. (hyperbole) _____
3. (simile) _____
4. (metaphor) _____

A's Are Back

It's Major

Main ideas can be anywhere in a paragraph. **Write** the main idea for each paragraph on the blank line. Choose from the main ideas listed below.

> They had to get Fudge to the hospital.
> Peter had to sit and wait alone.
> Someone did care that he had lost Dribble.
> Fudge had eaten Dribble.
> They waited for news about Fudge.
> After spending all day in the hospital waiting room, Peter was hungry.

1. Peter walked home from school. It was a spring day, and he was thinking about Dribble. Something was wrong when he got to his room. The bowl was there but not Dribble. When he asked Fudge where he was, Fudge just smiled and pointed to his tummy. _____

   _____

2. Peter grabbed blankets while his mother called the ambulance. Henry made no other elevator stops on the way down. _____

   _____

   Two men in white were waiting with a stretcher and the ambulance.
3. _____

   There were no magazines or books. He watched the clock. He read all the wall signs. He found out he was in the Emergency Room.

4. _____

   Mother joined him in the hospital coffee shop for a hamburger. He didn't eat much after he found out that Fudge might need an operation if the castor oil, milk of magnesia and prune juice didn't work soon.
5. The next day was Saturday. Peter's grandmother came to stay with him.

   _____

   Every hour the telephone rang with a report about Fudge. The good news came late at night.
6. Fudge came home with many presents. He was having fun and getting lots of attention. When Mr. Hatcher arrived home from work, he gave the biggest present to Peter.

_____

Synonyms and Antonyms

Write a synonym for each **bold** word. You may want to use a thesaurus.

1. Mattie and Toni find a **beautiful** pin for Mattie's mother. _____
2. Matt is **thrilled** to be on the basketball team. _____
3. Mrs. Benson works very hard to keep everything **done** around the apartment building. _____
4. Mrs. Stamps is a **friendly** person to visit. _____
5. Mr. Ashby tries to be a **fair** teacher. _____
6. Angel is **wicked** toward everyone around her. _____
7. The Bacon family really **enjoyed** Mattie's babysitting service. _____
8. Charlene took the bracelet from Angel because she was **envious** of Angel. _____
9. Mr. Phillips was **amazed** by Mattie's story. _____
10. Mattie had been very **helpful** to her mother. _____

Now, use the thesaurus to find an antonym for each synonym you wrote above.

1. _____
2. _____
3. _____
4. _____
5. _____

6. _____
7. _____
8. _____
9. _____
10. _____

Learn at Home, Grade 4

Multiplication

Come on, this is easy!

1. 32
    x 3

2. 21
    x 4

3. 43
    x 3

4. 20
    x 3

5. 11
    x 3

6. 34
    x 3

7. 21
    x 3

8. 33
    x 3

9. 24
    x 2

10. 22
    x 4

11. 40
    x 2

12. 32
    x 2

13. 13
    x 3

14. 22
    x 2

15. 20
    x 4

16. 23
    x 2

17. 11
    x 3

18. 41
    x 2

19. 31
    x 3

20. 44
    x 2

21. 23
    x 3

22. 12
    x 4

23. 33
    x 2

24. 30
    x 3

25. 21
    x 2

26. 13
    x 2

27. 42
    x 2

28. 12
    x 3

29. 14
    x 2

30. 22
    x 3

Learn at Home, Grade 4

Regrouping

1. Multiply the ones column. Ask: Do I need to regroup?

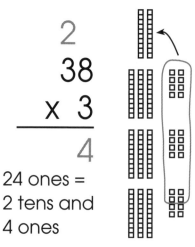

$$
\begin{array}{r}
2 \\
38 \\
\times\ 3 \\
\hline
4
\end{array}
$$

24 ones =
2 tens and
4 ones

2. Multiply the tens column. Ask: Do I need to regroup?

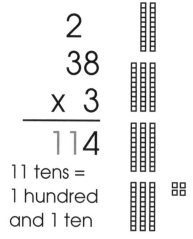

$$
\begin{array}{r}
2 \\
38 \\
\times\ 3 \\
\hline
114
\end{array}
$$

11 tens =
1 hundred
and 1 ten

$$
\begin{array}{r}
38 \\
\times\ 3 \\
\hline
\end{array}
$$

is the
same as

$$
\begin{array}{r}
38 \\
38 \\
+\ 38 \\
\hline
\end{array}
$$

Multiply.

1. $\begin{array}{r} 29 \\ \times\ 3 \\ \hline \end{array}$
2. $\begin{array}{r} 62 \\ \times\ 4 \\ \hline \end{array}$
3. $\begin{array}{r} 39 \\ \times\ 4 \\ \hline \end{array}$
4. $\begin{array}{r} 86 \\ \times\ 7 \\ \hline \end{array}$
5. $\begin{array}{r} 43 \\ \times\ 6 \\ \hline \end{array}$

6. $\begin{array}{r} 28 \\ \times\ 6 \\ \hline \end{array}$
7. $\begin{array}{r} 48 \\ \times\ 2 \\ \hline \end{array}$
8. $\begin{array}{r} 31 \\ \times\ 9 \\ \hline \end{array}$
9. $\begin{array}{r} 25 \\ \times\ 5 \\ \hline \end{array}$
10. $\begin{array}{r} 55 \\ \times\ 5 \\ \hline \end{array}$

Moon Logs

Keep a log of the Moon's phases.

You will need:

four sheets (8" x 12") of black construction paper, a stapler, a white crayon, a large calendar

Directions:

Create a Moon log by folding four sheets of black construction paper in half and stapling them together. Using a white crayon, create a title and decorate the cover.

It is best to begin the Moon observations with a "new Moon." Observe the Moon twice a week (or every 3 days), weather permitting. If clouds interfere with your planned dates to observe the Moon, you may be forced to postpone it.

In your log, record the date of observation, and use half of a page on which to draw the shape of the Moon. Pay careful attention to which side of the Moon is illuminated. Be sure to draw it exactly as you see it. As the month progresses, record your findings on a calendar.

Look up vocabulary such as waxing, waning, new, crescent, full, first quarter, etc.

Find out why the Moon shines. Why its shape seems to change. Why we see only one side of the Moon. What does the surface of the Moon look like from Earth? What has NASA recently discovered regarding the Moon?

When the log is complete and you are observing another new Moon, discuss with an adult the amount of time that has passed since you began logging

the Moon. Relate the cycle of the Moon phases to the calendar. Make predictions regarding specific phases of the upcoming month (i.e., How much time will pass between the new Moon and the full Moon? Predict the date we will see the next full Moon, etc.). You can glue the final draft on the inside cover of your Moon log.

Learn at Home, Grade 4

	Language Skills	Spelling	Reading
Monday	Help your child create a "story map" of a familiar nursery rhyme by listing the following information: *setting, characters, problem, events* and *solution. See* Language Skills, Week 8, number 1. Have your child use the information from the completed "story map" as a guide for writing a make-believe story.	Pretest your child on these spelling words. agree easel preach between greenery season breathe greetings wheat disease meek wheel eagle people yeast Have your child correct the pretest, add personalized words and make two copies of this week's study list.	With your child, review and practice the use of *similes.* Read chapters 1–3 of *The Whipping Boy.* Make a copy of **Story Organizer** (p. 101). Have your child fill in as much as he/she can. Have him/her complete the page over the next 2 weeks while reading the book.
Tuesday	Have your child write the days of the week in cursive several times. Remind him/her that each day should be capitalized.	Have your child use each of this week's spelling words correctly in a sentence.	Have your child match sentence beginnings with endings to form similes. *See* Reading, Week 8, number 1. Then, ask your child to write some original similes. Give him/her a starter to get going, such as "The boy was as timid as…." Read chapters 4–6 of *The Whipping Boy.* Have your child explain in his/her Reading Journal why Jemmy did not want the prince to tell the robbers who he was.
Wednesday	Discuss the meanings of several *affixes. See* Language Skills, Week 8, number 2. Have your child create several new words using the affixes listed. Have him/her write a definition for each new word and use the word in a sentence.	Have your child complete **Still Easy** (p. 100).	Review and practice writing *metaphors. See* Reading, Week 8, number 2. Read chapters 7–10 of *The Whipping Boy.* Have your child describe Jemmy's plan in his/her Reading Journal.
Thursday	Review prefixes. Have your child complete **The Beginning** (p. 98).	Have your child look up the words in the dictionary and write a brief definition for each on an index card. (Write ONLY the definition—not the word.) Then, mix up the cards and ask your child to name the word that each card defines. Encourage him/her to use the words in a sentence.	Have your child look through poetry books, looking for metaphors and similes. Read chapters 11–14 of *The Whipping Boy.* Ask: *Why does the prince not want to go back to the castle?* Have your child write a detailed explanation in his/her Reading Journal.
Friday	Review suffixes. Have your child complete **The End** (p. 99).	Give your child the final spelling test. Have him/her record the pretest and final test words in his/her word bank.	Read chapters 15–17 of *The Whipping Boy.* Discuss the prince's new attitude. Ask: *In what ways is he changing?* Have your child complete **Like…a Simile** (p. 102).

Learn at Home, Grade 4

Math	Science	Social Studies
Following the same process as in Week 7, show your child how to multiply a 4-digit number by a 1-digit number. Have him/her practice problems both with and without regrouping.	**Stars** Using library resources and an encyclopedia, locate information about stars. Have your child write a list of interesting facts about stars. *See* Science, Week 8. Have your child complete **Star Light, Star Bright** (p. 105).	Discuss areas that are left to be explored, such as the ocean floor and outer space. Ask your child to name any other frontiers. Discuss what an explorer of these frontiers might hope to find or learn. *See* Social Studies, Week 8, number 1.
Have your child practice multiplying a 4-digit number by a 1-digit number, using the process described in last Friday's lesson. Have your child complete **Amazing Arms** (p. 103).	Visit a planetarium. Afterward, ask your child for his/her impressions of the visit. What did he/she find most interesting? Review some of the constellations. Then, have your child imagine that he/she has just discovered a new constellation. Ask him/her what it would look like and what it would be called. Provide black construction paper and white chalk for your child to draw and label his/her new discovery.	Introduce the explorers of space and the ocean. *See* Social Studies, Week 8, number 2. Help your child create a chart showing the explorers, their countries of origin, where they explored, the years they explored and other relevant information.
Show your child how to multiply by 1, 10, 100 and 1,000. Create a grid on the chalkboard with five rows and eight columns. In the first row, write 1-, 2-, 3- and 4-digit numbers (two of each). In the second row, have your child write the product of each number x 1; in the third row, x 10; in the fourth, x 100; and in the fifth, x 1,000. He/she may want to solve the problems on paper first. Examine the grid for patterns. Ask your child what he/she notices.	Help your child follow the directions on the activity sheets to make a Star Gazer. Tell your child to take the completed Star Gazer outside to help identify constellations on a clear night. Turn the disk to the current month, date and time that you are star-gazing. Have your child match the stars on the disk to those in the sky. Make a copy of **Star Gazer (cover)** and **Star Gazer (disk)** (pgs. 106 and 107).	Read about the space station Mir. Discuss the goals of the mission and predict what will result from the research.
Demonstrate how to multiply a 2-digit number by another 2-digit number. *See* Math, Week 8, number 1. Have your child complete **Elephant Escapades** (p. 104).	Discuss *asteroids, comets* and *meteors,* which may be seen in our solar system. Have your child complete **Space Snowballs** (p. 108) and **A Black Hole** (p. 109).	**Art:** Have your child make a stabile of an explorer. Use wire, tape and tagboard to build a structure representing the work of an explorer. You will need a rectangular piece of foam for a base. *See* Social Studies, Week 8, number 3.
Give your child several story problems that involve multiplication. *See* Math, Week 8, number 2 for examples. Have your child write and solve a multiplication problem involving 2-, 3- or 4-digit factors.	Have your child write a haiku about our solar system. *See* Science, Week 8, number 1. Have your child complete the KWHL chart started at the beginning of the unit. Have your child write sentences in the final column telling what he/she has learned about the topic. Then, look over the information written in the other columns and determine if any information is incorrect. Help your child correct those mistakes at this time.	Let your child finish his/her art project. Ask him/her to name the stabile and add the title to the foam base.

TEACHING SUGGESTIONS AND ACTIVITIES

LANGUAGE SKILLS (Prefixes and Suffixes)

▶ 1. In the following sample of a completed story map from "Jack and Jill," notice that missing details were filled in with a little imagination.

Setting: In the country
Characters: Jack and his sister Jill
Problem: The well on their farm was empty.
Events: They walked a long distance to the community well. They climbed the hill to fetch some water. They were so tired, they fell down the hill. Jill ran for help.
Solution: A neighbor picked them up in his wagon and took them back to the farm.

▶ 2. Copy the following lists of prefixes and suffixes. Have your child look up the meaning of some of them in the dictionary. Help him/her brainstorm a list of words containing these affixes.

Prefixes: *anti, astro, auto, bi, con, de, dis, en, ex, fore, hemi, macro, micro, mono, non, pre, pro, re, sub, tri, un, uni*
Suffixes: *ance, en, ent, ese, ess, ful, ion, ish, ist, ite, itis, less, ment, ness, ly*

READING (Story Analysis)

▶ 1. Write sentence halves on the chalkboard. Have your child put together one beginning and one ending to form a simile. Repeat.

Sentence Beginnings	*Sentence Endings*
The black rain cloud looked . . .	. . . like a mountain peak.
Mr. Tretheway was . . .	. . . as blue as a cornflower.
The snow pile reached high into the sky . . .	. . . as mean as skunks.
The Connolly brothers are . . .	. . . like coyotes peering into a henhouse.
The darkness was soothing . . .	. . . like a heavy bag of coal hanging in the sky.
Maria's eyes were . . .	. . . as strong as an ox.
The sneaky boys looked in the window . . .	. . . like a comfortable blanket.

▶ 2. Use this brainstorming activity to help your child learn to form metaphors. Say a word, such as *South Pole*. Have your child name any words associated with the word that pop into his/her head. He/she might respond with the words *cold, ice, icicle, white* and *frozen*. From those words, have your child create metaphors. **Examples:** Peter's nose was ice. Susan was an icicle.

MATH (Multiplication)

▶ 1. Write problems similar to the one at right on the chalkboard. Model the procedure for your child, explaining each step. First, multiply the first number (47) by 5. Then, multiply 47 by 3. Explain that because 3 is in the tens place, you will place a 0 in the ones place to hold that place. Add the products to get the answer for 47 x 35. Guide your child as he/she completes other similar problems. Alternately, multiply in the manner described on Friday of Week 7.

$$\begin{array}{r} 47 \\ \times\ 35 \\ \hline 235 \\ +\ 1,410 \\ \hline 1,645 \end{array}$$

▶ 2. Sample story problems:

a. There were 12 busloads of fans who went to the baseball game. Each bus held 48 people. How many people rode the bus to the game?

b. A track and field relay team of 4 is competing with the track club of another school. Each relay participant will run 100 yards. How many yards total will the relay team run?

c. The Maple City Choir camp sent 356 people to the ball game. They each spent an average of $10 on snacks and souvenirs. How much money did the choir group spend at the ball park?

SCIENCE (Stars)

BACKGROUND

A star is a huge ball of glowing gas. Stars appear very small because they are so far away. They appear to twinkle because their light comes to us through moving layers of air. Stars do move, but their positions relative to each other do not, so we can recognize patterns or constellations night after night, year after year.

▷ 1. Review the elements of a haiku. The topic is usually something in nature. A haiku contains 17 syllables: 5 on line one, 7 on line two and 5 on line three. Encourage your child to write several poems about the solar system. Then, have him/her paint a watercolor background on 9" x 12" paper. When the paint is dry, have your child copy the poems onto the painting using a fine, black felt-tip marker.

SOCIAL STUDIES (Explorers)

▷ 1. Discuss some of the following issues with your child:

   a. Until recently, only men had been recognized in history as being explorers. Why?

   b. How do food provisions today differ from those used on earlier expeditions?
   — Shorter trips mean less food needed
   — Refrigeration allows people to bring healthier foods such as fruits and vegetables
   — Packaged foods
   — Innovations such as powdered drinks and dehydrated foods for astronauts

   Call NASA's Information Resources office: (713) 483-8694. They can send you a teacher's pack on food used for space flight.

▷ 2. Space and ocean explorers include:

   Edwin E. Aldrin, Jr.
   Jacques-Yves Cousteau
   Valentina Tereshkova
   William Anderson
   Yuri Gagarin
   Eileen M. Collins
   Neil Armstrong
   James Lovell
   John Young
   William Beebe
   Jacques Piccard
   Sally Ride

▷ 3. **Art:** A stabile is like a mobile but with no moving parts. Show your child how to bend and insert wires of different lengths into foam and attach paper cutouts with tape. Have your child think about one explorer's adventure and its components. Have him/her draw several pictures that capture the experience on poster board, cut them out and draw the same pictures on the backs of the cutouts. Attach the cutouts to the ends of the wires.

The Beginning

Add a prefix to each word in the list to make a new word. **Write** the new word on the trunk that has that prefix.

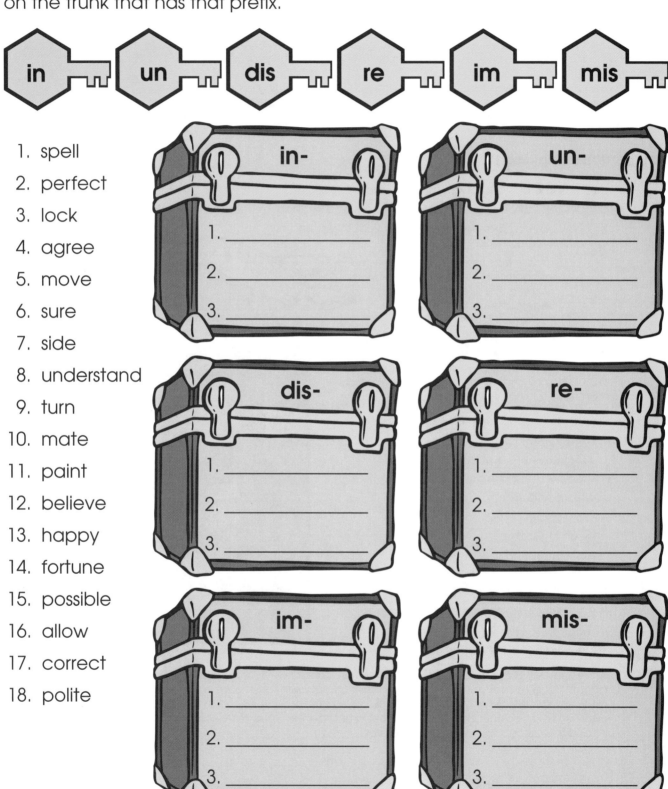

in   un   dis   re   im   mis

1. spell
2. perfect
3. lock
4. agree
5. move
6. sure
7. side
8. understand
9. turn
10. mate
11. paint
12. believe
13. happy
14. fortune
15. possible
16. allow
17. correct
18. polite

in-
1. _____
2. _____
3. _____

un-
1. _____
2. _____
3. _____

dis-
1. _____
2. _____
3. _____

re-
1. _____
2. _____
3. _____

im-
1. _____
2. _____
3. _____

mis-
1. _____
2. _____
3. _____

Learn at Home, Grade 4

The End

Add a suffix from the box to each word in parentheses to make a new word. The new word must make sense in the sentence. **Write** the new word in the blank.

ly	less	ion
ful	ing	ed

1. The snow fell _____ and covered the trees.
   (quick)

2. We _____ our dog Duke to roll over.
   (train)

3. It's fun to go _____ in a tent.
   (camp)

4. Who will be running for president in the next _____ ?
   (elect)

5. Be extra _____ with that knife.
   (care)

6. My mom was so excited that she was _____ .
   (speech)

7. We _____ for hours but caught nothing.
   (fish)

8. It is my _____ that it will rain tomorrow.
   (predict)

9. Jack is _____ on a hunting trip.
   (go)

10. Grandma's homemade chocolate cake tastes _____ .
    (wonder)

11. The opera star sang _____ .
    (loud)

Still Easy

Put a check to the left of the spelling words in which the letters **ea** make the **long e** sound.

Put a star to the right of the spelling words in which the letters **ee** make the **long e** sound.

Which word uses the letters **eo** for the **long e** sound? _____

agree	easel	preach
between	greenery	season
breathe	greetings	wheat
disease	meek	wheel
eagle	people	yeast

Fill in the blanks.

1. During the holiday _____, our family sends lots of _____.

2. The Reverend Smith will _____ to _____ a shorter time because of extra musical selections.

3. In earlier times, _____ was ground into flour with a large stone _____ .

4. The soaring _____ is a proud creature, not _____ or timid.

5. In the park surrounded by _____ stood the artist painting at his _____ .

6. The swimming coach taught the swimmers to _____ evenly _____ strokes.

7. Two topics or terms studied in life science are _____ and _____ .

Story Organizer

Date _____ Title _____

Vocabulary   **Definitions**

_____   _____

_____   _____

_____   _____

_____   _____

_____   _____

Setting: _____

Characters: _____

_____

Problem: _____

_____

Events: _____

_____

_____

_____

_____

Solution: _____

_____

_____

Did you enjoy this story?   1   2   3   4   5   6
                             Not   Very
                             at all   much!

Like . . . a Simile

In the sentences below, underline the two things or persons being compared. In the blank, **write** simile or metaphor. Remember, a simile uses **like** or **as**; metaphors do not.

1. Angel was as mean as a wild bull. _____

2. Toni and Mattie were like toast and jam. _____

3. Mr. Ashby expected the students to be as busy as beavers.

   _____

4. The pin was a masterpiece in Mattie's mind. _____

5. The park's peacefulness was a friend to Mattie. _____

6. The words came as slow as molasses into Mattie's mind. _____

7. Mrs. Stamp's apartment was like a museum. _____

8. Mrs. Benson was as happy as a lark when Mattie won

   the contest. _____

9. Mr. Phillip's smile was a glowing beam to Mattie and Mrs. Benson.

   _____

10. Mattie ran as fast as the wind to get her money. _____

11. Angel's mean words cut through Charlene like glass. _____

12. Mr. Bacon was a fairy godmother to Mattie. _____

13. The gingko tree's leaves were shaped like fans. _____

Complete the following sentences using similes.

1. Matt was as artistic as _____.

2. Hannibal's teeth were like _____.

3. Toni's mind worked fast like _____.

4. Mattie was as sad as _____.

5. Mrs. Stamp was like _____.

Star Light, Star Bright

Lie on your back. Gaze up into the night sky. Which star is the brightest? On a clear night you can see hundreds of stars, some are bright and others are dim. Why are some stars brighter than others? Let's try to find out by looking at the picture on this page.

1. Look at the two streetlights in the picture. Which streetlight appears brighter? _____
Why? _____
_____

2. Look at the bicycle and the truck. Which headlights appear brighter? _____
Why? _____

3. Some stars appear brighter than other stars for the same reasons as those stated above. What are the two reasons?
a. _____
b. _____

Color Me Hot

Stars differ not only in brightness but also in color. As a star gets hotter, its color changes. **Color** these stars. Use the chart to find the correct color.

Star Colors	
36,000°F Blue	18,000°F White
9,000°F Yellow	5,400°F Red

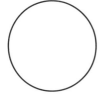

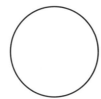
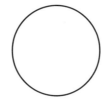
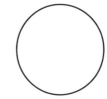

Spica 36,000°F   Sirius 18,000°F   Sun 9,000°F   Betelgeuse 5,400°F

Star Gazer (cover)

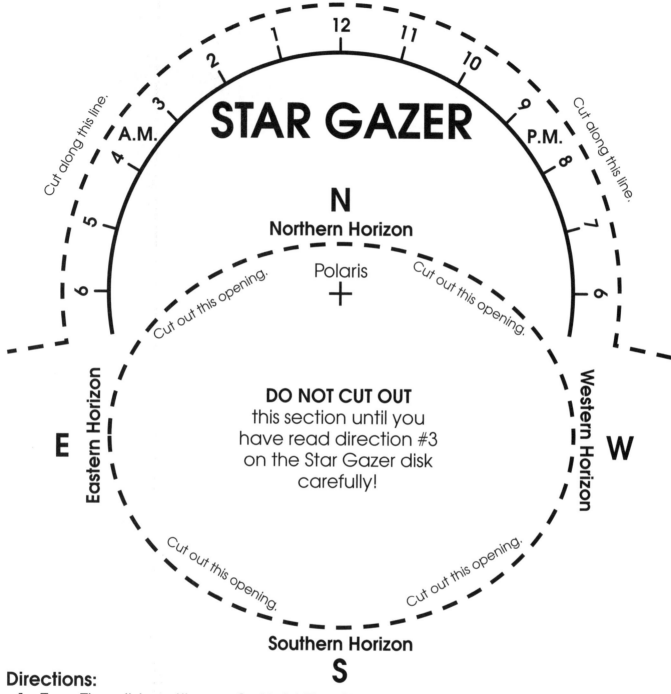

Directions:

1. Turn The disk until the approximate time of viewing and approximate date of viewing are set.

2. Hold The Star Gazer overhead with North towards the North Pole and South towards the South Pole.

3. The stars on the chart and the stars in the sky will match.

The Star Gazer is made for latitude 40°N., but it will be helpful for any mid-latitude areas in the Northern Hemisphere.

Star Gazer (disk)

1. **Cut out** Star Gazer disk and the Star Gazer cover.
2. Lay the cover on an 8" x 11" sheet of tagboard (or other sturdy paper). Line up and tape the bottom edge.

3. Make a pin hole through the cover and tagboard at the point marked "Polaris."

tape

pinhole

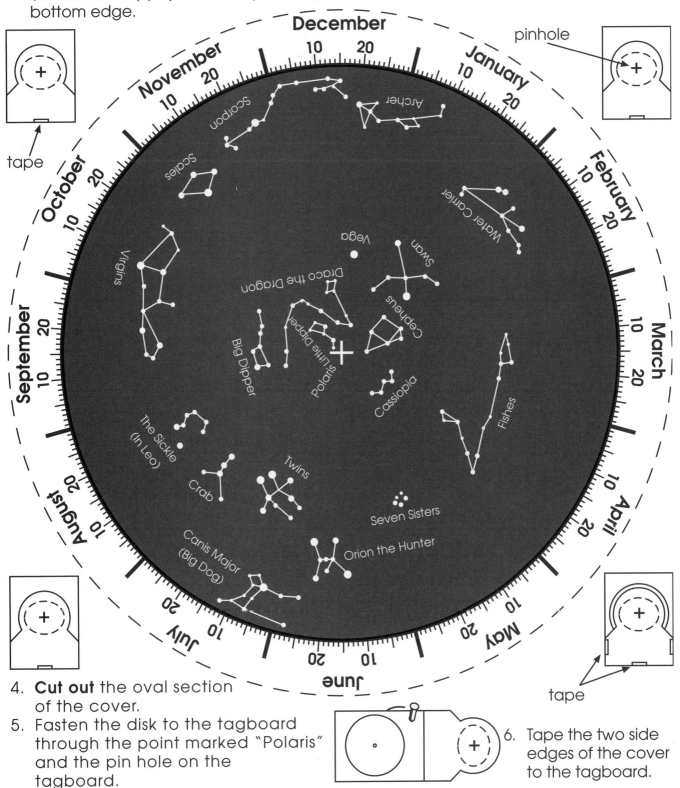

4. **Cut out** the oval section of the cover.
5. Fasten the disk to the tagboard through the point marked "Polaris" and the pin hole on the tagboard.

6. Tape the two side edges of the cover to the tagboard.

tape

Learn at Home, Grade 4

Space Snowballs

Planets and moons are not the only objects in our solar system that travel in orbits. Comets also orbit the Sun.

A **comet** is like a giant dirty snowball that is $\frac{1}{2}$ to 3 miles wide. It is made of frozen gases, dust, ice and rocks.

As the comet gets closer to the Sun, the frozen gases melt and evaporate. The dust particles floating in the air form a cloud called a **coma**. The "wind" from the Sun blows the coma away from the Sun. The coma forms the comet's tail.

There are more than 800 known comets. Halley's comet is the most famous. It appears about every 76 years. The last scheduled appearance in this century was in 1985. When will it appear next?

Find the words from the box in the word search. (They are horizontal or vertical.) When you are finished, **write** down the letters that are not circled. Start at the top left of the puzzle.

```
S P M E L T L A N H E
O T S S H A C O M A V
L E N O R D B I T L S
A L O I K U E C I L R
R C W L E S S C O E M
S E B T S T H A V Y E
Y O A R O R B I T B I
S T L S S H A P E D L
T I L K T A I L E A F
E O O T I C E B A L L
M S K Y S H I N I N G
```

dust	Halley
coma	snowball
melt	orbit
tail	ice
sky	shining
solar	system

— — — — — — — —   — — — —   — — — — — —

— — — —   — — — — — — — — — ,   — — — — — —

— — — —   — — — — — — — —   — — — —

— — — —   — —   — — — — — — — — .

A Black Hole

Have you ever heard of a mysterious black hole? Some scientists believe that a black hole is an invisible object somewhere in space. Scientists believe that it has such a strong pull toward it, called gravity, that nothing can escape from it!

These scientists believe that a black hole is a star that has collapsed. The collapse made its pull even stronger. It seems invisible because even its own starlight cannot escape! It is believed that anything in space that comes near the black hole will be pulled into it forever. Some scientists believe there are many black holes in our galaxy.

Check: Some scientists believe that:

☐ a black hole is an invisible object in space.
☐ a black hole is a collapsed star.
☐ a black hole will not let its own light escape.

Write:

| A - gravity |
| B - collapse |

_____ To fall or cave in
_____ A strong pull toward an object in space

Draw what you think the inside of a black hole would be like.

Language Skills	Spelling	Reading
Monday **Review Week** Assess your child's ability to identify parts of speech. Reteach, if necessary. Write the parts of speech on a chart, leaving space beneath each heading: nouns, pronouns, verbs, adjectives, adverbs, prepositions, interjections, conjunctions and articles. Give your child various sentences. Have him/her write each word from each sentence under the appropriate category on the chart.	**Review Week** Choose words from the last 8 weeks for the pretest. Pretest your child on these spelling words. Have your child correct the pretest and make a study list of misspelled words, if any. Have him/her study the words each day this week.	**Review Week** Assess your child's punctuation skills. Copy a paragraph from *The Whipping Boy*, leaving off all punctuation. Have your child replace the missing punctuation. Reteach, if necessary. Read chapter 18 of *The Whipping Boy*. Have your child imagine what will happen to Jemmy in the future. Then, have him/her write a paragraph describing Jemmy's life 5 years in the future.
Tuesday Review the different types of verbs: action, linking and helping. Have your child complete **Action and Linking Verbs** (p. 114).	Have your child sort the spelling words from the last 8 weeks into meaningful categories. Categories might include vowel sounds, parts of speech (nouns, verbs, adjectives, etc.) or number of syllables.	Assess your child's knowledge of prefixes and suffixes. Reteach, if necessary. Have your child complete **Fore and Aft** (p. 116).
Wednesday Assess your child's ability to use irregular verbs. Reteach, if necessary. Play the "Irregular Regularity" game. You will need a copy of **Irregular Regularity Game Board** (p. 115). *See* Language Skills, Week 9, number 1 for game directions.	Have your child list all the spelling words from the last 8 weeks that are nouns. Ask him/her to write an appropriate adjective in front of each noun.	Read chapters 19 and 20 of *The Whipping Boy*. Assess your child's classification skills. Work together with him/her to list the actions of the prince throughout the book. Have your child classify his actions as selfish or generous.
Thursday Assess your child's ability to use similes and metaphors. First, give your child a few examples of similes. Then, have him/her transform nondescriptive sentences by adding similes. **Example:** I am cold, *I am as cold as an ice cube.* Next, give your child a few examples of metaphors. Then, give him/her several sentence starters to turn into metaphors. **Example:** The bustling city was *a whirlwind of color.*	Have your child write a story using as many of the spelling words from the last 8 weeks as possible. Ask him/her to underline each of these words in the story.	Assess your child's knowledge of antonyms, synonyms and homophones. Give him/her a series of word pairs, such as *small—little.* Have your child mark each pair as antonyms (A), homophones (H) or synonyms (S). Reteach, if necessary. Have your child complete **Double Trouble** (p. 117) for homophone practice.
Friday Assess your child's ability to use idioms and personification. Read several examples of idioms. *See* Language Skills, Week 9, number 2. List them on a sheet of posterboard. Have your child think of others to add to the list. Keep the list posted for a few weeks and add to it. Have your child write four sentences using personification, then draw a picture of each literal interpretation.	Give your child the final spelling test.	Assess your child's ability to read with expression. Read some exciting parts of *The Whipping Boy* aloud with your child as if you were Jemmy and the prince. Urge your child to use expression and to leave off unnecessary words such as "he said." Have your child complete **Story Organizer** (p. 101), started last week.

Math	Science	Social Studies
Review Week Assess your child's understanding of place value. Play the "Big Numbers" game. *See* Math, Week 9, number 1. Copy **Game Parts for Big Numbers Game** (p. 118), glue the page onto light cardboard and cut out the pieces.	**Review Week** Have your child draw and label a picture of each of the six simple machines. Based on the drawings, assess whether the concept needs reteaching.	**Review Week** Have your child make a mural representing explorations since 2500 B.C. *See* Social Studies, Week 9, number 1.
Assess your child's understanding of greater than and less than. Read aloud two numbers. Have your child write the numbers on one line, leaving a space between them. Ask him/her to determine whether the first number is greater than or less than the second number and write in the appropriate symbol. Have your child read the number sentence aloud. Repeat with other number pairs and, for a challenge, with simple addition or subtraction problems.	On paper, have your child design a compound machine that performs a useful task. Ask him/her to label each simple machine in the drawing.	Have your child write a poem about discovering something down the road. *See* Social Studies, Week 9, number 2.
Assess your child's ability to round. Make a shopping list that includes some very expensive items (new car: $18,579) as well as some inexpensive items (t-shirt: $9). Show each item and its price (in dollars only) on an index card. Have your child round the price of each item to different places, then combinations of items (adding first, then rounding). Challenge: About how much money would your child need to buy everything on the list (to the nearest ten)?	Have your child sketch and label the solar system. Assess whether he/she knows the names and order of the planets. Reteach if necessary.	Have your child name four explorers of North America. Have him/her explain where they traveled and what they discovered or saw. Then, have your child trace the explorers' routes on a map. Ask how the findings of these explorers influenced the settlement of the U.S. Reteach if necessary.
Assess your child's ability to multiply by powers of ten. *See* Math, Week 9, number 2. Have your child complete **Wheels of Wonder** (p. 119).	Have your child write a Moon riddle. The riddle should consist of several clues about the Moon and should end with the question, "What am I?" Assess your child's understanding of the Moon, based on his/her clues.	Play a game in which your child asks questions and tries to guess the name of an explorer. Write the name of an explorer on an index card and tape it to your child's back. Your child may ask only yes/no questions to determine who he/she is. Also try reversing the game, giving your child the opportunity to *answer* questions.
Assess your child's ability to multiply with regrouping. Give him/her several problems to solve. Use a variety of numbers (1-, 2-, 3- and 4-digit numbers) in the problems.	From the library, borrow a variety of children's stories with the theme of space and the solar system. Read several stories together with your child. Then, have him/her write a fictional story on that theme.	Using the meter of a familiar poem, have your child write verses about explorers. *See* Social Studies, Week 9, number 3.

TEACHING SUGGESTIONS AND ACTIVITIES

LANGUAGE SKILLS

▷   1.   Make a copy of the **Irregular Regularity Game Board** (p. 115). Color each square as indicated. Those with arrows remain white. Use construction paper to make ten game cards ($2^1/_2$" x $1^1/_2$) in each of the following colors: yellow, blue, red and white.

   On each yellow card, write a present-tense irregular verb.
   On each white card, write a past-tense irregular verb.
   On each red card, write a regular verb, past or present tense.
   On each blue card, write directions for using a given verb in a sentence.

Example: Use the present tense of _____ in a sentence.

<u>Present-Tense Irregular Verbs</u>

awake	choose	feed
beat	come	fight
begin	cost	find
bend	creep	flee
bite	dig	fly
blow	do	forget
break	draw	freeze
bring	drink	get
buy	drive	give
catch	eat	go

<u>Past-Tense Irregular Verbs</u>

grew	meant	shone
had	paid	shook
heard	ran	shot
held	read	shut
hurt	rode	sold
knelt	rose	sought
knew	rung	spoke
left	said	stood
lost	sat	stole
made	saw	stuck

A player moves around the board by rolling a die and moving the number of spaces indicated. Then, he/she chooses the top card from the pile in the color of the space on which he/she landed. In order to roll again, the player must respond to the direction on the card as follows: *Yellow cards*—state the present tense of the given irregular verb. *White cards*—state the past tense of the given irregular verb. *Red cards*—state the present tense if the verb is in the past or the past tense if the verb is in the irregular present. *Blue cards*—create a sentence as indicated.

▷   2.   Idioms:

   • Robert was <u>down in the dumps</u> when he saw his grades.
   • The rumor was <u>nipped in the bud</u>.
   • Mom <u>flies off the handle</u> when we don't clean our rooms.
   • He certainly <u>pulled the wool over my eyes</u>.
   • The class was <u>in hot water</u> when they didn't settle down after recess.
   • They had to <u>face the music</u>.
   • Dad is <u>in the doghouse</u> because he was late for dinner.

112

MATH

1. Play the "Big Numbers" game. To make each spinner, attach a large paper clip or safety pin to the spinner base with a brad or paper fastener. The paper clip (or safety pin) should spin freely. Cut out the three sets of number cards. Your child must spin the spinners, then place the number card on the game board as indicated by the spinners. Spin until each place is filled on the game board. Your child then reads the number aloud.

2. Count the number of zeros at the end of a number (or numbers) in a multiplication problem and write them down in the answer. Then, multiply the numbers that are left.

Examples:	162	2,307	1,690	3,500
	x 100	x 1,000	x 2,000	x 3,000
	16,2**00**	2,307,**000**	3,380,**000**	10,5**00,000**

SOCIAL STUDIES

1. Use a long sheet of plain shelf paper or butcher paper for the mural. Organize the mural like a time line. Study the explorers of the different times and regions. Have your child paint the ships, maps and people traveling across the mural—like a collage showing the progression of exploration. Also, have your child label the different images with names, dates and, if there is space, a brief statement about the event or person that is depicted.

2. Read "Roads" by Rachael Field. Discuss the poem with your child. Then, direct him/her to write an original poem in the same style, imagining that he/she were an explorer. Encourage your child to think about something new to discover and tell where the "road" might lead. The first verse of the new poem should begin with the first six words of Field's poem: "A road might lead to anywhere." Be sure to give credit to Rachael Field on the final copy of your child's poem.

3. Copy and read the first verse from "The History of the U.S." by Winifred Sackville Stoner: "In fourteen hundred ninety-two,/Columbus sailed the ocean blue. /And found this land, Land of the Free, /beloved by you, beloved by me." Then, have your child write verses about other explorers in the same meter. Compile the verses into a book about explorers. Have your child create a cover for the book and think of a clever title.

Action and Linking Verbs

An **action verb** is a word that shows action.
Examples: We **play** basketball. I **think** about my pet.

Underline the action verb in each sentence below.

1. Have you ever wished for a dog of your very own?
2. Choose the breed of your dog very carefully.
3. Puppies may grow to be very large or very small.
4. Your dog must receive good care, attention and exercise.
5. The right dog will give you years of pleasure and enjoyment.
6. Can you imagine yourself as a dog owner?

A **linking verb** does not show action. Instead, it links the subject with a noun or adjective in the predicate of the sentence. Forms of the verb **be** are common linking verbs.
Example: Puppies **are** cute.

Underline the linking verb in each sentence. Then, **fill in** the chart.
1. Tom's new puppy is playful and mischievous.
2. His dad's socks are a temptation to that puppy.
3. Mom and Dad were angry when the puppy chewed up a shoe.
4. They were surprised when the puppy got into Mom's flowers.
5. He was so happy rolling around in the dirt.
6. The puppy will be less trouble when he grows up.

Subject	Linking Verb	Noun or Adjective(s)	Subject	Linking Verb	Noun or Adjective(s)
1. _____			4. _____		
2. _____			5. _____		
3. _____			6. _____		

Irregular Regularity Game Board

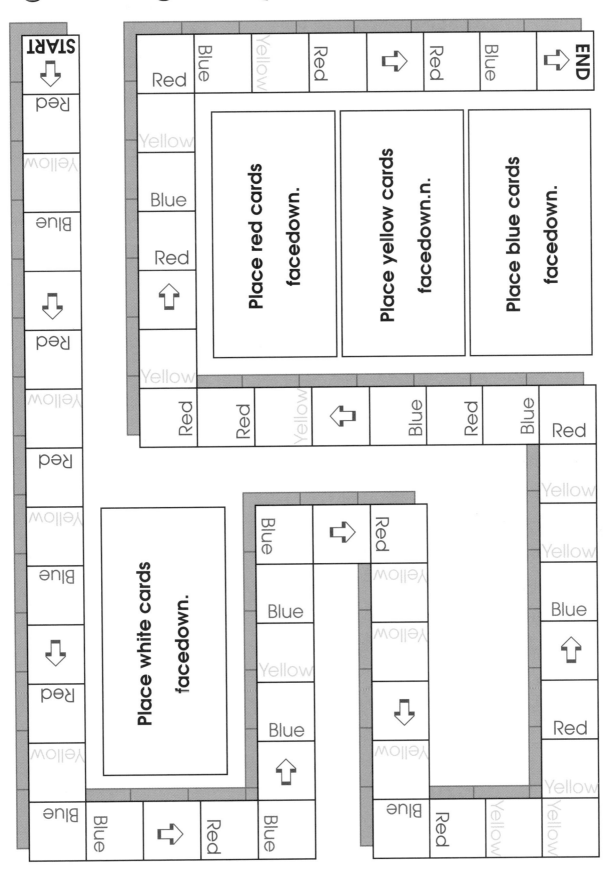

Fore and Aft

Fill in the blanks with the appropriate affixes.
Some will be used more than once.

Prefixes: dis im re un mis   Suffixes: ful ish ist less ly ness ward

Meaning	Root Word + Affix	New Word
1. having no fear	fear __ __ __ __	_____
2. to vanish	__ __ __ appear	_____
3. toward a lower level	down __ __ __ __	_____
4. having no friends	friend __ __ __ __	_____
5. an error in action	__ __ __ take	_____
6. to enter again	__ __ enter	_____
7. too many to count	count __ __ __ __	_____
8. not happy	__ __ happy	_____
9. perfection seeker	perfection __ __ __	_____
10. quality of being dark	dark __ __ __ __	_____
11. not possible	__ __ possible	_____
12. having doubts	doubt __ __ __	_____
13. without a care	care __ __ __ __	_____
14. sad from being alone	lone __ __	_____
15. not thinking	__ __ thinking	_____
16. without shoes	shoe __ __ __ __	_____
17. in a mysterious way	mysterious __ __	_____
18. appear again	__ __ appear	_____
19. in a quiet manner	quiet __ __	_____
20. call by wrong name	__ __ __ call	_____
21. somewhat yellow	yellow __ __ __	_____
22. cautious	care __ __ __	_____
23. to release	__ __ __ engage	_____

Double Trouble

Fill in the blanks with the correct definition number for each **underlined** word.

Example: __3__ I was covered with **pitch** after climbing the pine tree.

winding	1. having bends or curves
	2. the act of turning something around a central core
wolf	1. to gulp down
	2. a large carnivorous member of the dog family
pitch	1. to sell or persuade
	2. to throw a ball from the mound to the batter
	3. a resin that comes from the sap of pine trees

_____ 1. Do the children's clubs **pitch** cookies?

_____ 2. We are **winding** the top's string tightly.

_____ 3. The adult **wolf** returned to her lair.

_____ 4. Red didn't **pitch** after the fourth inning.

_____ 5. The Mather family had a **winding** driveway.

_____ 6. The young ball player **wolfed** down his lunch.

choke	1. to strangle
	2. to bring the hands up on the bat
hitch	1. obstacle
	2. to fasten or tie temporarily
wind-up	1. the swing of the pitcher's arm just before the pitch
	2. to close or conclude

_____ 1. We **hitched** the mule to the cart.

_____ 2. Skip would not **choke** up on his bat.

_____ 3. Paul wished to play, but there was just one **hitch**.

_____ 4. We wish to **wind-up** our program with more music.

_____ 5. Mom was afraid the dog would **choke** itself on its leash.

_____ 6. He has a great **wind-up** and curve ball.

ONES	
TENS	
HUNDREDS	
THOUSANDS	
TEN THOUSANDS	
HUNDRED THOUSANDS	
MILLIONS	
TEN MILLIONS	
HUNDRED MILLIONS	

0 0 0
9 9 9
8 8 8
7 7 7
6 6 6
5 5 5
4 4 4
3 3 3
2 2 2
1 1 1

Numeral Spinner

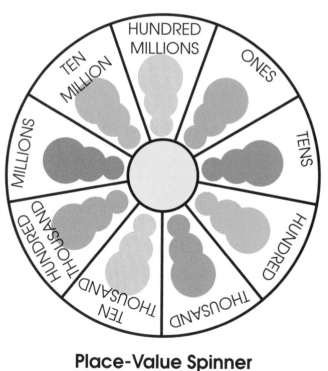

Place-Value Spinner

Wheels of Wonder

Solve the following problems by multiplying each number by the power of 10 in the center.

	Language Skills	Spelling	Reading
Monday	Guide your child in planning a make-believe story. Ask him/her to invent an unusual main character with some distinct attribute. Then, help your child create a problem for the character. Have him/her begin working on a rough draft of the story using the invented character and problem.	Pretest your child on these spelling words. account county mountain aloud doubt noun amount foul ounce boundary fountain pound couch hound south Have your child correct the pretest, add personalized words and make two copies of this week's study list.	**Syllables** Review the rules for dividing words into syllables. *See* Reading, Week 10, number 1. Introduce *Make Four Million Dollars by Next Thursday!* by Stephen Manes. Ask your child what he/she would do with four million dollars.
Tuesday	With your child, create a tongue twister or an alliterative sentence. Write it on the chalkboard. Have your child copy the sentence from the chalkboard in his/her best cursive handwriting.	Have your child use each of this week's spelling words correctly in a sentence.	Discuss the accented syllable in a word. Say a two-syllable word, then write it out phonetically. Ask your child to repeat the word, noting the syllable that receives more emphasis. Place an accent mark (') directly in front of the stressed syllable. Repeat with other two-syllable words. Read chapter 1 of *Make Four Million Dollars by Next Thursday!* Have your child begin filling in a copy of **Story Organizer** (p. 101).
Wednesday	**Commas:** Review commas in series. It is also correct to use a comma before the conjunction. **Example:** Jay, Fay, and Ray walked. Have your child complete **Series Commas** (p. 124).	Have your child complete **Ouch Words** (p. 126).	Have your child practice separating words into syllables. *See* Reading, Week 10, number 2. Read chapters 2 and 3 of *Make Four Million Dollars by Next Thursday!* Ask your child to make up a money joke about the way Jason is dressed.
Thursday	Review the proper use of commas in dates, letters, addresses and city/state combinations. *See* Language Skills, Week 10, numbers 1–3. Let your child practice these skills by writing a letter to a grandparent or other relative and addressing the envelope.	Ask your child to find any rhyming pairs in this week's list of words. Then, ask your child to think of a word that rhymes with each of the other words in the list.	Some words may have more than one stressed syllable. In this case, one stressed syllable has greater stress than the other. *See* Reading, Week 10, number 3 for more information. Read chapter 4 of *Make Four Million Dollars by Next Thursday!* Ask your child to predict what Dr. K. Pinkerton Silverfish will have Jason doing next.
Friday	Find a book that contains a lot of dialogue. Have your child identify where commas are in relation to the quotation marks. Have him/her formulate rules about the placement of commas in quotations. Let him/her check the rules against those stated in the activity sheet. Have your child complete **Direct Quotations** (p. 125).	Give your child the final spelling test. Have your child record the pretest and final test words in his/her word bank.	Read chapters 5 and 6 of *Make Four Million Dollars by Next Thursday!* Have your child brainstorm ten reasons NOT to be a millionaire.

Math	Science	Social Studies
Division Use flash cards to assess your child's knowledge of previously learned division facts. Encourage your child to practice division using flash cards and memorization. Have him/her solve the same set of problems again on Tuesday and Wednesday. Chart your child's performance in time and accuracy. Give your child a copy of **Division** (p. 127) for drill and practice.	**Earth Changes** Assess what your child already knows about Earth changes by asking questions and listening to his/her responses. *See* Science, Week 10, number 1. If your child is lacking knowledge or misunderstands concepts, focus your teaching in those areas.	**Native Americans** Introduce a unit on American Indians by discussing the term itself. Research to find out why they were called Indians and why they are called Native Americans today. Have your child make a topic web to show what he/she already knows about Native Americans. *See* Social Studies, Week 10, number 1.
Help your child discover the relationship between multiplication and division. Divide a given number of pennies evenly into a given number of sections in an egg carton. Name the two multiplication and two division sentences that the model represents. **Example:** Place 24 pennies in 6 sections of the egg carton so there are 4 in each section. The four sentences are $24 \div 6 = 4$, $24 \div 4 = 6$, $6 \times 4 = 24$, and $4 \times 6 = 24$. Let your child repeat with other quantities.	*Pangaea* is the name given to the original land mass that eventually became the seven continents we know today. Read about Pangaea in library resources or an encyclopedia. Scientists believe that, hundreds of millions of years ago, the seven continents were one. Slowly they have been drifting apart as the Atlantic Ocean grows larger and the Pacific grows smaller. *See* Science, Week 10, number 2.	Find a map of North America that shows the location of the different Native American culture areas (groups of similar tribes, such as Plains or Southwest). Have your child draw an outline of North America on a large sheet of butcher paper and shade in the regions occupied by the different cultures. Ask him/her to label the areas and fill in specific tribe names as they are discussed over the next several weeks.
Use the number line (0–144) from Week 6 to show that division with whole numbers is simply repeated subtraction. Practice division facts from $4 \div 2$ to $144 \div 12$. Give your child a problem such as $72 \div 9$. Starting at 72 on the number line, have your child use a piece of chalk to jump back to zero by increments of 9. Ask: *How many jumps did it take? How is this like repeated subtraction?*	Using library resources, science textbooks and the activity sheet (p. 129), study and discuss the composition of the Earth's layers. Help your child make the Earth-like layered dessert by following the directions on **Out of This World** (p. 129).	Have your child gather information for an alphabet book to be completed over the next several weeks. Use **Native American Alphabet Book** (p. 139) as a guide. Set aside one page of the book for each letter of the alphabet. Each page should include a colorful picture and an alliterative sentence about the tribe. Your child should also include information about the tribe in paragraph form. *See* Social Studies, Week 10, number 2.
Give your child a starting number such as 28. Ask him/her to subtract 7 repeatedly until he/she reaches zero. Then, have your child write the number of times 7 was subtracted as the answer (see example at right). Repeat with other equations. $$\begin{array}{r} 4 \\ 7\overline{)28} \\ -7 \\ \hline 21 \\ -7 \\ \hline 14 \\ -7 \\ \hline 7 \\ -7 \\ \hline 0 \end{array}$$	Study and discuss Earth's movements using **Twist and Turn** (p. 130).	As your child does research over the next several weeks, he/she will notice that the climate and resources of the areas in which the Native Americans lived had a major influence on housing materials, food, crafts and tools, leisure-time activities and culture. Discuss how climate affects our daily lives. Compare the lives of people in your area with the lives of people who live in a different climate. How are they the same? How are they different?
Teach your child how to divide a 2-digit number by a 1-digit number. *See* Math, Week 10, numbers 1 and 2. Have your child complete **Snowball Bash** (p. 128). Do NOT check it, but save the activity sheet for next Monday's lesson.	The continental plates that form the crust and the outer mantle of Earth are constantly moving. At times, the plates rub and crash together. Many years ago, the plates crashed into each other and caused great mountain ranges to form by folding layers of Earth's crust. Have your child complete **Majestic Mountains** (p. 131).	After studying Native American history, you will look at issues affecting Native Americans today. Over the next several weeks, look for pieces of their rich cultural heritage that remain today. Discuss ways in which the Native Americans might have been able to maintain some of their traditions, despite encroachment on their land and rights by European settlers.

TEACHING SUGGESTIONS AND ACTIVITIES

LANGUAGE SKILLS (Commas)

▶ 1. Show your child where to place the comma when writing the date (November 12, 1999). Cite and show examples where the date is written in this manner: in the heading of a letter, dating a check or on the front page of a newspaper. Write the date in various sentences or headings without commas. Have your child fill in the commas.

▶ 2. Demonstrate how to write a city and state separated by a comma.

    I live in Portland, Oregon.   Address: Miss Elizabeth Jones
    We visited Boston, Massachusetts.   1209 S. 5th St.
                                         Aspen, Colorado

▶ 3. Demonstrate how commas are used in letter writing.

    greeting: *Dear Lili,*   closing: *Sincerely,   Love,   Your friend,*

READING (Syllables)

▶ 1. Make a chart for reference, listing the rules below for dividing words into syllables.

- Compound words divide between the two root words. **Example:** jackpot   jack/pot
- Words that have two vowel sounds separated by two consonants (not a blend or digraph) are divided between the consonants. **Example:** batter   bat/ter
- Words that have two vowel sounds separated by a blend or digraph are divided before the blend or digraph. **Example:** retrain   re/train
- Words that have two vowel sounds separated by a consonant and a blend are divided between the consonant and the blend. The blend is never split into separate syllables. **Example:** instant   in/stant
- Words that have two vowel sounds separated by one consonant are divided before the middle consonant. **Example:** redo   re/do
- When a word ends in *le*, the syllable break falls before the consonant preceding *le*. **Example:** startle   star/tle
- When the vowel in the first syllable is followed by *r*, divide the syllable after the *r*. **Example:** party   par/ty
- In a word with adjacent vowels, the word is split between the vowels only if both vowels each make a sound. **Example:** neon   ne/on

▶ 2. Write words with three syllables. Have your child read them aloud and clap out the syllables.

accident	carpenter	grocery	marvelous	quality
advertise	chocolate	harmony	medicine	telephone
annual	detective	hesitate	organize	tobacco
assembly	funeral	ignorant	peppermint	universe

Have your child rewrite each word, divide it into syllables and draw an accent mark before the accented syllable.

▶ 3. Write a list of four- and five-syllable words that have primary and secondary accent marks. Have your child rewrite the words, divide them into syllables and draw a primary (') or secondary (,) accent mark before each accented syllable. **Example:** \ ˌre-kə-ˈlek-shən \ (recollection)

caterpillar	corporation	enthusiastic	renovation	cauliflower	discontinue
illustration	respiratory	civilization	electricity	independently	situation
constitution	elevation	opportunity	ventilation		

Hint: Look in the dictionary for help.

Learn at Home, Grade 4

MATH (Division)

▶ 1. Work through a sample division problem with your child, such as 84 ÷ 4.

   a. First, ask if the digit in the tens place is greater than the divisor. In this case, it is. Divide the 8 by 4. Multiply the partial quotient (2) by the divisor (4) and subtract from the partial dividend (8).

   b. Carry down the 4 in the ones column. How many groups of 4 are there in 4? (1). Divide. Multiply the partial quotient (1) by the divisor (4) and subtract from the partial dividend (4).

   c. When you divide 84 into 4 groups, there will be 21 in each group.

▶ 2. Give your child other 2-digit division problems to solve:
       63 ÷ 3, 72 ÷ 2, 48 ÷ 4, 56 ÷ 2, 96 ÷ 3

SCIENCE (Earth Changes)

▶ 1. Ask your child: *What are continents? Can you name them? What are some natural landforms on Earth? What changes occur when a volcano erupts? What changes occur when an earthquake strikes? What is the effect of weathering? What impact have humans had on Earth?*

▶ 2. Discuss the movement of Pangaea. Scientists think the continents have been drifting for hundreds of millions of years and continue to drift apart today. Cut apart Continents from a copy of a world map. Have your child try to fit the pieces together like a puzzle (they do not fit exactly). Then, have him/her project how the continents will look 200 million years from now. Remember, new Earth is forming beneath the Atlantic Ocean, so the continents are drifting away from each other in the Atlantic.

SOCIAL STUDIES (Native Americans)

BACKGROUND
It is believed that the first inhabitants of North America came from Asia over a land bridge at the Bering Strait. They may have first arrived as early as 35,000 years ago. They traveled across the Americas following the animals they hunted. Indians are called Native Americans today because they were the first people known to inhabit the Americas.

▶ 1. Make a topic web together. Begin by writing the topic (e.g., Native Americans) at the center of a large sheet of paper. Draw four or more lines from the topic, and at the end of these spokes write subtopics. Draw lines from each subtopic to write details. Use the completed topic web as a guide in planning lessons. Review the web at the end of the unit to emphasize how much your child has learned.

▶ 2. Have your child start gathering words for each letter of the alphabet. The actual alphabet pages can be created over the next several weeks. Provide your child with a variety of resources for finding names of the many North American Native tribes. Have your child look through the books and list the names of tribes for each letter of the alphabet. If your child is missing letters of the alphabet, he/she may supplement the list with topic-related words, such as pottery, hogan or birch bark. There are no tribes whose names begin with *r, v* or *x. See also* **Native American Alphabet Book** (p. 139).

Series Commas

Commas are used to separate words or groups of words in a series of three or more.

Example: Martha had fried chicken, baked potatoes, green beans and a tossed salad for dinner.

Use commas to separate the items in a series in the sentences below.

1. John bought buttered popcorn diet soda peanuts and a hot dog at the game.

2. The vending machine contained candy bars crackers bags of popcorn peanuts and jelly beans.

3. The package of jelly beans held assorted flavors such as banana licorice strawberry watermelon and grape.

4. Sam put ketchup mustard onions lettuce and pickles on his hamburger.

5. Barbara Carol and John each ordered sweet and sour pork fried rice and wonton soup.

6. The picnic basket was filled with sandwiches pickles potato chips oranges apples and brownies.

Rewrite the sentences below. Place the commas so that the number of food items listed is the same as the number in parentheses.

1. Susan had chocolate ice cream peanut butter cookies and strawberry licorice. (3)_____

   _____

2. Megan had an orange juice cinnamon toast bacon and eggs for breakfast. (5)_____

   _____

3. Mrs. Clark put tuna fish soda crackers and salad dressing into the grocery cart.(5)_____

   _____

Direct Quotations

Use **quotation marks** to enclose the exact words of the speaker. The speaker's first word must begin with a capital letter. Also follow these rules:

1. When the speaker is named **before** the direct quotation, separate the speaker from the quotation with a comma.

2. When the speaker is named **after** the direct quotation, use a comma or the proper end mark inside the last quotation.

Examples: 1. *Mother said, "You must clean your room."*
             2. *"Sara is cleaning her room," said Mother.*
             3. *"Have you found your shoes?" asked Tina.*
             4. *"Hurry up!" yelled John.*

Punctuate these sentences correctly.

1. Father asked John, will you be home for dinner
2. No, I will be at football practice said John
3. When will you have time to eat asked Dad
4. I'll have to eat after practice grumbled John
5. Hurry up yelled Pete
6. Pete commented We'll be late for practice if you don't move faster

Rewrite these sentences. Punctuate and capitalize them correctly.

1. will you take out the garbage asked Mother

2. Mary answered I don't have time now

_____

3. is it alright if I do it later she added

_____

4. please do that job as soon as you get home Mother said

_____

125

Ouch Words

Fill in the blanks. Each spelling word is used only once.

account
aloud
amount
boundary
couch
county
doubt
foul
fountain
hound
mountain
noun
ounce
pound
south

1. Write the word with more than two syllables.

   _____

2. Write the synonym for "orally." _____

3. Two measurement words are _____ and

   _____ . Circle the lighter weight.

4. A synonym for "sofa" is _____ .

5. The opposite of north is _____ .

6. The name of a person, place or thing is called a

   _____ .

7. Which word could describe a violation of the rules

   in a sport? _____

8. Which word names a geographic landform?

   _____

9. Which word names an item often found in

   classrooms or hallways? _____

10. If you make a deposit at the bank, the teller

    will add that _____ of money to your

    savings _____ .

11. Three spelling words have not been used.
    Use those three in one sentence.

_____

_____

Learn at Home, Grade 4

Division

1. 5⟌30   2. 7⟌21

3. 4⟌28   4. 9⟌63   5. 5⟌35

6. 1⟌9   7. 4⟌24   8. 8⟌32   9. 6⟌36   10. 2⟌14   11. 7⟌56   12. 4⟌36

13. 9⟌27   14. 6⟌42   15. 8⟌8   16. 3⟌24   17. 7⟌63   18. 9⟌54   19. 3⟌27

20. 1⟌7   21. 8⟌24   22. 2⟌16   23. 7⟌42   24. 6⟌54   25. 8⟌56   26. 4⟌32

27. 9⟌72   28. 5⟌45   29. 3⟌21   30. 8⟌64   31. 5⟌45   32. 7⟌49   33. 9⟌54

34. 3⟌36   35. 8⟌72   36. 7⟌28   37. 5⟌40   38. 6⟌30

Snowball Bash

Help Pete climb down this mound of giant snowballs.

$7\overline{)84}$

$5\overline{)75}$

$3\overline{)45}$

$9\overline{)99}$

$4\overline{)88}$

$5\overline{)80}$

$4\overline{)64}$ $3\overline{)57}$

$3\overline{)78}$

$3\overline{)72}$

$8\overline{)96}$

$2\overline{)86}$

$2\overline{)38}$ $6\overline{)66}$

$5\overline{)65}$

$4\overline{)52}$

$4\overline{)68}$

$6\overline{)78}$

$7\overline{)91}$

$2\overline{)42}$ $6\overline{)72}$

Learn at Home, Grade 4

Out of This World

You will need:

an adult, a round cake pan, a rolling pin, a wooden spoon, a large wooden cutting board, a saucepan, measuring spoons, a long sharp knife, paper plates, plastic forks, the ingredients listed below

Cover the inside of the cake pan with a nonstick spray.

Ingredients:

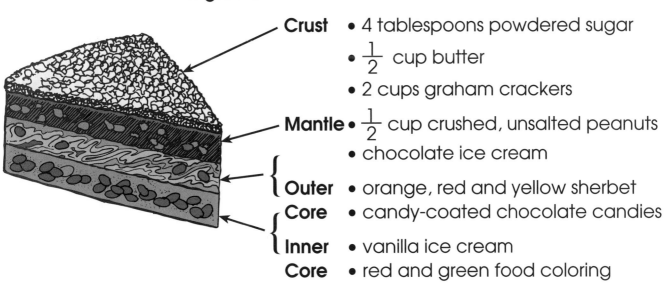

Crust
- 4 tablespoons powdered sugar
- $\frac{1}{2}$ cup butter
- 2 cups graham crackers

Mantle
- $\frac{1}{2}$ cup crushed, unsalted peanuts
- chocolate ice cream

Outer Core
- orange, red and yellow sherbet
- candy-coated chocolate candies

Inner Core
- vanilla ice cream
- red and green food coloring

Crust: Crush graham crackers on the cutting board. Mix powdered sugar with melted butter in the pan. Add graham crackers. Line all sides of the pan with the mixture. Pat it inside the pan to about $\frac{1}{4}$" to $\frac{1}{2}$" thickness. Put it into the freezer until frozen.

Make layers in the order shown above, one layer at a time. Freeze each layer in the pan before you go on to the next step. (Before mixing and adding each layer, let the ice cream soften, without completely melting.)

When the Earth's cross section is frozen, take it out of the freezer. Flip it over onto a cake plate. Cut it in half and then in fourths. Remove one quarter at a time. Slice it like a cake so that each serving has a little of each of Earth's layers. Put it on plates and serve.

Learn at Home, Grade 4

Twist and Turn

To observe how rocks shift when broken off inside Earth and how that movement can be felt, try the following demonstration.

You will need:
1 yard of $\frac{1}{2}$" wide elastic, a black pen, a ruler, a stapler, heavy-duty tape (duct tape), drinking straws, scissors

Directions:
Using a black pen, make a mark 6" from the end of the elastic. Make 11 more marks, one every 2". Place a straw across each mark, perpendicular to the elastic. Staple the center of each straw to the elastic. Tape one end of the elastic to the top of a door frame.

Hold the bottom of the elastic strip. Gently pull it down about a foot. Twist the bottom straw halfway around and then release it.

Observe the motions of the straws. Twisting straws can be compared to the strain placed on rocks within Earth's crust.

POW!

Seismic P-waves are movements in the Earth's crusts often caused by earthquakes. Use marbles, masking tape, string, a ruler, a table with overhang and scissors to observe how seismic waves are transmitted through Earth.

Directions: Cut five pieces of string, each 12" long. Tape each piece of string to a marble. Place the free end of the string even with the top of a table. Tape it to the edge of the table. Do this for each of the remaining four strings. Adjust the length of the strings so that the marbles are exactly the same height and are touching each other.

Raise one of the end marbles to the side and release it. Observe what happens. (Energy is transferred from the initial blow and spreads out in waves.)

Majestic Mountains

The word **mountain** means different things to different people. Some people who live on vast, level plains, consider a small hill a mountain. While others, who live in the mountains, would not consider a region mountainous unless it was very high and rugged.

Listed below are eight famous mountains of the world along with their heights. Graph each mountain's height. On the bottom of the graph, **write** the mountain's name and, on the side of the graph, **chart** the height. When you have finished graphing, use the results to answer the questions below.

Name	Height
Everest	29,022 feet
Lassen Peak	10,453 feet
Kenya	17,058 feet
Pikes Peak	14,110 feet
Fuji	12,388 feet
Mauna Loa	13,680 feet
McKinley	20,320 feet

30,000
28,000
26,000
24,000
22,000
20,000
18,000
16,000
14,000
12,000
10,000
8,000

1. Which mountain is the highest?_____

2. What is the average height of the mountains?_____

3. How much higher is McKinley than Pikes Peak? _____

4. What is the height of all the mountains?_____

5. What is the difference between the highest and shortest mountain?

_____

Learn at Home, Grade 4

	Language Skills	Spelling	Reading
Monday	Help your child create an outline for writing a biography. *See* Language Skills, Week 11, number 1. Then, have your child interview a family member or neighbor and write a biography about him/her.	Pretest your child on these spelling words. brook notebook wolf bush pudding woman could should wool cushion sugar would during understood yours Have your child correct the pretest, add personalized words and make two copies of this week's study list.	This week, have your child read *Squanto, Friend of the Pilgrims* by Clyde Robert Bulla. Strengthen your child's understanding of main idea with an accordion-book synopsis. Each page of the accordion book is dedicated to the main ideas of one chapter from the novel. *See* Reading, Week 11, number 1 for specifics. This project will take several days to complete.
Tuesday	Teach your child when to capitalize words, such as mother, grandfather, aunt and cousin. When used in place of a person's name, these words are capitalized. When preceded by a possessive, such as *my*, they are not. Dictate several sentences using family words, such as mother, uncle and grandfather. Let your child determine whether or not to capitalize the terms in each case.	Have your child use each of this week's spelling words correctly in a sentence.	Have your child continue to read *Squanto, Friend of the Pilgrims* and work on the accordion book.
Wednesday	**Abbreviations:** Many dictionaries list common abbreviations in an index. Select some of the abbreviations for words your child uses frequently. Teach him/her the correct spelling, capitalization and punctuation of those abbreviations. Add these to this week's spelling list.	Have your child complete **Book Words** (p. 136).	Have your child continue to read *Squanto, Friend of the Pilgrims* and work on the accordion book.
Thursday	**Acronyms:** Teach your child to recognize acronyms. *See* Language Skills, Week 11, number 2. What other acronyms has your child seen or heard? Have your child look up those acronyms to discover what they represent. Then, ask him/her to look for other acronyms to add to the list.	Assign each letter of the alphabet a numerical value (e.g., A = 4, B = 12). Say a spelling word. Have your child write out the word, write the value of each letter, then add the values. Which of this week's words are worth the most? Which are worth the least?	Have your child continue to read *Squanto, Friend of the Pilgrims* and work on the accordion book.
Friday	Have your child write a first-person story about viewing some kind of volcanic eruption. Have him/her describe where he/she is and what is going on. Remind him/her to involve as many senses as possible when describing and to use new volcano vocabulary.	Give your child the final spelling test. Have your child record the pretest and final test words in his/her word bank.	Finish reading *Squanto, Friend of the Pilgrims*. Your child should complete the final pages for the accordion book and design a cover. Help him/her assemble the book and display it.

Math	Science	Social Studies
Teach your child to use multiplication to check his/her work on division problems. **Example:** 45 ÷ 3 = <u>15</u> Check your work: Does 15 x 3 = 45? Have your child check his/her own division work from last Friday's assignment, **Snowball Bash** (p. 128).	**Geology** Study the three types of rock: *igneous, sedimentary* and *metamorphic*. Visit a rock shop and explore the variety of rocks and minerals formed on Earth. Ask for help identifying rocks as igneous, sedimentary or metamorphic. Let your child start a rock collection, maintaining the collection by sorting and labeling rocks as he/she obtains them.	Read about the Indians of Middle America, especially the Aztecs and Mayans. These tribes were probably the first farmers in North America. They also developed arts, government and religion, leaving behind beautiful cities and sophisticated works of art.
Give your child a calculator. Challenge him/her to find different methods for solving division problems without using the divide key. Do not give hints—let your child discover this on his/her own. **Example:** 56 ÷ 8 Trial and Error: 8 x 10 (too high), 8 x 5 (too low), 8 x 7 (just right) Repeated Subtraction: 56 − 8 = 48, 48 − 8 = 40, 40 − 8 = 32, . . .	Have your child read library books and textbooks to learn about earthquakes. Show him/her on a map where most earthquakes and volcanic eruptions occur. Observe the relationship between the location of tectonic plates and earthquake activity. Have your child develop a hypothesis about this relationship.	Have your child choose two tribes from this area to research. Give him/her a copy of **Native American Alphabet Book** (p. 139) to complete. He/she may want to include these tribes in the alphabet book.
Divide a 3-digit dividend by a 1-digit divisor. Use the same procedure as with 2-digit dividends. Practice with your child before assigning independent work. Give your child twenty division problems to solve, each with a 3-digit dividend, 1-digit divisor and no remainder.	Read about how scientists measure earthquakes using a seismograph. Seismographic stations must combine their data to locate the epicenter, or source, of an earthquake. Demonstrate how shock waves from an earthquake travel. *See* Science, Week 11, numbers 1 and 2.	Read about the advanced civilizations of the Mayans and the Aztecs. *See* Social Studies, Week 11, numbers 1 and 2. Look at pictures of structures they built. Discuss how we have learned about these civilizations that existed long ago. Have your child add pictures to the map (Week 20) of artifacts, tools, clothes and houses unique to the tribes of Middle America.
Teach the concept of remainders in division with word problems. **Example:** *Darnell has fourteen pieces of bubble gum. He wants to share the gum equally with five of his friends. How many pieces each will Darnell and his friends get? How many pieces will be left over?* Have your child write a story in which something is divided evenly. *See* Math, Week 11, number 1 for story starters.	Conduct an experiment to observe how wind affects the Earth's surface. *See* Science, Week 11, number 3.	Have your child draw and label a Mayan pyramid and an Aztec pyramid. Compare and contrast the purpose and construction of the the two types of pyramids. Ask: *Do any of these pyramids still stand today? Where?*
Teach your child how to solve a division problem with a remainder. *See* Math, Week 11, number 2. Have your child complete **Looking to the Stars** (p. 137).	Wind, water and ice are forces that slowly but continuously alter the surface of the Earth. Have your child read about hurricanes, tornadoes, monsoons, typhoons, dust storms and glaciers. Ask: *How can weathering and erosion change the surface of the Earth? Consider the Grand Canyon, valleys and river deltas.* Have your child complete **A Funnel Cloud–Danger** (p. 138).	The Aztecs adopted the religion of the Spanish conquerors and married the settlers. The Spanish built Mexico City over the ruins of the Aztec city, Tenochtitlán. Review the Aztec emperor Montezuma and the Tenochtitlán. Discuss how the Aztec culture has been lost to Spanish culture. *See* Social Studies, Week 4, number 1. Make tortillas together. *See* Social Studies, Week 11, number 3.

TEACHING SUGGESTIONS AND ACTIVITIES

LANGUAGE SKILLS (Abbreviations/Acronyms)

▷ 1. Help your child decide what each paragraph of the biography should contain. Topics might include early years, family experiences, school years, work years, recreation, present life and future plans. Have your child brainstorm a list of interview questions to ask the subject of the biography.

▷ 2. Help your child learn to distinguish acronyms from abbreviations. Acronyms are formed from the initial letters of a series of words, such as CAP from Civil Air Patrol. An acronym, unlike an abbreviation, reads like a word and does not use periods. Each letter of an acronym is capitalized to distinguish it from a word. Write a list of acronyms and the words they represent. Encourage your child to add to the list as he/she finds more acronyms.

NASA	National Aeronautics and Space Administration
SCUBA	Self-Contained Underwater Breathing Apparatus
WHO	World Health Organization
UNICEF	United Nations International Children's Emergency Fund
OPEC	Organization of Petroleum Exporting Countries
OSHA	Occupational Safety and Health Administration
SAC	Strategic Air Command
MASH	Mobile Army Surgical Hospital

READING (Main Idea)

▷ 1. As your child reads *Squanto, Friend of the Pilgrims* this week, have him/her keep track of the main idea in each chapter. Then, ask him/her to compile that information into book form, making the accordion-book synopsis following the directions below.

  a. Cut light-colored construction paper into four (or more) 6" x 18" strips.

  b. Accordion fold each strip to make three square panels.

  c. Attach the strips end-to-end with tape.

  d. Count the panels. The first panel is for the book title and cover. The subsequent panels are for each chapter of the book. Add strips as needed to have one panel per chapter.

  e. After reading each chapter, have your child write a sentence expressing the main idea of the chapter and draw a picture to illustrate it.

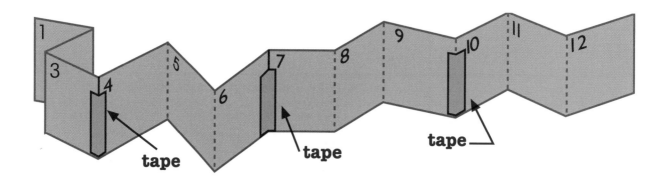

MATH (Division)

▶ 1. Each story starter below leads to an occasion where something is shared fairly. Have your child choose one story starter and finish the story, demonstrating how the items will be shared.

    a. Michael bought a bag of 100 jelly beans. He took them to the park, where he met. . . .

    b. Ms. Lee found a hundred dollar bill on her way to work. She put a notice on the bulletin board that she had found the money, but no one claimed it. Ms. Lee shared her luck with. . . .

    c. Lori made a batch of brownies in a 9-inch square pan. She set them out to cool before she cut. . . .

▶ 2. Work through a problem with your child that will have a remainder as shown here.

    a. Estimate how many 6's in 9 (think ___ x 6 = 9). Try 1 in the tens place.

    b. Multiply 1 x 6 = 6. Subtract 9 – 6 = 3.

    c. Bring down the 5 to make 35.

    d. Repeat these steps (estimate, multiply, subtract, bring down).

    e. Estimate how many 6's in 35 (think ___ x 6 = 35). Try 5 in the ones place.

    f. Multiply 6 x 5 = 30. Subtract 35 – 30 = 5.

    g. The quotient is 15.

    h. The remainder is 5.

SCIENCE (Geology)

▶ 1. Fill a pan with water. Tap the side of the pan with a knife or spoon. Have your child watch the surface of the water. What does he/she see? The waves produced are similar to the shock waves of an earthquake. Shock waves can cause much destruction on the surface of the Earth.

▶ 2. Standing on an uncarpeted floor, hold one end of a spring while your child holds the other. Push one end of the spring forward and back and have your child watch the movement from one end of the spring to the other. Have him/her describe the movement. This movement is like the primary wave of an earthquake traveling through the Earth.

▶ 3. Have your child pour about 1 inch of sand into a 2-inch-deep baking dish. Level the sand so that it covers the bottom of the pan evenly. Have your child predict what will happen when he/she simulates wind blowing across the sand. Using a hair dryer on low speed, try to simulate wind blowing across the Earth. Have your child hold the dryer horizontally, directed toward the pan of sand. Start with the nozzle about 2 feet away and gradually come in closer. Have your child describe what happens to the "surface of the Earth" as the "wind" blows. What happens when the speed of the "wind" is increased? As a variation, place rocks on top of the sand. Apply "wind." Ask your child how the surface has changed this time and what happened to the sand around and under the rocks. Relate this to how different surfaces of the Earth react to wind.

SOCIAL STUDIES (Native Americans)

▶ 1. The Mayans studied the stars and mathematics. They developed a yearly calendar. Have your child study the Mayan calendar and compare it to the one we use today.

▶ 2. The Mayans recorded important events on large stone monuments. These monuments are called *steles*. View pictures of these monuments with your child. Then, have him/her carve a stele to record important events in his/her own life thus far. Let your child carve the stele from a piece of clay using a knife and other clay tools.

▶ 3. One of the staples of the Aztec diet was the corn tortilla. Make corn tortillas with your child. Buy masa harina in the flour aisle of a grocery store. Mix the masa harina with water and salt (it will take some trial and error to achieve the right consistency). Roll a ball of dough about the size of a golf ball. Put the ball between two sheets of wax paper and roll into a thin disk. Remove the disk from the wax paper and fry it on a hot griddle. Serve warm with salsa.

Book Words

Use a spelling word to replace the **bold** words in the story. **Write** the replacement word on the corresponding numbered line below the story.

No Spelling Today

(1) **Throughout the time of** the afternoon Joan sat on a (2) **pad** near the babbling (3) **creek** that meandered through the pasture. She knew she (4) **ought to** have been studying the words for her spelling test, but instead she was doodling on the (5) **stack of paper** on her lap. Across the stream several sheep were grazing. Their soft (6) **fleece** was growing back after the spring shearing. Joan (7) **was able to** hear a chirping wren in the (8) **thicket** nearby. Suddenly, the peaceful scene was disturbed by a (9) **female** calling her name. "Joan, Joan," the voice called out. "Come eat some (10) **custard** I just cooked," continued the loud voice. Joan (11) **realized** she'd dozed off and her mom was calling her to the house. Tucking her list of spelling words under her arm, she walked back home in the late afternoon sun.

brook	notebook	wolf
bush	pudding	woman
could	should	wool
cushion	sugar	would
during	understood	yours

1. _____

2. _____

3. _____

4. _____

5. _____

6. _____

7. _____

8. _____

9. _____

10. _____

11. _____

Write two sentences using two of the four words not used above.

1. _____

2. _____

136

Looking to the Stars

Solve the problems. To find the path to the top, **color** the spaces where the answers match the problem number.

35. $4\overline{)57}$	36. $2\overline{)72}$					
32. $3\overline{)96}$	33. $2\overline{)66}$	34. $4\overline{)57}$				
27. $3\overline{)63}$	28. $3\overline{)84}$	29. $4\overline{)97}$	30. $6\overline{)74}$	31. $6\overline{)68}$		
22. $6\overline{)74}$	23. $2\overline{)46}$	24. $2\overline{)48}$	25. $3\overline{)75}$	26. $6\overline{)96}$		
15. $5\overline{)92}$	16. $3\overline{)41}$	17. $3\overline{)57}$	18. $4\overline{)84}$	19. $4\overline{)76}$	20. $7\overline{)86}$	21. $5\overline{)72}$
8. $5\overline{)57}$	9. $3\overline{)65}$	10. $2\overline{)87}$	11. $5\overline{)55}$	12. $7\overline{)84}$	13. $3\overline{)87}$	14. $7\overline{)93}$
1. $3\overline{)96}$	2. $6\overline{)94}$	3. $5\overline{)93}$	4. $9\overline{)36}$	5. $2\overline{)97}$	6. $6\overline{)84}$	7. $3\overline{)68}$

A Funnel Cloud—Danger!

Did you know that a tornado is the most violent windstorm on Earth? A **tornado** is a whirling, twisting storm that is shaped like a funnel.

A tornado usually occurs in the spring on a hot day. It begins with thunderclouds and thunder. A cloud becomes very dark. The bottom of the cloud begins to twist and form a funnel. Rain and lightning begin. The funnel cloud drops from the dark storm clouds. It moves down toward the ground.

A tornado is very dangerous. It can destroy almost everything in its path.

Circle:
A (thunder, tornado) is the most vicious windstorm on Earth.

Check:
Which words describe a tornado?
☐ whirling   ☐ twisting   ☐ icy   ☐ funnel-shaped   ☐ dangerous

Underline:
A funnel shape is: ◯   ▢   ⬭   ▽   〰

Write and Circle:
A tornado usually occurs in the _____ on a (hot, cool) day.

Write 1 - 2 - 3 below and in the picture above.

◯ The funnel cloud drops down to the ground.

◯ A tornado begins with dark thunder clouds.

◯ The dark clouds begin to twist and form a funnel.

138

Native American Alphabet Book

Copy the following outline to help your student organize information on different tribes. (*See* Week 10, Social Studies, number 2.)

Tribe Name: _____   Culture Area: _____

Type of House: _____   Language: _____

Clothing Material: _____   Transportation: _____

Foods: _____

Unique Tools, Crafts and Weapons: _____

_____

Interesting Fact(s): _____

_____

_____

_____

Tribe Name: _____   Culture Area: _____

Type of House: _____   Language: _____

Clothing Material: _____   Transportation: _____

Foods: _____

Unique Tools, Crafts and Weapons: _____

_____

Interesting Fact(s): _____

_____

_____

_____

139

	Language Skills	Spelling	Reading
Monday	**Poetry** Discuss the definition of poetry. Compare poetry with prose. Explore different types of poetry with your child. Have him/her memorize one poem and recite it tomorrow. Have your child write a color poem. *See* Language Skills, Week 12, number 1 for an example. Ask him/her to choose words carefully for the greatest impact. He/she may want to include figurative language as well.	Pretest your child on these spelling words. balloon cougar movable bruise drew route canoe group shoot cartoon lieutenant through choose loose troupe Have your child correct the pretest, add personalized words and make two copies of this week's study list.	**Cause and Effect** Introduce the concept of cause and effect. Read along with your child this week so that you can ask questions along the way. *What caused...?* *What was the effect of...?* Read chapters 1 and 2 of *Encyclopedia Brown, Boy Detective* by Donald J. Sobol. Introduce vocabulary prior to reading each chapter. *See* Reading, Week 12, number 1.
Tuesday	Have your child recite the poem he/she memorized yesterday. For handwriting practice, have your child copy the poem memorized for today in his/her neatest cursive handwriting. Then, have him/her go through the poem, underlining each subject and circling each verb.	Have your child use each of this week's spelling words correctly in a sentence.	Introduce vocabulary and read chapters 3 and 4 of *Encyclopedia Brown, Boy Detective*. Have your child complete **If . . . Then** (p. 147).
Wednesday	Discuss subject/verb agreement. When the subject is singular, the verb must also be singular. Read the sentences from yesterday's handwriting activity. Point out to your child that a present-tense singular verb ends in *s*. Have your child complete **Subject/Verb Agreement** (p. 144).	Have your child complete **Soup in a Canoe** (p. 146).	Introduce vocabulary and read chapters 5 and 6 of *Encyclopedia Brown, Boy Detective*.
Thursday	Write *I, you, he, she, it, we* and *they* on the chalkboard. Have your child sort the pronouns into two groups—singular and plural (*you* can be either). Like a noun, a pronoun must agree with the verb. Next, write several sentences on the board whose subjects are pronouns. Guide your child to change the verb in each sentence so that it agrees with the singular or plural pronoun. Have your child complete **Pronoun/Verb Agreement** (p. 145).	Have your child create a comic strip (five or six frames) using as many of this week's spelling words as possible in the dialogue.	Introduce vocabulary and read chapters 7 and 8 of *Encyclopedia Brown, Boy Detective*. Have your child complete **Case Rests** (p. 148).
Friday	Have your child practice writing sentences in past and future tenses. Discuss the subject/verb agreement (in the past and future tenses, the verb is the same for singular and plural). **Examples:** Two trees waved in the breeze. One tree waved in the breeze. One horse will march in the parade. Ten horses will march in the parade.	Give your child the final spelling test. Have your child record the pretest and final test words in his/her word bank.	Introduce vocabulary and read the final chapters of *Encyclopedia Brown, Boy Detective*. *See* Reading, Week 12, number 2 for an activity to review cause and effect.

Math	Science	Social Studies
Show your child how to divide a 4-digit dividend by a 1-digit divisor. Use the same procedure as with 2-digit dividends. Practice these with your child.	Volcanoes, like earthquakes, are caused by forces deep within the Earth. Volcanoes can cause destructive changes in the Earth's surface in a very short time. Obtain materials from the library about volcanoes and study the process of volcanic eruption. Discuss the meaning of the terms *magma* and *lava*. Add these words to this week's vocabulary list.	Read about the Native Americans of the Northeast. *See also* Social Studies, Week 12. Have your child list the tribes of this woodland area on the large map created in Week 10. Ask him/her to draw pictures on the map of artifacts, tools, clothes and houses unique to the tribes of the Northeast.
Demonstrate how to solve division problems with 3- and 4-digit dividends (with remainders). Follow the same procedure (estimate, multiply, subtract, bring down) as discussed last week. Note the placement of the quotient when the divisor does not fit into the first digit of the dividend. Have your child complete **To Catch a Butterfly** (p. 149).	Have your child study the library resources and **Fire Mountains** (p. 151). Then, have him/her complete **Volcanoes** (p. 152).	Have your child choose two tribes from this area to research. Your child may want to include these tribes in the alphabet book. Give him/her a copy of **Native American Alphabet Book** (p. 139) to complete.
Give your child the recipe for twenty-four dozen cookies. Help him/her reduce the ingredients to make only four dozen, then actually bake the cookies. *See* Math, Week 12, number 1 for a complete recipe.	Shake a bottle of soda before removing the cap (do this outside, if possible). Ask your child why the soda erupted. Pressure was building as the gas expanded, but the opening was blocked. When the cap was removed, the contents under pressure exploded. Relate this demonstration to the eruption of a volcano. Have your child do some research and write a description of how a volcano erupts or about a specific eruption, such as Mount St. Helens.	Study the houses built in this area. Observe the materials used and the method of construction. Help your child gather similar materials (bark, twigs, grass, leaves) and build a model of a wigwam or longhouse. Have your child begin thinking about a final project to do on the Northeastern Native Americans. *See* Social Studies, Week 12, number 1 for several project ideas.
Teach your child how to use a zero in the quotient. Explain the zero's importance as a place holder. Use the following problems and/or others to demonstrate: $520 \div 5$, $770 \div 7$, $636 \div 6$.	Sometimes volcanoes produce lava flows rather than eruptions. This happens when there is less gas in the lava. Eruptions and lava flows both produce volcanic rocks. Have your child read about pumice and obsidian, rocks produced from volcanoes. *See* Science, Week 12.	The Iroquois played the game of lacrosse, using a stick much like the stick still used today. Read about the game of lacrosse. Have your child write out the rules or directions for playing the game. Try it out for yourselves if you have access to the equipment. Let your child begin work on his/her final project. Allow time today and tomorrow for him/her to do the necessary research and preparation.
Show your child a method for checking division problems with remainders. Solve the problem $403 \div 8$. (*Answer: 50 R3.*) Have your child multiply 50×8 (just as he/she would to check a division problem without a remainder), then add the remainder of 3. The result: $400 + 3 = 403$. Have your child check his/her answers using the method discussed above. Have your child complete **A Visit to Space Camp** (p. 150).	Help your child build a physical model of a volcano. This may be as simple as a colorful diagram or as complex as a working three-dimensional clay or papier-mâché model. Look in library resources and science texts for ideas.	Have your child try to finish his/her project today. Have him/her present the final work and/or display it. Have your child complete **The Hunters** (p.153).

TEACHING SUGGESTIONS AND ACTIVITIES

LANGUAGE SKILLS (Poetry)

▶ 1. Here is an example of a color poem: *Red is anger.*
Yellow is the mighty lion's mane as he shakes his proud head.
Purple is the nighttime sky in summer.

Your child may wish to write a poem about a single color or a poem in which each line is dedicated to a different color. Let him/her choose.

READING (Cause and Effect)

▶ 1. Introduce vocabulary words before reading each chapter of *Encyclopedia Brown, Boy Detective.* Write the words on the chalkboard and discuss the meaning of each. Then, have your child watch for the words as he/she reads.
Vocabulary is listed by chapter

1. mastermind, detective, strike, method, observation, prove, reply, natty, dingy, mansion

2. mend, blackmail, shears, canal, kidnap, handbill, club, submarine, business, cash

3. agency, shed, chance, part, battle, hire, sword, blade, general, case

4. height, inheritance, challenge, dare, inning, claim, content, will, triumph, fame

5. run-down, resist, identify, haste, account, pug, backfire, handkerchief, exclaim

6. worry, proof, frown, robbery, hood, fender, clue, gravel, alibi, eyewitness

7. weak, racket, faint, refuse, soup, crook, instant, roommate, bid, blame

8. grocery, expense, carve, guilt, serious, argue, attempt, lead, thief, plunge

9. excuse, snoop, suspect, crime, collect, medical, pride, sprain, locker, certain

10. solve, soda, triple, match, counter, gang, taxidermy, foul, marble, telescope

▶ 2. Describe several unrelated events or situations, e.g., *Last night there was a thunderstorm.* Write each on an index card. Let your child choose one card and read the description aloud—this is the "cause." Have your child imagine a consequence of this event. *(The power went out for two hours.)* This is the "effect." Repeat with other cards. Then, have your child imagine a chain of events—i.e., he/she chooses a "cause" card and names a possible "effect," then the "effect" becomes the "cause" and so on. *(Sandra stopped to play soccer on her way home from school. She was an hour late getting home. Sandra's mother was very worried.)* Also try varying the activity by letting your child imagine a reverse chain of events, where the chosen card is the "effect" and your child must think of a "cause."

Learn at Home, Grade 4

MATH (Division)

▶ 1. Have your child reduce this recipe to make 4 dozen or 48 cookies.

SANDWICH COOKIES (Makes 24 dozen or 288 cookies.)

Ingredients:

6 cups butter	18 cups flour, sifted
6 cups sugar	3 tsp. salt
6 eggs	strawberry jam powdered sugar

Directions: In a mixing bowl, cream the butter with the sugar until light and fluffy. Beat in the eggs. Sift the flour and salt into the butter mixture and mix until well blended. Refrigerate for 1 hour. Preheat the oven to 375°. Divide the dough in half. To make the bottom cookies, roll out half the dough on a lightly floured surface until about $\frac{1}{8}$" thick. Cut the dough into 2- to 3-inch circles. Place circles on a cookie sheet and bake 10–12 minutes. Roll out the second half of the dough to make the top cookies. Cut into 2- to 3-inch circles. Use a bottle cap to cut a hole in the center of each cookie. Place on a cookie sheet and bake for 10–12 minutes.

While the cookies cool, sprinkle lightly with powdered sugar. Once cool, spread jam on each bottom cookie and cover with a top cookie.

SCIENCE (Earth Changes)

BACKGROUND

Volcanic rock is formed when lava comes to the surface and cools quickly. When a volcano *explodes*, the lava is full of gas. The gas bubbles are trapped when the rock cools. The rock that is formed, called *pumice*, looks like a sponge. When lava *flows* from a volcano, there is very little gas. The lava cools quickly and forms the dark, glassy rock called *obsidian*.

SOCIAL STUDIES (Native Americans)

BACKGROUND

The Northeastern Native Americans lived in an area of cold winters and warm summers. Their houses protected them from the cold of winter. Longhouses held many people. The longhouse was divided into many small living spaces for related family groups. Several longhouses formed a community. Some of the Northeastern Native Americans were farmers, while others relied mainly on hunting, fishing and gathering. Maple sugar was plentiful in the Northeast.

▶ 1. Let your child choose one of the following activities as a final project on the Northeast Indians.

a. Read about the Iroquois' sachems. Only men could be sachems, but women chose who would become a sachem. Women also removed a sachem if he did not perform up to expectations. Discuss their methods of decision making.

b. Read about the importance of religion in the lives of the Northeastern Native Americans. Read about their beliefs and practices. Compare their religions to a religion with which you are familiar.

c. The Northeastern Native Americans were some of the first to meet European settlers. Read about Squanto, a Pawtuxet Indian, who helped the settlers. Discuss what happened between the Natives and the early settlers that generated hostility. Write an imaginary letter to a Northeastern Native American on behalf of the European settlers. What can you say that might help improve relations?

d. Continue the **Native American Alphabet Book** (p. 139).

Subject/Verb Agreement

The **subject** and **verb** in a sentence must *agree*. If the subject is **singular**, add **s** to the verb. If the subject is **plural**, do not add an ending to the verb.

Examples:

Lava only **flows** when it is very hot. (singular)
Cinders **shoot** out of an active volcano. (plural)

Complete each sentence below using a form of the verb in parentheses.

1. Some volcanoes _____ quietly. (erupt)

2. The ground_____around a volcano just before an eruption. (swell)

3. Volcanoes _____ with great fury. (explode)

4. Tremors_____as magma works its way to the surface. (increase)

5. Magma_____ to the Earth's surface. (escape)

6. A volcano_____ so violently that the mountain can be blown apart. (erupt)

7. Obsidian_____when flying volcanic debris cools quickly in the air. (form)

8. Volcanoes_____ hot lava high into the air. (spew)

9. The sky _____from the ash and dust that explode out of a volcano. (darken)

10. Ash_____ the ground for many miles around a volcanic explosion. (cover)

11. Molten lava_____ bright red and yellow as it escapes from underneath the Earth's surface. (glow)

12. Steam_____when molten lava comes in contact with water (form)

Pronoun/Verb Agreement

The **subject pronoun** and the **verb** in a sentence must agree. If the subject pronoun is **singular**, add **s** to the verb. If the subject pronoun is **plural**, do not add an ending to the verb.

Examples:
He **wears** a helmet every time he rides his bike. (singular)
They **wear** helmets whenever they go roller-blading. (plural)

Circle the verb in parentheses that agrees with the subject pronoun.

1. She (ride, rides) her bike to band practice on Tuesdays.
2. They (zoom, zooms) down the hill to help them get up the steep incline on the other side.
3. He (glide, glides) nicely on his skateboard when he's going around the corners on the skating path.
4. We (travel, travels) as a family every Saturday to the park on our bikes.
5. It (rain, rains) sometimes while we're riding our bikes to school.
6. He (love, loves) to climb the hills on bikes with his mom and dad.
7. She (wear, wears) a helmet and kneepads whenever she goes roller-blading with her friends.

Write the subject pronoun that agrees with the verb.

1. _____ (They, We, He) tries very hard to skate backwards at the skating rink.
2. _____ (I, She, You) tells everyone about all the fun things there are to do at the park.
3. _____ (We, You, He) invites a friend every time he goes to the bicycle acrobatic demonstrations.
4. _____ (She, They, He) look both ways very carefully before crossing the street on their roller-blades.
5. _____ (It, We, He) send invitations to all our friends whenever there is a safety seminar at our school.

Soup in a Canoe

balloon
bruise
canoe
cartoon
choose
cougar
drew
group
lieutenant
loose
movable
route
shoot
through
troupe

Write the spelling words with **double o** that make the **oo** sound in alphabetical order.

1. _____   2. _____

3. _____   4. _____

5. _____

Write the spelling words with **ou** that make the **oo** sound in alphabetical order.

1. _____   2. _____

3. _____   4. _____

5. _____

For the remaining five spelling words, **circle** the letter or letters that make the **oo** sound.

Use the spelling words to complete the word search. The words are written horizontally, vertically and diagonally.

```
U J M Z O E H O V S Y K Y A Z
R V G M P O N R G R U C O X C
R C M U V T W S V H L S O P W
O D O G G W G W Y S O Y F F T
U R V U R O N Q M Y O E J N R
T E S U G O B R U I S E B B B
E W R W O A U G F O E H Y A K
O B B L Z T R P O B F X O T H
Q X L H V H L H H G P F K O B
K A E I D R C A N O E P Q V T
B O X Y E O A S S V G A W B Z
K Z W U V U R L Y X H G M A R
T Y E C F G T Z J S O L O Z A
D Y P Z X H O E G L N K V K Z
J F G S F U O R N S W O A K R
D K T T Y P N N H A D C B D I
B T A K J K A J Q L N Z L R Z
H E K N Z Y N H O L C T E R W
```

If . . . Then

Match the sentence parts that go together best. **Write** the number of the first sentence part on the line in front of the last sentence part for each one.

1. If you baby-sit for me Saturday night
2. If you are nice
3. If we leave work by 4:30
4. If you leave a note on your door
5. If you don't have enough money for the movie
6. If my father isn't too tired
7. If the wind keeps up
8. If you want to get a seat at the concert
9. If our neighbor cuts the grass early Sunday morning
10. If the plant doesn't feel damp
11. If my house were painted white
12. If everyone talked at the same time
13. If you don't get a haircut
14. If the tea kettle whistles
15. If no one answers the door
16. If the little boy crosses the street
17. If the horse is tired
18. If you have a long stick
19. If you don't want any dessert
20. If a king comes into a room
21. If it snows a lot tomorrow

___ the delivery man will leave the package.
___ it needs to be watered.
___ you could roast marshmallows.
___ probably no one is at home.
___ everyone will rise.
___ I'll pay you double.
___ the water is boiling.
___ tomorrow will be a great kite-flying day.
___ let him rest.
___ no one could hear directions.
___ we will avoid rush hour.
___ say "No, thank you."
___ the noise will wake me up.
___ we can build an igloo.
___ he said he would show me how to shoot baskets.
___ it would look like a miniature White House.
___ I'll loan you the rest.
___ he must hold onto his mother's hand.
___ you will have many friends.
___ you will have to be at the auditorium early.
___ you will have long hair.

Learn at Home, Grade 4

Case Rests

Select the correct main idea from the book
for each paragraph below by circling A, B or C.

1. In "The Case of the Scattered Cards," Encyclopedia noticed that cards
   on the floor of the tent were dry, not wet or muddy. It had been raining
   for two days.
   A. Encyclopedia had brought his own dry playing cards.
   B. The tent had been put up before it started raining.
   C. Bugs had fixed all the holes to keep the floor dry.

2. In "The Case of the Civil War Sword," Encyclopedia could tell the sword
   was a fake by writing on the blade. Bugs knew there had been two battles
   at Bull Run. He claimed that this sword belonged to General Stonewall
   Jackson.
   A. Bugs had found a valuable war memento.
   B. The writing used the Yankee name for the battle instead of the
      Confederate.
   C. Bugs was as smart as Encyclopedia.

3. In "The Case of Merko's Grandson," Encyclopedia realized that Fred
   Gibson was the real heir. The tall woman really was a relative, too, but not
   Fred's grandchild. The woman insisted that the Great Merko was not Fred's
   grandfather.
   A. Merko died in a circus accident.
   B. The tall woman was lying.
   C. The Great Merko was a woman—Fred's grandmother.

4. In "The Case of the Bank Robber," Encyclopedia figured out why the
   robber and Blind Tom had rolled on the ground. When they found the
   robber, he did not have the money. When Encyclopedia visited Blind Tom,
   the lights were on and a newspaper was on the bed.
   A. Blind Tom and the robber were working together and traded yellow
      bags.
   B. Encyclopedia buys bread in yellow bags.
   C. Blind people can see if the lights are on.

To Catch a Butterfly

Solve the problems. **Draw** a line connecting each **net** with the correct **butterfly**.

6 ⟌1279

5 ⟌843

168ʀ3

441ʀ6

5 ⟌3742

3 ⟌794

796ʀ7

213ʀ1

663ʀ1

9 ⟌3975

748ʀ2

264ʀ2

4 ⟌2653

149

422ʀ2

7 ⟌5230

2 ⟌1748

874

747ʀ1

691ʀ5

6 ⟌894

3 ⟌1268

8 ⟌6375

8 ⟌5533

Learn at Home, Grade 4

A Visit to Space Camp

Circle the correct problem and
write the answer on the line.

1. Five astronauts had flown a total of 637 hours so ___ ny
    hours did each astronaut fly?

    637 + 637   637 ÷ 5   5 x 5   637 x 5 _____

2. Terri's class ate 3 meals in the cafeteria at space camp. The cafeteria
    served 420 meals in all that day. How many people ate at each meal
    (breakfast, lunch and dinner) in the cafeteria the day Terri was there?

    420 x 2   3 + 420   420 ÷ 3   3 + 3 _____

3. Eight children can ride the moon gravitation simulator at a time. Ninety-
    seven children rode the simulator that day. How many groups of 8 rode
    the simulator?

    8 x 97   97 ÷ 8   8 x 8   97 ÷ 97 _____

4. At the souvenir shop, 9 children bought t-shirts. The total price was $106.
    They split the cost evenly. How much did each of the children spend on
    a space camp t-shirt?

    $106 + 9   9 x $106 $106 ÷ 9   9 x 9 _____

5. They drove 193 miles round trip. How many miles is it from the space camp
    to their hometown?

    193 ÷ 2   2 + 193   2 x 57   193 ÷ 193 _____

6. Terri was in a small group of 8 children who, in one day, spent an
    accumulated total of 82 hours in the museum. How many hours was that
    per child?

    8 x 82   82 ÷ 8   8 – 8   8 x 82 _____

7. The children stayed overnight in the dorms with their counselors. There
    were 124 girls and 8 counselors in the girls' dorm. How many girls was each
    counselor in charge of?

    124 ÷ 8   8 x 124   8 ÷ 8   124 + 124 _____

Use your calculator.

The Moon is 238,866 miles from Earth. It took 3 days for the rocket to get there
How many miles did the rocket go each day?

_____

Fire Mountains

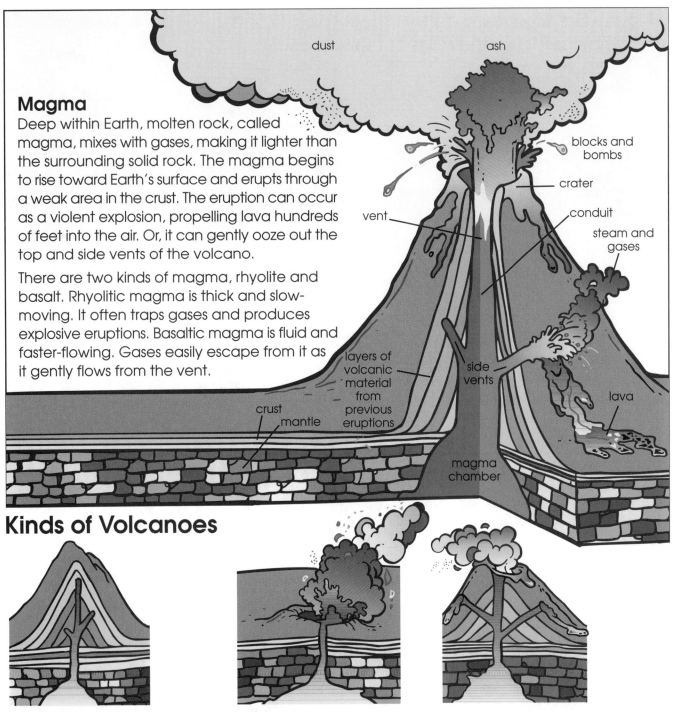

Magma

Deep within Earth, molten rock, called magma, mixes with gases, making it lighter than the surrounding solid rock. The magma begins to rise toward Earth's surface and erupts through a weak area in the crust. The eruption can occur as a violent explosion, propelling lava hundreds of feet into the air. Or, it can gently ooze out the top and side vents of the volcano.

There are two kinds of magma, rhyolite and basalt. Rhyolitic magma is thick and slow-moving. It often traps gases and produces explosive eruptions. Basaltic magma is fluid and faster-flowing. Gases easily escape from it as it gently flows from the vent.

dust · ash · blocks and bombs · crater · conduit · steam and gases · vent · layers of volcanic material from previous eruptions · side vents · lava · crust · mantle · magma chamber

Kinds of Volcanoes

Cinder Cone
Cinder cone volcanoes are formed from cinder and ash that are deposited around the vent after violent explosions. The layers of ash and cinder gradually build a cone-shaped mountain. The Paricutín Volcano in Mexico is a cinder cone volcano that grew to a height of over 1,300 feet in a cornfield.

Shield
Shield volcanoes are formed when lava flows gently from the vent, spreads and builds on a broad, gently sloping mountain. The Hawaiian Islands form a chain of shield volcanoes and include the famous Kilauea and Mauna Loa.

Composite
Composite volcanoes are some of the most spectacular mountains on Earth. These steep-sided, cone-shaped mountains can rise over 10,000 feet. They are made from alternating layers of gently flowing lava, ash, cinder, blocks and bombs. Some of the most beautiful mountains in the world, such as Mount Fuji in Japan and Vesuvius in Italy, are composite volcanoes.

Volcanoes

Using the **Fire Mountains** activity sheet (p. 151) and the box below, label the parts of the volcano.

Earth's crust	lava	side vent
Earth's mantle	crater	vent
magma chamber	ash and dust	conduit

The Hunters

Although they farmed and ate other foods besides meat, hunting was very important to most Woodland Native Americans, especially during the winter.

The information below shows the game that was caught by two Eastern Woodland tribes. Use the information to complete a double bar graph comparing the successes of the two tribes. Be sure to use a different color for each tribe.

Iroquois Tribe	**Mohawk Tribe**
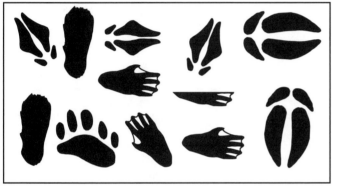	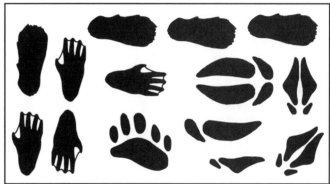

*Each print represents 4 animals caught.

Bear		
Beaver		
Deer		
Moose		
Rabbit		

0   2   4   6   8   10 12 14 16 18 20 22 24 26 28 30

☐ Iroquois   ☐ Mohawk

	Language Skills	Spelling	Reading
Monday	Have your child write a poem, imitating the style or format of a poem by another author. Encourage your child to use his/her own thoughts and words to create a similar rhythm, pattern or feeling.	Pretest your child on these spelling words. appointment enjoy rejoice avoid join royal choice loyalty soybean destroy moisture voice employer poison voyage Have your child correct the pretest, add personalized words and make two copies of this week's study list.	This week and next, have your child read *Little House in the Big Woods* by Laura Ingalls Wilder. Have your child make a character web for each character as he/she is introduced in the book. Incorporate appearance, actions, strengths and weaknesses as subtopics in the character web. *See* Social Studies, Week 10, number 1 for help making a topic (or character) web.
Tuesday	Have your child copy his/her poem from yesterday in neat cursive handwriting. Then, ask him/her to illustrate the poem.	Have your child use each of this week's spelling words correctly in a sentence.	Continue reading *Little House in the Big Woods*. Have your child verbally summarize what has happened so far in the book. Then, have him/her make three predictions as to what will happen in the rest of the book. Save the predictions for next week.
Wednesday	The *simple subject* is the most important word in the complete subject. It is a noun or pronoun that tells who or what the sentence is about. Identify the simple subject in a sentence. Then, have your child identify simple subjects in several sentences from a familiar book. Have your child write ten original sentences about zoo animals, then underline the complete subject and circle the simple subject in each.	Have your child complete **What's That Noise?** (p. 159).	Choose a chapter that covers several events. Write a one-sentence description of each event in the chapter on a strip of paper. Scramble the sentences. After your child has read the chapter, ask him/her to place the sentences in sequential order.
Thursday	The *simple predicate* is the most important word in the complete predicate. It is a verb that tells what the subject does. Identify the simple predicate in a sentence. Then, have your child do the same, using sentences from a familiar book. Have your child complete **Simple Subjects and Predicates** (p. 158).	Give your child a current news magazine or newspaper. Ask him/her to scan the articles for any of this week's spelling words. Challenge him/her to see how many he/she can find.	Continue reading *Little House in the Big Woods*. Have your child write down any words from the book that are unfamiliar, then look them up in a dictionary.
Friday	Sometimes sentences contain *compound subjects* or *predicates*. *See* Language Skills, Week 13, numbers 1 and 2. Have your child write ten sentences that contain compound subjects and/or predicates. *See* Language Skills, Week 13, numbers 3 and 4.	Give your child the final spelling test. Have your child record the pretest and final test words in his/her word bank.	Continue reading *Little House in the Big Woods*. Have your child write two paragraphs comparing and contrasting two characters from the book. He/she can use the character webs to get started.

Math	Science	Social Studies
Demonstrate how to divide 4- and 5-digit dividends by 1-digit divisors. Work through a couple of problems with your child before assigning independent work. Have your child complete **Yum-Yum!** (p. 160).	Have your child complete **Take It Away!** (p. 162).	Read about the Native Americans of the Plains. *See* Social Studies, Week 13, number 1. Have your child list the tribes of this area on the map created in Week 10. Ask him/her to draw pictures on the map of artifacts, tools, clothes and houses unique to the tribes of this area.
Teach your child to divide by multiples of ten. Show your child how to use estimation in solving the problems. *See* Math, Week 13, number 1. Work through several problems together. Then, let your child work independently. Assign the following problems: $80 \div 40$ $150 \div 20$ $180 \div 80$ $70 \div 40$ $120 \div 30$ $80 \div 70$ $590 \div 60$ $60 \div 20$ $240 \div 60$ $80 \div 10$ $90 \div 60$ $150 \div 50$	Conduct an experiment with your child to demonstrate how water affects the surface of the Earth. You may do this at the same time you are ready to finish the experiments from yesterday's activity sheet. *See* Science, Week 13, number 1.	Have your child choose two tribes from this area to research. Your child may want to include these tribes in the alphabet book. Give him/her a copy of **Native American Alphabet Book** (p. 139) to complete.
Have your child check yesterday's work by multiplying the quotient and divisor. Ask him/her to correct any mistakes he/she finds.	**Conservation:** Some people view humans as the most destructive creatures on Earth. Brainstorm a list of human developments that change the surface of the Earth, the air and the water. Ask your child: *If nature can be destructive in the form of volcanoes and earthquakes, why is it wrong for humans to be destructive?*	Refer to your child's completed information forms on the Native Americans of the Plains and of the Northeast. Help him/her create a Venn diagram comparing a tribe from each of these areas.
See **Puzzling Numbers** (p. 161) for a number puzzle activity. Your child must use both multiplication and division skills to fill in the missing boxes of each puzzle.	Help your child brainstorm possibilities, then research a career in conservation of natural resources. *See* Science, Week 13, number 2.	What influence did European settlers have on these tribes? *See* Social Studies, Week 13, number 2. Have your child draw a picture of a Plains native on a horse hauling a travois. What might they have transported using a travois?
Teach division with a 2-digit divisor. Solve several problems together with your child. Discuss the process step-by-step. Be sure your child places the digits carefully in the correct places. Show your child how to use multiples of ten when estimating. *See* Math, Week 13, number 2.	Have your child design ways to be a backyard conservationist. *See* Science, Week 13, number 3.	Study the sign language and picture writing of the Plains natives. *See* Social Studies, Week 13, numbers 3 and 4. Have your child complete **The Buffalo Hunters** (p. 163).

Learn at Home, Grade 4

TEACHING SUGGESTIONS AND ACTIVITIES

LANGUAGE SKILLS (Poetry)

▶ 1. Write a sentence on the chalkboard with two simple subjects: *Mary and her mother went shopping for a birthday present.* When there are two or more subjects, the sentence is said to have a compound subject. Have your child give some examples of compound subjects in oral sentences.

▶ 2. Write a sentence on the chalkboard with two simple predicates: *The circus tiger jumped through hoops and turned somersaults in the air.* When there are two or more predicates, the sentence is said to have a compound predicate. Have your child give some examples of compound predicates in oral sentences.

▶ 3. Have your child write five original sentences about personal interests or hobbies that contain compound subjects.

▶ 4. Have your child write five original sentences about sports that contain compound predicates.

MATH (Division)

▶ 1. Problem: 350 ÷ 80.

Estimate:	How many 80's are in 3? (none)
	How many 80's are in 35? (none)
	How many 80's are in 350? (Think 32 ÷ 8. Try 4.)
Multiply:	80 x 4 = 320.
Subtract:	350 − 320 = 30.
	The answer is 4r30.

▶ 2. Problem: 378 ÷ 75

Round the divisor up for estimating.

Estimate:	How many 80's are in 3? (none)
	How many 80's are in 37? (none)
	How many 80's are in 378? (Think 40 ÷ 8. Try 5.)
Multiply:	75 x 5 = 375
Subtract:	378 − 375 = 3
	The answer is 5r3.

SCIENCE (Conservation)

▶ 1. This experiment demonstrates how water can change the Earth's surface. Begin by asking your child to pour about an inch of dirt in a 2-inch-deep baking dish. Level the dirt so it covers the bottom of the pan evenly. Have your child predict what will happen when he/she simulates water flowing across the dirt. Using a sprinkling can filled with water, try to simulate water streaming over the surface of the Earth. Have your child describe what happens to the surface of the Earth as the water flows. Ask what happens when the volume of water is increased. Encourage your child to use the word *erosion* in his/her description. Have him/her tilt the pan and pour the water again. Ask how the angle of land affects erosion. Discuss how having grass and trees growing in the soil might affect the amount of erosion.

Learn at Home, Grade 4

2. Have your child brainstorm a list of careers that involve conservation of the Earth's natural resources. Have him/her choose one career to investigate more thoroughly. Here is a list to get started:

solid waste technician   geologist
oceanographer   air pollution inspector
ecologist   marine biologist
sewage plant worker   forester
forest naturalist   water treatment specialist
conservationist   park ranger

3. Being a backyard conservationist means that you look for ways that you personally can have a less negative impact on the environment. Some ways you can help: compost your yard waste and food garbage to keep down landfill volume; recycle plastics, paper products and cans; plant trees and other plants to add to the oxygen level; grow organic foods; avoid using chemicals in your yard.

SOCIAL STUDIES (Native Americans)

BACKGROUND
During the winter, spring and fall, Plains Native Americans lived in earth lodges along rivers. The women farmed in the tough sod of the grasslands. The men hunted. During the summer, they left their villages to follow the buffalo herds. They needed portable homes for this lifestyle—they carried tepees with them. The buffalo was very important to the lifestyle of these tribes.

1. Gather resources from the library on the Plains Native Americans. Let your child read through these materials. What aspect of their lifestyle most interests your child? Be sure to focus on that topic over the course of this week.

2. Read how European contact changed the Plains Indians' way of life. Not all European influence was negative. Compare their lives before and after the Europeans came, in terms of hunting, tools, weapons, disease and religion.

3. The Plains were home to a variety of native languages. Out of necessity, the natives who lived there developed a sign language so they could communicate with other tribes. Look at a chart of Native American sign language and practice some of the signs with your child. Try to have a conversation using only sign language.

4. The picture writings of the Plains Native Americans represented important events such as a good hunt, a warrior's bravery in battle and a successful harvest. Have your child write a picture story using these symbols.

Learn at Home, Grade 4

Simple Subjects and Predicates

The **simple subject** is the most important word in the complete subject. It is a **noun** or **pronoun** that tells who or what the sentence is about.

The **simple predicate** is the most important word in the complete predicate. It is a **verb** that tells what the subject is or does.

Example:

simple subject   simple predicate

Handmade pottery can be very beautiful.

complete subject   complete predicate

Underline the complete subject once and the complete predicate twice.

1. The science of pottery making is called ceramics.
2. Humans have been making pottery for thousands of years.
3. Early people made household utensils out of pottery.
4. Pottery has been made many different ways.
5. The earliest pottery making method was probably the hand-building method.
6. Clay coils were wound on top of one another.
7. Another method utilized the potter's wheel.
8. The Egyptians used the potter's wheel at least three thousand years ago
9. The ancient Greeks used the potter's wheel when making pottery.
10. Their vases are excellent examples of simplicity of color and shape.

Write the simple subjects and the simple predicates from the sentences above.

Simple Subject	Simple Predicate	Simple Subject	Simple Predicate
1. _____	_____	6. _____	_____
2. _____	_____	7. _____	_____
3. _____	_____	8. _____	_____
4. _____	_____	9. _____	_____
5. _____	_____	10. _____	_____

Learn at Home, Grade 4

What's That Noise?

Use the word list to complete the crossword puzzle.

Across

5. trip at sea
6. harmful substance
7. to express joy
9. to take pleasure from
11. an agreement to meet
13. faithfulness
15. sound produced by speaking

Down

1. to bring together
2. to stay away from
3. to ruin
4. farm crop
8. one who pays wages
10. dampness
12. selection
14. regal

appointment   moisture
avoid   poison
choice   rejoice
destroy   royal
employer   soybean
enjoy   voice
join   voyage
loyalty

Learn at Home, Grade 4

Yum-Yum!

What edible fungus is occasionally found on pizzas or in omelets? To find out, solve the problems. Then, **write** the corresponding letter above the answer at the bottom of the page.

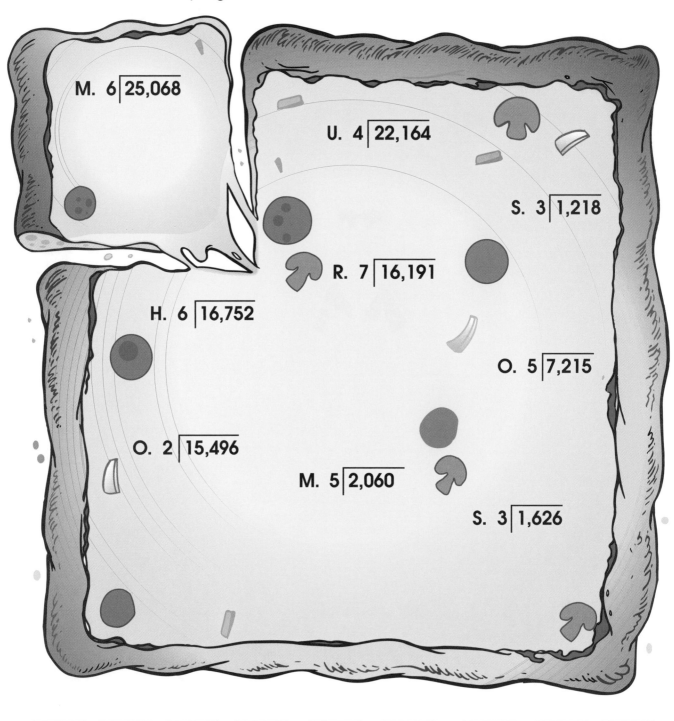

M. 6$\overline{)25,068}$

U. 4$\overline{)22,164}$

S. 3$\overline{)1,218}$

R. 7$\overline{)16,191}$

H. 6$\overline{)16,752}$

O. 5$\overline{)7,215}$

O. 2$\overline{)15,496}$

M. 5$\overline{)2,060}$

S. 3$\overline{)1,626}$

412	5,541	406	2,792	2,313	7,748	1,443	4,178	542

Puzzling Numbers

factor	factor	product
	4	180
16	8	
	5	275
4		104

factor	factor	product
3		123
	5	10
6		318
47	3	

factor	factor	product
5		125
	7	308
30	3	
	20	840

factor	factor	product
114	2	
6		198
	40	120
2		132

Shade in your answers below to reveal a picture.

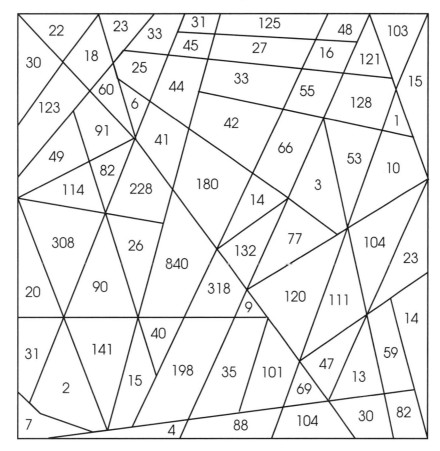

161

Take It Away!

Here is an activity to help you understand the effects of erosion on Earth.

You will need:
dirt, five 12" square pieces of thick cardboard, 5 roasting-type pans (you may wish to purchase disposable ones), grass seed, small rocks, leaves, twigs, paper towels, a small watering can, water, a quart-size jar

Directions:
Moisten dirt and cover the 5 pieces of cardboard with at least an inch or two of dirt. Then, do one of the following with each piece of cardboard:

1. Leave one piece of cardboard as is.

2. Set the leaves into the dirt in one.

3. Set the twigs into the dirt in one.

4. Set the rocks into the dirt in one.

5. Plant grass seed in one. Water it and wait for a good crop of grass to grow. When the board is dry and there is a good crop of grass, follow the directions below.

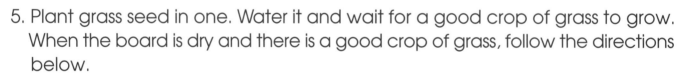

Lean the cardboard against the inside of the pan. Fill a quart jar with water and pour it into a watering can. Hold the spout about 2" above the cardboard, sprinkle water over it and observe the water flowing over the dirt into the pan. To compare the amount of dirt that has been eroded, fold a paper towel into a cone shape. Place it in the mouth of the jar and pour the muddy water from the pan into it. Compare what each piece of cardboard looks like and the amount of dirt on the paper towels. Why do you think there are differences?

Learn at Home, Grade 4

The Buffalo Hunters

The Plains Indians' survival depended on the buffalo. They killed only as many as they needed and wasted none of the animal. As a matter of fact, they had over 500 uses for the buffalo.

Below is a list of some of the buffalo body parts. Make a logical guess as to the function of each. Then, use an encyclopedia to find the actual uses. You may be very surprised!

Your Logical Guess

clothing, tepees, drums •   • teeth

decorations •   • brain

bowls for cooking •   • tongue

cups, spoons •   • hide

jewelry •   • large intestine

strings on bows •   • horns

bags for storage •   • muscles

ropes, belts •   • stomach

food •   • hair

tanning mixture for leather •   • tail

Name another buffalo part and its function. _____

_____

	Language Skills	Spelling	Reading
Monday	**Simple Sentences** Choose a topic or allow your child to choose a topic of interest. Topics might include a holiday, special event, friend or historical figure. Think of a word related to the chosen topic. Challenge your child to write about the topic, starting each sentence with a letter from the related word. *See* Language Skills, Week 14, number 1 for an example.	Pretest your child on these spelling words. beige fiend neighbor believe freight receive conceited friend sleigh eight height thief field leisure weigh Have your child correct the pretest, add personalized words and make two copies of this week's study list.	Have your child continue reading *Little House in the Big Woods* by Laura Ingalls Wilder. While reading this week, have your child write any unfamiliar words in his/her Reading Journal. Then, ask him/her to look up each word and write its pronunciation and a definition that fits the context. Add some of these words to this week's spelling list.
Tuesday	For this week's handwriting lesson, stress the importance of staying within the lines of the writing paper. Letters should touch the lines without going over. Have your child practice writing the following words: *answer, seam, crime, nervous, inner, mixer, voice, receive, move, over, music, sense* and *common*.	Have your child use each of this week's spelling words correctly in a sentence.	Continue reading *Little House in the Big Woods*. Choose a scene that contains mostly dialogue and act it out with your child.
Wednesday	A *simple sentence* contains one complete thought. A sentence may contain a compound subject or predicate and still be considered a simple sentence. The simple sentence may also contain descriptive words and prepositional phrases. *See* Language Skills, Week 14, number 2. Have your child turn phrases into simple sentences to form a story. *See* Language Skills, Week 14, number 3.	Have your child complete **I Before E or Not?** (p. 168).	Have your child write about an event from *Little House in the Big Woods*. Have him/her compose a paragraph describing the event as if for a newspaper article, addressing *who, what, when, where, why* and *how*.
Thursday	Have your child combine phrases to form sentences. Have him/her underline each subject and circle each predicate. *See* Language Skills, Week 14, number 4.	Have your child make up two or three tongue twisters using words from this week's spelling list. Have your child write out each tongue twister, then try to read it aloud quickly four times in a row.	Continue reading *Little House in the Big Woods*. Have your child compare and contrast Wilder's life with his/her own. Have your child think of four things that are nearly the same and four things that are very different.
Friday	Have your child add words and phrases to make the following dull sentences more interesting. Be sure that each sentence expresses only one complete thought. *I walked home.* *Matt likes cookies.* *Isabel wrote a letter.* *My dad helped me.* *He wore a hat.* *I listen to music.*	Give your child the final spelling test. Have your child record the pretest and final test words in his/her word bank.	Continue reading *Little House in the Big Woods*. Have your child paint or draw a scene from the book based on Wilder's descriptions.

Math	Science	Social Studies
Have your child practice division with 2-digit divisors. Write six or eight short story problems with a common theme for your child to solve. Encourage him/her to draw pictures to increase understanding of the problems. Have your child solve the problems.	**Physical Properties** Provide your child with a mystery object. Develop observation skills by having him/her make at least ten statements about the object's physical attributes. Observations may be quantitative (using measurement tools) or qualitative (using the senses). *See* Science, Week 14, number 1.	Read about the Native Americans of the Northwest Coast. Discuss their dependence on water and wood. Have your child list the tribes of this area on the map created in Week 10. Ask him/her to draw pictures on the map of artifacts, tools, clothes and houses unique to the tribes of this area.
Review the procedure for dividing with 2-digit divisors. Have your child complete **China's Dragon Kite** (p. 169).	Have your child make observations about an orange, using tools and the five senses. *See* Science, Week 14, number 2. Then, have your child write a detailed description of the orange using the measurements and observations.	Have your child choose two tribes from this area to research. Your child may want to use these same tribes in the alphabet book. Give him/her a copy of **Native American Alphabet Book** (p. 139).
Using copies of **Graph Paper** (p. 170), have your child cut out shapes to illustrate division problems. *See* Math, Week 14, number 1.	Teach your child to draw and label a model. Provide a variety of fruits and vegetables. Have your child draw two detailed cross sections (one lengthwise, one crosswise) of each object. Suggested foods: apple, squash, cucumber, potato, banana, star fruit, strawberry and kiwi. ***Note:*** *Refrigerate the fruits and vegetables for tomorrow's lesson.*	The Northwest is an area filled with many trees, including the giant redwoods. The Native Americans used the plentiful resources available to make many things out of wood. Have your child do some research on what types of things the Northwestern Native Americans created or built from wood.
Play "Math Bingo" with your child. You will need manipulatives, cards and problems. On the chalkboard or on a sheet of paper, write the letters *B, I, N, G* and *O* in a row. List fifteen division problems with 2-digit divisors beneath each letter. *See* Math, Week 14, number 2 for further instructions.	Use the fruits and vegetables from yesterday. Have your child predict what will happen to each food if it is cooked or frozen. Cook half of each food item (separately) and have your child observe the physical properties. Discuss the changes. Freeze the other half of each food item and have your child observe the physical changes. Discuss whether each food item remained that food item after the change (i.e., *Is the apple still an apple?*).	Study the totem poles of the Northwest coast. Ask: *What did they symbolize? Do we have something like a totem pole in our culture?* Let your child design a personal totem pole. Ask him/her to draw and paint a large version of the design. Use **Totem Poles** (p. 171) as a guide.
Once your child is dividing confidently with 2-digit divisors, ask him/her to form an accurate division problem given three or four numbers (*divisor, dividend, quotient* and *remainder*). Have your child arrange the following groups of numbers into division problems: 2, 102, 51 45, 540, 12 7, 183, 8, 22 6, 138, 23 49, 7, 345, 2 75, 3, 6, 12	Teach the importance of using specific language to describe physical attributes. Words such as *small* and *pretty* do not tell much about the attributes of an object. Have your child write a description of a familiar object using specific language. Encourage him/her to use senses other than sight. **Example:** *The elephant's trunk feels rough like a wool blanket. It looks like a gray tube about 5 feet long and 4 inches in diameter at the narrowest point.*	Potlatches are feasts held by wealthy Native Americans, designed to prove their wealth and social rank. Have your child read about potlatches. Then, ask him/her to write a description of the events at a potlatch.

TEACHING SUGGESTIONS AND ACTIVITIES

LANGUAGE SKILLS (Simple Sentences)

▶ 1. Example of this week's writing lesson:

Topic: feeding the birds   **Related word:** sunflower seeds

Sometime in the fall, I place sunflower seeds in my bird feeder.
Under the maple tree is where it hangs.
Now and then a chickadee or a nuthatch checks out the feeder.
For about a month, I don't see many birds.
Late in November, my feeder is visited by robins, chickadees and others.
Only in the early morning do I see a crowd at my feeder.
When the sun comes up, they must move on to someone else's feeder.
Early the next morning they are back.
Robins are my favorite guests.
Sometimes, I think that the same four robins are returning every morning.
Every once in a while I see six robins but usually it is my regular four.
Even the squirrels try to eat from my feeder.
Dropping seeds on the ground seems to keep the squirrels off the feeder.
Sunflower seeds are the favorite snack at my feeder.

▶ 2. Write the following simple sentences on the chalkboard and discuss the variations.

Theo ran to answer the telephone.
Theo and Margie ran to answer the telephone. (compound subject)
Theo ran and answered the telephone. (compound predicate)
My brother Theo ran quickly to answer the ringing telephone. (descriptive words added)
Theo ran from outside to answer the telephone. (prepositional phrase added)
Theo ran to answer the phone, then he talked for an hour. (This is NOT a simple sentence because it contains two complete thoughts.)

▶ 3. Reproduce the phrases below onto the chalkboard. Have your child write a story using ten of these phrases to form ten simple sentences.

the middle of the ocean	gathered driftwood along the beach
three sailors	split the coconut
a large volcano	were rescued
a small raft	shark-infested waters
in the hidden cave	heard a noise
the message in a bottle	tracks in the sand
behind the waterfall	a mountain of treasure

▶ 4. Copy the sets of phrases below. Have your child arrange each row of phrases into a simple sentence (including capitalization and punctuation). Then, have him/her underline the complete subject and circle the complete predicate.

a.	is being built	a huge new	in our neighborhood	shopping mall
b.	will be located	of the mall	a skating rink	in the center
c.	in the sports shop	my brother	was hired	to work
d.	there will be	in the new mall	by next year	forty-five stores
e.	at each end	there will be	a department store	of the mall

Learn at Home, Grade 4

MATH (Division)

▶ 1. Copy **Graph Paper** (p. 170) and write a division problem on each of several index cards. The problems for this activity should contain 2-digit divisors and should not have remainders.

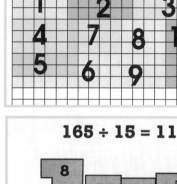

Directions for child:

a. Choose an index card and read the equation.

b. On the graph paper, lightly color the number of squares given as the dividend.

c. Using a pen, trace around the number of colored squares given as the divisor. Continue tracing that same number of squares in different shapes until all the colored squares are traced.

$$165 \div 15 = 11$$

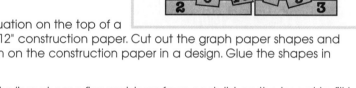

d. Count how many shapes are outlined. That number is the quotient.

e. Write the equation on the top of a sheet of 9" x 12" construction paper. Cut out the graph paper shapes and arrange them on the construction paper in a design. Glue the shapes in place.

▶ 2. Give your child a blank BINGO card. Let him/her choose five problems from each list on the board to fill in the spaces on the card. The problems can be in any order but should stay in the appropriate columns. Give your child beans, colored squares or other small manipulatives to use as markers for the cards. Read one problem at a time: "B—125 ÷ 25." Your child should place a marker over the problem if it is on his/her card. Repeat until your child has five markers in a row horizontally, vertically or diagonally. To win, your child must then solve the problems correctly. Offer him/her a small prize or treat as a reward.

SCIENCE (Physical Properties)

BACKGROUND

Understanding matter involves the study of properties that form the world around us. In this unit, your child will learn the language of sorting and describing physical attributes. Descriptions should include observable attributes, such as odor, size, weight, hardness, temperature, color and the more complex "states of matter." Your child will also learn that states of matter change—a liquid may become a solid—but the matter is still the same material.

▶ 1. Give your child an object that is not immediately recognizable, such as a sugar cube, a piece of apple, a slice of firm tofu or a chunk of cheese. Tell him/her to make at least ten qualitative and quantitative observations about the object. After he/she presents the list of attributes, discuss the tool or sense used to make each observation.

▶ 2. Give your child a whole orange and the following tools: string, a ruler and a balance scale. Have him/her measure the circumference of the whole orange using the string and ruler. Then, have your child measure the mass (weight) of the orange before and after it is peeled. He/she should record the weight of the whole orange, just the peel and just the fruit. Observations of each part may include: weight, circumference, area (of the peeling), color, number of sections, number of seeds, taste, texture, temperature, smell, sound and appearance.

Learn at Home, Grade 4

I Before E or Not?

Write the **ei** spelling words in alphabetical order.

1. _____   6. _____

2. _____   7. _____

3. _____   8. _____

4. _____   9. _____

5. _____   10. _____

How many **ei** words have a **long a** sound? _____

How many **ei** words have a **long e** sound? _____

Which of the **ei** words is left? _____

What sound does it have? _____

Write the **ie** spelling words in alphabetical order.

beige
believe
conceited
eight
field
fiend
freight
friend
height
leisure
neighbor
receive
sleigh
thief
weigh

1. _____

2. _____

3. _____

4. _____

5. _____

What sound do you hear in four of the **ie** words? _____

What sound do you hear in the remaining **ie** word? _____

Write the word. _____

Fill in the blanks with four different letters in this helpful spelling rule.

The letter ____ comes before ____ except after ____, or if it sounds like _____ .

Learn at Home, Grade 4

China's Dragon Kite

Solve the problems in this incredible dragon kite!

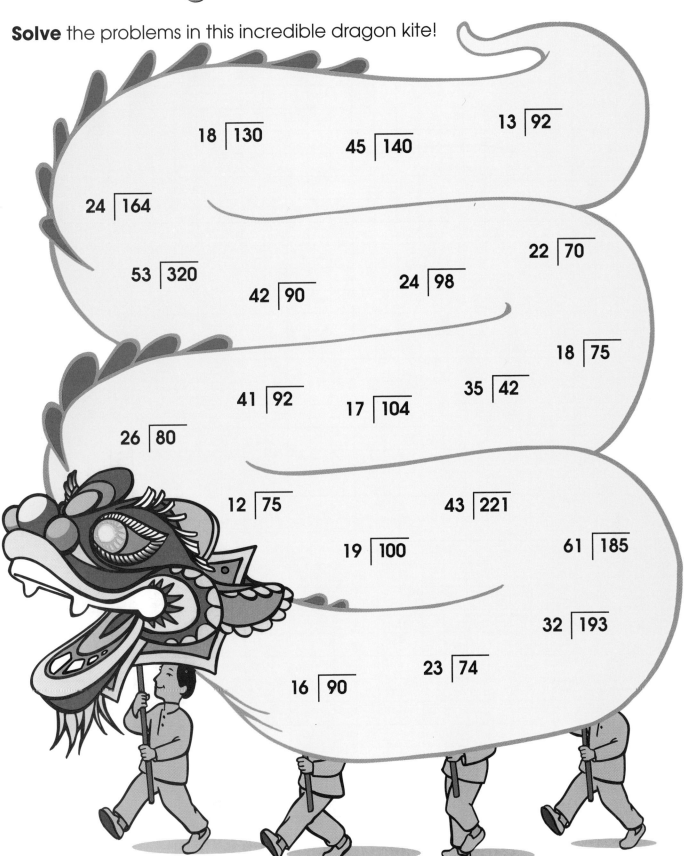

18 ⟌130

45 ⟌140

13 ⟌92

24 ⟌164

53 ⟌320

42 ⟌90

24 ⟌98

22 ⟌70

18 ⟌75

41 ⟌92

17 ⟌104

35 ⟌42

26 ⟌80

12 ⟌75

43 ⟌221

19 ⟌100

61 ⟌185

32 ⟌193

23 ⟌74

16 ⟌90

Learn at Home, Grade 4

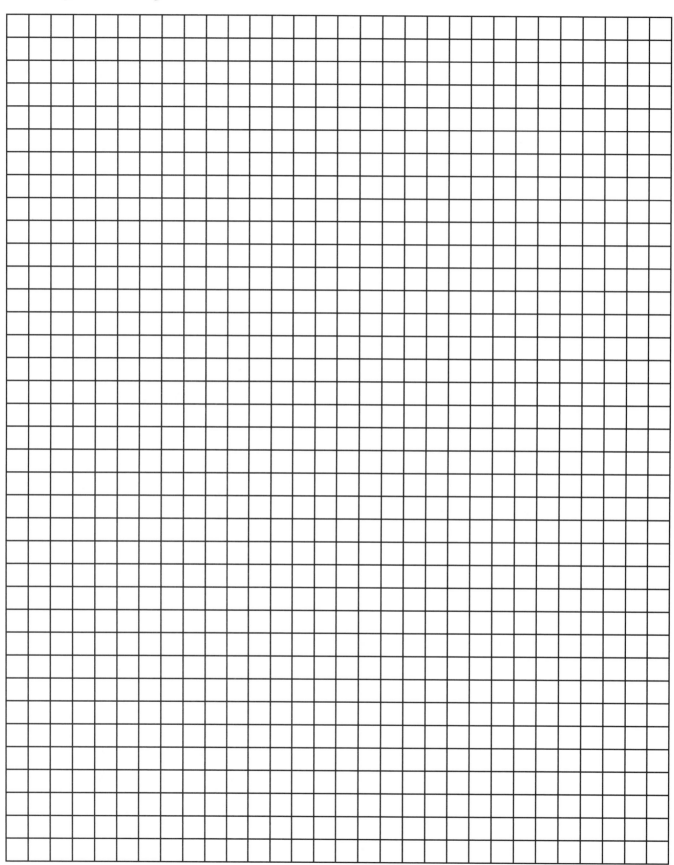

Totem Poles

Many Native American tribes painted symbols to tell stories. Others wove designs into blankets to remind them of legends. The tribes in Washington state and parts of Alaska carved their family crests into trees. We call these totem poles. You can make a personal totem pole, too. Draw your totem pole on another sheet of paper.

1. For the bottom of your totem pole, draw a human figure. It could be you.

2. On the top of the human figure, draw a symbol of your father's occupation or something he does that has special meaning to you.

3. Above that, draw a symbol to depict your mother. The symbol could show her occupation or it could show something she does that has special meaning to you.

4. Next, draw a favorite animal, which will be your family crest. It could be your family pet or an animal your family especially likes, such as a special bird.

5. The next section should include a symbol of the type of job you want to do when you become an adult.

6. Next, draw a hobby that you really enjoy, such as a sport, music or computers.

7. On top of your totem pole, draw a symbol that stands for something very important to you.

8. Now, color your totem pole.

9. Then, think of a way to make your totem pole out of scraps of construction paper, play dough, tissue paper or other odds and ends.

10. Use your design to create a 3-D totem pole.

	Language Skills	Spelling	Reading
Monday	Discuss the difference between a story and a journal entry. Sometimes a journal entry can be a story starter. Have your child choose a topic from a previous entry in his/her journal. Have him/her develop a story about that topic, adding details to make it more interesting.	Pretest your child on these spelling words. alphabetize memorize service arise office surmise concise police surprise enterprise price twice justice prize wise Have your child correct the pretest, add personalized words and make two copies of this week's study list.	Review the role of guide words at the top of a dictionary page. Have your child complete **Guide-Worthy Words** (p. 179).
Tuesday	Have your child tell you what he/she has learned in Social Studies this week. Write your child's words on the chalkboard. Have your child copy these dictated sentences for handwriting practice.	Have your child use each of this week's spelling words correctly in a sentence.	For the next three weeks, have your child read *The Borrowers* by Mary Norton. Ask him/her to write about the story in his/her Reading Journal (*see* **More Reading Suggestions**, p. 11). Suggestions for journal starters are offered in the lesson plans. Have your child read chapter 1 to find out who met the Borrowers and where. Ask him/her to think about who Mrs. May and Kate are in relation to that person.
Wednesday	Two simple sentences can be joined with the words *and, while, because* and *but* to form a single sentence. These words are called conjunctions. *See* Language Skills, Week 15, number 1. Have your child complete **Combining Sentences** (p. 176).	Have your child complete **Prize Words** (p. 178).	Review dictionary skills. *See* Reading, Week 15, number 1 for a dictionary activity involving compound words. Read chapter 2 of *The Borrowers*. **Reading Journal:** Describe the Borrowers' apartment and its contents.
Thursday	Have your child combine several sentences in a paragraph to make the paragraph more interesting to read. *See* Language Skills, Week 15, number 2. Encourage your child to vary the length of sentences in his/her own writing.	Have your child make up a song using some of this week's spelling words. He/she can use the melody of a familiar tune like "Frère Jacques" or "Pop! Goes the Weasel."	Read chapters 3 and 4 of *The Borrowers*. Have your child complete **Weird Words** (p. 180).
Friday	Teach your child to write cause and effect sentences. These combination sentences may be joined with the word *because* or *so*. Work together on **Cause and Effect Sentences** (p. 177).	Give your child the final spelling test. Have your child record the pretest and final test words in his/her word bank.	Read chapter 5 of *The Borrowers*. **Reading Journal:** Give examples of how the Clock family is different from other borrowers. Give your child practice reading guide words. Name a word. Have your child find the word in a dictionary and name the guide words at the top of the page.

Math	Science	Social Studies
Geometry Introduce your child to the basics of geometry. Begin your study of geometry with angles. Describe the three types of angles and draw an example of each. *See* Math, Week 15, numbers 1–3. acute right obtuse	Matter can exist in the form of a solid, liquid or gas. Provide your child with examples of each state. Explore each material to help him/her write a working definition for each state of matter. *See* Science, Week 15, number 1. This exploration can take 3 days, exploring one state of matter each day. Focus on solids today.	Read about the Native Americans of the Southwest, especially the Pueblos. *See* Social Studies, Week 15, number 1. Have your child list the tribes of this area on the map created in Week 10. Ask him/her to draw pictures on the map of artifacts, tools, clothes and houses unique to the tribes of this area.
Look at the figures on **Figure Finding** Have your child point to and name the different angles shown (*acute, obtuse* and *right*). Have your child complete **Figure Finding**. (p. 181).	Continue Monday's lesson, exploring liquids.	Have your child choose two tribes from this area to research. Give him/her a copy of **Native American Alphabet Book** (p. 139). Your child may want to use the same tribes in the alphabet book.
Teach the definition and provide examples of *lines, line segments, rays, angles* and *vertices*. See Math, Week 15. angle line vertex line segment ray	Continue Monday's lesson, exploring gases.	Read about the importance of rain to the Pueblo culture. Your child should explore the following questions: *What did this tribe do to bring rain? Why was rain so important?* Have your child draw a picture of a Kachina dancer.
Polygons are closed figures made up of three or more line segments or sides. Have your child define and illustrate the following terms in his/her geometry glossary: *triangle, square, rectangle, parallelogram, trapezoid, pentagon* and *hexagon*. Have your child complete **Connect the Dots** (p. 182). Tell your child he/she will probably not use all the dots for each shape.	After experimentation, have your child name the ways that each state of matter can be measured (described quantitatively). Ask: *Can a solid be measured with a ruler? Can a gas be measured with a ruler?*	The Pueblos were skilled at a variety of crafts. With your child, read about the different crafts and look at pictures of their handiwork. Let your child choose a Pueblo craft idea and create the product using similar materials. *See* Social Studies, Week 15, number 2.
Review shapes and polygons. Have your child complete a copy of **The Rocket Puzzle** (p. 183).	Explore a substance that could be considered either a solid or a liquid and have your child decide which state it is. What criteria will he/she use to decide? Ask him/her to write an explanation of his/her decision. *See* Science, Week 15, number 2.	Refer to your child's completed information forms on various tribes. Have your child create a Venn diagram comparing a tribe from the Southwest to a tribe from the Northwest Coast.

Learn at Home, Grade 4

TEACHING SUGGESTIONS AND ACTIVITIES

LANGUAGE SKILLS (Simple Sentences)

▶ 1. Write the following compound sentence on the chalkboard: *Dean bought chicken at the meat market, and he barbecued it for dinner.* Underline the two independent clauses. In this compound sentence, two simple sentences are connected by a comma and the word *and.* Write other compound sentences on the board. Have your child first underline the two independent clauses in each sentence, then identify the subject and verb in each clause.

▶ 2. Copy the following paragraph for your child to read. All the sentences are short. The paragraph would be more interesting if some of the sentences were combined. Have your child join some of the sentences together, then read the paragraph aloud to hear the improvements.

   Brad rode his bike to Isaac's house. He wanted to play baseball. He took his ball and glove. He knocked on Isaac's door. Nobody answered. He rode his bike to Fran's house. Nobody was home there. He stopped at Sonia, Greg and Todd's homes. Nobody was home anywhere. Sadly, he rode his bike to the baseball field. He saw Isaac, Fran, Greg, Sonia and Todd throwing a ball around the bases. He parked his bike. He ran to join them. They played all afternoon at the baseball field.

READING (Story Analysis)

BACKGROUND
Compound words are often written incorrectly, not because they are spelled wrong, but because the word may need a hyphen, a space between the two words or written with no space or hyphen. If you are unsure about these types of words, the dictionary is the place to look.

▶ 1. Give your child the following list of compound words to look up in the dictionary. Are they written correctly? If not, have your child write the words correctly, using the dictionary for help.

grandfather	one half	bird-watching	great grandfather
head ache	green house	textbook	vice president
mother in law	stomach ache	world wide	mini bike
checkbook	half-hearted	steam boat	police-officer

MATH (Geometry)

BACKGROUND
A *line* has an arrow at each end. A *line* continues in both directions indefinitely. A *line segment* is a portion of a line between two definite points. A *ray* is a line with one end point. An *angle* is formed where two lines meet or intersect. The meeting point is called the *vertex* of the angle. *Vertices* is the plural of vertex.

Obtuse	Right	Acute

▶ 1. Have your child keep a glossary of geometry terms. Every time a new geometry word is introduced, have him/her write it in a notebook along with a definition and an example.

▶ 2. Draw a circle with a right angle. Explain to your child that a circle measures 360 degrees all the way around. A right angle covers one-fourth of a circle, totaling 90 degrees. Any angle less than 90° is an acute angle. Any angle greater than 90° is an obtuse angle. Demonstrate with a protractor.

▶ 3. Have your child go "angling." Make a large table like the one shown to the right. Set a time limit and physical limits where your child may go. He/she should look for and list every angle he/she sees under the appropriate column. Have your child be specific. For example, if he/she sees a right angle on a table, he/she should not write "the table," but rather, "4 corners of the paint table."

174

SCIENCE (Physical Properties)

BACKGROUND

Solid: A solid maintains its shape (can only be altered using a tool), has mass, takes up space and other objects cannot pass through it easily. Examples of solids: a pencil, blocks, a book, a nail, an apple, a desk, a computer.

Liquid: A liquid takes up space, has mass, takes the shape of its container and other objects can move through it easily. Examples of liquids: water, milk, dishwashing soap, oil, vinegar, juice, shampoo, soda, syrup.

Gas: A gas takes the shape of its container (filling all space available in the container), has mass, takes up space and objects can move through it easily. Examples of (readily available) gases: oxygen, carbon dioxide, helium.

▶ 1. Read the definitions above. Have your child experiment with each material and prove the distinctions through exploration. For example, ask him/her to try passing a pencil through each liquid. Try passing a pencil through each solid. You can prove that a gas takes up space by blowing up a balloon. To show that a gas has mass, balance an empty balloon with an inflated balloon. The inflated balloon will be heavier because the carbon dioxide inside has mass.

▶ 2. Some substances are difficult to define because they may take the shape of a container but also maintain their own shapes. Explore the properties of play dough with your child. Let your child concoct a mystery substance of cornstarch and water, adding cornstarch until the substance has a very thick consistency.

SOCIAL STUDIES (Native Americans)

▶ 1. The Southwest is a varied region, but it is characterized by hot, dry weather. Some of the area is desert, some is mountainous and other areas consist of steep canyons. The Pueblo tribes of this region had a highly developed civilization. Find resources on the Pueblos to share with your child.

▶ 2. Help your child make a coil pot. Directions for the child:

a. Flatten a small ball of clay with a rolling pin until it is about a quarter of an inch thick. Cut out a 3-inch circle to form the base of the pot.

b. Take another small piece of clay. Roll it between your hands at first to get it into a cylinder shape. Then, put it on the table and roll it back and forth to make a thin snake shape.

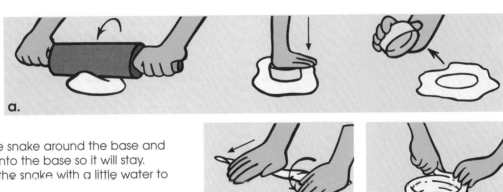

c. Wrap the snake around the base and pinch it into the base so it will stay. Smooth the snake with a little water to secure.

d. Make another snake and attach it where you left off from the last snake. Continue coiling the snakes up and around. Keep pinching and smoothing with water. You may want to smooth the outside as you work so you cannot see the coils.

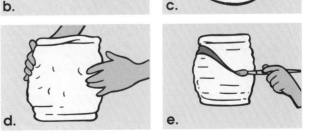

e. Let the finished pot dry for at least a week. Paint a Pueblo design on the dry pot.

Learn at Home, Grade 4

Combining Sentences

Two sentences can be written as one sentence by using **connecting words**.

Choose one of the words in the box to combine the two sentences into one sentence.

I am happy *when* *I go to school.*

1. We can eat now. We can eat after the game.

while
or
because

_____

_____

2. We stood on the cabin's deck. The sun rose over the deck.

as
or
but

_____

_____

3. Sarah wanted to watch TV. She had lots of homework to finish.

because
when
but

_____

_____

4. The concert did not begin on time. The conductor was late arriving.

until
because
while

_____

_____

5. The spectators cheered and applauded. The acrobats completed their performances.

when
if
but

_____

_____

6. The baseball teams waited in their dugouts. The rain ended and the field was uncovered.

or
until
after

_____

_____

Cause and Effect Sentences

A **cause and effect sentence** has two parts: a **cause**, which tells why, and an **effect**, which tells what happened. It can be written two ways.

Example: Today is Saturday, so I don't have to go to school.
          cause   effect

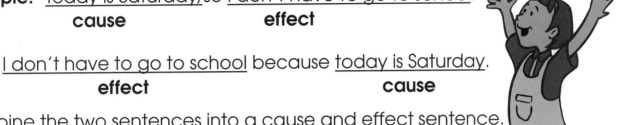

          I don't have to go to school because today is Saturday.
                    effect   cause

Combine the two sentences into a cause and effect sentence. **Write** the sentence two ways: **A. cause-effect, B. effect-cause**

1. I could not eat my dessert. I was full from dinner.

    A. _____

    B. _____

2. I forgot to take my umbrella. I got wet in the rain.

    A. _____

    B. _____

3. The astronomer could not see clearly. The night was cloudy.

    A. _____

    B. _____

4. I love animals. I want to be a veterinarian someday.

    A. _____

    B. _____

Write two sets of cause and effect sentences about any subject.

    A. _____

    B. _____

    A. _____

    B. _____

Learn at Home, Grade 4

Prize Words

Fill in the blanks. Each spelling word is used only once.

1. **One** is to **once** as **two** is to _____.

2. **Reverse** is to **forward** as **sit** is to _____.

3. **Book** is to **library** as **typewriter** is to _____.

4. **Shiny** is to **dull** as **foolish** is to _____.

5. **Teacher** is to **education** as **judge** is to _____.

6. **Illness** is to **doctor** as **crime** is to _____.

7. **Tag** is to **label** as **cost** is to _____.

8. **1, 2, 3** is to **count** as **A, B, C** is to _____.

9. **Imagine** is to **think** as **guess** is to _____.

10. **Wordy** is to **long-winded** as **brief** is to _____.

alphabetize	memorize	service
arise	office	surmise
concise	police	surprise
enterprise	price	twice
justice	prize	wise

Use the remaining words from the list to **answer** each question.

1. What do you usually get when you win a contest?

   _____.

2. What do actors do with their lines? _____.

3. What is a risky or important project? _____.

4. What is a synonym for "helpfulness"? _____.

5. What is a synonym for "astonish"? _____.

Guide-Worthy Words

Use a pencil to **write** ten vocabulary words from the box under each of the guide words. Remember to put them in alphabetical order.

Reflection	Syllable

Abrupt	Authority

Babyhood	Crest

Defense	Exult

burrow	commerce	cordial	corporal	accustom
accidently	barracks	barometer	explosive	schoolmaster
stealth	allow	calamity	stance	defiant
epidemic	ancient	scowl	discard	ammunition
disturbance	subside	salute	reindeer	consternation
assign	demoralize	disposition	appoint	beneficial
resolute	enormous	ashamed	retort	entirely
earthenware	additional	commotion	almanac	surpass

Learn at Home, Grade 4

Use a dictionary to help you **answer** the questions using complete sentences.

1. Which would you use to treat a sore throat: a **gargoyle** or a **gargle**?

_____

2. Which might be used on a gravestone: an **epiphyte** or an **epitaph**?

_____

3. Which is an instrument: **calligraphy** or a **calliope**?

_____

4. Would a building have a **gargoyle** or an **argyle** on it?

_____

5. If you trick someone, do you **bamboozle** him or **barcarole** him?

_____

6. If you studied handwriting, would you learn **calligraphy** or **cajolery**?

_____

7. What would a gondolier sing: a **barcarole** or an **argyle**?

_____

8. If you tried to coax someone, would you be using **cajolery** or **calamity**?

_____

9. Which might you wear: **argyles** or **calliopes**?

_____

10. In Venice, Italy, would you travel in a **gondola** or a **calamity**?

_____

Figure Finding

Find Figure 1 in Design 1 and shade it. Do this for each shape. The figure may be turned, and it may not be the same size.

Learn at Home, Grade 4

Connect the Dots

Connect the dots to make each shape.
Note: not all dots will be used.

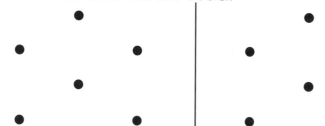

a rectangle	a kite	a different 4-sider
a different 4-sider	a triangle	a different triangle
a different triangle	a different triangle	a 5-sider
a 6-sider	a different 6-sider	a 7-sider

Learn at Home, Grade 4

The rocket has four parts. **Cut** them apart.
The rocket can change itself into many shapes.

Use all 4 pieces to make each shape below.

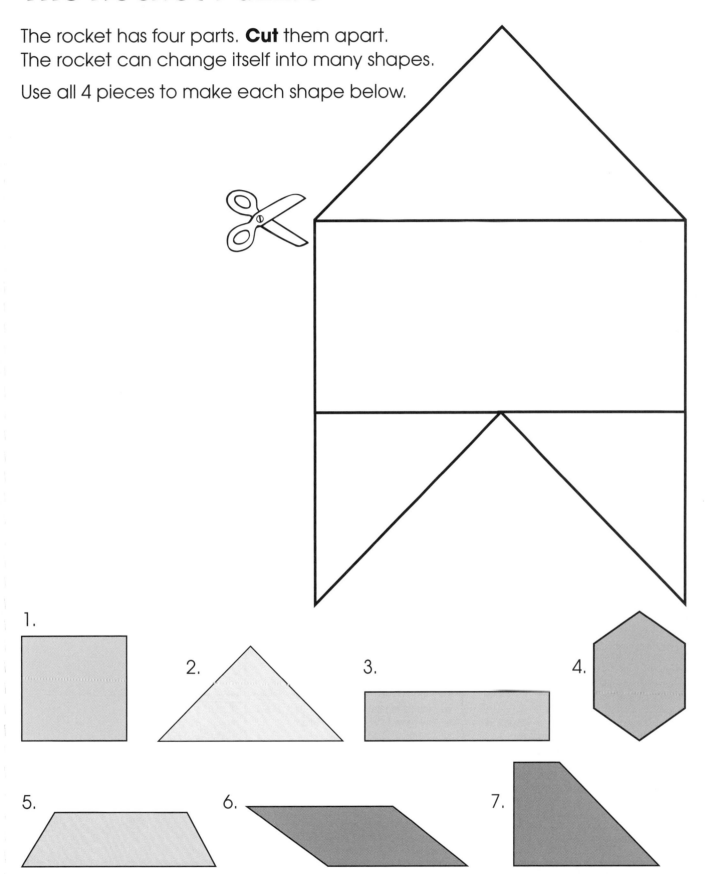

1.

2.

3.

4.

5.

6.

7.

Learn at Home, Grade 4

	Language Skills	Spelling	Reading
Monday	Have your child choose a character from history that he/she has studied. Help him/her gather reference books and biographies about this person from the library. Ask him/her to write about this character in the form of a dialogue. Encourage your child to be creative but true to history (historical fiction). Have your child work on a rough draft of a conversation between the historical figure and another person (possibly him/herself).	Pretest your child on these spelling words. coffee enough photo cough graph rough different half sniffle elephant laughter telephone elf oneself tough Have your child correct the pretest, add personalized words and make two copies of this week's study list.	Have your child continue reading *The Borrowers* this week (chapter 6). Reading Journal activities are included in the lesson plans.
Tuesday	Have your child tell you what he/she is learning in Science this week. Write his/her words on the chalkboard. Have your child copy the dictated sentences for handwriting practice.	Have your child use each of this week's spelling words correctly in a sentence.	**Reading Journal:** (chapter 7) Have your child draw a picture of the house from Arrietty's perspective beginning at the doormat.
Wednesday	A sentence fragment is missing either a subject or a predicate. Provide examples of sentence fragments and have your child identify what is missing. Then, have him/her turn the fragments into complete sentences. *See* Language Skills, Week 16, number 1.	Have your child complete **Elf on an Elephant** (p. 189).	**Reading Journal:** (chapter 8) What would happen if someone closed the front door while Arrietty was outside?
Thursday	Run-on sentences contain more than one complete thought without proper punctuation or connecting words. *See* Language Skills, Week 16, numbers 2 and 3. Have your child complete **Run-On Sentences** (p. 188).	Have your child write a short story about an adventure that Arrietty (from *The Borrowers*) might have, using several of this week's spelling words. After the story is complete, have your child underline each of the spelling words used.	Continue reading *The Borrowers* (chapters 9 and 10).
Friday	Write ten run-on sentences on the chalkboard. Have your child correct the sentences by either adding ending punctuation or a comma and a connecting word.	Give your child the final spelling test. Have him/her record the pretest and final test words in his/her word bank.	**Reading Journal:** (chapter 11) Have your child write a letter to Arrietty recommending how she should handle the letter and the boy. Should she talk to the boy again? Should she tell her parents? Encourage your child to be persuasive and argue his/her point of view.

Math	Science	Social Studies
Define *perimeter*. The perimeter of a closed figure is its outside boundary. Measure the perimeter of a figure by measuring each side and adding the measurements together. *See* Math, Week 16, number 1. Have your child measure the perimeter of objects around the room, recording each measurement on paper in the units used to measure each (cm, in., ft., etc.).	Help your child prove that different amounts of matter can fill the same amount of space. *Density* is defined as the amount of matter in a given space. *See* Science, Week 16, numbers 1 and 2.	Native Americans today have a very different lifestyle from that of their ancestors. Some tribes living on reservations have been able to maintain some of their traditions. Most Native Americans, however, live in urban areas. If possible, have your child interview a Native American living in your community. Help your child generate a list of questions prior to the interview. Make sure your child writes a thank you note after the interview.
Define *area*. Area is a measure of the surface of an object. Area is the number of square units that will fit inside a flat figure. Discuss when it would be useful to know the area of a shape (measuring a floor for carpeting or a wall for paint). *See* Math, Week 16, number 2. Have your child measure the area of several square and rectangular objects (a name tag, a stamp, a desktop, the floor, a bulletin board).	Compare the densities of water and maple syrup. Pour a half cup of each liquid into two identical containers and place the containers on a balance scale. Your child should note that the syrup is heavier. Discuss that more particles of matter are packed into the denser (heavier) liquid. Have your child pour the water into a clear glass, then pour the syrup into the water and observe. Have your child describe and explain the interaction in writing.	Many Native Americans have become famous figures in the areas of sports, entertainment, politics and literature. Read about Native Americans that have become famous. *See* Social Studies, Week 16, number 1.
Have your child imagine that he/she has a present to wrap. He/she will need a box and will need to purchase wrapping paper that is sold by area. Help your child measure the area of each surface on the box and add the measurements together to determine the total area. Then, have your child write a sentence telling how much wrapping paper he/she will need.	Solids are usually more dense than liquids, and liquids are usually more dense than gases. Draw pictures to illustrate how the particles of matter in each are spread apart or tightly packed together. Is ice (solid water) more or less dense than liquid water? Have your child explain.	Pose the following question: *If a certain activity is not allowed off reservations, should it be allowed on reservations because of agreements made long ago?* Read about a current issue such as gambling or net fishing. *See* Social Studies, Week 16, number 2. Have your child write an argument supporting his/her beliefs on an issue.
Introduce *volume*. Volume can be measured as the number of cubes needed to fill a box. Give your child a small box and many square blocks (cubes). Ask him/her to fill the box with blocks and count the total number of blocks.	Different liquids have different densities. Conduct an experiment to demonstrate this concept. Work together to pour a variety of liquids into a clear glass cylinder, then float objects in the various layers. *See* Science, Week 16, number 3. Have your child record the results of the experiment with drawings and written explanations.	Discuss whether Native American children should go to public schools or separate schools where they experience their own culture. Discuss the advantages and disadvantages of each type of school.
Have your child build three-dimensional rectangular structures with blocks. Have your child determine volume by counting the number of blocks used.	Add kosher salt to tap water to make the water more dense. Have your child find objects that float in the salt water but do not float in the tap water. (Try an egg.) If your child has ever been in the ocean, he/she may relate this concept to floating in the ocean compared to floating in a lake or pool. Challenge your child to think of a magic trick using the two densities of water to amaze his/her friends.	Many Native Americans are concerned about losing their culture in mainstream society. Only a few of the over 300 original languages are still spoken today. This is a result of many different factors. The extended family cannot stay together in urban settings. The environmental focus of Native Americans has become difficult to maintain as well. What would your child do if your family stopped practicing some of his/her favorite family traditions?

Learn at Home, Grade 4

TEACHING SUGGESTIONS AND ACTIVITIES

LANGUAGE SKILLS (Simple Sentences)

▶ 1. Review what it takes to make a complete sentence: a *subject* and a *predicate*. Write some sentence fragments on the chalkboard. Help your child identify what is missing from each fragment. Encourage him/her to supply a creative subject or predicate to complete each sentence fragment.

Sample fragments:

Ran all the way home from the store.
Went to the game together.
The big green ball on Bobby's porch.
Needed to be watered.
The police officer in the middle of the street directing traffic.
The two-toed, green monster.
Ate mushroom stew quickly and greedily.

▶ 2. Write the following run-on sentence on the chalkboard: *Mom made a chocolate cake for my birthday she put nine candles on it.* Have your child read the sentence without taking a breath until the period. Ask him/her to explain what is wrong with the sentence. Discuss how to correct the problem: either add ending punctuation to make two sentences or add a comma and a conjunction to make a compound sentence.

Mom made a chocolate cake for my birthday. She put nine candles on it.
Mom made a chocolate cake for my birthday, and she put nine candles on it.

▶ 3. Sample run-on sentences:

Marvin and Toby went to the movies they shared popcorn and soda.
They laughed through most of the movie it was funny.
After the movie they went home for dinner they were not hungry.
Toby ate supper later that night Marvin skipped supper.

MATH (Geometry)

▶ 1. Provide your child with measuring tools and objects to measure. Measuring tools may include a ruler, meterstick, yardstick or a non-standard unit such as a Unifix cube. Objects may include tables, desks, books, toys, small drawn shapes and appliances. To record the perimeter measurements, have your child write the name of the object measured followed by its measurement and the units used.

▶ 2. To find the area of a rectangle or square, multiply length times width.
Write the answer in square units:

```
  4 cm
x 3 cm
 12 square cm (cm²)
```

SCIENCE (Physical Properties)

▶ 1. Have your child compare a bag of flour and a bag of potato chips (about the same size). He/she should observe that the flour is much heavier, even though the bags are nearly the same size. Explain that the flour is more dense or has a greater density. Have your child find other pairs of objects that have different densities. (Compare a bowling ball to a beach ball. Compare a cement block to a wooden block. Compare a pillow to a folded blanket.)

2. Relate density observations to Social Studies. Discuss population density. Compare the number of people living within a square mile in the country to the number of people living within a square mile in the city. Also compare population densities of different cities (e.g., New York, NY and Pierre, SD) or countries (e.g., China and Canada).

3. Use a clear glass cylinder such as a vase. Pour equal amounts of each of the liquids listed below into the cylinder. (Use between 2 tablespoons and $1/2$ cup, depending on the diameter of the cylinder. The liquid should be about $1/2$-inch deep in the cylinder.) Pour the liquids in the order listed. Pour them slowly down the side of the tilted cylinder to prevent mixing. Since the syrup is sticky, it should be poured directly in the bottom and not along the side. Have your child drop small pieces of the objects listed below into the liquid layers. Ask him/her to observe and record where each item settles. Discuss the relative densities of the objects. Have your child observe and record the layers of liquids as he/she determines which liquids are most dense.

Liquids:
maple syrup
glycerin
(can be found at a drug store)
blue dishwashing liquid
water
vegetable oil
rubbing alcohol

Solid objects:
foil pressed into a small ball
rubber
hardwood such as oak
a cork
softwood such as pine
plastic
lead such as a fishing sinker
a raisin

SOCIAL STUDIES (Native Americans)

1. Have your child research a famous Native American from the twentieth century. Have him/her write a brief biography of that person's accomplishments and draw a portrait. Possible subjects might include Jim Thorpe (athlete), Wilma Mankiller (chief) and Graham Greene (actor).

2. Several Native American reservations have used their lands for commercial endeavors. Some get oil from the land. Others have built golf courses or filling stations on them. Still others have established gambling casinos. All bring money to the tribe. Discuss several of these issues with your child. Then, ask him/her to choose a position (for or against) on one of these issues and argue it.

Run-On Sentences

A **sentence** expresses a clear thought. But if two or more sentences are written together without punctuation, their meaning is confusing. This is called a **run-on sentence**.

Example: The artist has painted twenty portraits the paintings will be displayed in the new museum.

The artist has painted twenty portraits.

The paintings will be displayed in the new museum.

Read each diary entry below. **Rewrite** each run-on sentence as two or more good sentences.

Dear Diary,

After lunch we went to the animal shelter the cages were full of adorable pets to adopt we chose a frisky two-year-old brown dog.

_____

_____

_____

_____

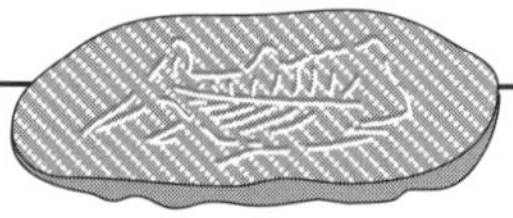

Dear Diary,

While we were on our field trip my friend, Joe, found an animal fossil Mrs. Roberts is taking it to the university tomorrow.

_____

_____

_____

_____

Elf on an Elephant

Use the spelling words to **fill in** the blanks.
Look for a cause/effect relationship in each situation.

1. **cause:** cutting in _____
   effect: sharing a candy bar

2. **cause:** having a _____
   effect: covering your mouth

3. **cause:** hearing the _____
   effect: answering "hello"

4. **cause:** reading about an _____
   effect: enjoying a fairy tale

5. **cause:** telling a joke
   effect: hearing _____

6. **cause:** having a _____
   effect: blowing your nose

coffee
cough
different
elephant
elf
enough
graph
half
laughter
oneself
photo
rough
sniffle
telephone
tough

Complete these statements by **filling in** the blanks.

1. An antonym for "alike" is _____.

2. An antonym for "fragile" is _____.

3. An antonym for "smooth" is _____.

4. A kind of beverage is _____.

5. The word that is a pronoun is _____.

Four words have not been used. Use two of them in one sentence and the
other two in a separate sentence. Underline the words.

_____

_____

_____

189

	Language Skills	Spelling	Reading
Monday	Copy the story outline for writing fiction from Language Skills, Week 17, number 1. With your child, brainstorm some characters and possible problems. Have your child take a character from a familiar story and create a new problem for the character. Have your child write a fictional story, following the fiction outline as a guide.	Pretest your child on these spelling words. argue few queue beautiful hue review beauty mew view cue newt you feud pew yule Have your child correct the pretest, add personalized words and make two copies of this week's study list.	**Digraphs** *Digraphs* are made of two consonants that, when paired, lose their individual sounds. Digraphs include *ph, gh, gn, kn, ch, sh* and *ck*. Write words containing digraphs on the chalkboard. Have your child say each word aloud and identify the digraphs. How would the word be pronounced if the letters of the digraph retained their individual sounds? Read chapters 12 and 13 in *The Borrowers*.
Tuesday	For handwriting practice, have your child write his/her mailing address. Have your child use his/her best cursive handwriting to write the address several times. Encourage correct capitalization and punctuation.	Have your child use each of this week's spelling words correctly in a sentence.	Read words containing digraphs. Then, have your child look for digraphs in *The Borrowers*. *See* Reading, Week 17, numbers 1-6. **Reading Journal:** (chapter 14) What do you think happened to Aunt Lupy?
Wednesday	Teach your child to avoid using double negatives in his/her writing. *See* Language Skills, Week 17, number 2. Have your child complete **Double Negatives** (p. 194).	Have your child complete **You Are Beautiful** (p. 195).	Read chapters 15–17 in *The Borrowers*. **Reading Journal:** Describe the characters in the book. What are they like? Describe their personalities. Are they careful, adventurous, tidy, friendly, snooty? Does Arrietty remind you of someone you know?
Thursday	Teach the proper placement of negative words in a sentence. *See* Language Skills, Week 17, number 3.	Have your child write a rhyme using this week's spelling words. Use the meter of a familiar rhyme, such as "Jack and Jill."	**Reading Journal:** (chapter 18) Predict how the boy will help the Borrowers now that Mrs. Driver has found them. Do you think the Borrowers are stealing?
Friday	Publish your child's revised and edited fictional story. Ask him/her to copy the story neatly on the pages of a blank book, adding illustrations if desired. Have your child decorate the cover and make a title page for the book. Add the book to your personal library.	Give your child the final spelling test. Have your child record the pretest and final test words in his/her word bank.	With your child, finish reading *The Borrowers*. **Reading Journal:** (chapters 19 and 20) Read the last sentence of the book. Did the Borrowers really exist or did Mrs. May's brother make it all up? Make a decision and write supporting arguments for your choice.

Math	Science	Social Studies
Teach your child how to use a compass to make circles of different sizes. Give him/her time to practice. Have your child draw a picture of overlapping circles. *See* Math, Week 17, number 1.	Sometimes a scientist needs to determine the elements that form a substance. In order to identify the parts that make up the whole, a scientist needs to be able to separate a mixture and identify matter by its measurable and observable attributes, state (solid, liquid or gas) and density. Teach your child different methods for separating mixtures. *See* Science, Week 17, number 1.	Before 1924, when the Indian Citizenship Act was passed, Native Americans were not necessarily citizens of the U.S. Have your child imagine that he/she is living prior to 1924. Have him/her write a letter to a newspaper editor arguing for Native American citizenship. Remind him/her to give supporting reasons.
Define *radius* and *diameter*. Draw circles of various sizes. Draw in the radius and diameter of each. Have your child measure each. Lead him/her to discover that all points on a circle are the same distance from the center and that the diameter of a circle is always twice the length of its radius.	Provide your child with a substance that is difficult to separate such as rice and flour. Challenge him/her to find different ways to separate the mixture (e.g., turn a fan on to blow away the flour, use a mesh sieve).	Discuss whether the U.S. government acted fairly by moving the Native Americans from their homelands to reservations. What are some arguments for and against this action? Ask your child how the area in which he/she lives would be different if there were no reservations.
Have your child draw several circles by tracing objects such as lids or glasses. Have him/her find the radius and diameter of each circle.	Provide your child with a mixture such as sugar and sand. Challenge him/her to find different ways to separate the mixture. To separate this mixture, your child must try a process such as dissolving or heating.	Native Americans legends are passed on orally from generation to generation. The legends keep alive beliefs, tribal laws and culture. Legends often explain the spiritual and physical worlds. Read several Native American legends with your child. You can find a variety at the library or bookstore. After reading, have your child write a summary of the story and a description of the main idea or lesson of the legend.
Review patterns and shapes. Have your child complete **Circles and Squares** (p. 196).	Read about Robert Boyle in an encyclopedia. Boyle was a founder of modern chemistry. He worked with gases and explored the makeup of basic elements. Have your child write an essay about Robert Boyle, including an explanation telling why his work is important.	Read more Native American legends together and have your child write summaries as described yesterday.
Review patterns and shapes. Have your child complete a copy of **The Weird Worm Puzzle** (p. 197).	Finish yesterday's lesson.	Let your child choose from the activity suggestions related to legends. *See* Social Studies, Week 17, numbers 1–5.

TEACHING SUGGESTIONS AND ACTIVITIES

LANGUAGE SKILLS (Writing)

▶ 1. Use the outline below to help your child get ready to write fiction.

Subject: _____

Setting: where _____

_____

when _____

Characters: Name _____ Description _____

Name _____ Description _____

Name _____ Description _____

Main Plot: _____

Subplot(s): _____

_____

_____

Climax: _____

Ending: _____

▶ 2. List words that are negatives (*not, no, never, none, no one, nobody, nothing, nowhere*) and contractions containing a negative such as *can't (cannot), doesn't (does not)* and *won't (will not)*. Explain that it is never correct to use two negatives in a sentence. Write the following sentences on the board and discuss the difference:

The store didn't have no paper plates.
The store didn't have any paper plates.
Write several sentences containing double negatives. Have your child correct each sentence.

▶ 3. Write the following examples to show that the words *no* and *any* appear in a sentence before the noun:

There were no *cookies in the cookie jar.*
No leaves were on the trees.
I do not have any *candy left.*
Brenda doesn't want any *broccoli salad.*

Write the following examples to show that the word *not* usually appears before a verb in the sentence:

We will not *play in the rain.*
Flowers will not *grow without water and sunlight.*
I can't understand why the bus is late.

READING (Diagraphs)

▶ 1. Write the words *elephant, photograph, telephone* and *phonics*. Have your child read the words and identify the digraph in each (*ph*). Look for other words that contain the *ph* digraph.

▶ 2. Write the words *enough, laughter, tough* and *rough*. Have your child read the words and identify the digraph in each (*gh*).

▶ 3. Write the words *through, thought, sigh, fighter* and *straight*. Have your child read the words and indicate what letters are silent (*gh*).

▶ 4. Write the words *ghost, ghetto* and *ghastly*. Have your child read the words and state the second sound that the *gh* digraph makes.

▶ 5. Write the words *chair, pitcher, lunch* and *reach*. Have your child read the words and identify the digraph in each (*ch*).

6. Write the words *school, chemistry, architect, chorus* and *choir*. Have your child read the words and state the second sound that the *ch* digraph makes.

MATH (Geometry)

1. On a sheet of white drawing paper, have your child draw several overlapping circles of different sizes. Ask him/her to choose one circle to be the top circle and color it completely and dark. Using different colors, have your child color the other circles, but only the parts that do not fall behind already colored circles.

SCIENCE (Physical Properties)

1. Provide your child with a simple mixture such as rocks and sand. Challenge him/her to find a way to separate the mixture. He/she may pick out the rocks by hand, shake the mixture in a pail to let the sand settle to the bottom, use a sieve or try another creative method. Encourage your child to think of other ways he/she might have separated the mixture. Explain that scientists look at each mixture to determine the best method of separation.

SOCIAL STUDIES (Native Americans)

1. Compare and contrast Native American legends with other legends, myths and fables. How do legends and myths explain natural phenomena?

2. Have your child practice reading a legend until he/she can tell it from memory. Remind him/her to use expression and a variety of voices to make the story interesting. You may have him/her tell the legend to a group of young children at a local story hour.

3. Compare and contrast the recurring characters of Native American legends to characters in other myths and legends (e.g., coyote and rabbit).

4. Help your child perform a legend as a puppet show.

5. Compare stories that offer different explanations for the same spiritual or physical event or phenomenon.

Learn at Home, Grade 4

Double Negatives

Only use one negative word in a sentence.
Not, **no**, **never** and **none** are negative words.

Examples:

Incorrect: No one nowhere was sad when it started to snow.
Correct: No one anywhere was sad when it started to snow.

Incorrect: There weren't no icicles hanging from the roof.
Correct: There weren't any icicles hanging from the roof.

Underline the word in parentheses to say no correctly.

1. There wasn't (no, any) snow on our grass this morning.

2. I couldn't find anyone (nowhere, anywhere) who wanted to build a snowman.

3. We couldn't believe that (no one, anyone) wanted to stay inside today with all the beautiful snow outside to play in.

4. We shouldn't ask (anyone, no one) to go ice skating with us.

5. None of the students could think of (nothing, anything) to do at recess except play in the newly fallen snow!

6. No one (never, ever) thought it was a waste of time to go ice skating on the pond.

7. Not a single student skiing (nowhere, anywhere) was unhappy yesterday!

Replace the negative in parentheses.

1. You shouldn't (never)_____ play catch with a snowball unless you like to be covered with snow.

2. Isn't (no one) _____ going to join me outside to eat icicles?

3. There wasn't (nothing)_____ wrong with using the clean, fresh snow to make our fruit drinks.

4. The snowman outside isn't (nowhere)_____ as large as the statue in front of our school.

5. Falling snow isn't (no) _____ fun if you can't go out and play in it.

You Are Beautiful

argue
beautiful
beauty
cue
feud
few
hue
mew
newt
pew
queue
review
view
you
yule

Write the spelling words that contain the letters **ew** or **iew** (as the **yoo** sound) in alphabetical order.

1. _____   4. _____
2. _____   5. _____
3. _____   6. _____

Use the spelling words to **fill in** the blanks. Not all words are used; one is used twice.

1. TV announcers read from ☐ __ __ cards.

2. It's good manners to say "Thank __☐__"

    when someone gives you something.

3. A cat says ☐ __ __.

4. A church seat is called a ☐ __ __.

5. Christmas is sometimes called __ __ ☐ __.

6. Roses are __ __ __ __ __ ☐ __ __ __ flowers.

7. A hungry kitten says ☐ __ __.

8. Look at the __ __ ☐ __ out the window.

9. A salamander is related to a ☐ __ __ __.

10. __ __ __ __ ☐ __ is only skin-deep.

Read the letters in the box to **answer** the question: What have you received if someone says, "You are beautiful"? _____

What three spelling words have not been used?

_____   _____   _____

Circles and Squares

Shade the correct shapes to keep each pattern going.

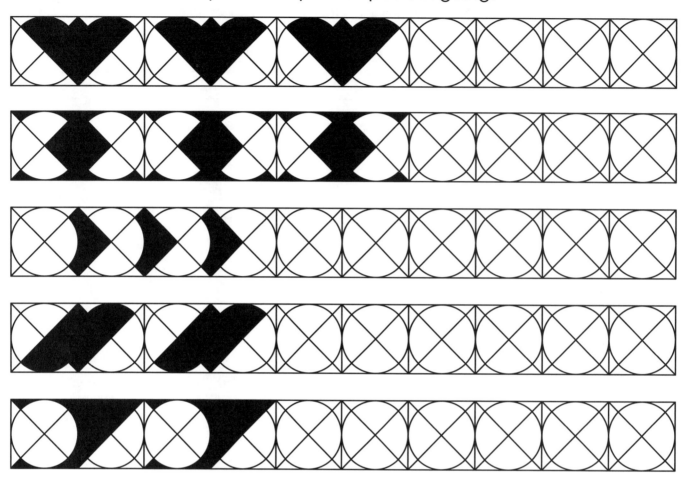

Make your own patterns using two colors.

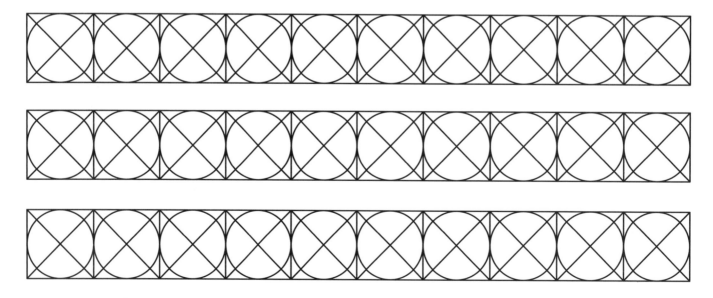

Learn at Home, Grade 4

The Weird Worm Puzzle

- **Cut out** the Weird Worm.
- **Fold** on the dashed lines.
- **Trace** the fold lines on the back.
- **Fold** flat to make each shape below.

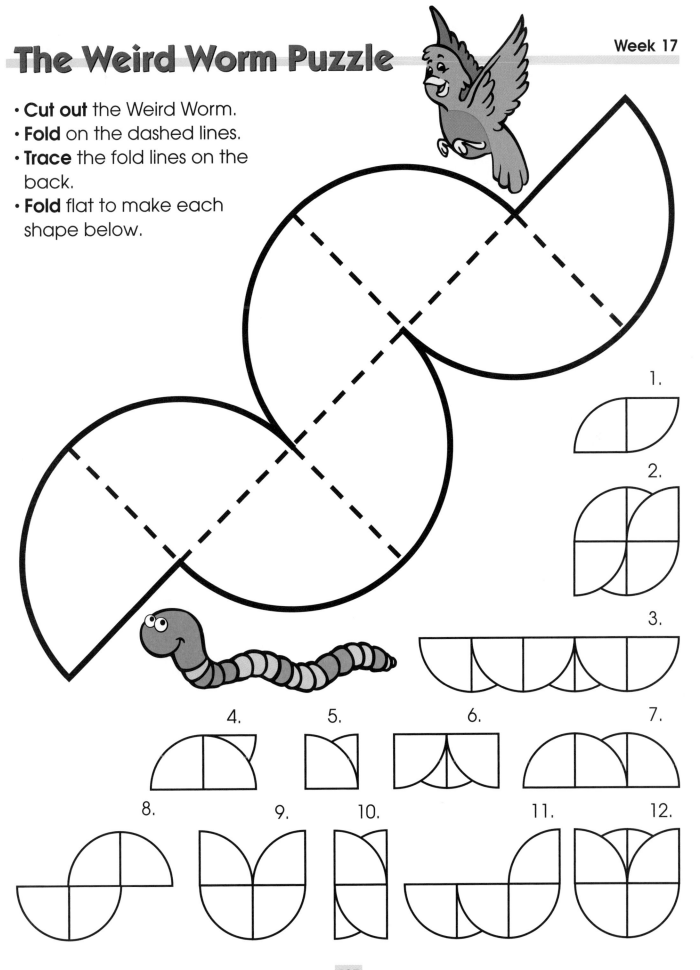

1.

2.

3.

4.   5.   6.   7.

8.   9.   10.   11.   12.

Language Skills	Spelling	Reading
Monday **Review Week** Review with your child the proper use of commas. Write sentences using commas in the following ways: commas in series, commas in a friendly letter, commas in a date and commas in a direct quotation. Write several sentences on the chalkboard, omitting all commas. Assess your child's understanding by having him/her add missing commas to your sentences.	**Review Week** Choose words from the past 8 weeks for the pretest. Pretest your child on these spelling words. Have your child correct the pretest. Make a study list of misspelled words, if any. Remind your child to study the words each day this week.	**Review Week** Review main idea. Discuss why it is important to recognize the main idea of a paragraph, chapter or conversation. Have your child complete **What a Day!** (p. 204).
Tuesday Review capitalization and abbreviations. Have your child correct these sentences: *the bus was late.* *We saw mr keeler at the store.* *The local library is not open on mondays.* *the recipe calls for 1 tsp of vanilla.* *when gretchen was ill, we called dr lee.* Have your child complete **Capitalize I, Names and Initials** (p. 202).	Scramble the letters of each spelling word from the past 8 weeks. Have your child unscramble the words and write them.	Review cause and effect. The ability to recognize cause and effect in a story will help your child read more critically. Give your child several groups of sentences that include both a cause and an effect. **Example:** *The snow came down harder than anyone could ever remember. For days the people of the village were housebound.* Base your sentences on *The Borrowers.* Have your child identify the cause and effect in each group.
Wednesday Assess your child's understanding of subject/verb agreement. *See* Language Skills, Week 18, number 1.	Make up a code with your child's help. Use the code to write review spelling words. Have him/her decode the words.	Review character analysis. Guide your child to think about characters in books read recently. Discuss your child's favorite characters and ask him/her to explain what he/she likes about them. Have your child complete **Lucky Beth or Lucky Kim?** (p. 205).
Thursday Assess your child's ability to identify complete sentences. A complete sentence must contain a subject and a predicate. *See* Language Skills, Week 18, number 2.	Have your child look up spelling words in the dictionary. Then, have him/her write the proper pronunciation on cards in the word bank.	Review dictionary skills. Write ten sentences on the chalkboard. Include a word in each sentence that is unfamiliar to your child. Erase the unfamiliar words from the sentences and write them in a different order in a word bank. Have your child look up the words in the dictionary and write them in the correct sentences.
Friday Review compound sentences. Have your child complete **Commas With Compound Sentences** (p. 203).	Give your child the final spelling test.	Review guide words. Have your child complete **Shootin' Hoops** (p. 206).

Math	Science	Social Studies
Review Week Review the relationship between division and multiplication. Provide your child with a division fact (24 ÷ 6). Have him/her draw a representation or build a model of the fact and solve it. Then, ask him/her to write two related multiplication facts. Reteach, if necessary.	**Review Week** Assess your child's knowledge of Earth changes. Ask him/her to name some ways that Earth changes. Reteach, if necessary. Using a blank sheet of paper, have your child draw the seven continents in the correct locations without looking at a map.	**Review Week** Ask your child questions to review the study of Native Americans. Reteach concepts, if necessary. *See* Social Studies, Week 18, number 1.
Discuss reasons for finding the average of several numbers (baseball scores, test scores, temperatures over time). Teach the procedure of adding the numbers and dividing by the number of "events" (or addends). Have your child complete **Work It Out** (p. 207).	Have your child diagram how forces from within the Earth cause Earth changes in the form of volcanoes and earthquakes.	Let your child select one of the tribes studied. Have him/her make a mobile to show the homes, tools, clothing, artifacts, customs and other aspects of that tribe. Use two wire hangers as the frame of the mobile. Put one hanger inside the other at a 90° angle. Hold the hangers together using wire twisties. Hang pictures or objects from the hangers with pieces of yarn.
Have your child complete **Number Puzzles** (p. 208).	Help your child review the Earth's composition by making a model. *See* Science, Week 18, number 1.	Have your child complete the alphabet book of Native American tribes. Be sure he/she includes a cover and title page.
Review geometric shapes. Show your child cutouts of different geometric shapes. Ask him/her to identify each shape. Have your child create a picture of an object or a scene using only geometric shapes. He/she may use as many of each shape as desired.	Assess your child's understanding of the importance of conservation. Have your child design and carry out an effort to recycle a material that is not currently being recycled. Ask him/her to do this either in your home or through an organization to which he/she already belongs.	Review the **Native American Alphabet Book** your child completed on different tribes begun in Week 10. Have your child compile information from the cards in meaningful ways. For example, he/she could draw a map of the United States that includes illustrations of the typical homes of different tribes or areas.
Review the formula for finding area. Look at an atlas with your child. Teach him/her to estimate the size of a state both lengthwise and crosswise. Have your child practice finding an approximate area in square miles for one or two states. Highlight between ten and thirty states on the activity sheet for your child to complete on his/her own. Give your child a copy of **"State"istics** (p. 209).	Assess your child's use of observation skills to determine the identity of some "mysterious white powders." *See* Science, Week 18, number 2.	Review the topic web your child made on the first day of the unit. Discuss what your child has learned. Have your child write what he/she has learned about Native Americans or add to the topic web (*see* Social Studies, Week 10, number 1).

Learn at Home, Grade 4

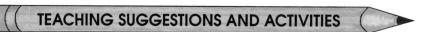

TEACHING SUGGESTIONS AND ACTIVITIES

LANGUAGE SKILLS

▶ 1. Copy the sentences below on the chalkboard. Have your child complete them by filling in the correct form of the present-tense verb in parentheses.

Troy	to ride his bike in the woods. (like)
My family and I	on vacation every summer. (goes)
Sunday, my brothers	football on TV. (watches)
The boy	his fingernails when he is nervous. (chew)
We	to the lake on Saturdays. (drives)

▶ 2. Write the sentences below on the chalkboard. Have your child use colored chalk to draw a line dividing the subject from the predicate in each sentence. Then, have him/her circle the simple subjects and simple predicates in each.

The porcupine makes its home in many parts of the world.
Porcupines eat plants and other foliage.
A porcupine uses sharp quills to ward off enemies.
An enemy will turn and run away from a porcupine.
Dogs and cats that grow up together may play well together.
We baked bread and cooked soup for dinner.
Brian and his father flew a kite at the beach.
In the summer, we like to fish and lie in the sun.

SCIENCE

▶ 1. Help your child make this clay model for a review lesson on the Earth's composition.

   You will need: green, blue, red, gray, white and yellow plasticine clay; knives; a small lemon, a medium apple, a navel orange, a grapefruit (or objects their equivalent sizes); paper; pen or chalk.

   Directions for your child:

   a. Make the Earth's inner core using the gray clay. Roll it into a ball the size of the lemon.

   b. Add red clay around it to make the outer core. The total size should be the size of the apple.

   c. Add yellow clay to make the mantle. This should make the model the size of the orange.

   d. The last layer of the Earth is the crust. Put a $\frac{1}{4}$" white layer of clay around the mantle.

   e. Put on what is visible—a thin layer of blue for water and green for land.

   f. Cut out a wedge to see the cross section of the Earth's different layers.

▶ 2. Place four safe, white household products (i.e., flour, sugar, salt, baking soda, cornstarch, baking powder, epsom salts) in four small plastic cups. Label each cup with a number and record what powder is in each on a separate sheet of paper. Do not tell your child what is in the cups. The purpose of this activity is for your child to use experimentation and observation to identify the mystery powders.

   a. Have your child observe one powder at a time and record all observations in a lab book.

   b. First, have your child describe the powder's appearance and feeling or texture. Emphasize that he/she should not taste the powders or inhale them. Here are some words to get him/her started: lumpy, crystalline, soft, sharp, smooth, dusty, sandy, gritty, grainy, feathery.

   c. Next, have your child place a few drops of water on some of the powder and describe the appearance of the wet powder. Here are some words to get him/her started: lumpy, muddy, clear, slippery, dissolved, greasy, smooth, sticky, soft, streaky.

   d. Then, allow your child to make other observations that will help him/her identify the powders. For example, your child may add vinegar to a powder or stir the powder into a glass of water.

   e. Have your child guess the identity of each powder before you disclose the powder's name.

SOCIAL STUDIES

▶ 1. Ask your child questions that will spark discussion while at the same time review some of the information learned about the history of Native Americans.

   How long ago did the Native Americans enter the Americas? From where did they come?
   How were they able to cross over to the Americas?
   Why didn't they all stay together in one place?
   Before the arrival of the Europeans, how did the Native Americans travel?
   What mode of transportation did the Europeans introduce?
   In what ways did life change for the Native Americans after the arrival of the Europeans?
   Propose what America might be like today if the Europeans had not come.

Capitalize I, Names and Initials

The pronoun **I** is always capitalized. Each part of a person's or pet's name begins with a capital letter.

Examples: I, Mary Ann Smith, Lassie

An initial (the first letter of a name) is always capitalized and is followed by a period.

Example: M. A. Smith

Rewrite each sentence using capital letters correctly.

1. Where did molly parsons get her dog, laddie?

_____

2. Her grandmother, louella cane, bought it for the family.

_____

3. The most unusual pet is tom simpson's parrot named showboat.

_____

4. I have heard showboat say words quite clearly.

_____

5. Tom says his parrot's full name is a. h. showboat.

_____

6. What do the initials a. h. stand for?

_____

7. tom told me that his parrot's first name is always and his middle name is hungry.

_____

8. i call my dog "m. m." instead of megan mae.

_____

Follow each direction carefully.

1. Write your full name. _____

2. Write the full name and initials of one of your parents.

_____

3. Use the pronoun "I" to tell what you like to eat best.

_____

Commas With Compound Sentences

A **compound sentence** contains two simple sentences joined by a comma and a connecting word such as "and." The simple sentences must be about the same topic.

Example: Jane helps prepare dinner, and Pat sets the table.

Write compound on the line if it is a compound sentence and add the needed comma. **Write no** on the line if it is not a compound sentence.

1. The porpoise looks very much like a fish. _____

2. It is a mammal and it bears its young alive. _____

3. The porpoise resembles and is closely related to the dolphin. _____

4. The top of a porpoise is mostly black and its underside is white. _____

5. It searches out and eats small fish and shellfish. _____

6. A mother porpoise has just one baby and that baby is large. _____

7. The mother nurses the baby while swimming through the water. _____

8. Porpoises seem to like humans and they have saved people who were drowning. _____

9. Porpoises are social animals and swim in large groups. _____

10. Porpoises often travel with tuna and they are sometimes caught in the tuna nets. _____

Use a comma and the word *and* to combine each pair of sentences.

1. Most species of dolphins live only in salt water. They can be found in almost all the oceans. _____

_____

2. The word "dolphin" also refers to a big game fish. This fish is good to eat.

_____

What a Day!

Read the story that goes with each picture. **Write** the word which best describes each day on the line.

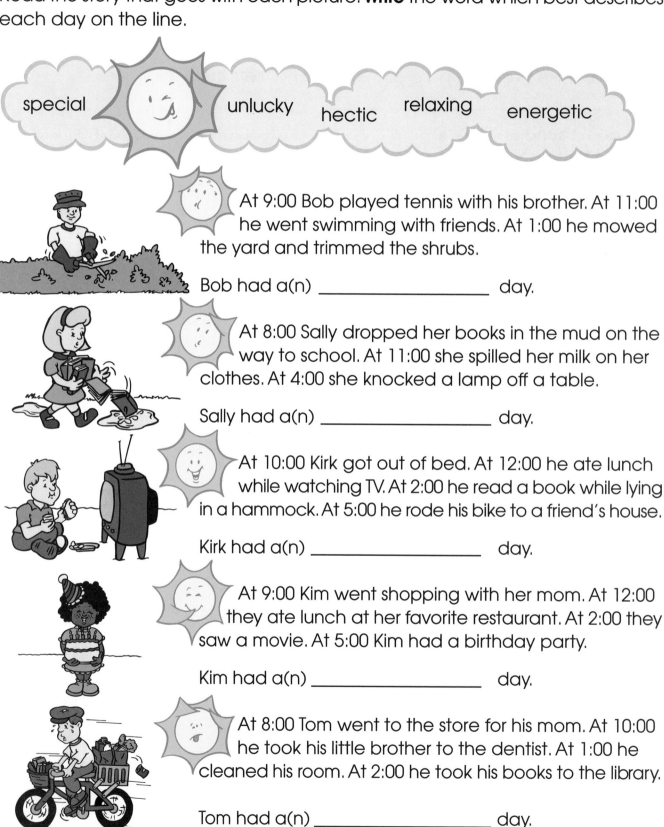

special   unlucky   hectic   relaxing   energetic

At 9:00 Bob played tennis with his brother. At 11:00 he went swimming with friends. At 1:00 he mowed the yard and trimmed the shrubs.

Bob had a(n) _____ day.

At 8:00 Sally dropped her books in the mud on the way to school. At 11:00 she spilled her milk on her clothes. At 4:00 she knocked a lamp off a table.

Sally had a(n) _____ day.

At 10:00 Kirk got out of bed. At 12:00 he ate lunch while watching TV. At 2:00 he read a book while lying in a hammock. At 5:00 he rode his bike to a friend's house.

Kirk had a(n) _____ day.

At 9:00 Kim went shopping with her mom. At 12:00 they ate lunch at her favorite restaurant. At 2:00 they saw a movie. At 5:00 Kim had a birthday party.

Kim had a(n) _____ day.

At 8:00 Tom went to the store for his mom. At 10:00 he took his little brother to the dentist. At 1:00 he cleaned his room. At 2:00 he took his books to the library.

Tom had a(n) _____ day.

Lucky Beth or Lucky Kim?

Kim thinks Beth is so lucky. Almost every day, Beth comes to school with something new. One day, she might be wearing a new outfit her mom bought her at the department store where her mom works. The next day, Beth may have something really unique from her father, like a watch that has the days of the week in a foreign language. He brings her gifts when he comes home from traveling on business.

Beth, however, does not think she is so lucky. Beth's mom works until 7 p.m. every night and also has to work every Saturday. Her father travels so much with his job, that Beth is lucky if she gets to see him one week a month. Beth loves her parents, but she wishes they were both home every night and every weekend like Kim's parents so they could do special things together. She also wishes she had a little brother like Kim does so she wouldn't be so lonely.

Check:
Kim thinks Beth is lucky because Beth . . .

☐ gets lots of neat gifts.

☐ doesn't have a brother or sister.

☐ has a father who travels a lot.

Circle:
Beth thinks Kim is lucky because . . .

Kim has a little brother.

Kim doesn't get a lot of new clothes.

Kim's parents are home at night and on the weekends.

Underline:
When something is unique, it is . . .

ugly   special   small   unusual   different

Write:
Who do you think is luckier, Kim or Beth? Why? _____

_____

_____

Learn at Home, Grade 4

Shootin' Hoops

Shoot some hoops but make sure that you shoot them alphabetically into the correct basket. **Write** the words from the basketballs into the correct hoop.

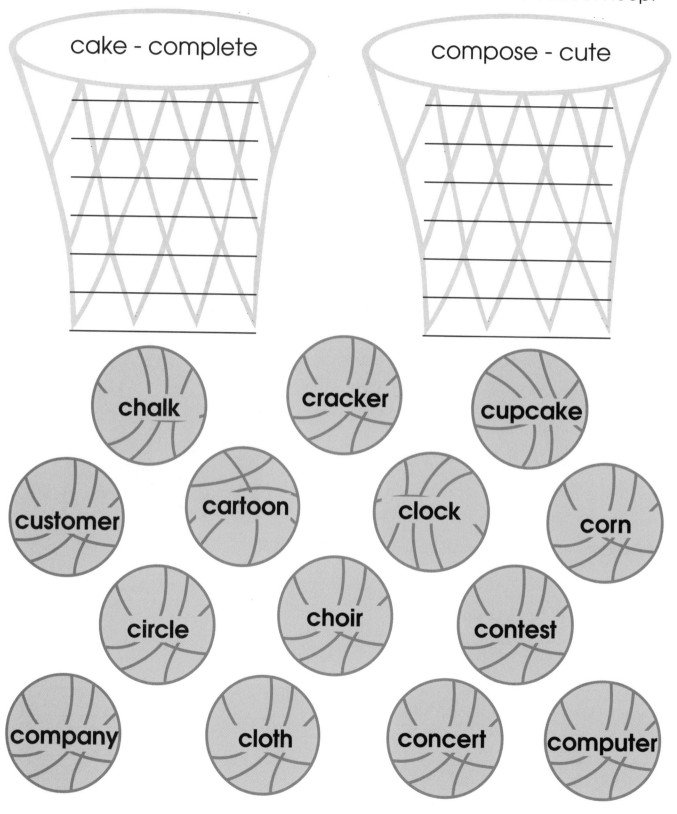

cake - complete

compose - cute

chalk

cracker

cupcake

customer

cartoon

clock

corn

circle

choir

contest

company

cloth

concert

computer

Work It Out

The **average** is the result of dividing the **sum** of addends by the **number** of addends. **Match** the problem with its answer.

1. 80 + 100 + 90 + 95 + 10   _____   A.   53

2. 52 + 56 + 51   _____   B.   190

3. 85 + 80 + 95 + 95 + 100   _____   C.   410

4. 782 + 276 + 172   _____   D.   75

5. 125 + 248 + 214 + 173   _____   E.   93

6. 81 + 82 + 91 + 78   _____   F.   55

7. 40 + 60 + 75 + 45   _____   G.   83

8. 278 + 246   _____   H.   33

9. 75 + 100 + 100 + 70 + 100   _____   I.   3

10. 0 + 0 + 0 + 0 + 15   _____   J.   262

11. 21 + 34 + 44   _____   K.   89

12. 437 + 509 + 864 + 274   _____   L.   94

13. 80 + 80 + 100 + 95 + 95   _____   M.   8

14. 4 + 6 + 7 + 12 + 11   _____   N.   90

15. 75 + 100 + 100 + 100 + 95   _____   O.   521

Number Puzzles

1

Write your age. _____

Multiply it by 3. _____

Add 18. _____

Multiply by 2. _____

Subtract 36. _____

Divide by 6.(your age) _____

2

Write any number. _____

Double that number. _____

Add 15. _____

Double again. _____

Subtract 30. _____

Divide by 2. _____

Divide by 2 again. _____

3

Write any 2-digit
number. _____

Double that number. _____

Add 43. _____

Subtract 18. _____

Add 11. _____

Divide by 2. _____

Subtract 18. _____

4

Write the number of
children in your
neighborhood. _____

Double that number. _____

Add 15. _____

Double it again. _____

Subtract 30. _____

Divide by 4. _____

"State"istics

State Name	Approximate Miles E - W	Approximate Miles N - S	Area in Square Miles	State Name	Approximate Miles E - W	Approximate Miles N - S	Area in Square Miles
Alabama				Montana			
Alaska				Nebraska			
Arizona				Nevada			
Arkansas				New Hampshire			
California				New Jersey			
Colorado				New Mexico			
Connecticut				New York			
Delaware				North Carolina			
Florida				North Dakota			
Georgia				Ohio			
Hawaii				Oklahoma			
Idaho				Oregon			
Illinois				Pennsylvania			
Indiana				Rhode Island			
Iowa				South Carolina			
Kansas				South Dakota			
Kentucky				Tennessee			
Louisiana				Texas			
Maine				Utah			
Maryland				Vermont			
Massachusetts				Virginia			
Michigan				Washington			
Minnesota				West Virginia			
Mississippi				Wisconsin			
Missouri				Wyoming			

Learn at Home, Grade 4

Language Skills	Spelling	Reading

Monday

Language Skills: Have your child choose a favorite sports personality, then brainstorm that person's qualities and accomplishments. Help him/her organize the information and write an outline for the story. Then, have your child write a rough draft of his/her nonfiction story.

Spelling: Pretest your child on these spelling words.

anxious	except	sixteen
ax	excuse	sixth
boxes	exercise	taxes
coax	Mexico	Texas
example	saxophone	toxic

Have your child correct the pretest, add personalized words and make two copies of this week's study list.

Reading: **Nonfiction**
Nonfiction books are based on facts. They provide information about people, places and how to make or do things. Introduce *Jackie Robinson and the Story of All-Black Baseball* by Jim O'Connor. Read pages 5–9 together. Is this book fiction or nonfiction? Have your child write in his/her Reading Journal about the events that made it difficult for Jackie to cross the "color line."

Tuesday

Language Skills: Brainstorm a list of six to ten unusual animals with your child. Ask him/her to copy the list of animals in alphabetical order in his/her best cursive handwriting.

Spelling: Have your child use each of this week's spelling words correctly in a sentence.

Reading: Look up Jackie Robinson in an encyclopedia. Talk about how people are listed in encyclopedias by the first letter of their last names. Look at the end of the article for "related articles" and find those as well. Read pages 10–18 of *Jackie Robinson*. **Reading Journal:** How did the baseball careers of blacks in early pro baseball differ from those of white players? What was barnstorming? What made it a hard life? What made it worthwhile?

Wednesday

Language Skills: **Sentence Types:** Teach your child to identify four kinds of sentences: *statement, command, question* and *exclamation*. Give him/her an example of each sentence type. Discuss word order and final punctuation. Have your child write an example of each kind of sentence. Then, read various sentences to the child, and ask him/her to identify the type of each.

Spelling: Have your child complete **"X"citing Words** (p. 215).

Reading: An almanac can be a quick reference for finding facts. Teach your child to use an almanac by helping him/her find references to Jackie Robinson. Read pages 19–24 of *Jackie Robinson*. **Reading Journal:** What tricky pitches were allowed in black baseball? What were some of the stadium difficulties?
Have your child complete **Recalling Details** (p. 216).

Thursday

Language Skills: Write any number of the four kinds of sentences on the chalkboard. Practice fractions by asking your child questions about sentence punctuation. **Examples:** *What fraction of the sentences end with a period? What fraction of the sentences are questions? What fraction of the sentences begin with the word "will"?*
Have your child complete **End Punctuation** (p. 214).

Spelling: Have your child study this week's spelling words by doing some stamp pad spelling. You will need a stamp pad, a pencil with a new eraser and sheets of unlined paper. *See* **Background Information and Supporting Activities** (p. 8).

Reading: Look at a variety of nonfiction books. Study how they are arranged at the library. *See* Reading, Week 19, numbers 1 and 2. List ten to twelve fiction and nonfiction titles. Write each title, along with the author's name and a brief summary, on a sheet of paper. Have your child classify each book as fiction or nonfiction. Read pages 25–34 of *Jackie Robinson*.
Have your child complete **Is It Fiction or Nonfiction?** (p. 217).

Friday

Language Skills: Have your child practice final punctuation and recognizing sentence types with a fun activity. Follow the directions to play "Riddle Match." *See* Language Skills, Week 19, number 1.

Spelling: Give your child the final spelling test. Have your child record pretest and final test words in his/her word bank.

Reading: Read pages 35–48 of *Jackie Robinson and the Story of All-Black Baseball*.
Have your child complete **Skill Search** (p. 218).

Learn at Home, Grade 4

15

Math	Science	Social Studies
Fractions Review the simple fractions $\frac{1}{2}$, $\frac{1}{4}$, $\frac{1}{3}$ and $\frac{1}{10}$. Show models of each fraction and have your child name them. *See* Math, Week 19, number 1. Write each fraction as he/she names it. Model fractions with round candies. Using twelve pieces of candy, have your child divide the candies into two equal groups. What is the fraction symbolized by one group? Both groups? Repeat with thirds, fourths, sixths and twelfths.	**Meteorology** Discuss the science of meteorology and the reasons that people are so interested in weather reports. Help your child build a weather station and learn how to use it this week. Have your child keep a glossary of weather-related words throughout this unit. Help your child make a rain gauge. *See* Science, Week 19, number 1. This gauge will measure all types of precipitation—not just rain.	**Your State** Introduce the state unit. Have your child complete a KWHL chart (*see* Science, Week 4, number 1). Using the state's outline, have your child make a cover for a state book. Encourage him/her to be creative. Keep it in a folder for later use.
Model eighths with orange slices and teach your child how to write a fraction symbolically. Cut an orange into eight equal pieces. Have your child show you one-eighth of the orange. Write $\frac{1}{8}$ on the board and read it aloud. Then, have your child read it aloud for you. Repeat with other fractions. Have your child draw pictures that illustrate the fractions $\frac{1}{8}$, $\frac{2}{8}$, $\frac{3}{8}$, $\frac{4}{8}$, $\frac{5}{8}$, $\frac{6}{8}$, $\frac{7}{8}$ and $\frac{8}{8}$.	Help your child make a barometer. *See* Science, Week 19, number 2 for directions. Explain that a barometer measures air pressure and can be used to predict a change in weather. Store-bought barometers measure air pressure in inches, but the balloon barometer will show if the pressure goes up or down. High pressure usually means good weather. A drop in pressure may indicate a coming storm or strong winds.	Discuss why states have symbols. Find out the meaning behind the symbols for your state. Have your child research and draw your state's symbols, including the state flag, flower, tree and bird, as well as the official seal of the state and any other symbols. Have your child draw each symbol on 9" x 12" paper and explain why each one was selected. Save these pages in the student's state book folder.
Use two colors of blocks to build fractions. Place the blocks in a pile. Have your child choose any five blocks. Have him/her identify the fraction of blocks that are a given color, place them on a sheet of paper, then write the fraction on the paper. Repeat, asking your child to choose another five blocks.	Discuss humidity. Then, help your child build a tool to measure it—a hygrometer. *See* Science, Week 19, number 3 for directions.	Let your child continue working on the state's symbols. Are there any symbols that your child feels do not accurately represent the state? What are they? What would your child suggest as an alternative?
Have your child complete **What Fraction Am I?** (p. 219).	Help your child determine the direction the wind blows by making a weather vane. *See* Science, Week 19, number 4.	Have your child find out what Native American tribes currently live in your state. What tribes used to live in the area? Have your child write a page about the Native Americans who lived or are still living in your state. Have him/her include related illustrations.
Have your child practice naming fractions from various models. First, ask him/her to draw specific pictures, then answer questions about them. *See* Math, Week 19, number 2. Second, have your child name fractions based on different attributes shared by objects. *See* Math, Week 19, number 3.	Have your child make a line graph charting temperature changes over several days. Record the morning temperatures in red and the evening temperatures in blue. Ask the child to plot the data on a graph and analyze it. Continue recording temperatures over the next couple of weeks. Also, help your child design a chart for recording other information gathered at his/her weather station.	Read about the first settlers in your state. Talk about why they settled there. What were the natural resources that attracted them? What was going on in the country as a whole at the time? On 9" x 12" paper, have your child draw a picture of an area of your state that would have been attractive to settlers. Ask your child to draw the area as it might have looked at the time.

Learn at Home, Grade 4

TEACHING SUGGESTIONS AND ACTIVITIES

LANGUAGE SKILLS (Sentence Types)

▷ 1. **Riddle Match**

Preparation: Find or create ten riddles. Write the questions from each riddle on yellow index cards or construction paper squares. Omit the question marks. Write the answers from each riddle on pink index cards or construction paper squares. Omit the final punctuation. Scramble the cards.

Directions for your child: Read the cards and match each question and answer to form the original riddle. Add the final punctuation to each card with a marker or pen.

READING (Nonfiction)

▷ 1. Gather a variety of nonfiction books. Have your child locate the table of contents, index and glossary in each book, if included. Discuss the arrangement and usefulness of each.

▷ 2. Create a scavenger hunt activity sheet to teach your child how to use the table of contents and index of a nonfiction book. Design the activity sheet to be used with one or two specific books. Sample questions: *How many chapters are in this book? In which chapter will you learn about the Revolutionary War? On what page would you look to find the specific causes of the American Revolution? Where would you look to find the meaning of a loyalist? What is the title of the chapter that tells about settling America? On what page does it begin?*

MATH (Fractions)

▷ 1. You can purchase fraction bars, Cuisenaire rods or pattern blocks at a school supply store. These models help your child create fraction models that are consistently sized. These models make adding fractions and illustrating equivalent fractions more concrete for your child.

▷ 2. Give your child directions to draw pictures. Then, ask him/her the questions indicated.

    a. Draw 3 balls on a table and 2 balls on the floor.
    How many balls are on the floor?
    What is the total number of balls?
    What fraction of the balls is on the floor? — $2/5$

    b. Draw 4 apples on the ground and 8 on a tree.
    What fraction of the apples is on the ground? — $4/12$
    What fraction of the apples is on the tree? — $8/12$

    c. Draw 6 black balls and 4 white balls.
    What fraction of the balls is white? — $4/10$
    What fraction of the balls is black? — $6/10$

▷ 3. Collect several buttons. You will need boxes or bags to hold the buttons in small groups. Put a different number of buttons in each box or bag. Write one color or attribute on the outside of the box or bag such as *blue* or *two holes*. Your child should write the color or attribute on a sheet of lined paper, then name the fraction of buttons in that bag or box that shares the named attribute.

SCIENCE (Meteorology)

▷ 1. Help your child make a rain gauge to measure all types of precipitation.

Directions for the child: Obtain a straight-sided, clear container that will hold water. Tape a ruler to the outside with zero at the base. Face the ruler out so you can read the numbers. Place the rain gauge outside in an open area. To read the rain gauge, measure the height of any collected water in centimeters or inches. Discard any precipitation after each reading.

2. Help your child make a barometer to measure air pressure and predict changes in the weather.

Materials: wide-mouth jar, a round balloon, rubber bands (use more than one to secure the balloon to the jar), broom straw, scissors, tape, black felt-tip pen, paper, tagboard

Directions: Blow up a balloon. Let the air out. Cut the balloon in half and throw away the part with the neck. Stretch the top part over the mouth of the jar. Secure it with a rubber band. Tape a broom straw on top of the stretched balloon. Cut a piece of tagboard a little taller than the jar. Set it up against a wall. Put the barometer next to it with the straw in front of the tagboard.

To Use: Each time you read the barometer, make an extension of the broom straw and write the date and time using a marker. If the broom straw is higher than the last time the barometer was read, mark an up arrow on the weather chart. If it is lower, mark a down arrow. If it is the same, write "steady." Predict what the weather might be in the next 24 hours.

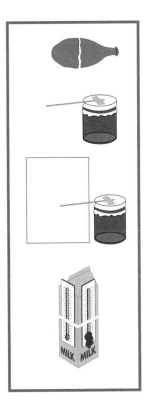

3. Help your child make a hygrometer to measure the humidity in the air.

Materials: 2 room thermometers, a scrap of cotton material, a 1-quart milk carton, string, rubber bands, scissors

Directions: Read the two thermometers first to confirm that they both record the same temperature. Cover the bulb of one thermometer with cotton material and leave a piece of the material hanging an inch below the thermometer. Secure the material to the bulb with string. Use rubber bands to hold the thermometers to two sides of a milk carton. Cut a small hole in the carton just below the covered thermometer. Put the loose end of material into the hole. Pour water in the carton up to the bottom of the hole to keep the material wet. This thermometer is called the wet bulb thermometer. The other is called the dry bulb thermometer. Read the temperature on both thermometers. The wet bulb should be lower.

To Use: Record the temperatures from each thermometer in degrees Fahrenheit. Look in the *World Book Encyclopedia* under "Humidity" for a chart that shows the relative humidity based on the two temperature readings.

4. Help your child make a weather vane to observe the direction of wind flow.

Materials: a 6" x 6" x 2" piece of wood, a long nail, a hammer, a cork, a ruler, scissors, glue, a pen cap, a feather, a directional compass, a black felt-tip pen

Directions: Measure the halfway point of all four sides of the block of wood and mark each one with a dot. Label the four directions (N, S, W and E) over each dot. Draw a diagonal line from one corner to the opposite corner. Repeat this on the other two corners. Hammer a nail in the center where the two diagonals cross. The nail should stick straight up 2 inches. Using scissors, dig a hole in the cork. The hole should be large enough for most of the pen cap to fit in. If it isn't a tight fit, glue the cap into the cork, open end out. Glue a feather across the top of the cork. Put the cork over the nail in the wood block. Refer to a compass to line up N on your weather vane with magnetic north. You will be able to tell which way the wind is blowing because the quill end of the feather will point into the wind.

End Punctuation

A **statement** ends with a period. (.)
A **question** ends with a question mark. (?)
A **command** ends with a period. (.)
An **exclamation** ends with an exclamation point. (!)

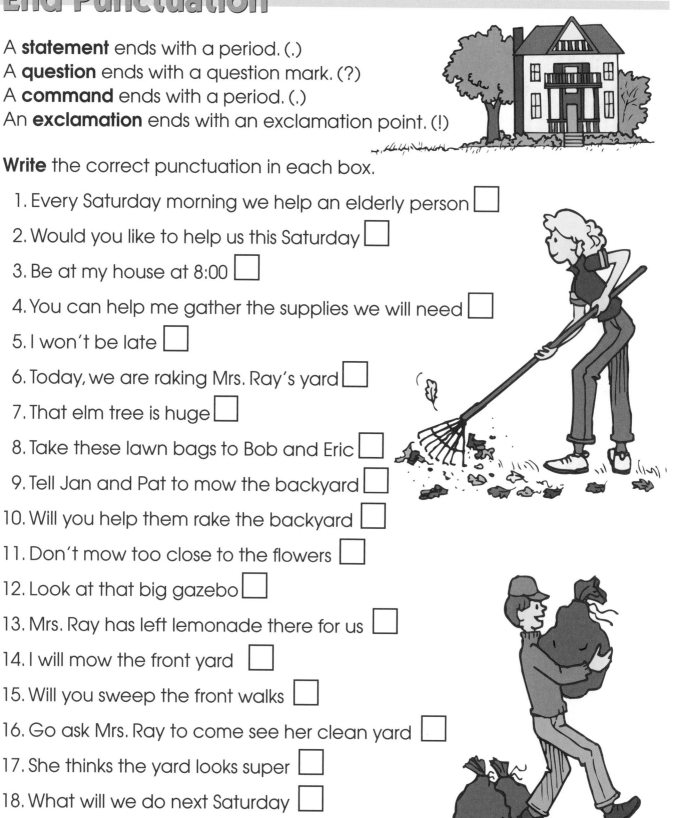

Write the correct punctuation in each box.

1. Every Saturday morning we help an elderly person ☐

2. Would you like to help us this Saturday ☐

3. Be at my house at 8:00 ☐

4. You can help me gather the supplies we will need ☐

5. I won't be late ☐

6. Today, we are raking Mrs. Ray's yard ☐

7. That elm tree is huge ☐

8. Take these lawn bags to Bob and Eric ☐

9. Tell Jan and Pat to mow the backyard ☐

10. Will you help them rake the backyard ☐

11. Don't mow too close to the flowers ☐

12. Look at that big gazebo ☐

13. Mrs. Ray has left lemonade there for us ☐

14. I will mow the front yard ☐

15. Will you sweep the front walks ☐

16. Go ask Mrs. Ray to come see her clean yard ☐

17. She thinks the yard looks super ☐

18. What will we do next Saturday ☐

19. We are helping Mr. Scott shop for groceries ☐

20. Would you like to work with us again ☐

214

"X"citing Words

anxious
ax
boxes
coax
example
except
excuse
exercise
Mexico
saxophone
sixteen
sixth
taxes
Texas
toxic

Fill in the blanks.

1. Write the two proper nouns and circle the country.

   _____   _____

2. A synonym for "eager" is _____ .

3. One _____ of a reed instrument is a _____ .

4. A synonym for "persuade" is _____ .

5. Another word for "hatchet" is _____ .

6. Which word is a preposition? _____

7. Which word refers to poison? _____

8. Which word refers to money collected by the

   government? _____

9. There were _____ _____ of toys for

   the children in the flooded town.

10. Jogging is a type of _____ .

11. He celebrated his _____ birthday on

    the last day of kindergarten.

12. Jane's father did not believe her _____ .

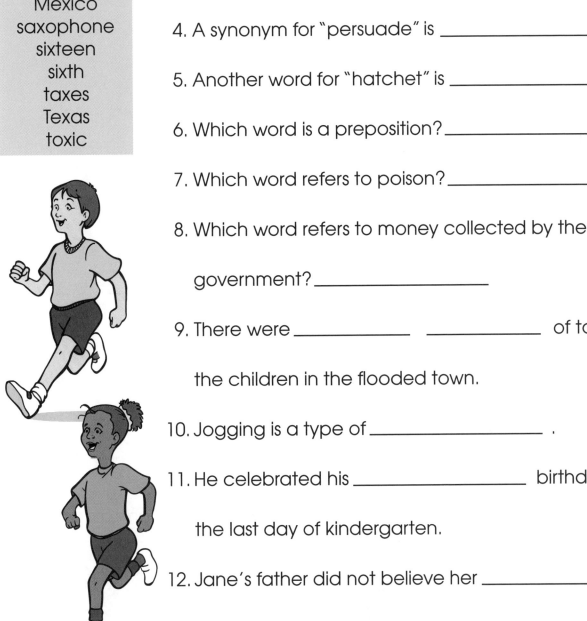

Recalling Details

Read *Jackie Robinson.* Then **write** the answer to each question on the lines.

1. Where is the Baseball Hall of
   Fame located? ◯_ _ _ _ _ _ _ _ _ _ _ _ , _ _ _ _ _ _ _ _

2. Who was the first African American
   to play professional baseball? _ ◯ _ _ _ _ _ _ _ _

3. What is it called when baseball teams travel
   the countryside playing games? ◯_ _ _ _ _ _ _ _ _ _ _

4. What did Rube Foster start
   in 1920? _ _ _ _ _ _ _ ◯_ _ _ _ _ _ _ _ _ _

5. What baseball team made history on April 15, 1947, by having Jackie
   Robinson in the lineup? _ _ _ _ _ _ ◯ _ _ _ _ _ _ _

6. Who was called the "Black Babe Ruth" because
   he hit so many home runs? _ _ _ _ ◯_ _ _ _

7. What position did Satchel Paige play? _ ◯_ _ _ _ _

8. Who was the president and general manager of the
   team that hired Jackie Robinson? _ _ ◯_ _ _ _ _ _ _ _

9. Who was the first African American elected to
   to the Baseball Hall of Fame? _ _ _ _ _ _ _ _ _ _ _ _ _ ◯

10. For what team did Judy Johnson, Oscar Charleston, and Cool Pappa
    Bell play? _ _ ◯_ _ _ _ _ _ _ _ _ _ _ _ _ _ _

11. In 1948, Satchel Paige helped what American League team win
    the World Series? _ _ _ _ _ _ _ _ _ _ _ _ _ _ ◯

Write the circled letters in order on the lines to find out the name of the first
all-black baseball team. _ _ _ _ _ _ _ _ _ _ _ _ _

Is It Fiction Or Nonfiction?

Write on the blank **fiction** or **nonfiction**.

1. *The Chicken and the Dragon* by Arthur C. Feather. This is the story of a dragon who helps a chicken remember his way home.

   _____

2. *The Planets* by Peter Starlight. This book describes the planets in our solar system. Descriptions and pictures of each planet are included.

   _____

3. *Explorers Go to America* by James Boat. This book gives the routes the explorers took to America. Maps and illustrations are given.

   _____

4. *Pinky, the French Poodle* by James Poof-Poof. This is the story of a French poodle with pink fur.

   _____

5. *Dinosaurs of Long Ago* by Peter Tail. This book tells the types of dinosaurs that lived long ago.

   _____

6. *Dogs and Their Owners* by Roger Leash. This book describes the types of ways to train your dog.

   _____

7. *How To Start Your Aquarium* by Peter Fish. This book tells what to buy and how to put it together.

   _____

8. *Sports Legends* by Alvin Bat. This book describes the lives of famous sports stars.

   _____

9. *Flower Designs* by Hilda Vase. This book tells how to arrange flowers for special occasions.

   _____

10. *Hamsters! Hamster! Hamsters!* by Roger Pellet. This book tells how to train and care for your hamster.

    _____

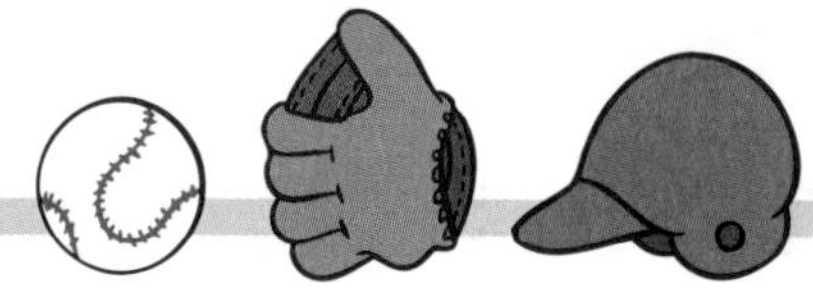

Search through *Jackie Robinson* to find the following:

(p. 5)   1. Four proper nouns: _____

(p. 6)   2. The words before each question mark: _____

(p. 7)   3. Three number words: _____

(p. 9)   4. Two contractions: _____

(p. 10)   5. The name of a train: _____

(p. 11)   6. Five words with three syllables: _____

_____

(p. 12)   7. The name of a war: _____

(p. 14)   8. Four Giant teams: _____

(p. 15)   9. Two hyphenated words: _____

(p. 18)   10. Two color words: _____

(p. 19)   11. Five words with **ed** suffixes: _____

_____

(p. 20)   12. Three compound words: _____

(p. 21)   13. A three-syllable word: _____

(p. 22)   14. Five **long a** words: _____

(p. 23)   15. Words beginning with these consonant blends:

           bl _____ pl _____ st _____ cr _____

(p. 24)   16. Four different years: _____

(p. 26)   17. Three adjectives to describe Satchel Paige: _____

_____

(p. 36)   18. The name of a state: _____

(p. 39)   19. Seven words with double consonants: _____

_____

What Fraction Am I?

Identify the fraction for each shaded section.

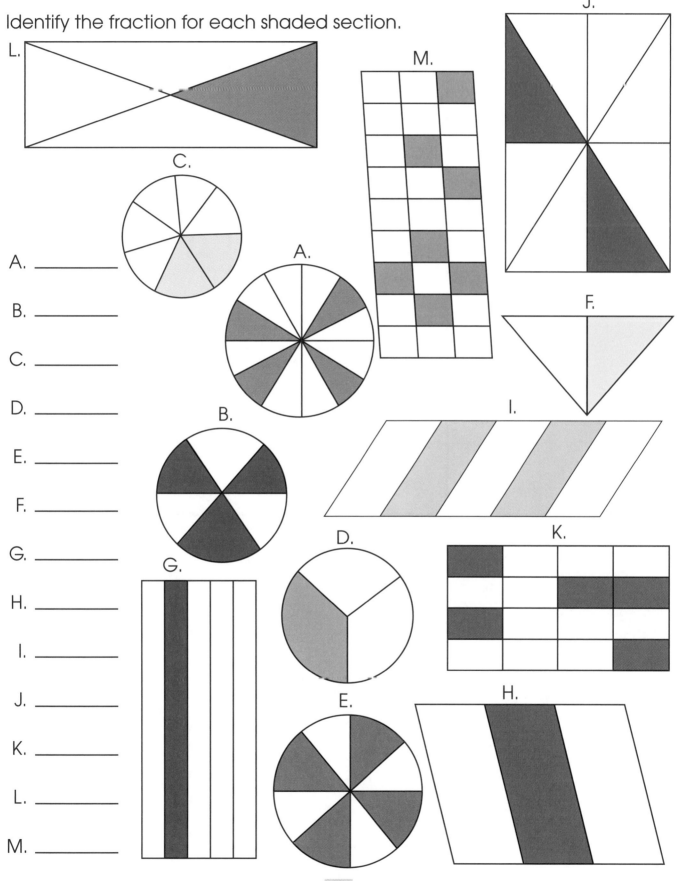

A. _____

B. _____

C. _____

D. _____

E. _____

F. _____

G. _____

H. _____

I. _____

J. _____

K. _____

L. _____

M. _____

Learn at Home, Grade 4

	Language Skills	Spelling	Reading
Monday	Have your child brainstorm traits of an imaginary creature. Prompt him/her with the following questions: *Where does it live? When did it live? What does it look like? Smell like? What does it eat? What is it called?* Have your child draw a picture of the imaginary creature, then write a story about it.	Pretest your child on these spelling words. across · difference · recess afford · difficult · success battle · gallon · suppose goddess · message · terrible copper · official · traffic Have your child correct the pretest, add personalized words and make two copies of this week's study list.	**Library Skills** Teach your child how to use the library card catalog. *See* Reading, Week 20, numbers 1 and 2.
Tuesday	Brainstorm a list of six to ten foods with your child. Have him/her copy the list of foods in alphabetical order in his/her best cursive handwriting.	Have your child use each of this week's spelling words correctly in a sentence.	Review the Dewey decimal system of organizing nonfiction books in the library. *See* Reading, Week 20, number 3. Read *Annie and the Old One* by Miska Miles.
Wednesday	Have your child read a short article from a newspaper or magazine. Then, have him/her write five questions based on the article. Finally, have your child write a statement in response to each question.	Have your child complete **No Troubles With Doubles** (p. 224).	Return to the library. Have your child look for nonfiction books on topics related to *Annie and the Old One*. Possible topics include weaving and Navajo Indians.
Thursday	Building on last week's lesson, introduce the following vocabulary: *declarative sentences* (statements) *interrogative sentences* (questions) *imperative sentences* (commands) *exclamatory sentences* (exclamations) Have your child make sentence necklaces. *See* Language Skills, Week 20, number 1.	Study this week's spelling words. Play the "Silly Sybil" game with syllables. *See* **Background Information and Supporting Activities** (p. 9).	Have your child complete a project based on his/her library research. A project may include a diorama, poster, artwork or puppet show.
Friday	Set out five pictures cut from magazines and newspapers. Have your child look carefully at each picture, then write four sentences about it: one statement, one question, one command and one exclamation.	Give your child the final spelling test. Have your child record the pretest and final test words in his/her word bank.	Allow your child to finish and then present his/her final project. Reread *Annie and the Old One*.

Math	Science	Social Studies
Make two copies of **Fraction Bars** (p. 225). Have your child color the bars of each size the same color. Allow him/her to compare the bars and make discoveries about fractional parts. Your child may discover that the bar that is one-sixth of the longest bar, is one-half of the one-third bar. Encourage this creative exploration.	Brainstorm ways that weather affects different people. What jobs depend on certain weather? How does weather affect feelings? Why do people listen to or read weather forecasts? Why do people talk about the weather? Ask how the weather affects your child personally. Have him/her write about weather. *See* Science, Week 20, number 1.	Find the current population of your state and compare it to the population of the largest city. Compare the population of your state to other states approximately the same size. Have your child make a graph showing population comparisons.
Introduce counting fractions. Identify the longest fraction bar as one whole. Have your child identify the bars that make up sixths. Then, have him/her count by sixths as he/she places the six sixths along the whole bar ($^1/_6$ . . . $^6/_6$). Continue beyond the whole bar with the other sixths ($^7/_6$ . . . $^{12}/_6$). Lead your child to discover that $^{12}/_6$ is the same as two whole bars. Repeat this counting activity with halves, fourths, etc.	Pose questions about the basics of weather for your child to research and answer. Possible questions might include: *Where does weather develop? How many miles above the Earth is weather formed? What four conditions are necessary for making weather?*	Help your child measure the mileage of your state in all directions. Determine the area of your state. Compare the area of your state with the area of other states. Then, compare it with the area of other countries, such as Germany or Canada. Have your child make a graph comparing the areas of several states. You may want to use the information gathered for **"State" istics** (Week 18, p. 209).
Have your child count aloud by fourths as you write the fractions on the chalkboard. Repeat for other parts as well (sixths, thirds). $^1/_4$, $^2/_4$, $^3/_4$, $^4/_4$, $^5/_4$, $^6/_4$, $^7/_4$, $^8/_4$ $^1/_6$, $^2/_6$, $^3/_6$, $^4/_6$, $^5/_6$, $^6/_6$, $^7/_6$, $^8/_6$, $^9/_6$, $^{10}/_6$, $^{11}/_6$, $^{12}/_6$ $^1/_3$, $^2/_3$, $^3/_3$, $^4/_3$, $^5/_3$, $^6/_3$, Ask your child questions about the fractions. *See* Math, Week 20, number 1.	Teach your child about the atmosphere and how the earth is heated. *See* Science, Week 20, number 2.	Have your child research the major industries in your state. On a 9" x 12" sheet of paper, have your child draw and label pictures of products of the major industries in your state.
Introduce fraction addition. Have your child show you $^1/_4 + ^1/_4$ and name the total ($^2/_4$). Then, have him/her show you $^2/_6 + ^3/_6$ and name the total ($^5/_6$). Continue this adding activity with other fractions. Remember to use the same denominator in each problem.	Teach your child about air pressure and moving air. Explain that air has mass and takes up space (it is made up of gases). Therefore, it creates pressure. Air pressure varies but is greatest at sea level. It is also greater when saturated with water or when it is cold. Have your child explain how he/she knows that air moves. He/she may describe evidence of wind such as leaves moving. *See* Science, Week 20, number 3.	Have your child research the ethnic makeup of your state. Have him/her make a pie chart showing the current ethnic population.
Challenge your child to think of other ways to name fractions. *See* Math, Week 20, number 2. Use manipulatives such as fraction bars or Cuisenaire rods.	Teach your child about wind and air pressure. Ask him/her to look at the barometer readings for the past week. *See* Science, Week 20, number 4. Have your child list ways that wind can be helpful and ways that it can be harmful.	Teach your child your state's song. Have your child design a state slogan that could appear on a bumper sticker. The slogan should promote some unique aspect of your state.

Learn at Home, Grade 4

TEACHING SUGGESTIONS AND ACTIVITIES

LANGUAGE SKILLS (Sentence Types)

▶ 1. **Sentence Necklaces**

Preparation: Cut 9" x 1" strips of construction paper in four colors. You will need about ten of each color. Copy and enlarge the four "medals" (below) onto white construction paper. Punch a hole near the top of each medal and thread a piece of yarn through the hole.

Directions for your child: Write declarative sentences on paper strips of one color. Write interrogative sentences on a second color. Write exclamatory sentences on a third color. Write imperative sentences on the last color. Interlock the strips to form chains, one color per chain. With the yarn, attach the appropriate medal to each chain to indicate the type of sentence represented.

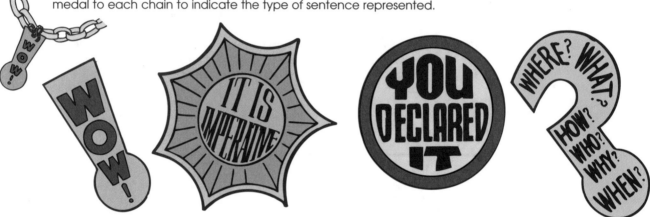

READING (Library Skills)

▶ 1. Most libraries today have an electronic catalog of books. With this system, your child can type in a subject, title or author to find the location of a desired book. Some libraries still depend on traditional card catalogs with cards representing the books on the shelves. Teach your child both systems. There are three types of cards in the card catalog: Each book in the library has a title card, a subject card and an author card. The cards are named for the information that is listed first on the card (title, author or subject) and are filed in alphabetical order.

▶ 2. Find an example of each type of card or entry (author, subject and title) in the card catalog. Look over each one with your child and discuss the information given on each card: author, illustrator, title, subject, Dewey decimal number, publisher, printing date and number of pages. Then, have your child find these books on the shelves.

▶ 3. Dewey decimal system

000–099	General Works	encyclopedias, magazines, newspapers
100–199	Philosophy	human ideas
200–299	Religion	the Bible, denominations, world religions
300–399	Social Studies	laws, governments, fairy tales, folktales, customs
400–499	Language	dictionaries, grammar, languages
500–599	Science	rocks, animals, insects, mathematics, solar system
600–699	Technology	how things work, cooking, pet care, farming
700–799	Fine Arts	painting, photography, arts and crafts, sports, music
800–899	Literature	poems, plays, short stories
900–999	History and Geography	history, travel, geography, biography, atlases

MATH (Fractions)

▶ 1. Ask the following questions about the rows of fractions you have written on the chalkboard:

   How is each row alike? What part of the row is like counting? Why does the bottom number stay the same? What does the top number in a fraction tell you? (It counts.) *What does the bottom number in a fraction tell you?* (It tells what is being counted.)

▶ 2. Sample questions to challenge your child's thinking:

   How many eighths will it take to make as much as one and a half? Build three-halves. What else can you call this fraction? (one whole and a half) If the red bar is a whole, what bar is a half? If eight counters are a whole set, how many is one-fourth of a set?

SCIENCE (Meteorology)

▶ 1. Write the weather sentence starters below on the chalkboard for your child to copy and complete. He/she may complete each one as a single sentence or together as a poem. Encourage your child to be creative both linguistically and visually by writing in the form of a design or shape.

   Blue skies and sunshine are . . .   *In foggy weather, I . . .*

   A rainy day makes me . . .   *When I hear thunder, I . . .*

   Lightning streaking across the sky is . . .   *Black clouds cause me . . .*

   When I wake and see snow on the ground, I . . .   *Fluffy white clouds are . . .*

▶ 2. Have your child explain how he/she thinks the Earth and the air around it is heated. Then, research the question together. Energy from the sun passes through the air and strikes the Earth. The Earth absorbs some heat energy and reflects some into the air around the surface of the Earth.

   Have your child measure the air temperature accurately in several different rooms and spaces in the same building or house. Ask why it is warmer in some places than in others. Listen to your child's response and relate it to why some places on Earth are warmer than others. Sunlight is more direct in some places during certain times of the year. Different colors reflect or absorb heat and light from the sun differently. Have your child relate an incident when he/she noticed that one surface was hotter than another (stepping on black tar, walking in sand).

   Consider how heat gets trapped in a closed car or greenhouse. The same thing happens with the Earth's atmosphere. The atmosphere, a blanket of air surrounding the Earth, traps heat and keeps the warm air around the Earth. The *greenhouse effect* is a theory that pollutants increase the amount of carbon dioxide in the atmosphere, causing it to absorb too much heat.

▶ 3. The following is a dramatic demonstration of the presence of air pressure. You will need an empty can with a screw-on lid. ***Do not use a can that held turpentine, gasoline or any other flammable liquid!*** You can purchase an empty can at a hardware store.

   Pour about an inch of water into the can. Put the can on a burner on your stove, uncovered, and heat until steam comes from the can. Have your child explain what is happening. *(As the water heats, it turns into a gas that fills the can with water molecules.)* Using pot holders, screw the lid on tightly. Turn off the heat so the water in the can cools. Ask your child what will happen as the steam in the can cools. Observe what happens. The can should crush itself. As the steam cools, it will condense into a liquid. The liquid did not fill the space like the gas did. Since the cover was on, no air filled the space vacated by the gas molecules. Because there was no air in the can, the greater air pressure outside crushed the can. This shows that air has pressure.

▶ 4. Wind is caused by the uneven heating of the Earth. Your child has learned that the Earth is not heated evenly and that warm air has less pressure than cool air. *(Cold air molecules are closer together, therefore cold air is denser and weighs more.)* Wind is created when air moves from an area of high pressure (warm air) to an area of low pressure (cold air).

   Have your child think about the wind felt near a lake or ocean. Remind him/her that air over the land is quite warm during the day and air over the water is cooler. Ask him/her to explain why the wind blows toward shore.

No Troubles With Doubles

Fill in the blanks. One spelling word is used twice.

across
afford
battle
goddess
copper
difference
difficult
gallon
message
official
recess
success
suppose
terrible
traffic

1. Write the three-syllable words and divide them into syllables. _____ _____

_____ _____

2. Our secretary wrote down the telephone _____ for our boss.

3. Which word names a metal? _____

4. Which word refers to a lot of vehicles? _____

5. The in-line skates were so expensive that Jill had to save money before she could _____ them.

6. Write the four words which do not have syllable divisions between some of their double letters. _____

_____ _____ _____

7. Of the three words that have not been used, which one is always a verb?

_____

8. Which word names a measurement? _____ Name an item sold in this quantity. _____

9. Use the remaining spelling word in a sentence.

_____

Fraction Bars

	Language Skills	Spelling	Reading
Monday	**Descriptive Sentences** Read the first line of a novel aloud to your child. Ask: *Does the first line create a mood? Does it grab your interest?* Read the first line from several novels for discussion. Have your child write a fictional story, carefully wording the first line to grab the reader's attention and set the mood for the story.	Pretest your child on these spelling words. bare groan pain stair bear grown pane stare berry hall raise wait bury haul rays weight Have your child correct the pretest, add personalized words and make two copies of this week's study list.	Locate the biography section at the library. Guide your child in choosing a biography to read this week. *See* Reading, Week 21, number 1. Brainstorm some questions for your child to keep in mind as he/she reads. This will help focus your child's reading and make it more meaningful. Have your child begin reading the biography. Ask him/her to keep notes as he/she reads because he/she will be making a presentation on this person on Friday.
Tuesday	Brainstorm a list of six to ten flowers with your child. Have him/her copy the list of flowers in alphabetical order in his/her best cursive handwriting.	Have your child use each of this week's spelling words correctly in a sentence.	Plan a way for your child to share the information learned from the biography. For example, you could have your child write an imaginary interview with the person. Continue reading the biography together.
Wednesday	Discuss the importance of word choice in expressing a feeling clearly. Avoid language that is too vague or general. Opt instead for specific language. *See* Language Skills, Week 21, number 1. Have your child write a paragraph on a topic that he/she feels strongly about. Encourage him/her to choose words to match those feelings.	Have your child complete **Is the Bear Bare?** (p. 231).	Practice reading and interpreting the Dewey decimal numbering system. *See* Reading, Week 21, number 2. Finish reading the biography.
Thursday	Certain words are overused in writing: *nice, good, pretty, many, go, some, said* and *like*. These bland words can often be replaced with more interesting or specific words. *See* Language Skills, Week 21, number 2 for examples. Have your child look up the eight words above in a thesaurus and find five synonyms for each. Then, have your child use the synonyms in a descriptive paragraph about spring.	Write sentences on the chalkboard using words from this week's spelling list. Erase the spelling words in each sentence. Have your child fill in the missing words—spelled correctly—then read the sentences aloud.	Let your child work on the biography presentation planned on Tuesday.
Friday	Encourage your child to use descriptive words to make his/her writing more interesting. Give your child five sentences. After each sentence, write three descriptive words in parentheses. Have your child rewrite the sentences, incorporating the descriptive words. Ask: *Which set of sentences sounds better? Why?* Have your child complete **Descriptive Sentences** (p. 230).	Give your child the final spelling test. Have your child record the pretest and final test words in his/her word bank.	Let your child complete the biography project and make his/her presentation.

Learn at Home, Grade 4

Math	Science	Social Studies
Challenge your child to make his/her own fraction models. Propose problems for your child to solve by drawing or creating fraction models. Provide him/her with the means for making models: paper and pencil, manipulatives, construction paper, scissors. *See also* Math, Week 21, number 1.	Wind direction is affected by the turning of the Earth. Read about prevailing and trade winds. *See* Science, Week 21, number 1. **Note:** Make arrangements for a field trip next week to a local television station, airport or newspaper office to meet with a meteorologist. (*See* Science, Week 22, Thursday.)	With your child, look at travel brochures from your state. What are some points of interest? List natural sites, museums, communities, parks and other locations that attract visitors. Help your child plan a trip within your state. Ask him/her to record what you will see, the route you will take, your itinerary for each day and how long you will be gone. Use a state map for reference in making the plans.
Have your child practice adding fractions. Provide written equations and have him/her build models of the fractions to solve. *See* Math, Week 21, number 2. Have your child complete **Bubble Math** (p. 232).	Weather is determined by several factors, including temperature, wind, air pressure and moisture. Explore the role of moisture in weather. *See* Science, Week 21, number 2.	Read a biography about a famous person that was born or lived in your state. Have your child create a state Hall of Fame and choose five famous or legendary individuals to induct. Have your child draw a portrait of each candidate with a caption describing his/her greatest accomplishments.
Teach your child how to subtract fractions. Encourage your child to draw pictures to help, if necessary. Work together to solve the word problems on **Crazy Quilts** (p. 233).	Using the temperature data collected since Week 19, have your child make another line graph, this one showing the changes in temperature over several weeks. Record morning temperatures in red and evening temperatures in blue. Have your child plot the temperatures and analyze the fluctuations between morning and evening.	Help your child make a time line of your state's history. Choose at least ten events since the earliest settlers to note on the time line. Then, have your child choose one interesting event to study in-depth. Have him/her write a descriptive paragraph or two about the historical event, then construct a diorama to represent the event visually.
Using the fraction bars from last week, have your child model subtraction problems with fractions. Here are a few to get you started: $$^5/_6 - ^3/_6 = \underline{\quad}$$ $$^6/_4 - ^3/_4 = \underline{\quad}$$ $$^7/_8 - ^4/_8 = \underline{\quad}$$ $$^{10}/_5 - ^5/_5 = \underline{\quad}$$ $$^4/_3 - ^2/_3 = \underline{\quad}$$ $$^3/_2 - ^2/_2 = \underline{\quad}$$	Discuss the difference between weather and climate. Compare the climate where you live with polar climates and climates at different latitudes. Explore whether longitude makes a difference in climate. Have your child write a description of your climate. Encourage him/her to use specific and interesting language (*see* Language Skills, Week 21, numbers 1 and 2).	Research your child's (and your) family history. Help your child think of questions to ask a grandparent or older relative in an interview. The questions should relate to the family's early experiences of life in the state. If the family recently moved to the state, have your child learn, then explain their reasons for moving.
Give your child a set of small objects such as pennies or small round candies. Ask him/her to model and solve addition and subtraction problems with fractions. **Example:** *You have twelve cookies to share with friends. There are four of you. How many cookies does each person get? What fraction of the cookies do two friends get?*	**Creative Writing:** With your child, brainstorm familiar expressions containing weather words. *See* Science, Week 21, number 3 for examples. Have your child draw literal interpretations of a few of the expressions.	Have your child write an acrostic poem about your state. *See* Social Studies, Week 21, number 1.

Learn at Home, Grade 4

TEACHING SUGGESTIONS AND ACTIVITIES

LANGUAGE SKILLS (Descriptive Sentences)

▶ 1. Some words are more exact than others. Write a sentence that is vague next to a sentence that is exact. Discuss the words that can be avoided.

   Example: I put my things on the table. (The word *things* is very vague.)
   I put my *backpack* and *raincoat* on the *dining* room table.

   Give your child several vague sentences. Ask him/her to rewrite each one using exact language.

▶ 2. Writing is more interesting when words are not overused. Write the following paragraph on the chalkboard: *We went to visit our grandparents in New York. Our grandparents are nice. They were good to us. We saw the Statue of Liberty and the East River, and we went on a boat ride. We like to visit our grandparents.*

   Have your child rewrite the paragraph. Words such as *nice, like* and *good* are overused and nonspecific. Encourage your child to write more colorfully.

   Example: *We went to visit our grandparents in New York. They are so fabulous. They took us all over the city. We saw the Statue of Liberty and the East River, and we went on a boat ride. We enjoyed everything we did with them and can't wait to go back.*

READING (Library Skills)

▶ 1. Biographies and autobiographies can be found in the nonfiction section but often follow the 900's section. They all have the same call number (920) and are arranged by the last name of the subject of the biography (or autobiography). Some libraries do not use the numbering system and simply use the last name of the subject. Find a biography that interests your child. Books by Jean Fritz are grade-appropriate and interesting.

▶ 2. Point out the call number on the spine of a nonfiction library book. The Dewey decimal system is like an address book. It tells the "address" of every nonfiction book in the library. Compare the number on the spine to the chart of the Dewey decimal numbers (*see* Reading, Week 20, number 3). Discuss the meaning of the numbers and letters in the call number. Ask your child where in the Dewey decimal system (to the hundreds place) he/she would look for books on specific topics. For example, ask where to look for a book that teaches German, a book about painting a bedroom or a book about the Olympics.

MATH (Fractions)

▶ 1. Provide your child with a model for each problem. Ask him/her to solve the problem.
   a. If this rectangle is one whole,
      • find one-fourth.
      • find two-thirds.
      • find five-thirds.
   b. If this bar is one-fourth, what could the whole look like? (Show at least two options.)
   c. If this shape is a whole, what would four-thirds look like?
   d. If these four buttons are one-half of a set, how big is the whole set?
   e. If twelve marbles are two-fifths of a set, how many marbles are in a whole set? How many are in a half set?

▶ 2. Provide your child with fraction models. Designate the whole before he/she begins solving the problems.

   $4/5 + 2/5 =$ ____ $2/4 + 2/4 =$ ____ $4/8 + 2/8 =$ ____ $3/3 + 2/3 =$ ____

   $1/4 + 5/4 =$ ____ $1/2 + 3/2 =$ ____ $2/6 + 5/6 =$ ____ $3/10 + 6/10 =$ ____

SCIENCE (Meteorology)

▶ 1. Wind and weather systems in the United States generally move from west to east. The United States is located in the *prevailing westerlies* belt. Prevailing winds are influenced by the turning of the Earth. To demonstrate how the *prevailing westerlies* move, use a globe and chalk (see A). Show how the Earth rotates from east to west. Have your child turn the globe slowly in this direction. While the globe is turning, put a piece of chalk on the equator and draw a line straight up to the North Pole. Have your child observe the line the chalk made and tell which direction the line moved (west to east).

A.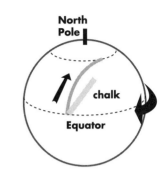

The *trade winds* blow in the area from the south of the United States to the equator. To demonstrate how the trade winds move, once again use a globe and chalk (see B). Have your child turn the globe slowly from east to west. While the globe is turning, put a piece of chalk at the top of the globe and draw straight down from the North Pole to the equator. Have your child observe the line the chalk made and tell which direction the line moved (east to west).

The prevailing westerlies blow in a belt above the trade winds through most of Canada. There is another band of prevailing winds called the *polar easterlies*. They are above the prevailing westerlies in the northern hemisphere and blow in the same direction as the trade winds. These three belts also exist in the southern hemisphere.

B.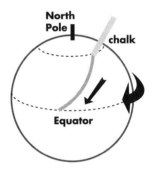

▶ 2. Review the water cycle. Have your child draw a diagram of the cycle and explain how rain forms.

▶ 3. **Creative Writing:** Discuss the literal and idiomatic meaning of each weather word expression. Have your child write sentences using some of them.

cool cat	razor-sharp winds	thundering hooves
hot number	dancing raindrops	head in the clouds
greased lightning	fair-weather friend	cold shoulder

SOCIAL STUDIES (Your State)

▶ 1. Have your child write an acrostic poem about your home state. Have him/her begin by writing the title "(your state), the Beautiful" accross the top of a large sheet of writing paper. Then, have your child write the state's name in large capital letters—one letter at the start of each line—down the left side of the paper. He/she will write a sentence about the state beginning with each letter of the state's name. Each sentence should tell something about the state or describe something beautiful about it.

IDAHO THE BEAUTIFUL

I ncredibly beautiful mountains
D efinitely a skier's paradise
A gem of a state
H ell's Canyon is a sight to see
O h, how beautiful!

Learn at Home, Grade 4

Descriptive Sentences

Turn a good sentence into a great sentence by using more descriptive words.

Example: The dog chased the boy.
The big brown dog playfully chased the little boy.

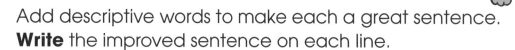

Add descriptive words to make each a great sentence.
Write the improved sentence on each line.

1. The man climbed the mountain.

_____

_____

2. The group found a buried tomb.

_____

_____

3. The girls painted a sign.

_____

_____

4. The sunlight came through the window.

_____

_____

5. Ice cream dripped down the cone.

_____

_____

6. The snake moved down the tree.

_____

_____

7. The storm rocked the boat.

_____

_____

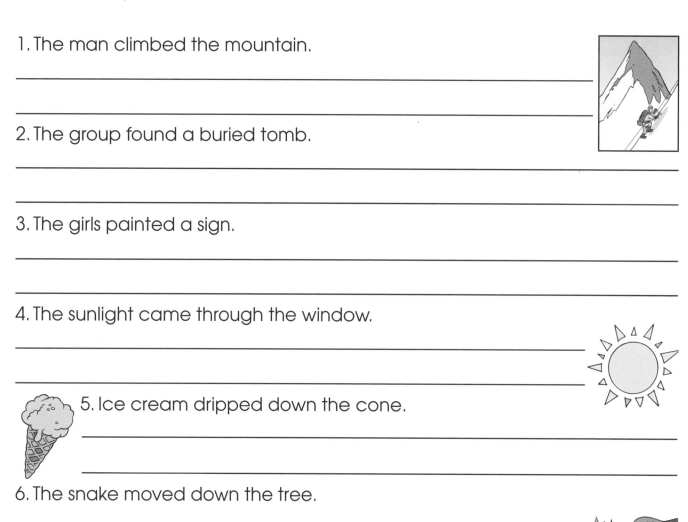

Learn at Home, Grade 4

Is the Bear Bare?

bare
bear
berry
bury
groan
grown
hall
haul
pain
pane
raise
rays
stair
stare
wait
weight

Use each pair of homophones correctly in the sentences. Indicate the part of speech in the parentheses.

1. When my brother moved into the dormitory, he had to

_____ (   ) all his belongings down the

_____ (   ).

2. The camper was _____(   ) when he swam in the

lake, but only a _____(   ) saw him.

3. I decided to _____(   ) the blinds to let in the sun's

_____(   ) .

4. My dad let out a _____ (   ) when he discovered he had _____

(   ) too large for his pants.

5. I felt a small _____ (   ) when I cut my hand on the _____(   ) of

glass.

6. It's not polite to _____(   ) when someone stumbles on a _____

(   ).

7. When our pet canary died, we decided to _____ (   ) it near the

bush with the one red _____ (   ) on it.

Bubble Math

Reduce each sum to a whole number or a mixed number in lowest terms.

$\frac{6}{9}$
$+ \frac{6}{9}$
_____

$\frac{5}{11}$
$+ \frac{8}{11}$
_____

$\frac{3}{4}$
$+ \frac{2}{4}$
_____

$\frac{8}{11}$
$+ \frac{8}{11}$
_____

$\frac{2}{5}$
$+ \frac{3}{5}$
_____

$\frac{4}{5}$
$+ \frac{6}{5}$
_____

$\frac{5}{7}$
$+ \frac{6}{7}$
_____

$\frac{5}{9}$
$+ \frac{5}{9}$
_____

$\frac{8}{9}$
$+ \frac{3}{9}$
_____

$\frac{2}{4}$
$+ \frac{2}{4}$
_____

$\frac{4}{8}$
$+ \frac{4}{8}$
_____

$\frac{4}{8}$
$+ \frac{6}{8}$
_____

$\frac{6}{8}$
$+ \frac{6}{8}$
_____

$\frac{3}{6}$
$+ \frac{3}{6}$
_____

$\frac{5}{4}$
$+ \frac{2}{4}$
_____

$\frac{3}{9}$
$+ \frac{7}{9}$
_____

$\frac{3}{12}$
$+ \frac{10}{12}$
_____

$\frac{8}{11}$
$+ \frac{3}{11}$
_____

$\frac{7}{11}$
$+ \frac{7}{11}$
_____

$\frac{7}{14}$
$+ \frac{8}{14}$
_____

$\frac{6}{12}$
$+ \frac{8}{12}$
_____

$\frac{4}{3}$
$+ \frac{2}{3}$
_____

$\frac{5}{7}$
$+ \frac{6}{7}$
_____

$\frac{13}{16}$
$+ \frac{7}{16}$
_____

$\frac{8}{15}$
$+ \frac{14}{15}$
_____

$\frac{4}{11}$
$+ \frac{9}{11}$
_____

$\frac{7}{13}$
$+ \frac{6}{13}$
_____

$\frac{7}{12}$
$+ \frac{7}{12}$
_____

$\frac{5}{12}$
$+ \frac{10}{12}$
_____

$\frac{5}{12}$
$+ \frac{8}{12}$
_____

Soap

Learn at Home, Grade 4

Crazy Quilts

Toni and her mother made a crazy quilt. It doesn't have a set pattern; the pieces are many colors and sizes. Read each story problem. **Circle** the correct problem, and **write** the answer on the line.

1. Toni had $\frac{6}{8}$ of a yard of yellow gingham. She used $\frac{3}{8}$ of a yard to make two triangles for the quilt. How much yellow gingham did she have left?

$$\frac{3}{8} - \frac{2}{8} \qquad \frac{6}{8} - \frac{3}{8} \qquad \frac{6}{8} + \frac{2}{8} \qquad \rule{4cm}{0.4pt}$$

2. Toni's mother found $\frac{5}{10}$ of a yard of red velvet material. She made a rectangle from $\frac{2}{10}$ of a yard. How much red velvet did she have left?

$$\frac{5}{10} - \frac{2}{10} \qquad \frac{5}{10} + \frac{2}{10} \qquad \frac{5}{10} \times \frac{5}{10} \qquad \rule{4cm}{0.4pt}$$

3. Mother and Toni liked to sew black satin between the red and yellow pieces. They had $\frac{3}{4}$ of a yard of black satin. They used $\frac{1}{4}$ of a yard to place between the red and yellow pieces. How much black satin did they have left?

$$\frac{3}{4} - \frac{1}{4} \qquad \frac{3}{4} - \frac{3}{4} \qquad \frac{2}{4} + \frac{3}{4} \qquad \rule{4cm}{0.4pt}$$

4. Toni had $\frac{2}{3}$ of an hour before her piano lesson. She wanted to make one more blue piece. It took her $\frac{1}{3}$ of an hour to make the blue piece. What fraction of an hour did she have left to get ready for her piano lesson?

$$\frac{1}{3} + \frac{1}{3} \qquad \frac{2}{3} - \frac{1}{3} \qquad \frac{2}{4} + \frac{3}{4} \qquad \rule{4cm}{0.4pt}$$

5. Mother and Toni finished $\frac{4}{8}$ of the quilt. Toni did $\frac{1}{8}$ of it herself. How much did Mother do?

$$\frac{1}{8} + \frac{4}{8} \qquad \frac{3}{8} + \frac{4}{8} \qquad \frac{4}{8} - \frac{1}{8} \qquad \rule{4cm}{0.4pt}$$

6. Toni and her mother wanted to give the quilt to Grandmother for her birthday. They used purple cotton to make the edging. They had $\frac{6}{8}$ of a yard of the purple cloth. They used $\frac{5}{8}$ of a yard to make the edging. How much purple cloth did they have left?

$$\frac{6}{8} \times \frac{5}{8} \qquad \frac{6}{8} - \frac{5}{9} \qquad \frac{6}{8} - \frac{5}{8} \qquad \rule{4cm}{0.4pt}$$

Language Skills	Spelling	Reading
Monday Teach your child to use a story frame to organize a narrative. He/she may write in first or third person. *See* Language Skills, Week 22, numbers 1 and 2. Have your child write a narrative based on his/her story frame.	Pretest your child on these spelling words. airport earthquake landlord barefoot farewell northwest birthday flyswatter scarecrow cardboard forenoon teakettle downstairs iceberg throughout Have your child correct the pretest, add personalized words and make two copies of this week's study list.	**Bibliography** Help your child choose an interesting topic (perhaps a meteorological phenomenon) to research. Go to the library and gather several books related to the topic. Look in the back of a nonfiction book for a bibliography. Show your child how to use this information to locate other resources.
Tuesday Brainstorm a list of six to ten different types of trees with your child. Have him/her copy the list of trees in alphabetical order in his/her best cursive handwriting.	Have your child use each of this week's spelling words correctly in a sentence.	Continue yesterday's lesson. Teach your child how to make a bibliography. Then, help him/her become familiar with reading a bibliography by asking directed questions. *See* Reading, Week 22, numbers 1 and 2.
Wednesday Give your child several simple sentences. Ask him/her to expand the sentences by adding information. Encourage your child to ask questions such as *how, who, what, where, when* and *why*. The answers will help fill out the sentences. Have your child complete **Expanding Sentences** (p. 238).	Have your child complete **Twice the Fun** (p. 239).	Help your child form some questions on the chosen research topic. Have him/her write each question on an index card.
Thursday Read sentences from a book or magazine. Discuss what information (*who, what, when, where, why*) is given in each sentence. Discuss which words give which information. **Example:** *My brother and I played basketball all day at the park.* "At the park" tells where, "all day" tells when and "my brother and I" tells who.	Divide each of this week's compound words into two root words. Write each root word on an index card. Mix up the cards. Have your child put the cards back together to form the fifteen words.	Have your child read (sometimes skimming) the books on the chosen topic and answer the questions on the index cards. When your child finds an answer to a question, have him/her write the answer on the card and write the number of the resource (*see* Reading, Week 22, number 1) after the answer.
Friday Show your child how to combine the information in two sentences to form one sentence. *See* Language Skills, Week 22, number 3.	Give your child the final spelling test. Have your child record the pretest and final test words in his/her word bank.	Have your child continue reading and answering the questions on index cards. If he/she quotes directly from a source, he/she should use quotation marks, copy the words exactly and give credit to the source. If your child finds conflicting answers to a question, have him/her write down both answers on the index card (including the source) and look for a third source to confirm one of the answers.

Learn at Home, Grade 4

Math	Science	Social Studies
Practice mental fraction math. Say problems for your child to visualize such as "one-sixth plus four-sixths minus three-sixths." Have your child work the problem in his/her head, then state the answer.	Save newspaper weather maps from several consecutive days. Write the date on each map. Compare the information with your child's weather charts from the same days. Have your child analyze the accuracy of the meteorologists' forecasts. Have your child write an analysis of the accuracy of the forecasts. Look especially for the information that is most often correct.	**Field Trip:** Visit your city or community government center (city hall or township hall). Interview the mayor, if possible. Find out how the government is organized. *See* Social Studies, Week 22, number 1.
Introduce your child to comparing fractions. Ask him/her to build two fractions with the same denominator ($^2/_3$ and $^1/_3$). Your child should be able to see from the model which number is greater. Show the fractions in written form next to the models so that your child can see the comparison symbolically. Repeat this process with several different fractions, always comparing two fractions with the same denominator.	Observe weather maps to learn how fronts affect weather. *See* Science, Week 22, numbers 1 and 2. Have your child draw diagrams explaining cold fronts and warm fronts.	Discuss the rights and responsibilities of an individual in his/her community, state and country. Have your child write a statement of commitment for being a responsible citizen in the community. Have your child write a thank you note to the community leader you visited yesterday.
Ask your child if he/she would rather have two-tenths or two-sixths of a favorite candy bar (or other special treat). Ask for an explanation to assess your child's comprehension of the size of fractions. Model two-tenths and two-sixths of the candy bar (using two candy bars). Model and discuss other comparisons where the numerator is the same in both fractions.	Have your child watch a televised weather report and compare and contrast it with that day's newspaper weather report. Discuss the similarities and differences in the information and the means of reporting it. Have your child make a weather map and predict the weather. *See* Science, Week 22, number 3.	Have your child locate the state capital on a map of your state. Discuss why a state needs a capital. Have your child draw and label a picture of your state's capitol building.
Discuss your child's responses for each problem on the activity sheet. Have your child complete **Picture the Problem** (p. 240).	**Field Trip:** Visit a local television station, airport or newspaper office to meet with a meteorologist. Have your child form a list of questions prior to the visit.	Find out how the state government is organized. Together, compare and contrast your city government to the state government.
By using physical models, your child can see which fraction of a pair is larger. Allow your child to use models while working on the activity sheet if he/she needs reinforcement. Have your child complete **Dare To Compare** (p. 241).	Discuss the information learned from the meteorologist. Have your child write a thank you note to the meteorologist. Write the word *meteorology* on the chalkboard. Set a time limit and tell your child to write as many words as possible using only the letters in *meteorology*. He/she may manipulate cutout letters to help with this activity.	Have your child make a poster about your state's capital. Ask him/her write the name of the capital in outlined letters, then fill in the letters with words and pictures. *See* Social Studies, Week 22, number 2.

Learn at Home, Grade 4

TEACHING SUGGESTIONS AND ACTIVITIES

LANGUAGE SKILLS (Descriptive Sentences)

▶ 1. Teach your child to complete a story frame in order to organize a story. He/she may write the episodes from an actual event or create something new.

Introduction:
    Setting
    Time
    Characters

Body:
    Plot
    Events
    Climax

Conclusion/Solution:

▶ 2. A narrative is a story that may be true or fictional. It may be told in the first person (I) in which the storyteller is part of the story. Or, it may be told in the third person (he, she, they) in which the teller is an observer. Give a short example of each perspective and discuss the differences.

First Person: Once when I was walking in the woods, I stumbled on a rock. "Ouch!" I cried as I stood up and brushed myself off. But that was no rock! The rock turned out to be a rabbit, and it was rubbing its eyes and whimpering. "I'm sorry," I said to the rabbit. The rabbit stopped crying and. . . .

Third Person: Once upon a time there was a little boy named Oliver. Oliver was staying with an uncle while his mother and father were away on a business trip. Oliver's uncle was very busy and Oliver was lonely. He tried to keep busy and stay out of the way but somedays he couldn't think of anything quiet to do.

One day. . . .

▶ 3. Sometimes you can expand a sentence by combining information from two sentences. Information can be combined in the subject or predicate.

Example (subject):   Eric played football after school. Mike played football after school.
                                    Eric and Mike played football after school.

Example (predicate):   Our team won the tournament. Our team received a trophy.
                                      Our team won the tournament and received a trophy.

Write the following pairs of sentences on the chalkboard. Have your child rewrite each pair to form one sentence by combining subjects or predicates.

The quarter rolled under the sofa. The dime rolled under the sofa.

The twins are in the play. Jane is in the play.

The children went to the library. The children checked out books.

The chips are in the picnic basket. The sandwiches are in the picnic basket.

Katy folded her camp clothes. Katy packed them in her luggage.

Mom came to see me in the play. Dad came to see me in the play.

Our teacher gave us an assignment. Our teacher told us to work quietly.

236

READING (Bibliography)

▶ 1. Help your child make a bibliography from the books collected on the research topic. First, have him/her list each source in the format shown here:

Author (last name, first name).

Title.

Publisher's location.

Publisher, date of publication.

Note that the format for book and articles is slightly different:

Book: Henry, Marguerite. *Misty of Chincoteague*. Chicago: Rand McNally, 1947.

Article: Jaroff, Leon. "Crunch Time at the Canyon." *Time* 3 July 1995: pgs. 46–47.

Then, have your child arrange the sources alphabetically by author. Number the alphabetized sources for easy reference.

▶ 2. Look at a bibliography with your child and pose the following questions:

Which resources in this bibliography are articles?

What is the name of the book written by _____?

When was _____ published?

SCIENCE (Meteorology)

BACKGROUND
Large air masses form over areas where the temperature remains fairly constant. When a cold air mass and a warm air mass meet, a front or an area of rapidly changing weather occurs. Fronts are largely responsible for changes in weather. Cold fronts cause sudden changes while warm fronts cause more gradual changes.

▶ 1. Challenge your child to find information on fronts at the library. Have your child draw diagrams and write explanations for cold fronts and warm fronts.

▶ 2. Together, look at the fronts on the weather maps. Ask your child the following questions: *What kind of fronts are shown? Did each one bring a change? Explain what the change was and why it occurred. If no change occurred, explain why not.*

▶ 3. Have your child trace an outline of the United States or Canada from a newspaper weather map. While he/she watches a televised weather report, have your child draw the weather fronts, note some temperatures and shade in precipitation if there is any. Have your child indicate his/her approximate location on the map in red. Then, ask him/her to predict the weather and record the prediction in the Science Log. Note the actual weather for the next two days and record it in the log. Compare the actual weather with your child's prediction.

SOCIAL STUDIES (Your State)

▶ 1. Have your child draw a diagram of the city government, labeling each office and describing its duties. Then, have him/her explain how ideas for improvement are introduced and how laws are made.

▶ 2. Have your child write the name of your state's capital in large block letters on plain shelf paper.

Tell your child to write a different fact about the state capital inside each letter.

Learn at Home, Grade 4

Expanding Sentences

You can s-t-r-e-t-c-h a sentence by adding more information. Stretch these sentences by adding words to **answer** each question.

Example: The plane landed. When? The plane landed at 1:30 p.m.

1. We are all going to the airport. How?

_____

2. I am taking three pieces of luggage. Why?

_____

3. The passengers are lined up. Why?

_____

4. The baggage was stacked. Where?

_____

5. She bought her ticket. How?

_____

6. We will arrive in Los Angeles. When?

_____

7. Our flight was delayed for forty-five minutes. Why?

_____

8. The tourists brought plenty of film. Why?

_____

9. Our flight attendant is helping us. How?

_____

10. We will fasten our safety belts. When?

_____

11. The plane is beginning to move. Where?

_____

12. Our cautious pilot avoided the stormy clouds. How?

_____

Twice the Fun

airport
barefoot
birthday
cardboard
downstairs
earthquake
farewell
flyswatter
forenoon
iceberg
landlord
northwest
scarecrow
teakettle
throughout

Fill in the blanks.
Look for a cause/effect relationship in each situation.

1. **cause:** a _____
   effect: receiving gifts

2. **cause:** using a _____
   effect: dead insects

3. **cause:** an _____
   effect: a shipwreck

4. **cause:** an _____
   effect: toppled buildings

5. **cause:** going _____
   effect: cutting a toe

6. **cause:** have a _____
   effect: a good harvest

7. **cause:** using a _____
   effect: boiled water

Complete these statements by **filling in** the blanks.

1. Which word names a part of the day? _____

2. A synonym for "goodbye" is _____ .

3. Boxes are often made of _____ .

4. As the plane took off from the _____ , it flew in a _____ direction.

5. The _____ who owns the duplex lives upstairs, and my family lives _____ .

6. Which word is a preposition? _____

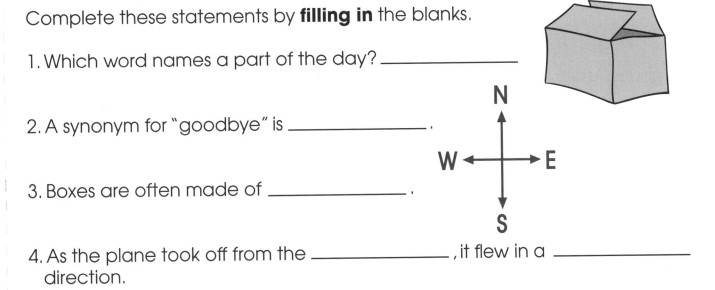

239

Picture the Problem

Week 22

Use the picture to solve the problem.

1. Andy had two ropes of the same length. He cut one rope into 2 equal parts and gave the 2 halves to Bill. The other rope he cut into fourths and gave 2 of the fourths to Sue. Circle who got the most rope.

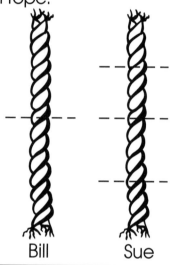

Bill   Sue

2. Henry cut an 8-foot log into 4 equal pieces and burned 2 of them in the fireplace. Joseph cut an 8-foot log into 8 equal pieces and put 3 of them in the fireplace. Circle who put the most wood in the fireplace.

Henry   Joseph

3. Mr. Johns built an office building with an aisle down the middle. He divided one side into 6 equal spaces. He divided the other side into 9 equal spaces. The Ace Company rented 5 of the ninths. The Best Company rented 4 of the sixths. Circle which company rented the larger space.

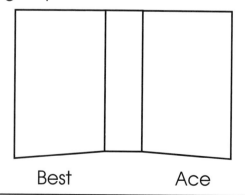

Best   Ace

4. The 4-H Club display area at the state fair was divided into 2 equal areas. One of these sections had 12 booths, the other had 9 booths. The flower display covered 2 of the ninths, and the melon display covered 4 of the twelfths. Circle which display had the most room.

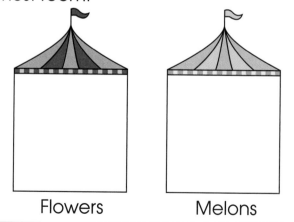

Flowers   Melons

240

Learn at Home, Grade 4

Dare To Compare

Compare the fractions below. Use >, < and =.

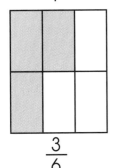 $\frac{3}{6}$ ◯ 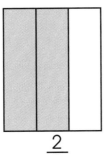 $\frac{2}{3}$ 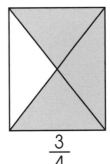 $\frac{3}{4}$ ◯ 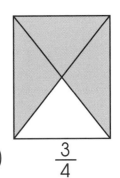 $\frac{3}{4}$

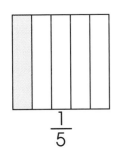 $\frac{1}{5}$ ◯ 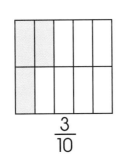 $\frac{3}{10}$ 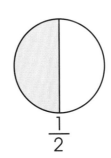 $\frac{1}{2}$ ◯ 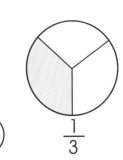 $\frac{1}{3}$

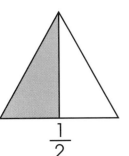 $\frac{1}{2}$ ◯ 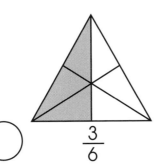 $\frac{3}{6}$ 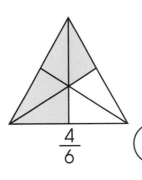 $\frac{4}{6}$ ◯ 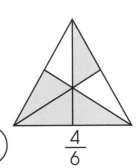 $\frac{4}{6}$

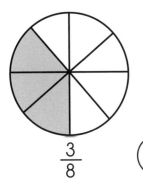 $\frac{3}{8}$ ◯ 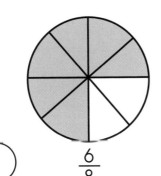 $\frac{6}{8}$ 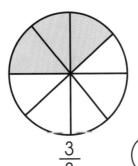 $\frac{3}{8}$ ◯ 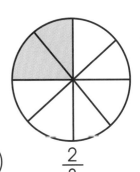 $\frac{2}{8}$

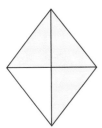 $\frac{3}{4}$ ◯ $\frac{1}{2}$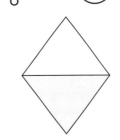

241

Learn at Home, Grade 4

	Language Skills	Spelling	Reading
Monday	**Paragraphs** Give your child a photo from a newspaper article. Help him/her list details and make up a story about the photo. Have your child plan a story based on the photo. Have your child organize his/her ideas into a beginning, middle and ending. Then, he/she can write a rough draft from the plan.	Pretest your child on these spelling words. batteries ivies stories cowboys ladies trays delays Mondays Tuesdays donkeys pennies valleys gravies ponies Wednesdays Have your child correct the pretest, add personalized words and make two copies of this week's study list.	Your child should continue reading and answering questions about his/her research topic begun last week until enough material is collected to write the report. Then, help your child organize the index cards into a meaningful order.
Tuesday	Brainstorm a list of six to ten book titles with your child. Have him/her copy the list of book titles in alphabetical order in his/her best cursive handwriting.	Have your child use each of this week's spelling words correctly in a sentence.	With the index cards as reference, have your child write a report in his/her own words. If he/she copies a passage directly from a source, he/she must use quotation marks and identify the source.
Wednesday	Teach your child to identify the topic sentence in a paragraph. *See* Language Skills, Week 23, number 1.	Have your child complete **Tricky Y** (p. 246).	Read the first draft with your child and offer constructive suggestions for improving fluency, organization and language. Leave it to your child to decide which revisions to make. These are only stylistic changes. Let your child continue working on the report.
Thursday	Provide your child with several photos and written paragraphs. Have him/her write a topic sentence to express the main idea of each. *See* Language Skills, Week 23, numbers 2 and 3.	Have your child choose ten words from this week's list. Have him/her write each word neatly in the center of a sheet of paper, then illustrate its meaning with a picture.	Read your child's second draft and provide necessary instruction on grammar, punctuation and spelling. Have him/her make all necessary corrections and copy the report neatly on lined paper or print out a clean copy. Once the written portion is finished, have your child make a diorama, poster, filmstrip or mobile to accompany the report.
Friday	Teach your child to write topic sentences for given topics. Generate a varied list of topics: family, school, vacations, early settlers, sports heroes, friends, etc. Guide your child in writing a topic sentence for a paragraph about each topic. He/she does not need to write the rest of the paragraph.	Give your child the final spelling test. Have your child record the pretest and final test words in his/her word bank.	Allow your child to complete and present his/her report.

Math	Science	Social Studies
Make several fraction bars for comparing equivalent fractions. *See* Math, Week 23, number 1. Have your child compare the fractions.	Have your child observe and draw cloud shapes and movements. *See* Science, Week 23, number 1.	**Field Trip:** Visit your state capital. Have your child prepare questions ahead of time to ask his/her representative. *See* Social Studies, Week 23, numbers 1 and 2. Make sure to have your child write a thank you note to anyone who met with you.
Have your child find equivalent fractions using a set model. Give him/her a set of twenty-four blocks that includes sixteen of one color and eight of another. Using these blocks, model several different fractions. All these fractions will be equivalent to $8/24$ (or $16/24$). *See* Math, Week 23, number 2.	Have your child read about how clouds are formed. Discuss the information by asking the questions found in Science, Week 23, number 2. Help your child research the answers in library resources and encyclopedias.	Teach your child the role of the legislative branch of government. Help your child draw a map of your state with district boundaries, writing in the names of the current representatives for each district.
Equivalent fractions are the same size when the whole is the same size. Look at the activity sheet with your child. Note that all the bars (the whole) are the same size, though each bar is divided up differently. Propose that your child cut out the fractions in the right column and line them up under the fraction bars on the left. Have your child complete a copy of **Match the Fractions** (p. 247).	Discuss the names of different types of clouds and where each type forms. Read about weather prediction and its relation to clouds. *See* Science, Week 23, numbers 3 and 4. Have your child hypothesize why a cloudy day might be cool, while a cloudy night might be warm. Have him/her write out the hypothesis.	Discuss the purpose of the state's constitution. Should the constitution be unchangeable? Discuss justifiable reasons for amending the state constitution. *See* Social Studies, Week 23, number 3.
Compare fractions in volume. Have your child compare the volume of a $1/4$-cup measure to a 1-cup measure. Allow your child to pour water or flour from one measure into the other. Repeat with other fractional measuring tools (measuring cups or spoons). Compare $1/4$ cup to $1/3$ cup. Which holds more? Have your child add two quantities together and name the total amount ($1/4 + 1/4 = 2/4$). Have your child record his/her discoveries.	Continue yesterday's lesson.	Talk about a controversial issue in your state. What are the opposing views? How is the state dealing with the issue? How do politicians feel about the issue? Have your child write a summary of the issue, then his/her own opinion on that issue.
Find a recipe that uses fractions. Read the recipe together. Follow the recipe to make the food.	Have your child draw and label a cloud diagram showing the different types of clouds and where they form (at what altitude). *See* Science, Week 23, number 5.	Have your child think of something he/she would like to see changed in your state. Help him/her write a persuasive letter to your local representative. In the letter, your child should clearly state his/her view and what he/she thinks should be done.

Learn at Home, Grade 4

TEACHING SUGGESTIONS AND ACTIVITIES

LANGUAGE SKILLS (Paragraphs)

BACKGROUND

A paragraph consists of several sentences that tell about one main idea, but the sentence that best expresses the main idea is called the topic sentence. The topic sentence is often the first sentence in a paragraph.

1. Discuss and define *topic sentence.* Give your child a science or social studies textbook. Ask him/her to read a given paragraph and point out the topic sentence.

2. Cut out pictures from magazines and newspapers. Mount each picture onto a sheet of construction paper. Glue lined paper under each picture. Have your child look at the photos and determine the main idea of each picture. What is the photographer trying to express? Have your child write an appropriate topic sentence beneath each picture.

3. Copy paragraphs from books and textbooks. Leave out the topic sentences. Glue each paragraph on a lined index card or a sheet of writing paper, leaving space at the top for your child to write. Have your child read each paragraph and write a topic sentence on the lines provided.

MATH (Fractions)

1. Cut six 18" x 2" strips of construction paper. Mark each strip with a different set of fractions. Fold the first strip in half and mark $^1/_2$ on the fold line. Fold and mark the second strip with $^1/_4$, $^2/_4$ and $^3/_4$. Fold and divide the third strip into thirds. Repeat with sixths, eighths and twelfths. Line up the strips and compare fractions. Your child should be able to see that $^1/_2$ and $^2/_4$ represent the same part of the whole. What other equivalent fractions can your child find?

2. Have your child look at the set of twenty-four blocks. Ask: *What is the whole?* (24) *What fraction of the set is black* (or whatever color you have eight of)? ($^8/_{24}$)

   a. Arrange the blocks in equal groups of eight, keeping the colors in separate groups. *How many groups are there?* (3) *What fraction is black?* ($^1/_3$)

   b. Arrange the blocks in equal groups of four, keeping the colors in separate groups. *How many groups are there?* (6) *What fraction is black?* ($^2/_6$)

   c. Arrange the blocks in equal groups of two, keeping the colors in separate groups. *How many groups are there?* (12) *What fraction is black?* ($^4/_{12}$)

Learn at Home, Grade 4

SCIENCE (Meteorology)

▶ 1. On a partly cloudy day, walk to an open area like a park. Have your child study the shapes of the clouds and watch them move. Discuss your child's observations. Ask him/her to draw the clouds using a piece of white chalk on light blue construction paper. Repeat this activity on other days so your child has the opportunity to observe a variety of cloud types.

▶ 2. Questions to ask during a discussion about the formation of clouds:

Does cold or warm air hold more water?
What happens to the amount of water air can hold if it is cooled? Warmed?
How does water get from land into the air?
What happens to water vapor as it rises from the Earth?
Under what conditions does it rain, snow, sleet or hail?
What is fog and how is it formed?
What happens when warm air moves over a cold surface?

▶ 3. Obtain books with photos of different types of clouds. There are three basic cloud types: *cirrus, cumulus* and *stratus*. Clouds may also be combinations or variations of these three types.

Cirrus (cirro) are high feathery clouds usually 20,000 feet or higher. They are called ice clouds because they are composed mostly of ice crystals.

Cumulus (cumulo) clouds are formed by rising air currents. They look like piles of cotton balls. The name means accumulated.

Stratus clouds blanket the sky, forming when a layer of air is cooled below the saturation point without vertical air movement. They are called stratus because they are in layers. The bases of these clouds are less than 6,000 feet above sea level.

Alto is a prefix attached to the name of a cloud to indicate it is in the middle range of clouds (between 15,000 and 20,000 feet). They are blue or gray opaque.

Nimbus (nimbo) is a prefix or suffix added to the names of clouds that usually produce a form of precipitation. Nimbus means *rain cloud*.

▶ 4. Given the definitions above, Have your child extrapolate what the clouds listed here look like and at what altitude they are found:

cirrus	cirrocumulus
altocumulus	stratus
cumulonimbus	cumulus
cirrostratus	altostratus
nimbostratus	stratocumulus

▶ 5. Show pictures of clouds or look at actual clouds. Have your child identify each type.

SOCIAL STUDIES (Your State)

▶ 1. If possible, arrange to visit the state capital when the legislature is in session. Arrange to meet with your district's representative or with a senator for a tour of the capitol building, a visit to the legislature in action and possibly an introduction to the governor. Your child should bring questions and write the answers for his/her state notebook. Ask him/her to write down any other bits of information learned and sketch or take pictures of some of the things seen. If a trip is not possible, your child could write to a representative and send his/her questions.

▶ 2. Have your child look in the local paper for articles about events happening in the capital city. Discuss the articles. Have your child cut out the articles and write summaries of the articles for the state notebook.

▶ 3. Have your child define the following terms (he/she may have to look them up in a dictionary): *bill, policy, tax, law* and *veto*. Discuss the process of how a law is passed. Have your child create a diagram of the legislative process to demonstrate his/her understanding of it. Who may introduce a new law, amendment, policy or tax? Have your child record the answers.

Tricky Y

batteries
cowboys
delays
donkeys
gravies
ivies
ladies
Mondays
pennies
ponies
stories
trays
Tuesdays
valleys
Wednesdays

Write the singular (S) form of each spelling word. Then, **write** its plural (P) form below it. The first one is done for you.

1. (S) battery
   (P) batteries

2. (S) _____
   (P) _____

3. (S) _____
   (P) _____

4. (S) _____
   (P) _____

5. (S) _____
   (P) _____

6. (S) _____
   (P) _____

7. (S) _____
   (P) _____

8. (S) _____
   (P) _____

9. (S) _____
   (P) _____

10. (S) _____
    (P) _____

11. (S) _____
    (P) _____

12. (S) _____
    (P) _____

13. (S) _____
    (P) _____

14. (S) _____
    (P) _____

15. (S) _____
    (P) _____

What part of speech is each of these words?_____

Which word can also be used as a verb?_____

How do you know when to change the **y** to an **i** before adding **es**?

_____

246

Match the Fractions

Match the Fractions

Week 23

Above each bar, **write** a fraction for the shaded part. Then, **match** each fraction on the left with its equivalent fraction on the right.

1. _____

a. _____
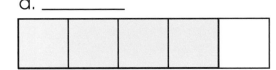

2. _____
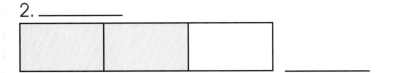

b. _____
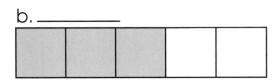

3. _____
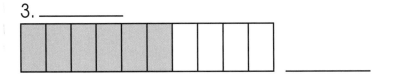

c. _____
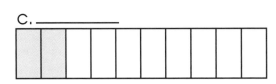

4. _____

d. _____

5. _____

e. _____
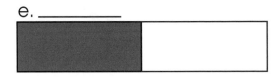

6. _____
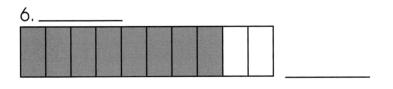

f. _____

7. _____

g. _____

Learn at Home, Grade 4

247

	Language Skills	Spelling	Reading
Monday	Building on work done in Weeks 12 and 13, explore more poetry with your child. *See* Language Skills, Week 24, number 1. Have your child write a rhyming poem. *See* Language Skills, Week 24, number 2. As he/she revises and edits, your child will find just the right words to express the desired meaning and mood.	Pretest your child on these spelling words. prearrange reappear reform predict rebuild reload preface recover remodel prepay redecorate repaint preview refill restore Have your child correct the pretest, add personalized words and make two copies of this week's study list.	**Diagrams and Charts** Provide your child with a model kit. Teach him/her the process of making a model: 1. Read through the instructions once. 2. Set up an appropriate workspace. 3. Make sure you have all the pieces. 4. Gather all necessary materials, such as glue, newspaper, paint shirt, paper towels and a bright light.
Tuesday	For handwriting practice, have your child copy a favorite poem in cursive. Be sure the author gets credit.	Have your child use each of this week's spelling words correctly in a sentence.	Let your child begin work on building the model. Remind your child to read the instructions carefully as he/she constructs the model.
Wednesday	Look at a page of a book to study paragraphs. With your child, discuss which paragraphs are full, which are continued from a previous page and which are continued on the next page. Have your child find and point to the first full paragraph on a page you indicate. Repeat with other pages until your child becomes familiar with paragraphs.	Have your child complete **Using Prefixes** (p. 253).	Have your child read the text and diagram to learn the box step. Directions are found in Reading, Week 24, number 1. Also, allow time for your child to continue working on the model.
Thursday	Paragraphs consist of sentences that support a main idea. Read two paragraphs on a page. Talk about why the author chose to break the paragraph where he/she did. How does the focus of the second paragraph differ from the first? Have your child complete **Paragraph Form** (p. 252).	Have your child write six predictions using words from this week's spelling list. The predictions can be about anything—from "Dad will wear a blue shirt tomorrow" to "Suzanne will be president someday."	Show your child how to read charts and diagrams to gain information. Newspapers, magazines and textbooks are excellent sources for tables, charts and graphs. Also look for movie timetables and bus schedules. Assemble several of these charts and diagrams for your child. Ask questions that require your child to read and interpret the information presented.
Friday	The United States has historically been called a melting pot. Immigrants from all over the world have come to live in the U.S. Now the term *melting pot* is being questioned because it implies that each person loses his/her identity and becomes part of a homogeneous mixture. Have your child write a paragraph explaining why *tossed salad* is a better image for this land of immigrants. Include a topic sentence and supporting sentences.	Give your child the final spelling test. Have your child record the pretest and final test words in his/her word bank.	Read an information-packed story to your child. Then, teach him/her how to make a chart to organize the information. *See* Reading, Week 24, number 2. Have your child make a chart listing the pros and cons for each of Beth's options. Based on what he/she knows about Beth, what does your child think Beth would do?

Learn at Home, Grade 4

Math	Science	Social Studies
Measurement Have your child measure given lengths in both centimeters and inches. *See* Math, Week 24, number 1. Have your child complete **It Suits Me to a Tee!** (p. 254).	Read about storms and extremes in weather: thunderstorms, tornadoes, hurricanes, floods, heat waves and others. What are the positive effects of such weather? What are the destructive elements? *See* Science, Week 24, number 1.	Help your child define the location of your state. Determine its latitude and longitude, its relative position in the U.S. and any other information that could help a foreigner find the state on a map. Have your child complete **Near My State** (p. 255).
Teach your child to measure precisely and to write linear measurements with fractions. Select several objects for your child to measure. Include measurements such as $2^1/_2$ in., $4^1/_4$ in., $7^3/_8$ in., $6^3/_{10}$ cm and $5^6/_{10}$ cm.	Many famous scientists have had an impact on the science of weather forecasting. Read about the weather-related work of Aristotle, Edmund Halley, Abbe Cleveland, Vilhelm Bjerknes, Gabriel Daniel Farenheit and others. Look under "Weather" in *The World Book Encyclopedia*. Have your child write about the weather-related work of one scientist.	Look at a map of the United States. Ask questions that will challenge your child to study the map carefully and use the mileage scale and compass rose. *See* Social Studies, Week 24, number 1.
Have your child identify a foot, a yard and a meter. Discuss when it would be appropriate to use inches or centimeters and when it would be appropriate to use feet, yards or meters. What unit would you use to measure: *the length of the room?* *the height of the door?* *the width of your desk?* *the length of your pencil?* *the distance to your friend's house?*	Analyze the data on the weather charts your child has maintained so far. Have him/her make a graph showing the changes in one area and explain the graph to you.	Obtain a physical map of your state/ province. Study the landforms found in your area. Help your child make a relief map. *See* Social Studies, Week 24, number 2.
Look through the kitchen and bathroom cupboards for containers of liquids. Read the measurements listed. Some products list in ounces, others in milliliters. Have your child line up the bottles in order of volume from smallest to largest capacity. This activity should give your child a sense of the size bottle for a given capacity. It is valuable for him/her to have a sense of one liter. *See* Math, Week 24, number 2.	Sing songs related to weather. Suggestions include "Raindrops Keep Falling on My Head," "You Are My Sunshine" and "Singin' in the Rain."	Allow time for your child to finish the relief map.
Experiment: You will need several bowls or pie tins, a milliliter measuring cup and a variety of liquids (tap water, different juices, vinegar, boiling water and cooking oil). Have your child measure the same amount of each liquid and pour into pie tins or bowls. Leave the liquids on a sunny windowsill for several days. Have your child take a measurement each day for several days and graph the data. Discuss the results.	Have your child create a comic strip, song or mural that teaches one weather-related concept. The intended audience should be someone your child's age who has not learned about weather yet. Have your child present his/her creation to a real audience (it can be one person) if possible. Allow the audience to ask questions.	Study a state map. Look at the variety of type (large, bold, thin, light) used to indicate the size of a city or town. Discuss the terms *city, town, village, suburb* and *metropolis*. Create a Venn diagram with your child to compare two places in your area.

Learn at Home, Grade 4

TEACHING SUGGESTIONS AND ACTIVITIES

LANGUAGE SKILLS (Paragraphs)

▷   1.   Read poetry with lots of expression. Choose age-appropriate poems that convey a variety of moods. Model your enjoyment of reading poetry and playing with words. Have your child read a poem aloud. Encourage him/her to be expressive. Read several kinds of poems with your child. After looking at humorous poems, rhyming poems, descriptive poems and others, have your child make lists of rhyming words, words that describe, sound words and nonsense words. Copy the lists onto chart paper and display them in the room for future reference.

▷   2.   Guide your child as he/she writes a rhyming poem. Have him/her select a topic for the poem, then brainstorm a list of related words.
   Example: night—stars, dark, moon, Milky Way, galaxy, sleeping, dream, shining, quiet, shadows, still, midnight, meteor, twinkle, prayers

   Then, have your child pair adjectives and nouns to create images of the topic.
   Examples: dancing stars, dark sky, sweet dreams, shooting star, still air, flashing light, black shadows, full moon, milky path

   Your child can choose some of the images to write about. Look at lists of rhyming words to help. Have him/her write in couplets, rhyming the final words of the lines.
   Examples: Sitting did I see from afar
   A flash that was a shooting star?
   The shooting star made a yellow streak
   And my eyes could only catch a peek.

READING (Diagrams and Charts)

▷   1.   Sometimes it is easier to follow directions if there is a picture or diagram to accompany the text. Let your child practice moving between text and a diagram. Here is a diagram of the box step with text. Copy this for your child and have him/her read and demonstrate the step.

a. Start with both feet together.

b. Move your right foot to the right.

c. Slide your left foot next to your right.

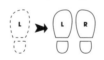

d. Move your right foot back.

e. Move your left foot next to your right.

f. Slide your left foot to the left.

g. Slide your right foot next to your left.

h. Move your left foot forward.

i. Move your right foot forward.

▷   2.   Read the story below aloud to your child.

   Beth is excited for the approaching summer—three months off! She would like to read and go swimming, biking and hiking. Beth's dad offered to send her to Creativity Camp for the summer. Creativity Camp specializes in the arts. Beth would learn how to draw, paint, play an instrument, sculpt, cook, dance and more. Her good friend Kim is going to Creativity Camp.

Beth's mom suggested that they rent a cabin at a lake for the summer. Beth and her mom would go for the summer, and her dad would come for the weekends. At the cabin, she can swim, bike, hike, and learn to water-ski, canoe and sail.

Since this is a difficult decision for Beth, she decided to make a chart of the pros and cons of the two alternatives.

Now, help your child create a chart like Beth's, organizing the information from the story to show the pros and cons of each alternative.

MATH (Measurement)

▶ 1. Give your child a ruler and a yardstick. Have him/her identify the units of measurement on each. Compare them to a centimeter ruler and a meterstick. Discuss what units are on each. Put the two rulers next to one another, comparing their lengths and size of units. Have your child measure and record the length of some common objects such as a pencil, book or sheet of paper. Ask if there seems to be any advantage to using one unit of measurement over the other. The metric system is divided into units of 10 at every level making it simpler to use than U.S. Customary. When you need to measure lengths of a fraction more or less than an inch, it becomes very difficult to name with U.S. Customary standards.

▶ 2. Write the U.S. Customary and metric units used for measuring liquids on the chalkboard:
U.S. Customary: cup, fluid ounce, pint, quart, gallon
Metric: milliliter (mL), liter (L)

Center: Create a measuring center with tools, a sink and liquids for your child to explore. Have your child record any relationships discovered (e.g., 2 cups = 1 pint).

SCIENCE (Meteorology)

▶ 1. Ask some of the following questions in a discussion about storms.

When do most thunderstorms take place?   *What is an ice storm?*
What kind of clouds usually produce them?   *What is a blizzard?*
What produces lightning and thunder?   *In what areas do tornadoes occur?*
What kind of storms occur in winter?   *Who must watch out for heat waves?*
What areas of the world will probably   *Can a flood be prevented?*
*   never see an ice storm?*   *How can people be prepared for a flood?*

SOCIAL STUDIES (Your State)

▶ 1. While your child is looking at the map, ask questions such as the following:

What state/province is north of your state? In what direction would you travel to reach _____?
Is the state capital south of your present location? How far is it from city A to city B?
What highway would you take to get from city A to city B?

▶ 2. Help your child make a relief map.

Preparation: Mix flour, water and salt to make a wet dough.
Making the map: Draw the state/province outline on a sheet of 15" square piece of cardboard. Apply the flour and salt mixture in various thicknesses to create raised areas on the map. Paint a thin layer of the dough over the entire state outline. Allow it to dry. Apply thicker dough in areas where the land is higher. Your child can shape mountains by hand and scrape into the first layer of dough to make rivers. Let the dough dry. Look at a physical map again. Note the colors used to show land formations. Have your child paint the map using the same colors.

Learn at Home, Grade 4

Paragraph Form

A **paragraph** is a group of sentences about one main idea.
When writing a paragraph:
1. **Indent** the first line.
2. **Capitalize** the first word of each sentence.
3. **Punctuate** each sentence.

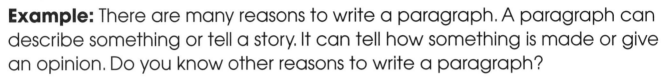

Example: There are many reasons to write a paragraph. A paragraph can describe something or tell a story. It can tell how something is made or give an opinion. Do you know other reasons to write a paragraph?

Read the paragraphs below. They contain errors. **Rewrite** the paragraphs correctly on the lines by following three basic rules:
    1. Indent 2. Capitalize   3. Punctuate

the number of teeth you have depends on your age a baby has no teeth at all gradually, milk teeth, or baby teeth, begin to grow later, these teeth fall out and permanent teeth appear by the age of twenty-five, you should have thirty-two permanent teeth

_____

_____

_____

_____

_____

my family is going to Disneyland tomorrow we plan to arrive early my dad will take my little sister to Fantasyland first meanwhile, my brother and I will visit Frontierland and Adventureland after lunch we will all meet to go to Tomorrowland

_____

_____

_____

_____

_____

Learn at Home, Grade 4

Using Prefixes

prearrange
predict
preface
prepay
preview
reappear
rebuild
recover
redecorate
refill
reform
reload
remodel
repaint
restore

Fill in the blanks.

1. After the tornado destroyed the barn, the neighbors helped us _____ .

2. If you try to guess what a story is about by looking at the pictures, you are trying to _____ .

3. When Dad decided to _____ the family room he had to tear down walls and install new windows.

4. My folks selected new wallpaper and drapes when they decided to _____ .

5. You have to _____ the photographer for your school pictures before he will take them.

6. We had to _____ the chair because my cat clawed the fabric.

7. It's difficult to _____ a bicycle to its original condition if a truck runs over it.

8. The room parents worked with the teacher to _____ the details of the field trip.

9. We helped to _____ the ice-cream machine when it ran out of ingredients.

10. The _____ of the book gives an introduction.

11. The magician hid the coin and then made it _____ .

12. I was so thirsty that I asked for a _____ of lemonade.

13. When my brother's new car got scratched, he wanted to _____ it immediately.

14. Before watching the afternoon movie, we saw a _____ of coming attractions.

15. My clay project in art class started to fall apart, so I had to _____ it.

253

It Suits Me to a Tee!

How many inches and centimeters from the tee to the flag?

Example:

12 cm

5 in.

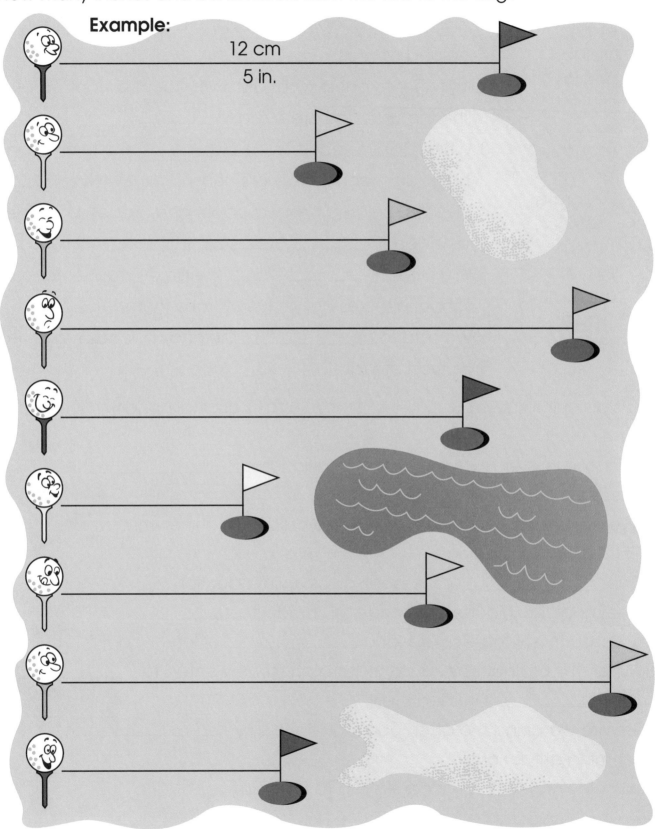

Near My State

Use a map of the United States to locate your state. **Write** the names of the bordering states/countries and/or bodies of water on the chart below. **Write** each one in its correct location relative to your state.

Northwest	North	Northeast
West	My State Draw an outline of your state.	East
Southwest	South	Southeast

	Language Skills	Spelling	Reading
Monday	With your child, brainstorm onomatopoetic words, such as *grr, hiss, buzz* and *moo*. Have your child create a book entitled *Onomatopoeia*. Each page of the book should include one sound word and a picture (drawn by your child) of an object that makes that sound. For the final page of the book, have your child write a poem using onomatopoetic words.	Pretest your child on these spelling words. bicycle quadruplet trio bifocals triangle tripod bimonthly tricep unicorn binoculars tricorn unicycle quadrangle tricycle uniform Have your child correct the pretest, add personalized words and make two copies of this week's study list.	The setting of this week's novel is Norway during World War II. Find Norway on a map. Give your child a little background on World War II. With your child, read chapters 1 and 2 of *Snow Treasure* by Marie McSwigan. Have your child make a prediction: *What do you think Uncle Victor's plan is?*
Tuesday	For handwriting practice, have your child copy a list of onomatopoetic words onto a chart. Hang the chart for reference.	Have your child use each of this week's spelling words correctly in a sentence.	Introduce vocabulary from chapters 3 and 4: *scheme, fjords, navigator, rickety, logic, restless, primer, schoolmaster, precaution, lieutenant, audience, defense, mantle, secrecy, caution, appoint, uppermost, invasion, foreign, character, ordinary, unreal, confidential, inspect, stagger, suspect, explosive.* Have your child add these to his/her Reading Journal. Read chapters 3 and 4 of *Snow Treasure.*
Wednesday	Have your child write a paragraph from a given topic sentence. Write a topic sentence on the chalkboard about a subject that interests your child. Then, ask him/her to write a paragraph to support the topic sentence.	Have your child complete **Number Words** (p. 261).	Read chapters 5 and 6 of *Snow Treasure.* Have your child imagine he/she were given a responsibility as big as Peter's. Would your child feel as brave? Has there been a time when your child was entrusted with a big responsibility? How did your child feel about it?
Thursday	Have your child arrange scrambled sentences to form into paragraphs. *See* Language Skills, Week 25, number 1.	Have your child write a silly story using words from this week's spelling list. Encourage your child to include onomatopoetic words as well. Have him/her underline each spelling word, then illustrate the story.	Read chapters 7–9 of *Snow Treasure.* **Reading Journal:** *What did the four children learn on the first night that they must remember to teach their individual teams?*
Friday	Help your child write a descriptive paragraph by brainstorming words related to a chosen topic. *See* Language Skills, Week 25, number 2. Have your child complete **Topic Sentences—Paragraphs** (p. 260).	Give your child the final spelling test. Have your child record the pretest and final test words in his/her word bank.	Read chapters 10–13 of *Snow Treasure.* **Reading Journal:** *Write a description of the sled journey the children take down the mountain. Include the stops, the people they meet and the return trip.*

Math	Science	Social Studies
Weight can be measured in grams, kilograms, metric tons, ounces, pounds and tons. Using a balance scale, set one unit (a pound) on one pan and look for familiar objects to place in the other pan. Have your child sort the objects into three groups: less than a pound, about a pound and more than a pound. Repeat this exercise with other units. *See* Math, Week 25, number 1.	Read *The Lorax* by Dr. Seuss. In this story the main character discovers that living things depend upon each other and that the impact of human actions can set off a chain reaction of destruction. Have your child think about the specific cause of the demise of each plant and animal in the book. Relate this story to what's happening today in our own world.	**Landforms** Teach your child the definition of *landform* (a natural feature of the Earth's surface). Discuss actions, such as erosion from wind and water, glaciers, earthquakes and volcanoes, that contribute to the formation of different landforms. Have your child name examples of well-known landforms or look for them on an atlas. *See* Social Studies, Week 25, number 1.
Provide your child with several objects to weigh in ounces and pounds. A kitchen pantry is full of items of various weights. Have your child estimate the weight of each object before weighing. Then, have your child weigh each item on the scale, then record the name of the object and its weight on a sheet of paper. Today, use U.S. Customary units.	Each biome or ecosystem is a delicately balanced web of interconnected life. Choose a biome such as desert, mountain, rainforest or swamp. This week, have your child study the living organisms found there. Have your child list some of the plants and animals that live in the chosen biome.	Have your child make a glossary of landforms. Have him/her write each landform on an index card, define it, name an example and sketch a picture on the card. Then, have your child file the cards in alphabetical order. *See* Social Studies, Week 25, number 2.
Repeat yesterday's lesson using metric measurements (grams).	Have your child describe in writing the climate of the area you are studying. Ask him/her to explain how the climate affects the types of plants and animals living there.	Using a physical map of North America, teach your child to use the key to understand how the landforms are shown symbolically. Ask him/her to locate major landforms that you name, such as Cape Cod, the Grand Canyon, the Mississippi River, the Gulf of Mexico, the Bering Strait and the Florida peninsula.
Teach your child to read a thermometer in Celsius and Fahrenheit. Notice the difference in units between each degree. Use a teaching thermometer to give your child practice reading temperatures. You can make a teaching thermometer by drawing the scale carefully on paper. Use a strip of red paper to act as the mercury. Move the "mercury" to different degrees and have your child read the temperature.	Teach your child about food chains and food webs. Include plants, animals and decomposers in the discussion. Have your child diagram several food chains that exist in the biome you are studying. Show your child how several interconnecting food chains form a food web.	While referring to a world map, have your child group given landforms into categories. *See* Social Studies, Week 25, number 3.
You can purchase a thermometer for reading the temperature of liquids at a science supply store or teacher's store. Place the thermometer in boiling water and in water near freezing. Have your child read and record the temperatures of liquids in Celsius and Fahrenheit. *See* Math, Week 25, number 2.	Have your child choose an animal from the biome he/she is studying and find out what type of home the animal makes for itself. Have your child write a fictional account of this animal. The story should include an incident that affects the animal's home and tell how the animal reacts. Give the story a happy ending.	Have your child group his/her glossary cards, putting similar landforms together and naming the category. For example, river, bay, sea, lake and gulf could all be placed under the category *bodies of water*. Encourage your child to group creatively but insist that each landform within the category fit the title.

TEACHING SUGGESTIONS AND ACTIVITIES

LANGUAGE SKILLS (Paragraphs)

▶ 1. Copy each sentence from the following four paragraphs onto a separate strip of paper or index card. Write the topic sentences (in bold here) in a different color so they stand out. Scramble the sentences and give them to your child. Ask him/her to sort the sentences into groups related to the same subject. Then, using the topic sentence as the first sentence, have your child arrange the sentences in each group to form a coherent paragraph.

> I—**The seals at the zoo were hungry**. They were making a lot of noise, because they knew it was almost feeding time. When their keeper opened the gate to their pen, they dove into the water and swam over to him. They jumped out of the water to catch the fish he threw at them. All was quiet as they swam back to their island and basked contentedly in the sun.

> II—**We packed our car with everything we thought we would need on our camping trip**. We took more than enough food and plenty of clothes to last a week without doing laundry. When we got to the site where we planned to set up camp, we unloaded the car. We put our clothes inside the tents and set the food and cooking supplies on a table nearby. When it was time to fix dinner, Dad soon discovered he had forgotten charcoal, so we gathered sticks and built a great fire.

> III—**The runners had gathered downtown for the big race**. The gun sounded and they were off, running down the streets of the city that were usually crowded with traffic. Along the way, people stood by the roadside to cheer. As the runners came within sight of the finish line, they saw what seemed to be hundreds of people. The mob of people rushed forward to congratulate the winner when she crossed the finish line.

> IV—**Emily and her mother went to the animal shelter**. They were looking for a new dog. Emily wanted one just like their old dog, Baby, but her mom wanted a smaller one. Finally, they found one that looked like Baby but was much smaller. They named their new dog Big Baby.

▶ 2. Before writing a descriptive paragraph, it helps to organize one's ideas. Teach your child to choose a topic, then brainstorm descriptive and related words, keeping in mind all the senses.

Topic: A sandy desert   **Related words:** sandy, hot, dry, cactus, desolate, oasis, camel, caravan, parched, blinding, thirsty, windy, silence

a. Have your child think about the image of the desert and write an appropriate topic sentence. *The hot, desolate desert stretches for miles ahead of the well-prepared traveler.*

b. Then, have your child write three or four supporting sentences incorporating the remaining brainstormed words. Let your child choose from one of the following topics: music, magic, movies, computers and summer. Have him/her brainstorm descriptive and related words for the chosen topic, then write a topic sentence and supporting sentences to form an organized paragraph.

MATH (Measurement)

▶ 1. U.S. Customary: 16 ounces (oz.) = 1 pound (lb.)
2000 pounds = 1 ton (T.)

Metric System: 1000 milligrams (mg) = 1 gram (g)
1000 grams = 1 kilogram (kg)

▶ 2. Have your child measure the temperature of different liquids using both Celsius and Fahrenheit scales. Fill cups with different liquids (see below). Have your child measure and record the temperature of each.

tap water	____ °C	____ °F
rain water	____ °C	____ °F
boiling water	____ °C	____ °F
milk from refrigerator	____ °C	____ °F
fresh-squeezed orange juice	____ °C	____ °F
water near freezing	____ °C	____ °F
_____	____ °C	____ °F

SOCIAL STUDIES (Landforms)

▶ 1. Obtain pictures of some well-known landforms. Discuss their heights or lengths and how they were formed. Examples might include the Rocky Mountains, the Grand Canyon, Mount Everest, Monument Valley, the Nile River, Maine's seacoast and Crater Lake.

▶ 2. Have your child include the following landforms in his/her glossary:

archipelago	cliff	floodplain	mesa	prairie
arroyo	coastline	geyser	monument	reef
atoll	continent	glacier	mountain	savanna
bay	cordillera	gorge	natural bridge	steppe
beach	crater	gulf	pampa	strait
brook	crevasse	headland	peninsula	stream
butte	delta	highland	piedmont	tableland
canyon	dune	hill	pinnacle	tributary
cape	estuary	island	plain	tundra
cave	fault	isthmus	plateau	valley
chimney	fjord	lowland	promontory	waterfall

▶ 3. Write the following categories across the chalkboard: *desert, mountain, river, archipelago, island* and *sea.* The following proper nouns each name a particular landform. Have your child list each name under the appropriate category on the board.

Mediterranean	Alps	North Bering	Madagascar	Hawaii
Galapagos	Kalahari	Congo	Beaufort	Japan
Jamaica	Yangtze	Arkansas	Gobi	Atlas
Australia	Baffin	Canary	Ural	Atacama
Philippine	New Guinea	Appalachian	Andes	Caribbean

Learn at Home, Grade 4

Topic Sentences—Paragraphs

Read each topic listed below. **Write** a topic sentence for each topic.
Example: Topic: Seasons

       Topic Sentence: There are four seasons in every year.
    or: Of all the seasons, my favorite is summer.

1. Topic: Winter
   Topic Sentence: _____

   _____

2. Topic: Skateboards
   Topic Sentence: _____

3. Topic: America
   Topic Sentence: _____

4. Topic: Horses
   Topic Sentence: _____

5. Topic: Books
   Topic Sentence: _____

Choose two of your best topic sentences from above. **Write** each as the beginning sentence for the two paragraphs below. **Write** at least four support sentences to go with each topic sentence to make two complete paragraphs.

_____

_____

_____

_____

_____

_____

_____

_____

_____

Learn at Home, Grade 4

Number Words

bicycle
bifocals
bimonthly
binoculars
quadrangle
quadruplet
triangle
tricep
tricorn
tricycle
trio
tripod
unicorn
unicycle
uniform

Complete the crossword puzzle.

Across
2. three-sided figure
4. mythical horse with one horn
6. rectangular area with buildings on four sides
7. eyeglasses having two focal lengths
8. three-wheeler
12. every two months
13. three-cornered hat in early times

Down
1. field glasses
2. group of three musicians
3. two-wheeler
5. three-legged camera support
6. one of four babies born at a single birth
9. one-wheeler
10. all the same
11. arm muscle with three points of origin

	Language Skills	Spelling	Reading
Monday	Teach your child the format for writing a business letter. Use the block style and compare the style to that of a personal letter. *See* Language Skills, Week 26, numbers 1 and 2. Also show your child how to address the envelope. Have your child write a letter to the United States Geological Survey (USGS) or local tourist office requesting materials (maps, brochures, etc.) of your area.	Pretest your child on these spelling words. discolor nonfat unfold dislike nonsense unfriendly disobey unbreakable unhappiness distrust uncertain unlucky nondairy unfair unselfish Have your child correct the pretest, add personalized words and make two copies of this week's study list.	Read chapters 14–17 of *Snow Treasure*. Discuss events from the reading: *Why did the Germans want the children in school? How did the doctor help them solve the problem? What might have happened if the German doctor had checked on the patients?* Have your child complete **Who Is It?** (p. 269).
Tuesday	For handwriting practice, have your child copy a descriptive paragraph from a book in his/her best cursive handwriting.	Have your child use each of this week's spelling words correctly in a sentence.	Read chapters 18–20 together. Draw a picture of the *Cleng Peerson* as described at the end of chapter 20. Then, quickly review cause and effect. Have your child complete **What Made It Happen?** (p. 270).
Wednesday	Have your child write a descriptive paragraph about a still life. Set up a still life (such as a bowl of fruit) as if you were going to paint it. Then, have your child paint the picture with words by writing a detailed paragraph.	Have your child complete **Don't Be So Negative** (p. 268).	Read chapters 21–24. Does your child believe Jan Lasek's story? Have your child write a letter to Uncle Victor either convincing him to take Jan or persuading him that Jan is lying. Use supporting arguments.
Thursday	Sometimes the topic sentence is not the first sentence in a paragraph. Teach your child how to recognize the topic sentence. Guide him/her through the first two paragraphs on **Main Ideas—Location** (p. 266).	Have your child make spelling stairs using several or all of this week's words. *See* **Background Information and Supporting Activities** (p. 8).	Read chapters 25–28. Discuss whether Peter did the right thing. Have your child complete **Creative Endings** (p. 271).
Friday	Teach your child how to write an organized paragraph. The supporting sentences should support the main idea. *See* Language Skills, Week 26, number 3. Have your child complete **Support Sentences** (p. 267).	Give your child the final spelling test. Have your child record the pretest and final test words in his/her word bank.	Read chapters 29 and 30. Have your child write an imaginary newspaper article for a U.S. newspaper telling about the bravery of Peter and the journey of the gold bullion.

Math	Science	Social Studies

Assess if your child needs more practice with reading a clock. *See* Math, Week 26, number 1. Periodically throughout the day, have your child report the time to you. Then, ask him/her to tell you what time it will be…
    in an hour or 2 hours.
    in 20 minutes.
    when play time begins.
    when… (be creative).
	There are many types of relationships found in nature, some based on the need for nourishment. Some animals eat plants while others eat animals. Some animals eat dead plants and animals. Teach your child about scavengers. Scavengers are important to the food chain because they clean up food or decaying material left behind. Have your child name some scavengers he/she has seen.	Some landforms are very similar. An ocean and a sea are so similar that these terms are often used interchangeably. Have your child look through the definitions of landforms in his/her glossary and pair any landforms whose definitions are almost identical.

Think of some "events" that your child experiences often. Make a list of these events and have your child guess how long each one lasts. Then, have him/her time the events the next time they occur. **Examples:** How long does a commercial last? How long does it take to walk to a friend's house. How long does it take to eat breakfast? dinner?	Teach your child about parasites. In a parasitic relationship, one organism (plant or animal) gets its food from another organism (host) and harms the host in the process. A common parasitic relationship is between a flea and a cat. The cat in this relationship is called the host. The flea is called the parasite and causes the cat to itch by sucking its blood.	Looking at a map of the country, have your child refer to his/her glossary cards and locate an example of the different landforms in your state or province. If he/she cannot find an example of a particular landform, ask him/her to explain why. For example, you cannot have a seacoast if the state is landlocked.
Make up time-related story problems for your child to solve. **Example:** If it was 8:00 a.m. when we left for Grandma's house, and it took five-and-a-half hours to drive there, when did we arrive? Have your child complete a copy of **Minute Monsters** (p. 272).	Teach your child about mutualism. In this relationship, the two organisms involved both help each other. One may provide food while the other provides shelter.	Large cities were often established because the natural resources were attractive to a large number of people. Have your child locate major cities on a map of your state. What geographic features might have attracted the settlers? Why?
For other measurement activities, *see* Math, Week 26, numbers 2–4. Have your child complete **How Far Is It?** (p. 273).	Teach your child about commensalism. Sometimes two organisms live together but only one of the two benefits. When the other (host) is not harmed by the relationship, it is called commensalism. Have your child draw a picture of one plant growing on another without harming the host. Look for specific species that exhibit this relationship.	Choose two very different locations in the country. Study the climate and landforms in each area with your child. Have him/her compare the areas and decide which place would be a more desirable place to be in a given month. Consider how the climate and landforms influence things such as clothing, recreation, types of jobs and foods.
Continue Thursday's activities.	Read about food producers, consumers and decomposers. A food chain depends on all these elements. Plants are usually food producers. Have your child illustrate and label the cycle of decomposition. Include the living organisms that die, the decomposer that breaks them down into nutrients and the new life that benefits from the nutrients.	Have your child draw a physical map of an imaginary place including at least ten landforms on the map. Have your child name the place and each of the landforms.

Learn at Home, Grade 4

TEACHING SUGGESTIONS AND ACTIVITIES

LANGUAGE SKILLS (Paragraphs)

▶ 1. Teach your child to use the business letter format when writing to a person that he/she does not know personally. He/she would use this format to write . . .

to an author	to the city mayor
to an editor	giving ideas for improvement
a complaint letter	a complimentary letter
to a U.S. government official	requesting information or materials

▶ 2. Use the block style shown here for writing business letters.

Your name
Your address

Today's date

Name of person to whom you are writing
Name of company or organization
Address of company or organization

Greeting,

Do not indent paragraphs.

Place an extra return between paragraphs.

Closing,

Your signature

Your name

Ask your child: *How does a business letter differ from a friendly letter? What elements are the same? What elements are different?*

▶ 3. Teach your child this basic outline for writing an organized paragraph.

Writing a Basic Paragraph
  I. Choose a topic.
  II. Brainstorm supporting ideas.
  III. Write a topic sentence.
  IV. Use the ideas from Step II to write supporting sentences.
  V. Write the topic and supporting sentences together in paragraph form.

Example:
  I. Helping with household chores
  II. Cleaning room
    Taking out trash
    Washing dishes
    Feeding pets
  III. Most children help their families by doing household chores.
  IV. Some children take out the trash every day. Many children feed their pets and help with the dishes. Almost every child must keep a neat room.
  V. Most children help their families with household chores. Some take out the trash every day. Many children feed their pets and help with the dishes. Almost every child must keep a neat room.

Learn at Home, Grade 4

MATH (Measurement)

▶ 1. The best approach to teaching time on an analog clock is to teach your child to begin looking only at the hour hand. From the hour hand alone, your child can tell if it is near to an hour or halfway to the next hour. Teach him/her to read the hour hand first, then look to the minute hand for precision. Do not relate the minutes to the numbers on the clock face. Teach your child to count the minutes. Help him/her see the clock face in fractions. Also, teach your child to count minutes before the hour.

▶ 2. Using a ruler and the scale of miles/kilometers on a map, have your child estimate distances between cities.

▶ 3. Have your child complete the activity on **How Far Is It?** (p. 273) as directed. Then, have him/her create a new scale (1 cm = 1 km) and measure the distances again.

▶ 4. Sometimes we use non-standard units of measurement when precision is not important. Have your child measure different distances by pacing. You can measure the length of a pace by walking along a yardstick or by measuring length between footprints. Place the end of the stick at the back of one heel. Take a normal step and note the measurement from the heal to the tip of the front foot.

Learn at Home, Grade 4

Main Ideas—Location

The **main idea** of a paragraph can be located anywhere in the paragraph. Although most main ideas are stated in the first sentence, many good paragraphs contain a topic sentence in the middle or even at the end.

Draw two lines under the topic sentence.
Draw one line under each support sentence.

We had a great time at the basketball game last Friday night. My dad took four of my friends and me to the gym at seven o'clock. We sat with other kids from our class. Our team was behind at the half but pulled ahead to win by eight points. After the game, we stopped for burgers before going home.

The alarm rang for a full minute before Jay heard it. Even then, he put his pillow over his head, rolled over and moaned loudly. Getting up in the morning was always hard for Jay. As usual, his mom had to take the pillow off his head and make him get up for school.

On the lines below, **write** three paragraphs. Put the topic sentence in the correct place. **Underline** each topic sentence.

Paragraph 1 (Topic Sentence—Middle)

_____

_____

_____

Paragraph 2 (Topic Sentence—Beginning)

_____

_____

_____

Paragraph 3 (Topic Sentence—End)

_____

_____

_____

_____

Learn at Home, Grade 4

Support Sentences

The **topic sentence** gives the main idea of a paragraph. The **support sentences** give the details about the main idea. Each sentence must relate to the main idea.

Read the paragraph below. **Underline** the topic sentence. **Cross out** the sentence that is not a support sentence. On the line, **write** a support sentence to go in its place.

Giving a surprise birthday party can be exciting but tricky. The honored person must not hear a word about the party! On the day of the party, everyone should arrive early. A snack may ruin your appetite.

_____

Write three support sentences to go with each topic sentence.

Giving a dog a bath can be a real challenge!

1._____
2._____
3._____

I can still remember how embarrassed I was that day!

1._____
2._____
3._____

Sometimes I like to imagine what our prehistoric world was like.

1._____
2._____
3._____

A daily newspaper features many kinds of news.

1._____
2._____
3._____

discolor
dislike
disobey
distrust
nondairy
nonfat
nonsense
unbreakable
uncertain
unfair
unfold
unfriendly
unhappiness
unlucky
unselfish

Write the spelling word that closely matches each definition.

1. unjust _____

2. foolishness _____

3. stain _____

4. unfortunate _____

5. open; spread out _____

6. aversion to _____

7. suspicion; no confidence _____

8. sadness _____

9. cannot be easily broken _____

10. misbehave _____

11. lacking grease _____

12. generous _____

13. doubtful; questionable _____

14. lacking milk _____

15. hostile _____

What do all three prefixes mean? _____

Learn at Home, Grade 4

Who Is It?

Write the correct descriptions below each character's name.

- a very thorough planner
- knew the weather was in for a change
- risked his life to save a life
- always seems to get everything right
- was daring enough to throw a snowball
- daring as any boy
- destroyed the snowman
- became a very good leader
- wanted a chance for freedom in America
- loved the *Cleng Peerson*
- helped the children learn to load the gold
- wanted a shoe polisher

Uncle Victor

_____

_____

Peter Lundstrom

_____

_____

Per Garson

_____

_____

Jan Lasek

_____

_____

Helga Thomsen

_____

_____

The Commandant

_____

_____

What Made It Happen?

Each set of sentences includes a cause and an effect. Remember: The cause is what makes something happen, and the effect is the result.

Write the cause on the line and **circle** the effect.

1. The snow came down harder than anyone could ever remember. For days the people of the village were housebound.

   _____

2. Many of the soldiers decided to learn to ski. The children called one soldier "Lieutenant Sit-Down," because he fell down more than he stood.

   _____

3. The Commandant kept kicking the snowman covering the gold. Peter threw a snowball to distract the Commandant from discovering the gold.

   _____

4. Per Garson was skiing in crazy patterns around and around the Lundstrom's house. Uncle Victor had been there earlier on his skis.

   _____

5. Peter was sailing down the slope at high speed. In his path, he could see approaching soldiers. Peter was going so fast he could not stop his sled. The soldiers scattered to let Peter through.

   _____

6. Mrs. Holms seemed very excited to see the Lundstroms coming to her home. She acted as though she could not wait to speak. Earlier in the day a German soldier had been in the Holms's barn.

   _____

Learn at Home, Grade 4

Creative Endings

Many events occurred in the story because of well thought-out plans. Now it is your turn to do the thinking. Each of the following events have been given a new twist. **Write** what happens.

1. Uncle Victor was really a German Spy. With all of the gold he . . .

_____

_____

_____

2. Peter Lundstrom was unable to escape from the camp. The Commandant has called for him . . .

_____

_____

_____

3. Per Garson was wrong about the rain changing to snow. The children then decided to take the gold . . .

_____

_____

_____

4. Jan Lasek accidentally led the troops to the hiding place of the Cleng Peerson . . .

_____

_____

_____

5. The Commandant ordered his doctor to examine the patients . . .

_____

_____

_____

Minute Monsters

The Minute Monsters have their pairs of shoes mixed-up. **Cut out** the shoes. **Glue** the matching pairs onto another paper.

45 min. after 2:35

8:20

2 hrs. 5 min. after 1:10

8:00

3 hrs. 10 min. before 10:00

2:20

2 hrs. 10 min. before 4:00

6:50

45 min. after 1:45

4:20

1 hr. 50 min. before 6:10

2:30

1 hr. 25 min. before 9:45

3:20

55 min. before 3:15

3:45

3 hrs. 15 min. before 7:00

1:50

2 hrs. 35 min. after 5:25

3:15

272

Learn at Home, Grade 4

How Far Is It?

Use your ruler to measure each distance on the map. Then, use the letters on the tires and your answers to solve the message at the bottom of the page.

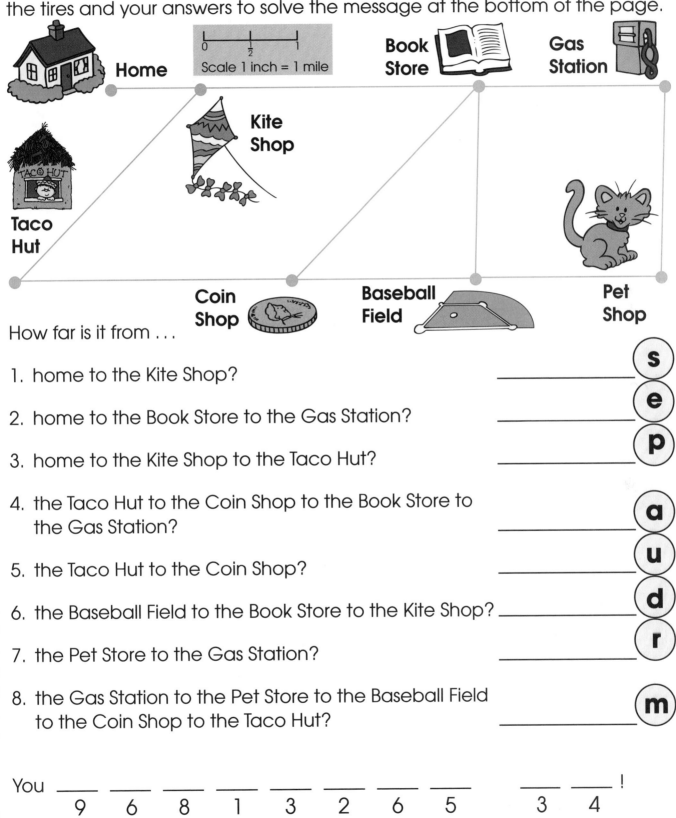

Home

Scale 1 inch = 1 mile

Book Store

Gas Station

Kite Shop

Taco Hut

Coin Shop

Baseball Field

Pet Shop

How far is it from . . .

1. home to the Kite Shop? _____ **s**

2. home to the Book Store to the Gas Station? _____ **e**

3. home to the Kite Shop to the Taco Hut? _____ **p**

4. the Taco Hut to the Coin Shop to the Book Store to the Gas Station? _____ **a**

5. the Taco Hut to the Coin Shop? _____ **u**

6. the Baseball Field to the Book Store to the Kite Shop? _____ **d**

7. the Pet Store to the Gas Station? _____ **r**

8. the Gas Station to the Pet Store to the Baseball Field to the Coin Shop to the Taco Hut? _____ **m**

You __ __ __ __ __ __ __ __ __ __ !
   9   6   8   1   3   2   6   5   3   4

Learn at Home, Grade 4

Language Skills	Spelling	Reading

Monday

Language Skills — Review Week
Review the four kinds of sentences. Have your child write five declarative sentences, five imperative sentences, five interrogative sentences and five exclamatory sentences. Check that your child understands and uses the correct word order and punctuation for each.

Spelling — Review Week
Choose words from the past 8 weeks for the pretest. Pretest your child on these spelling words. Then, have your child correct the pretest and make a study list of misspelled words, if any. Remind him/her to study the words each day this week.

Reading — Review Week
Review the meaning of *fiction* and *nonfiction*.
Have your child write a nonfictional account of a recent event in which he/she was involved.

Tuesday

Language Skills — Review the elements of a good sentence: expressing a complete idea, subject/verb agreement, word choice, capitalization and punctuation. *See* Language Skills, Week 27, number 1. Assess whether your child is writing "good" sentences. Reteach, if necessary.

Spelling — Have your child write words from the past 8 weeks in colorful paint or markers.

Reading — Review library and research skills. *See* Reading, Week 27, numbers 1–3.

Wednesday

Language Skills — Review how to expand sentences to add more interesting information. *See* Language Skills, Week 27, number 2. Check that each sentence contains the five parts required. Reteach, if necessary.

Spelling — Have your child look up spelling words in the dictionary, then write sentences for the words in the word bank (on the note cards).

Reading — Review comprehension skills. Cut out a newspaper or magazine article that is of interest to your child. Black out every tenth word. Have him/her read the article aloud, filling in the missing words with words that fit the context.

Thursday

Language Skills — Have your child define *topic sentence* and *supporting sentences*. Provide topic choices and ask him/her to write a topic sentence for three of the topics. Assess whether your child has written a broad enough topic sentence to support an entire paragraph. *See* Language Skills, Week 27, number 3.

Spelling — Have your child write a poem using several spelling words from the past 8 weeks.

Reading — Review reading diagrams and charts. Look in a current newspaper for charts and diagrams for your child to read and interpret.

Friday

Language Skills — Review the outline for organizing a paragraph. Have your child choose a subject of interest and write a paragraph. Help him/her assess whether he/she followed the outline to write a successful paragraph. *See* Language Skills, Week 26, number 3.

Spelling — Give your child the final spelling test.

Reading — Review the skill of evaluation. Discuss the need to read critically, thinking about the actions of the characters.
Have your child complete **Dudley's Doing It Again!** (p. 278).

Math	Science	Social Studies
Review Week Review fractions with your child. Model different fractions with fraction bars and have your child name them. Have your child complete **The Mystery of the Missing Sweets** (p. 279).	**Review Week** Have your child list ten reasons why people might read or watch a weather report.	**Review Week** Have your child complete the KWHL chart started in Week 19. Have your child list the things he/she has learned about the state. Discuss any misconceptions that were clarified.
Assess your child's ability to compare pairs of fractions. Use the fraction bars from Math, Week 23, Monday.	Have your child write a double cinquain poem about different kinds of clouds. *See* Science, Week 27, number 1. Assess your child's knowledge of cloud types, based on his/her poem. Reteach, if necessary.	Have your child complete **Your State** (p. 280).
Assess your child's ability to add and subtract fractions. Cut two apples into evenly sized wedges. Have your child model given addition and subtraction problems. **Examples:** a) Show me $^4/_8$ of the apple. Add $^2/_8$ and count the total. b) Start with $^{10}/_8$. Take away $^4/_8$. What do you have left?	Have your child analyze the data on the weather charts he/she has maintained so far. Have him/her make a graph showing the changes in one area, then explain the graph to another person. Assess your child's interpretation of the data. Reteach, if necessary.	Play "Tic-Tac-Toe" to review facts about the state. Write game questions related to state facts on index cards. Take turns drawing cards. The player who answers a question correctly may place an X or O on the tic-tac-toe grid.
Assess your child's linear measurement skills. Have him/her draw a simple maze using straight paths. Then, have your child write specific directions for solving the maze. **Example:** Use a toy car to travel through this maze. Start at the garage and drive your car 5 cm west. Turn and drive 2 cm south….	Have your child draw and label a food chain of plants and animals common to your area.	Review key statistics about your state. Have your child complete **State Fact Sheet** (p. 281).
Determine what types of measurement (linear, weight, capacity, time or temperature) your child needs to review and practice. Repeat activities from previous weeks to review these skills.	Have your child define the following terms: *scavengers, parasites, mutualism* and *commensalism.* Have him/her cite an example of each to demonstrate his/her understanding.	Use the completed landform glossary cards to quiz your child. Have your child define a landform or read the definition and ask him/her to name the landform. Allow your child time to review the cards, if necessary.

Learn at Home, Grade 4

TEACHING SUGGESTIONS AND ACTIVITIES

LANGUAGE SKILLS

▶ 1. Write the following questions on the chalkboard. Have your child write a complete sentence in response to each question.

What is our state most famous for?
What does our family do just for fun?
What would you do to make our school a little better?
What did you eat for dinner last night?
What do you hope to be doing in the year 2010?
What do you think exists beyond our solar system?
What event would you choose if you could compete in the next Olympic Games?
What makes you a good friend to others?
What foreign country would you most like to visit?
What do you admire the most in someone famous?

▶ 2. Write the following sentence on the chalkboard and underline as shown.

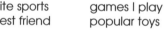

The kids read books at the library after school to prepare for tests.

Ask your child which parts of the sentence tell who, what, when, where and why. Then, give your child the following sentence starters. Ask him/her to complete each sentence by adding words that tell who, what, when, where and why (in any order that makes sense).

The president . . .	*My dog . . .*
The cheering crowd . . .	*Two neighbors . . .*
The bald eagle . . .	*A famous movie star . . .*
The newborn baby . . .	*My best friend and I . . .*
The umpire . . .	*The zookeeper . . .*

▶ 3. Give your child a topic and ask him/her to write a topic sentence about it. Possible topics include:

bicycling	wolves	my bedroom
favorite books	my sister	arts and crafts
my birthday	favorite sports	games I play
a pet	my best friend	popular toys

Learn at Home, Grade 4

READING

▶ 1. List the following reference materials on the chalkboard:

    encyclopedia   dictionary   thesaurus   magazine
    newspaper   almanac   atlas   regional map

Ask your child which type of reference material to use to find . . .

current information about world affairs.   *synonyms for the word* help.
the longest river in the United States.   *information on Thomas Edison.*
which countries are south of the Equator.   *the world population.*
how to get from your house to the airport.   *yesterday's baseball scores.*
the history of a European country.   *the definition of* theatrics.

▶ 2. Give your child a nonfiction book that contains an index and table of contents. Ask him/her to locate information using the index or table of contents.

Examples: Where are the Sierra Madre Mountains?
               What is the mantle of the Earth?
               In which chapter will you find information about how the Earth formed?

▶ 3. Provide your child with three to six nonfiction books on a single topic. Have him/her prepare a bibliography of the books.

SCIENCE

▶ 1. A double cinquain poem has four syllables in the first line, eight in the second, twelve in the third, sixteen in the fourth and four in the last. Have your child list the names of different kinds of clouds and brainstorm cloud-related words. Ask him/her to write a rough draft of the poem on a sheet of practice paper. Revise and edit the poem with your child. When the poem is finished, have your child copy it neatly onto a gray paper cloud using a black felt-tip pen. Demonstrate how to stretch cotton balls out so they are airy and fluffy. To decorate the clouds, have your child glue around the outside edge of each cloud and lightly press the stretched cotton onto the glue. Punch a hole in the top center of each cloud and hang the poem from string on a clothesline.

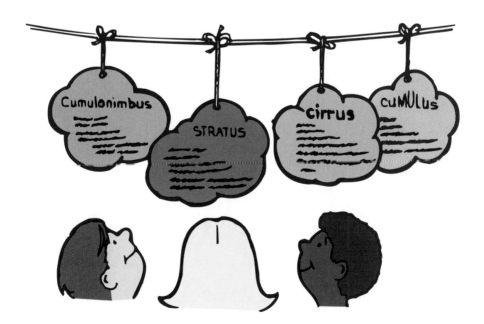

Dudley's Doing It Again!

Dudley is up to his old tricks again. He just finished dog school six weeks ago, and he had really been doing so well. He fetched when he was told to fetch. He heeled when Donald said, "heel." He sat when he was supposed to sit. He would even do tricks like roll over, play dead and speak to impress Donald's friends, if Donald gave him a doggy treat. But lately, Dudley hasn't been doing any of the things he was taught.

For the past several days, Dudley has been digging in the yard. This makes Donald's dad really mad. Dudley has also been chewing up the newspapers instead of bringing them to Donald's mom. One day, he chewed up all her grocery coupons. Boy, was she angry! And, Dudley won't sit or heel when Donald tells him to. Two days ago, Dudley knocked down Donald's friend Lee. Something has to be done about Dudley!

Circle:

Dudley seems to have forgotten . . .

how to chew newspapers.　　　　　everything Donald taught him.

everything he learned at dog school.　　how to learn new tricks.

Check:

	Good Dog	Bad Dog
Dudley is up to his old tricks.	☐	☐
Dudley finished dog school.	☐	☐
Lee was knocked down by Dudley.	☐	☐
Dudley did tricks for treats.	☐	☐
Dudley has been digging in the yard.	☐	☐

Write:

What has Dudley forgotten that he learned at dog school?

_____

_____

What do you think Donald should do about Dudley? _____

_____

The Mystery of the Missing Sweets

Some mysterious person is sneaking away with pieces of desserts from Sam Sillicook's Diner. Help him figure out how much is missing.

1. What fraction of Sam's Super Sweet Chocolate Cream Cake is missing?

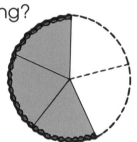

_____

2. What fraction of Sam's Tastee Toffee Coffee Cake is missing?

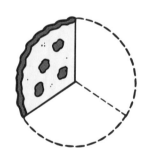

_____

3. What fraction of Sam's Tasty Tidbits of Chocolate Ice Cream is missing?

_____

4. What fraction of Sam's Heavenly Tasting Cherry Cream Tart is missing?

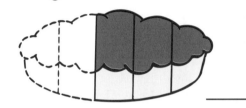

_____

5. Sam's Upside-Down Ice-Cream Cake is very famous. What fraction has vanished?

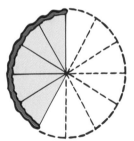

_____

6. What fraction of Sam's Luscious Licorice Candy Cake is missing?

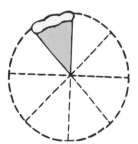

_____

Your State

1. Color your state on the map. Draw a star approximately where the capital is and a blue dot approximately where you live. In which direction do you live from the capital?_____ Name the capital._____

2. What borders your state on the north?_____ south?_____
   east?_____ west?_____

3. Are all the borders natural?_____ Explain._____
   _____

4. Circle the geographic descriptions below that apply to your state. Think of the word state following each description (**Example:** northwestern state).

   Northeastern   New England   Peninsular   Great Plains

   Border   Southwestern   Midwestern   Rocky Mountain

   Inland   Northwestern   Gulf Coast   Middle Atlantic   Southeastern

5. Write the names of several points of interest in your state._____
   _____

6. Select one of the points of interest you would like to visit. Write a sentence or two about it. On the map, put a red dot approximately where it is located._____
   _____

State Fact Sheet

My state is _____ .

The date my state entered the Union. _____

It was the _____ state to join the Union.

How many years has it been one of the United States? _____

How many states were already part of the Union when my state entered it? _____

How many states joined the Union after my state? _____

Total area in square miles _____

Rank in size among states _____

How many states are smaller than my state? _____

How many states are larger than my state? _____

Population _____

Rank in population among states _____

How many other states have more people living in them? _____

How many other states have fewer people living in them? _____

What are the names of my state's five largest cities and their population?

City	Population
_____	_____
_____	_____
_____	_____
_____	_____
_____	_____

Is the state capital one of the five largest cities? _____

How many people live in these five cities altogether? _____

How many people live in the rest of the state? _____

What are the names of several famous people from my state? _____

_____

_____

Select one of these people about whom to write a few sentences.

_____

_____

_____

Learn at Home, Grade 4

	Language Skills	Spelling	Reading
Monday	**Articles** Have your child write a book report on a book he/she has read recently. Show your child the steps involved in writing a book report. Follow the guidelines on **Book Review** (p. 286).	Pretest your child on these spelling words. beliefs elves loaves calves halves roofs chiefs knives scarves cliffs leaves shelves cuffs lives wives Have your child correct the pretest, add personalized words and make two copies of this week's study list.	Read a variety of poetry with your child. *See* Reading, Week 28, number 1. *A Light in the Attic* by Shel Silverstein is a very popular (and fun) poetry book.
Tuesday	Write a paragraph on the chalkboard with punctuation and capitalization errors. For handwriting practice, have your child copy the paragraph, fixing all the errors, in his/her best cursive handwriting.	Have your child use each of this week's spelling words correctly in a sentence.	Gather a variety of poetry books, including collections and books that illustrate just one poem. Allow time for your child to browse through the books and choose one poem. Then, ask him/her to read the poem aloud with lots of expression. Tape record another reading of the poem and play it back for your child to hear.
Wednesday	Teach your child the format of an outline. Discuss the value of using an outline for organizing information as a prewriting activity. *See* Language Skills, Week 28, number 1. Have your child choose a writing topic or choose one for him/her. Help him/her create an outline on the topic before writing. Have the child write five sentences on the topic, then illustrate it.	Have your child complete **Plurals With F** (p. 287).	Look carefully at a book that contains just one poem. Note how the poem is interpreted through illustrations. There may be only a single line of poetry per page. Challenge your child to choose one poem from an anthology and illustrate it in this manner.
Thursday	Have your child write an article about camping, following the outline from yesterday but completing it with details from his/her own experiences or imagination.	Have your child write out this week's words, each in a different color or using a different medium (paint, crayons, markers, pastels). Challenge your child to write the singular forms of these words.	Have your child continue work on the illustrated poem.
Friday	Explore how articles are organized. Help your child make simple outlines from well-organized articles. *See* Language Skills, Week 28, number 2. Have your child write an outline for a topic in which he/she is interested. Then, have him/her write an article based on the outline.	Give your child the final spelling test. Have your child record the pretest and final test words in his/her word bank.	A critical reader often predicts upcoming events as he/she reads. Practice this skill by offering opportunities for your child to make predictions. *See* Reading, Week 28, number 2.

Math	Science	Social Studies
Money Review different ways to write money. Teach your child the meaning of the decimal point. Review that dollars are placed before the decimal point and cents after. *See* Math, Week 28, numbers 1 and 2. Dictate different amounts of money for your child to write on the board. Ask him/her to write each amount at least two different ways. Check his/her placement of the decimal point.	**Plants** Plants are food producers. They take the sun's energy and convert it into food. Teach your child the process of photosynthesis. *See* Science, Week 28, numbers 1 and 2.	**The Middle Ages** Introduce the Middle Ages. Discuss the importance of land ownership at that time and the central role it played in medieval society. Also stress the importance of the church. Look at maps showing Europe during the Middle Ages. Place the Middle Ages on a time line that also includes the explorers previously studied.
Estimating amounts is important when buying more than one item. The easiest way to estimate is to round to the nearest dollar or half-dollar before adding the two amounts. Give your child several scenarios involving the purchase of two or more items. Ask questions related to each scenario that require him/her to estimate.	Have your child draw and label a diagram explaining photosynthesis.	Obtain research materials from the library and museum about the Middle Ages. *See* Social Studies, Week 28, numbers 1 and 2. Have your child read about the Middle Ages.
Read the money-related story problems (or copy the written problems) for your child to solve, using addition, subtraction, multiplication and division. *See* Math, Week 28, number 3.	Provide resources that explain the different parts of plants and leaves and their functions. Have your child draw and label the parts of a plant and explain the function of each.	Write the words *king, nobleman, lord, vassal, knight* and *peasant* on the chalkboard. Discuss the social relationships and responsibilities established between them. Have your child draw a diagram showing the duties each person had to fulfill in the social and political hierarchy of the Middle Ages.
Teach your child to make change by counting up from the amount of a purchase to the amount given to a clerk. Model this skill using real money for this activity. *See* Math, Week 28, number 4.	Read about Carolus Linnaeus. He was a botanist who established the current method of scientifically naming plants and animals using two Latin words. Have your child write a one-paragraph biography of Carolus Linnaeus.	Learn about King Arthur, a legendary figure based on a real king from the Middle Ages. Though we know little about the actual man, the legend of King Arthur is well known. Have your child read books or watch a movie about King Arthur and Camelot. Discuss which events are believable and which are not.
With your child's help, set up a store in your home. Put a price tag on each item in the store. On index cards, write problems like the ones below. Let your child choose an index card and solve the problem independently. **Examples:** a) How much more does a ball cost than a book? b) What two toys can you buy with $5.00?	Obtain a flower that your child can dissect. (A geranium has flowers with easily identifiable parts.) Provide a diagram of a flower and have your child carefully take apart the actual flower, finding each part labeled in the diagram.	Have your child create a glossary of words related to the Middle Ages. Have him/her include the following terms: *aristocracy, battering ram, battlement, chivalry, Crusades, curtain wall, feudalism, fortress, gatehouse, heraldry, joust, knight, lance, lord, manor, moat, poleax, rampart, serf, uncial* and *vassal.* Include illustrations where practical.

TEACHING SUGGESTIONS AND ACTIVITIES

LANGUAGE SKILLS (Articles)

1. An outline is an organizational tool that can be helpful when writing a report or article. Read the following outline with your child and discuss the lettering and numbering system. Also point out that there are no complete sentences in the outline—only phrases.

    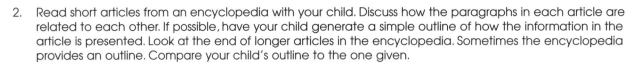

    Camping
    I.   Preparation
         A. Food
         B. Clothes
         C. Camping gear
    II. Setting up camp
         A. Tent
            1. Finding the best spot
            2. Procedure
         B. Food preparation area
    III. Activities
         A. Swimming
         B. Hiking
         C. Building a fire
            1. Finding firewood
            2. Starting the fire
            3. Evening fireside activities
               a. Roasting marshmallows
               b. Singing

2. Read short articles from an encyclopedia with your child. Discuss how the paragraphs in each article are related to each other. If possible, have your child generate a simple outline of how the information in the article is presented. Look at the end of longer articles in the encyclopedia. Sometimes the encyclopedia provides an outline. Compare your child's outline to the one given.

READING (Poetry)

1. Poetry is meant to be heard. The sound and rhythm of a poem engage the reader as much as, or even more so, than its content. Your child has probably been listening to poems since infancy and has joined in the telling and retelling of many verses. Poetry should be read (or sung) aloud. Model poetry reading for your child using a variety of rhythms and voices. Encourage your child to do the same.

2. Read the situations below (or make up your own). Have your child predict what might happen next.

    • When Mr. Tipton arrived late that night at the hotel where he had reserved a room, he was told there were no vacancies.

    • Bert told his teacher that he did not do his homework last night, because he had to take care of his baby sister.

    • Betsy had an eight o'clock haircut appointment on Saturday morning. She slept through her alarm and woke up at seven-thirty.

    • Mother could not read the telephone message written by Carlos.

Learn at Home, Grade 4

MATH (Money)

▷ 1. Write $2.08 on the chalkboard. Have your child show you, using real money, the number of whole dollars in this amount. Ask how many cents make a dollar. Add eight pennies to the $2. Help your child deduce what fraction of a dollar 8¢ is ($^8/_{100}$). Another way to write that fraction is 0.08. Anything less than a whole dollar is written after the decimal.

▷ 2. Review the different ways to write amounts of money.

six cents, 6¢, $0.06

fifty-three cents, 53¢, $0.53

ten dollars, $10, $10.00

four dollars and twenty-five cents, $4.25

Some people get confused and use the decimal sign along with the cent sign, such as .50¢ which actually means a half of a cent.

▷ 3. The following are examples of money-related story problems.

a. John bought a mask for 69¢ and a treat for 47¢. How much did he spend?

b. The Ready-Quick Oil Change Company charges $40.00 to change your car's oil. This week they made $480.00 on oil changes. How many oil changes did they perform this week?

c. Susan needs $8.75 to buy a T-shirt. She has $6.99. How much more does she need?

▷ 4. Linda bought a can of tennis balls for $8.95. She gave the clerk $10.00. Here is how the clerk counted her change back to her:

The clerk gave Linda:	The clerk counts:
1 nickel	$9.00
1 dollar	$10.00

Randy bought a candy bar for 49¢. He gave the clerk $5.00. Here is how the clerk counted back his change to him:

The clerk gave Randy:	The clerk counts:
1 penny	$0.50
2 quarters	$0.75, $1.00
4 dollars	$2.00, $3.00, $4.00, $5.00

SCIENCE (Plants)

▷ 1. *Photosynthesis* is a process that occurs in green plants. Photosynthesis is the basis of all we eat, because we eat plants and the animals who eat plants. The green leaf of a plant is the site of food production. The sun provides the energy to produce photosynthesis. Carbon dioxide and water also play important roles. Carbon dioxide enters the leaf from the air by way of the stomata, small openings on the leaf's surface. Water travels from the roots of the plant and enters the leaf through tiny veins (xylem).

▷ 2. Photosynthesis: Sunlight falls on a green leaf and is captured by the chloroplast in the leaf. Then, the chlorophyll (a green pigment) in the chloroplast absorbs the energy from the sun. The energy is used to split water molecules (H_2O) into hydrogen and oxygen. The oxygen is released into the air for us to breathe. The hydrogen combines with carbon dioxide to form a simple sugar (carbohydrate). The sugar travels through tiny veins (phloem) to other parts of the plant where it is used to help the plant grow.

SOCIAL STUDIES (The Middle Ages)

▷ 1. With your child, read about the history of the Middle Ages. Together, find out the answers to the following questions: What were the different systems of government? What was manorialism? What was feudalism? What were the high Middle Ages? What brought an end to the Middle Ages?

▷ 2. Visit a museum that has a display of medieval art. Notice that most of the art reflects the influence of the Christian church. Look for displays or pictures of armor and other knightly paraphernalia.

Learn at Home, Grade 4

Book Review

A **book review** is a good way to share a favorite book with others. Most good book reviews give facts about the book as well as the writer's opinions. There are many ways to write about a book, but it may be helpful to follow a basic plan.

1. Organize facts about the book.
2. Make notes of your opinions.
3. Write several paragraphs–combining facts and opinions.
4. End with a paragraph which tells why others should read the book.

Choose a favorite book. Use the plan to **write** a short book review.

FACTS

Title:_____

Author:_____Kind of Book:_____

Setting:_____

Main Characters:_____

Basic Plot:_____

Special Features:_____

OPINIONS

Which character did I like best and why?_____
_____

Was the plot interesting?_____

What was my favorite part?_____

Did the author use interesting language?_____

How would I change the book?_____

Other things I liked best about the book:_____
_____

Some things I did not like:_____
_____

WRITE REVIEW   SUMMARY

Use the information above to **write** a review of your book.

I have just read a fascinating book, _____
_____, by _____.

Finish writing your review on another sheet of paper.

Plurals With F

beliefs
calves
chiefs
cliffs
cuffs
elves
halves
knives
leaves
lives
loaves
roofs
scarves
shelves
wives

Cross out the word that does not belong in each group. **Write** the spelling word that fits the category. **Write** its singular form on the second line.

1. colts, kittens, hogs   _____ _____

2. pine cones, tulips, twigs   _____ _____

3. canyons, mountains, gorges   _____ _____

4. lawyers, aunts, husbands   _____ _____

5. totals, fourths, thirds   _____ _____

6. collars, shoes, sleeves   _____ _____

7. neckties, beads, belts   _____ _____

8. pixies, giants, fairies   _____ _____

9. followers, leaders, directors   _____ _____

10. hatchets, swords, pencils   _____ _____

Five words have not been used. **Write** both the singular (S) and plural (P) forms.

1. _____ (S)   2. _____ (S)   3. _____ (S)

     _____ (P)   _____ (P)   _____ (P)

4. _____ (S)   5. _____ (S)

     _____ (P)   _____ (P)

	Language Skills	Spelling	Reading
Monday	Help your child organize an outline for an article of several paragraphs on any subject of interest. If he/she needs to do research, *see* Reading, Weeks 22 and 23 for a review of the research process. Then, have your child write the article. It should be several paragraphs long, and each paragraph should be focused on one main idea.	Pretest your child on these spelling words. ailment employment multiplication attention germination statement basement limitation subtraction celebration measurement treatment movement disappointment vacation Have your child correct the pretest, add personalized words and make two copies of this week's study list.	Introduce the book *Iggie's House* by Judy Blume. Have your child recall a time when a friend moved away or when he/she moved away from a friend. Read chapters 1 and 2 together.
Tuesday	For handwriting practice, have your child copy a poem in his/her neatest cursive handwriting.	Have your child use each of this week's spelling words correctly in a sentence.	Read chapters 3 and 4 of *Iggie's House*. Discuss the way some people in the neighborhood are reacting to the Garber family. What would your child do if he/she were Winnie? Have your child complete **A Little More** (p. 293).
Wednesday	Read a picture book aloud to your child. Talk about the events in the beginning, middle and end of the story. Teach your child how to plot out the events of a story. *See* Language Skills, Week 29, number 1.	Have your child complete **What's Meant by Suffixes?** (p. 292).	Read chapters 5 and 6 of *Iggie's House*. Have your child imagine that he/she is Winnie. Have him/her write a letter to Iggie describing what happened on this day.
Thursday	Read another picture book. Have your child outline the story by plotting the events as discussed yesterday. The outline should include events from the beginning, middle and end of the story.	Have your child clap out the syllables in each of this week's words. Ask him/her to group the words by number of syllables (2, 3, 4 or 5) and write them out.	Discuss the issues raised in *Iggie's House*. *See* Reading, Week 29, numbers 1–3. Read chapters 7 and 8 of *Iggie's House*.
Friday	Have your child plan an original story, using the outline provided. *See* Language Skills, Week 29, number 2.	Give your child the final spelling test. Have your child record the pretest and final test words in his/her word bank.	Read chapters 9 and 10 of *Iggie's House*. Have your child complete **Who Says?** (p. 294).

Math	Science	Social Studies
Decimals Using a base-ten square, have your child shade a fraction and discuss the shaded amount. Introduce how a fraction can be renamed as a decimal. *See* Math, Week 29, numbers 1 and 2. Use a copy of **Base-Ten Squares** (p. 295).	Flowers produce seeds. Their beautiful colors often serve to attract the birds or insects needed to carry out reproduction. Read about the process of plant reproduction in a science book or an encyclopedia. Have your child draw and label a diagram of plant reproduction.	Review the social hierarchy of feudal government. The clothes people wore served as symbols of their social standing. Have your child draw people from each social class, illustrating the different styles of clothing. Label the class represented by each drawing.
Repeat yesterday's lesson with different fractions. Teach your child to see the fraction $^{45}/_{100}$ as 4 tenths and 5 hundredths. **Example:** $^{45}/_{100}$ 4 tenths, 5 hundredths 0.45	If seeds dropped and grew directly below the parent plant, only one species would grow in a small area. Fortunately, seeds get around in many different ways. This results in great plant diversity all over the world. Have your child read about seed dispersal in an encyclopedia or other reference book.	Have your child put him/herself in the position of a peasant farmer working at the fiefdom of a wealthy lord. Have your child defend his/her line of work to a modern factory worker who thinks the lord is exploiting his workers. Be sure your child explains how he/she benefits from the relationship with the landowner.
Use a meterstick to model the connection between fractions and decimals. *See also* Math, Week 29, number 3.	People spread seeds. In the past, people carried crops with them when they moved. Now we can buy seeds and plant them in places where they might not have grown naturally. Have your child plant some seeds in a small pot and observe their growth over several months. Ask him/her to keep a daily record of how he/she cares for the plants. Have your child record plant growth (height) and changes in appearance.	Read about the life of the clergy in feudal times. Some clergymen were also noblemen. Some were very wealthy and ruled over large fiefs. Others were very poor and served as priests in peasant villages. Have your child draw several pictures of clergymen. Have him/her label each drawing and indicate the social class of each figure.
Write a variety of decimal numbers and have your child shade in the number on a copy of **Base-Ten Squares** (p. 295) or point to the decimal on a meterstick. If a number has a whole number and a fraction, your child can use the appropriate number of whole squares plus the fractional part of one square.	Some seeds travel by wind and water. Maple seeds, often called helicopters, are shaped to ride on the wind a great distance from the parent tree. Dandelion seeds are extremely lightweight and ride easily on the wind. Other seeds are carried by water. Have your child explain why a neighbor might not want someone to blow on dandelions near his/her yard.	Read about and discuss the role of the lord's wife, the "lady." She had almost no rights and was expected to sew, supervise the servants and produce sons. Have your child compare and contrast the life of a "lady" with the life of a modern-day working woman. Have him/her conclude the comparison by stating which he/she believes is a better life.
Choose two of the decimal models made by your child. Ask him/her to decide which model represents a larger number. Have your child write the two decimals on lined paper with a greater than or less than symbol between them. Repeat with other pairs of models. Have your child create works of art using base-ten squares. *See* Math, Week 29, number 4. Have another copy of **Base-Ten Squares** (p. 295).	Some seeds are carried by animals. Sandburs cling to the fur of animals as they travel to different locations. Other seeds are sticky and travel the same way. Some fruit seeds are not digested and are transferred when an animal eliminates in a different location. Have your child propose several ways in which a bird might transfer a seed to someplace far away.	Have your child draw the home of a peasant. Be sure that he/she includes illustrations of the foods eaten, the beds and other furnishings.

TEACHING SUGGESTIONS AND ACTIVITIES

LANGUAGE SKILLS (Articles)

▶ 1. Look at the following story plot for *Make Way for Ducklings* by Robert McCloskey. The beginning of the story includes information about the setting and characters. The middle of the story contains the events leading up to the climax. The end includes the events following the climax or the closing. Point out that not all stories are organized in this manner.

   Using only the information from the story plot, have your child write a paragraph summarizing *Make Way for Ducklings*. Then, read the story with your child. How accurate was his/her summary?

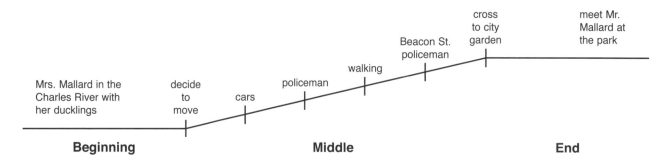

▶ 2. Have your child plan a story using the following story outline:

   Subject: _____

   Setting: where _____

   　　　　　 when _____

   Characters: Name _____ Description _____
   　　　　　　 Name _____ Description _____
   　　　　　　 Name _____ Description _____

   Main Plot: _____

   Subplots: _____
   　　　　　 _____
   　　　　　 _____

   Climax: _____

   Ending: _____

READING (Story Analysis)

▶ 1. *Iggie's House* is fiction, meaning it is a story created by the author. Though the characters and plot may be based on real people or events, the story itself is not true. The purpose of fiction may often be to entertain, but it can teach as well. From Blume's story, for instance, the reader may learn about race relations and the importance of getting to know people who are different. Discuss with your child whether this story could be true. Discuss whether he/she has ever encountered a situation where someone he/she liked was not liked by others. What is the best way to handle it?

▶ 2. Have your child research and write a report about a famous African American. Possible subjects include Jesse Owens, Maya Angelou, Reverend Jesse Jackson, Sidney Poitier, Rosa Parks, Thurgood Marshall, Billie Holiday and George Washington Carver.

▶ 3. Have your child write and send a letter to a friend who has moved away.

MATH (Decimals)

▶ 1. Decimals and fractions represent the same concept. They both represent parts of whole numbers. This can be a very difficult concept to grasp. The best way to help your child see the relationship is with base-ten models, such as squares of 100 blocks, a meterstick, a circle divided into tenths and hundredths or money.

▶ 2. Give your child a copy of **Base-Ten Squares** (p. 295). Each 100-box square is considered a whole. In one square, have your child shade in a given fraction ($^{70}/_{100}$). Explore the following questions with your child: *Is this fraction more or less than* $^1/_2$? *Is it closer to* $^1/_2$ *or* $^3/_4$? *What are some different ways to say this fraction using tenths and hundredths?* ($^7/_{10}$, seven tenths, $^{70}/_{100}$) Show your child that the quantity (which is less than the whole) can also be written as 0.7 (seven tenths) or 0.70 (seventy hundredths). Repeat this process with another square and a new fraction.

▶ 3. Place a meterstick on top of a long sheet of butcher paper or a series of smaller sheets taped together. Have your child think of the meterstick as one whole. Then, have him/her divide the meterstick into tenths, making marks on the paper. Have your child write the tenths as $^1/_{10}$ and 0.1, $^2/_{10}$ and 0.2 and so on. Repeat this process with hundredths. Have your child count by hundredths while pointing to the meterstick. Check where your child is pointing when he/she says $^{10}/_{100}$, $^{20}/_{100}$, etc. Ask him/her to name the fraction and decimal represented by 24 cm on the meterstick $^{24}/_{100}$, 0.24 or two tenths and four hundredths). Repeat with other points on the meterstick.

▶ 4. Give your child colored pencils to draw a picture on a copy of **Base-Ten Squares** (p. 295). The picture should be made up of squares and half squares so that the total number of colored squares will be easy to count. When the picture is finished, have your child count the colored squares and include the decimal point in the title of the artwork.

Examples: The 0.46 Flying Bird or A 0.82 Scuba Diver.

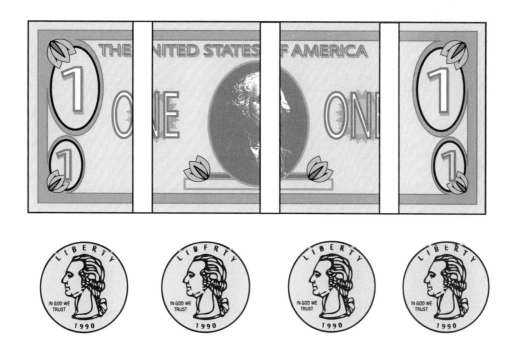

What's Meant by Suffixes?

ailment
attention
basement
celebration
disappointment
employment
germination
limitation
measurement
movement
multiplication
statement
subtraction
treatment
vacation

Write each word and **count** the number of vowels in it. Multiply that number by 5. Next, **count** the number of consonants and multiply that number by 2. Add the two numbers to get a point total for each word. The first one is done for you.

1. ailment (3 x 5) + (4 x 2)   =   23
2. _____   = _____
3. _____   = _____
4. _____   = _____
5. _____   = _____
6. _____   = _____
7. _____   = _____
8. _____   = _____
9. _____   = _____
10. _____   = _____
11. _____   = _____
12. _____   = _____
13. _____   = _____
14. _____   = _____
15. _____   = _____

Look at the totals and answer these questions.

1. Which word totals the most points?_____

2. Which word totals the fewest points?_____

3. Which three words are all worth the same point total?

_____   _____   _____

Learn at Home, Grade 4

A Little More

Draw a box around the root part of each word below.

1. moved   3. pushes   5. invited   7. jumpy   9. slapped
2. finally   4. reported   6. softly   8. privately   10. parents

Circle all the prefixes and suffixes in the words below.

1. signed   3. bushes   5. invisible   7. thinking   9. Saturdays
2. handful   4. asleep   6. running   8. wooden   10. spying

Add a prefix or suffix to each word below to make a new word. The new word may be one already used on this worksheet.

1. _____ report _____

2. _____ visible _____

3. _____ wood _____

4. _____ soft _____

5. _____ run _____

6. _____ jump _____

Circle the words that have prefixes.

1. He will recover by next week.
2. Go ahead and say what you're thinking.
3. It's not always easy to fall asleep.
4. Iggie's house was almost invisible through the trees.

Circle the words that have suffixes.

1. Winnie went running toward her house.
2. The treehouse floor was made of wooden planks.
3. Her binoculars were really powerful.
4. Glenn's voice was whispery as he read the sign.

Learn at Home, Grade 4

Who Says?

Write fact or **opinion** in the blanks
to show which each sentence is.

1. "Peanut butter makes everybody thirsty." _____

2. Because Winnie brought all the sandwiches, Glenn
   paid for the soda pops. _____

3. The blue lake looked sparkling and pretty to Winnie. _____

4. Glen rowed to the middle of the lake. _____

5. Winnie needed new shoes for school. _____

6. Winnie thought that Wednesday would be a good
   day to play. _____

7. Mrs. Barringer thinks that moving is too much trouble. _____

8. Mr. Barringer was snoring after reading the
   Sunday papers. _____

9. Winnie thought her parents didn't care about
   the Garbers. _____

10. The letter to Iggie said that Winnie missed her. _____

11. Winnie liked how her hair looked. _____

12. Winnie's family went to pick up her brother. _____

Base-Ten Squares

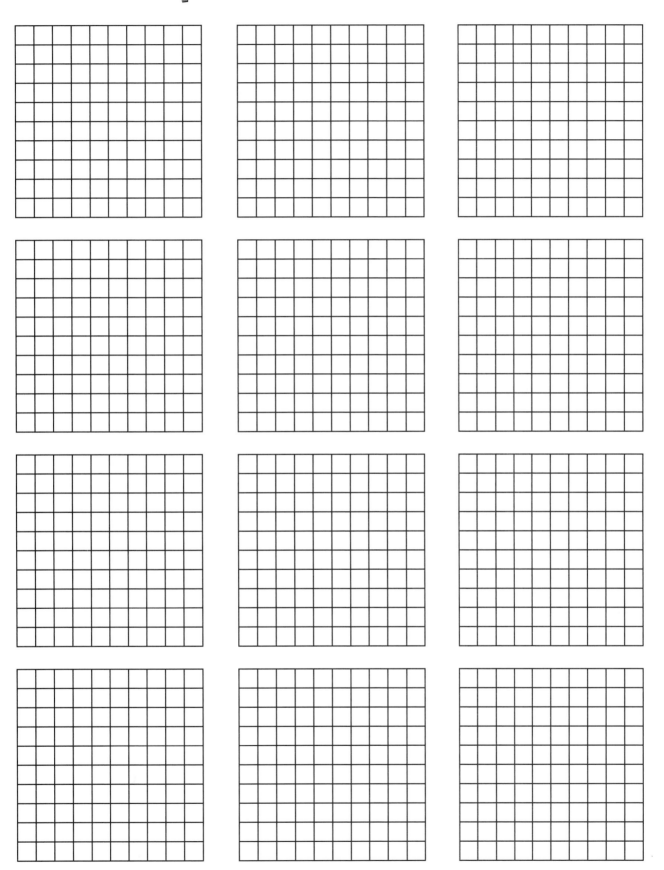

	Language Skills	**Spelling**	**Reading**
Monday	Have your child write a first draft of the story he/she outlined on Friday of Week 29.	Pretest your child on these spelling words. aren't I'd weren't couldn't she's what's doesn't should've who'd hasn't they'll won't he'd wasn't you've Have your child correct the pretest, add personalized words and make two copies of this week's study list.	**Tall Tales** Discuss tall tales. *See* Reading, Week 30. What is a tall tale? Are tall tales fiction or nonfiction? What tall tales does your child already know? Read *Paul Bunyan* by Steven Kellogg. Discuss the descriptions and events that are exaggerated. Have your child practice reading the tale aloud until he/she can read it fluently and with expression. Have him/her read the tale to a younger sibling or friend.
Tuesday	Assess your child's handwriting. Have him/her write each letter of the alphabet in upper-case and lower-case. Note any letters that are formed incorrectly. For the remaining weeks, have your child practice these letters. Reteach and practice as needed.	Have your child use each of this week's spelling words correctly in a sentence.	Read several tall tales. Identify the language of exaggeration: *He was as tall as…. She was as tough as…. He was fiercer than….* Let your child try writing his/her own tall tale lines. Have your child describe some of his/her own attributes through exaggeration.
Wednesday	**Directions:** Reading directions is a skill. When you buy something new, you must often read directions for care, installation or assembly. Read some directions with your child. Give him/her helpful suggestions for writing clear directions. *See* Language Skills, Week 30, numbers 1 and 2. Have your child write clear, step-by-step directions for a simple procedure such as brushing teeth or making a peanut butter sandwich.	Have your child complete **Shortening Words** (p. 300).	Have your child brainstorm a list of things he/she has done recently. Then, have him/her exaggerate something about each activity. Have your child write a tall tale about him/herself, using the exaggerated list of feats above.
Thursday	Allow your child to practice following and giving directions. Give your child verbal directions to perform a simple task. Assess how well he/she follows the directions. Then, switch roles and have your child give you verbal directions. How well does he/she describe the task? Does he/she leave out any important steps?	Write out the two words that form each contraction from this week's spelling list on an index card (e.g., she + is). Shuffle the cards. Have your child pick a card. He/she must read the words out loud, state the contraction that combines the two words, then write the contraction on the board. Repeat with other cards.	Read more examples of tall tales. *See* Reading, Week 30, numbers 1–3 for activity ideas.
Friday	Write unclear directions for a procedure that is familiar to your child. Include first and third person, steps that are out-of-order and confusing language. Have your child edit your directions and rewrite them clearly in second person.	Give your child the final spelling test. Have your child record the pretest and final test words in his/her word bank.	Through tall tales we gain an image of the main character. The details may not be accurate, but we can draw conclusions about the character. Being able to draw conclusions about something that is not overtly stated is an important reading skill. Have your child complete **A Picture Is Worth…** (p. 301).

Math	Science	Social Studies
Write out two decimals (0.34 and 0.67) and have your child determine which is the larger number. Encourage your child to look at a meterstick and see which is closer to a whole. Repeat with other pairs of decimals. *See* Math, Week 30, number 1.	Have your child make a mobile or poster to demonstrate what he/she has learned about plants and animals. Have him/her include an illustration of a food chain or one of the cycles or processes in nature. Have your child present the finished project to a friend or relative.	Read about the types of crops grown in Europe in the Middle Ages. What foods were common? Have your child create a menu of foods that might have been eaten in a manor house in the Middle Ages.
Explain that the number to the left of the decimal point is a whole number. The first number to the left is in the ones place. Everything to the right of the decimal represents a part of a whole (fraction or decimal). The first place is the tenths place, the second is the hundredths place and the third is the thousandths place. Write out several decimals with whole numbers and help your child read the numbers aloud.	Read in an encyclopedia to learn how an electric charge (static and current) occurs. Have your child keep a glossary of electricity terms. Have him/her write each term in the Science Log or on an index card, defining or explaining the term. Have your child keep the cards in alphabetical order. *See* Science, Week 30, number 2.	Introduce the topic of heraldry. Learn about the origins of heraldry and what it came to mean in later years. *See* Social Studies, Week 30. Have your child read more about heraldry in an encyclopedia.
Dictate decimals for your child to write, placing the decimal point accurately. Have your child draw a picture or build a model using base-ten materials to represent some of the dictated decimals. *See* Math, Week 30, number 2.	**Electricity:** Ask your child questions about electricity and have him/her explain how electricity works. Assess his/her understanding of the concept and note any misconceptions. Design experiments that will allow your child to experience firsthand the accurate information. *See* Science, Week 30, number 1.	Learn about the different elements of a coat of arms. *See* Social Studies, Week 30, numbers 1 and 2.
Teach your child to add and subtract decimals. Stress that the only difference from regular addition and subtraction is that he/she must align the decimal points when setting up the problem and must include the decimal point in the answer. Write a series of addition and subtraction problems with decimals on the board. Have your child solve them. *See* Math, Week 30, number 3.	Have your child begin work on a research project to be completed within 4 weeks. Your child should be prepared to present a biography on a scientist who contributed to the science of electricity. Have him/her prepare an article with a picture or diagram. Some famous scientists in this field include Thomas Edison, Benjamin Franklin, André Ampère, Michael Faraday, Hans Oersted, Samuel Morse and Alessandro Volta.	Have your child design a meaningful coat of arms for him/herself. Let your child choose colors, symbols and a motto that best represents him/her and his/her family. *See also* Social Studies, Week 30, number 3. Use a copy of **Heraldry Patterns** (p. 303) to get started.
After completing the activity sheet, have your child look at a meterstick to gain a sense of how long each measurement is. You may also have him/her compare these measurements with the U.S. standard measurements (here, inches). Have your child complete **Animal Trivia** (p. 302).	Discuss how life today would be different without electricity. Have your child describe what a typical day might be like if there were no electricity.	Have your child write a description of his/her coat of arms and the symbolic meaning of each element. In heraldry language, this description would be called the *blazon*.

TEACHING SUGGESTIONS AND ACTIVITIES

LANGUAGE SKILLS (Directions)

BACKGROUND

Directions should be written directly to the reader. This is called writing in the second person. The pronoun used is *you*, but it is not usually stated in a command. First person uses *I* and third person uses *he/she/they*.

1. Write the directions in a step-by-step format. Start with the first task and explain the tasks in order. It is helpful to try the directions yourself after you have written a rough draft.

   Example: How To Eat an Apple

   Select a ripe and firm apple from the refrigerator. Wash it thoroughly with cold water. You should also get out a plate for your apple slices. If the apple is waxy, you may need to scrub it clean. Find a sharp knife and a cutting board. Ask an adult to supervise while you use a knife. Cut the apple in half from the top to the bottom. Cut each piece in half again. Carefully scoop out the core and seeds with a spoon. Rinse the apple pieces and put them on your plate. You may eat the apple now or cut each fourth into smaller slices.

2. Write out directions for a common procedure or activity, such as doing the laundry or planting a garden. Write each step on a separate strip of paper. Mix up the strips of paper, then hand to your child. Ask him/her to arrange the steps in the proper order. Repeat with other common activities.

READING (Tall Tales)

BACKGROUND

Tall tales are wonderful stories of exaggeration mixed with truth and/or history. The central personalities of tall tales are usually real people about whom adventure stories have been told and retold until they are completely unrealistic. Davy Crockett, a subject of many tall tales, lived to hear the exaggerated stories of his own adventures. He actually started his own tall tales in the form of *backwoods brag*. Borrow from the library a variety of tall tales or find an anthology of tall tales which may include simple lines of exaggeration that are fun to read.

1. After reading a tall tale, discuss what makes the story a tall tale. Have your child draw two columns on a sheet of paper and write "Could Happen" and "Could Not Happen" at the head of the columns. Tell your child to list all the things from the story that could not possibly happen in one column and all the things that could happen in the other.

2. Have your child tell about the main character in a tall tale and list his/her characteristics. Using his/her imagination, your child may act out some of the character's feats or speak in a manner in which the character might have spoken.

3. Have your child read a tall tale many times to become familiar with the story line and language. Then, have your child tell the story as if relating the events for the first time.

MATH (Decimals)

1. Teach your child to round decimals to the nearest tenth. When he/she finds a decimal on a meterstick (0.34), ask your child if the number is closer to three-tenths or four-tenths.

2. Teach your child to round to the nearest whole number. Use the models your child has created to represent numbers such as 2.37. Have your child look at the model and determine if the number is closer to two or three. Repeat with other numbers.

3. Demonstrate addition and subtraction with decimals. Show your child how to line up the decimal points when setting up the problems.

   Examples:

$$3.6 \\ \underline{+\ 3.3} \\ 6.9 \qquad\qquad 6.8 \\ \underline{-\ 2.6} \\ 4.2$$

SCIENCE (Electricity)

▷ 1. Below is a suggested list of electricity terms for your child's glossary.

alternating current	atom	conductor	parallel circuit
direct current	ion	electron	positive pole
electric circuit	fuse	neutron	negative pole
filament	generator	proton	plug
electric field	insulator	static electricity	battery
electric induction	cables	current electricity	electrodes
electric power	voltage	electromagnetism	socket
semiconductor	watts	transformer	short circuit
series circuit	switch	ground wire	

▷ 2. Questions to guide reading and discussion:

Where does most electricity come from?
Where can it be found in nature?
What is the difference between static and current electricity?
How does electricity get into our homes?
Name places where electricity is used.
What are sources of electricity?

SOCIAL STUDIES (The Middle Ages)

BACKGROUND
Heraldry is a system of symbols used to represent individuals and families. Heraldry originated so knights could be recognized in battle. It was difficult to tell a friend from a foe behind armor, so identifying coats of arms were painted on each knight's shield and flag. Later, heraldry became a system of identification for members of the upper class.

▷ 1. Enlarge the coat of arms to the right or provide pictures of different coats of arms. On the coat of arms, locate each of the elements defined below.

1. **crest**—object placed on top of helmet or on top of shield
2. **mantling**—cape attached to helmet or draped around shield
3. **helmet**—shows rank of bearer
4. **shield**—main part of the coat of arms
5. **supporter**—animal or human being on either side of shield
6. **charge**—object or figure on the shield
7. **motto**—found below shield, also called the device
8. **cadency**—status symbols of individual members in a family

▷ 2. Study various coats of arms. Have your child identify the different elements and give their symbolic meanings. Discuss the different symbols and why they might have been chosen.

▷ 3. Discuss what your child might put on his/her own shield. The charge might refer to your child's name, where he/she lives, the occupation of someone in the family, personal interests, etc. Review the colors used in coats of arms (found in the *World Book Encyclopedia*).

Shortening Words

aren't
couldn't
doesn't
hasn't
he'd
I'd
she's
should've
they'll
wasn't
weren't
what's
who'd
won't
you've

Write each contraction and the two words that form it.

1. _____ _____ _____

2. _____ _____ _____

3. _____ _____ _____

4. _____ _____ _____

5. _____ _____ _____

6. _____ _____ _____

7. _____ _____ _____

8. _____ _____ _____

9. _____ _____ _____

10. _____ _____ _____

11. _____ _____ _____

12. _____ _____ _____

13. _____ _____ _____

14. _____ _____ _____

15. _____ _____ _____

Sometimes a contraction can represent different words. **Circle** the correct answer in each of the following.

1. In the sentence, "He'd had a cold," the **'d** stands for . . .

    a. would   b. had   c. did

2. In the sentence, "He'd like to go," the **'d** stands for . . .

    a. would   b. had   c. did

3. In the question "Who'd volunteer?" the **'d** stands for . . .

    a. would   b. had   c. did

4. In the question "Who'd you say it was?" the **'d** stands for . . .

    a. would   b. had   c. did

A Picture Is Worth . . .

Look at the first picture. Put a check in the box by each sentence which seems sensible. Look at the second picture. **Write** six sentences that tell your conclusions about the picture.

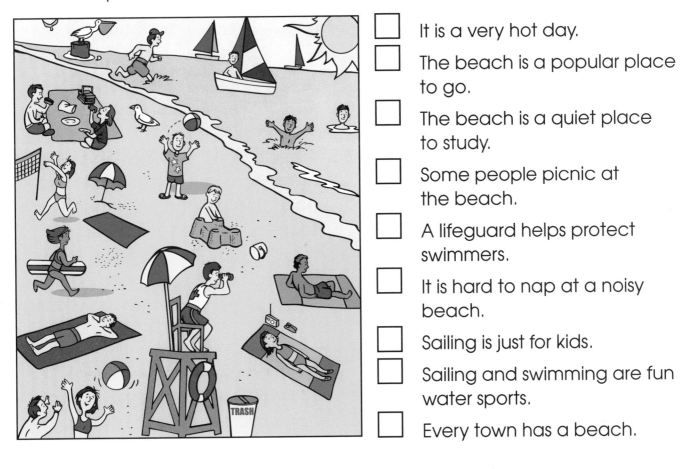

- ☐ It is a very hot day.
- ☐ The beach is a popular place to go.
- ☐ The beach is a quiet place to study.
- ☐ Some people picnic at the beach.
- ☐ A lifeguard helps protect swimmers.
- ☐ It is hard to nap at a noisy beach.
- ☐ Sailing is just for kids.
- ☐ Sailing and swimming are fun water sports.
- ☐ Every town has a beach.

Write your own conclusions.

1. _____

2. _____

3. _____

4. _____

5. _____

6. _____

Animal Trivia

1. An earthworm is 14.9 cm long. A grasshopper is 8.7 cm long. What is the difference?

2. A pocket gopher has a hind foot 3.5 cm long. A ground squirrel's hind foot is 6.4 cm long. How much longer is the ground squirrel's hind foot?

3. A porcupine has a tail 30.0 cm long. An opossum has a tail 53.5 cm long. How much longer is the opossum's tail?

4. A wood rat has a tail which is 23.6 cm long. A deer mouse has a tail 12.2 cm long. What is the difference between the two?

5. A cottontail rabbit has ears which are 6.8 cm long. A jackrabbit has ears 12.9 cm long. How much shorter is the cottontail's ear?

6. The hind foot of a river otter is 14.6 cm long. The hind foot of a hog-nosed skunk is 9.0 cm long. What is the difference?

7. A rock mouse is 26.1 cm long. His tail adds another 14.4 cm. What is his total length from his nose to the tip of his tail?

Learn at Home, Grade 4

Heraldry Patterns

Learn at Home, Grade 4

Language Skills	Spelling	Reading

Monday

Language Skills

Persuasive Writing
Children can be experts at persuasion if motivated. With your child, brainstorm things he/she feels strongly about. *See* Language Skills, Week 31, number 1. Have your child write a paragraph persuading someone of something. For example, have him/her try to persuade you that he/she needs a certain toy or food.

Spelling

Pretest your child on these spelling words.

scheme	scream	strainer
scholar	screw	strength
school	scrimmage	string
schooner	scrub	stripe
scratch	straight	struggle

Have your child correct the pretest, add personalized words and make two copies of this week's study list.

Reading

Discuss the differences between nonfiction and historical fiction. Many events in a book of historical fiction are accurate, but they are seen through the eyes of a fictional character. To introduce this week's book, look on a map for the country of Vietnam. As you read, locate the cities mentioned. Read chapters 1 and 2 of *Goodbye, Vietnam* by Gloria Whelan.

Tuesday

Language Skills

Read your child's persuasive paragraph together. Talk about the sentences that are strong and convincing. Which words are particularly strong? Discuss the sentences that do not convince, and help your child edit the paragraph to make it more convincing.
Have your child revise his/her paragraph to make it stronger. Make sure each sentence supports the opinion with solid reasons or examples.

Spelling

Have your child use each of this week's spelling words correctly in a sentence.

Reading

Read chapters 3–5 of *Goodbye, Vietnam*. Discuss the feelings of resentment harbored by the adults. Ask why they were forced to pay what the others demanded.

Wednesday

Language Skills

Collect other examples of persuasive paragraphs. Look in the editorial column of the newspaper. Read the back cover or inside flap of a book jacket. *See* Language Skills, Week 31, number 2.

Spelling

Have your child complete **Grouping Letters** (p. 308).

Reading

Read chapters 6–8 of *Goodbye, Vietnam*. Have your child write about one of the events aboard the boat as if he/she were a passenger. Find articles and books about the flight of the boat people from Vietnam to Hong Kong in the early 1990s. Discuss the plight of some of these people. Not all families were as lucky as Mai's.
See Reading, Week 31, number 1.

Thursday

Language Skills

When you see an advertisement on a billboard, in a magazine or on TV, have your child tell you what is being sold. Ask him/her to analyze how a business tries to convince people to buy its product. (You can't live without it, smart people do it, it's the best of its kind, etc.)

Spelling

Have your child write two or three tongue twisters using words from this week's spelling list.

Reading

Read chapters 9 and 10 of *Goodbye, Vietnam*. Have your child do a bit of cultural comparison. *See* Reading, Week 31, number 2.

Friday

Language Skills

Let your child design an advertisement for an imaginary product using persuasive language including supporting arguments.
Field Trip: Plan a tour of a newspaper, magazine or book publishing company. If possible, arrange for several different people (artists, writers, editors, advertising directors and press operators) to speak with you and your child about the publishing business.

Spelling

Give your child the final spelling test. Have your child record the pretest and final test words in his/her word bank.

Reading

Read chapters 11 and 12 of *Goodbye, Vietnam*. Discuss the disappointment the people must feel at having to stay at the camp. Have your child imagine that they had to stay there for a long time. What would life have been like? What options would they have had?
Have your child complete **From Whose Point of View?** (p. 309).

Learn at Home, Grade 4

Math	Science	Social Studies
Graphs There are many different types of graphs. Find examples of bar graphs, circle graphs (pie charts), picture graphs and line graphs in magazines, books and newspapers. Read the title and discuss the purpose of each graph. Look for the variables being compared or presented. Find labels and/or a key that explain the symbols used.	Current electricity relies on an uninterrupted flow of current through materials that conduct electricity. Set up a simple circuit and discuss the six points of contact necessary for "closing the circuit." *See* Science, Week 31, number 1.	Read about the steps necessary for a boy to become a knight. *See* Social Studies, Week 31. Have your child pretend that he/she is a boy in training as a page. Have your child write a letter home telling what he/she is doing and about his/her plans for the future. The letter should include details about the steps necessary to become a knight.
Assign topics for graphs and either provide the data or have your child gather data. *See* Math, Week 31, numbers 1–3 for examples. Have your child make three different graphs, labeling each one completely. Ask him/her to be prepared to explain the graphs and answer questions about the data presented.	Anything that blocks the flow of current in a closed circuit is called an *insulator*. Set up an experiment by altering the simple circuit you created yesterday. Cut one of the wires and strip the insulation off each of the two new ends. Have your child find items from around the house (nail, crayon, paper, chalk, eraser, paper clip, penny, nickel, ruler, salt water), test them in the simple circuit and sort them into conductors and insulators.	Read about and discuss what it means to be a knight. What is chivalry? Have your child list things that he/she does today that would have been considered chivalrous in the Middle Ages. Then, list those things that would have been considered unworthy of a knight.
Have your child complete yesterday's assignment.	Have you ever seen a whole string of lights go out at once? To reactivate the lights, you have to find the one light that does not work. Why does that happen? The Christmas tree lights are on a series circuit. For the next two days, experiment with series and parallel circuits. *See* Science, Week 31, numbers 2–4. Have your child write a definition of a series or parallel circuit.	Look at pictures of different armor worn by knights of the Middle Ages. Compare it to armor of different times and places. Using pencil drawings, have your child design armor that is comfortable yet protects the wearer from battle wounds. Have your child label the different parts of the armor and describe the materials used to make it.
Have your child study several graphs to learn the appropriate parts and their placement. Give your child four graphs to study. Ask questions that challenge him/her to order the information from the graphs. **Example:** Give your child a line graph showing a company's annual profits listed by month. Have your child list the months in order from greatest profit to lowest.	Continue working with circuits. Help your child create variations on series and parallel circuits by introducing more batteries.	During times of peace, knights needed to keep their fighting skills sharp. Tournaments were like real battles but were considered sport. Read about tournaments, jousts and tilting. Ask your child why kings and the church opposed tournaments. Have your child complete **Steps to Knighthood Crossword** (p. 311).
Today's independent activity will give your child practice finding points on a grid. Teach your child how to find the intersection of two axes. Have your child complete **Gliding Graphics** (p. 310).	What does it mean when there is a short circuit? Find out through experimentation. Help your child create a series circuit with two batteries and one light bulb. Strip the insulation near the center of the wires leading from each battery to the bulb. What happens when these two stripped areas touch? **Important:** *Do not touch the exposed wire!*	Let your child make a knight's helmet. *See* instructions in Social Studies, Week 31, number 1. Discuss how knights might have felt about wearing such a helmet in battle. Ask what the advantages and disadvantages of this particular helmet design are.

Learn at Home, Grade 4

TEACHING SUGGESTIONS AND ACTIVITIES

LANGUAGE SKILLS (Persuasive Writing)

▷ 1. When someone has a strong opinion about a subject and wants others to think the same way, he/she will try to persuade the others. Have your child recall a time that someone tried to persuade him/her to do something. Ask if your child has any strong feelings about a current event, style of clothes, a food, homework, chores, TV, video games or the environment. Discuss his/her opinions.

▷ 2. Look at persuasive articles together. Discuss the opinions the articles are trying to promote to the reader. Have your child circle the supporting arguments. Discuss whether the articles are truly persuasive and why.

READING (Story Analysis)

▷ 1. The following passage from page 62 of *Goodbye, Vietnam* speaks about communicating without words. Read it, then have your child brainstorm other things that communicate in this manner. Be specific.

Lying there squeezed into as small a shape as possible, I thought about Kim's music. I had never heard such sounds. They were a puzzle. How could something speak to you so well without words? Then, I thought, there are many things that do that: the fragrance of rice when you knew the harvest was near, the taste of ripe mangoes from the tree in our yard. For some things words were not needed.

▷ 2. Discuss and compare the setting (time and place) of the story with your own setting. Have your child draw pictures to illustrate the comparison. Discuss travel, common modes of transportation, dress, children's behavior and games they play.

MATH (Graphs)

Listed below are examples of several different graphing topics. Use these and/or others for a graphing activity. Have your child choose three topics to graph. Once the graph is completed, ask him/her specific questions about the data.

▷ 1. Spelling test scores: (line graph) Record your child's weekly test scores using his/her number correct out of 20.

▷ 2. Newspaper collection for recycling: (bar graph) Pounds of newspaper collected by each ecology club member: Tom collected 60 pounds, Jamie collected 130 pounds, Patty collected 95 pounds and Louis collected 107 pounds.

▷ 3. Favorite playground equipment: (circle graph) Take a survey of twelve children of various ages. Ask each person to name his/her favorite piece of playground equipment from the following list: swing, slide, basketball court, monkey bars or merry-go-round.

SCIENCE (Electricity)

BACKGROUND
The three main elements of a closed circuit are the source of energy, the conductor and the use (or a device that converts the electric energy into another form of energy). A battery is a source, the insulated wire is a conductor and the light bulb is the use. Encourage your child to explore different arrangements of the three elements. Add wires or batteries to increase the possible arrangements.

Use the descriptions that follow to help your child set up a simple, series and parallel circuits. You will need the following supplies: several batteries, insulated wire, pocket knife, flashlight bulbs and flashlight bulb sockets.
Note: If any of the components in an experiment feel hot, disconnect the circuit immediately. The parent need to strip the insulation from the wires with the pocket knife.

▷ 1. **Simple Circuit**

A simple circuit is created by making six points of contact. The wire's points of contact are its two bare ends. The battery's points of contact are its two poles. The bulb's point of contact are the base and the brass side. To make a simple circuit, use the pocket knife to strip off the

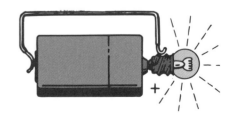

insulation on both ends. Then, have your child connect the wire, the battery and the bulb so that the bulb will light. Divide a sheet of blank paper into eight squares. In each square have your child draw a picture of different ways he/she tried to light the bulb. Have him/her write "yes" or "no" on the picture telling if the bulb did light up.

2. **Series Circuit**

   Put three bulbs in three sockets. Line up the three bulbs and a battery in a single row. Cut four pieces of insulated wire. Cut two wires about 4" long and two about 6" long. Strip the ends of each wire with the pocket knife. Connect the 6" wires to the poles of the battery using electrical tape. Attach the free end of one 6" wire to the end light bulb socket. Attach the free end of the other 6" wire to the light bulb socket on the other end of the row. Use one 4" wire to attach the first light bulb to the second light bulb. Use the other 4" wire to attach the second light bulb to the third light bulb.

3. **Parallel Circuit**

   Put three bulbs in three sockets. Line up the three bulbs and a battery cell in a single row. Cut six pieces of insulated wire. Cut two wires about 6" long and four wires about 4" long. Strip the ends of each wire with pocket knife. Connect the 6" wires to the poles of the battery. Attach the free ends to the two sides of the first light bulb socket. Using the 4" wires, attach the light bulb sockets. Connect the first to the second and the second to the third along one side. Then, attach the wires in the same manner on the other side of the sockets.

4. Have your child draw the series circuit and the parallel circuit in his/her Science Log. Unscrew one bulb in the series circuit and observe what happens. Repeat with the parallel circuit. Have your child record the results for each. Tell your child to add arrows to the diagrams to show the flow of current.

SOCIAL STUDIES (The Middle Ages)

BACKGROUND

Becoming a knight was a great honor. Only boys from families of nobility became knights. When a boy turned eight, he was sent to a neighboring castle where he was trained as a page. At the age of fifteen or sixteen, the boy became a squire in the service of a knight. At the age of twenty, the squire could become a knight if he proved himself worthy. A lord would dub him knight in a special ceremony. Read about the details of each step in an encyclopedia or a book about knighthood.

1. Use a sheet of stiff paper 12" wide and long enough to wrap around your child's head to form a cylinder (*see* drawing A). Have your child cut half-inch vertical slits across the top edge of the helmet (*see* drawing B) and fold them down toward the inside of the helmet. While your child holds the helmet in place on his/her head, mark where his/her eyes are. Have your child cut two horizontal rectangles for eyeholes. Cut some breathing holes beneath the eyeholes (*see* drawing C). Have your child paint the helmet. When it is dry, tape the helmet together at the back to form a cylinder. On a second sheet of stiff paper, have your child trace the circumference of the helmet, making a circle for the top. Put glue on the tabs along the top edge and secure the circle there. Tell your child to put the helmet on and see how well he/she can see. Ask if he/she thinks it would be easy to maneuver in battle wearing a helmet like this.

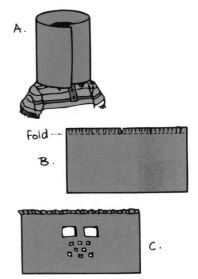

Grouping Letters

scheme
scholar
school
schooner
scratch
scream
screw
scrimmage
scrub
straight
strainer
strength
string
stripe
struggle

Cross out the word that does not belong in each group.
Write the spelling word that fits the category.

1. filter, mixture, sieve _____

2. polish, claw, rip _____

3. rope, leather, cord _____

4. college, academy, apartment _____

5. soil, wash, clean _____

6. power, weakness, force _____

7. tramp, pupil, learner _____

8. fight, conflict, agreement _____

9. laugh, yell, cry _____

10. plan, vacation, plot _____

11. nail, bolt, hammer _____

12. ship, locomotive, vessel _____

13. band, line, circle _____

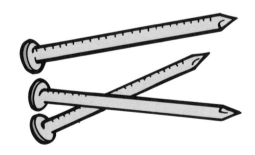

Which two words were not used? _____   _____

Write one sentence using both words. _____

_____

Learn at Home, Grade 4

Read each sentence below. Decide if it is the first or third person's point of view. If it is a first person's point of view, **rewrite** the sentence to make it a third person's point of view. If it is a third person's point of view, **rewrite** it to make it a first person's point of view.

1. I wanted to tell Anh and Thant the secret of our leaving, but I had given my word.

_____

2. The grandmother did not want to go aboard the boat.

_____

3. The people on shore were pushing to get on the deck of the boat.

_____

4. Though I had worked many days in the rice paddies watching planes fly over, I never thought I'd be on one.

_____

5. Loi made a net from pieces of string and caught a turtle with his new device.

_____

6. I know of a place where we can wash our clothes.

_____

7. The officer looked at them with great interest.

_____

8. When I looked into the harbor, I could see the shape of the sampan boats.

_____

9. This is my duck and I choose to share it with everyone for the celebration of Tet.

_____

Gliding Graphics

Draw the lines as directed from point to point for each graph.

Draw a line from:

F,7 to D,1
D,1 to I,6
I,6 to N,8
N,8 to M,3
M,3 to F,1
F,1 to G,4
G,4 to E,4
E,4 to B,1
B,1 to A,8
A,8 to D,11
D,11 to F,9
F,9 to F,7
F,7 to I,9
I,9 to I,6
I,6 to F,7

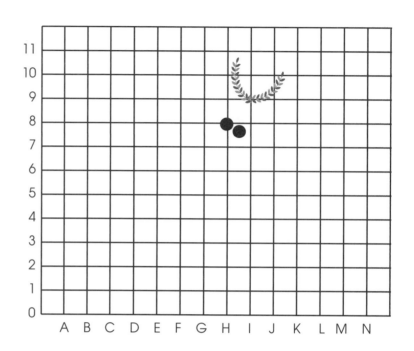

Draw a line from:

J, ◉ to N, ◣
N, ◣ to, U, ◣
U, ◣ to Z, ▦
Z, ▦ to X, ✤
X, ✤ to U, ◣
U, ◣ to S, ◈
S, ◈ to N, ◣
N, ◣ to N, ◈
N, ◈ to J, ◉
J, ◉ to L, ▦
L, ▦ to Y, ▦
Y, ▦ to Z, ▦
Z, ▦ to L, ▦
L, ▦ to J, ◉

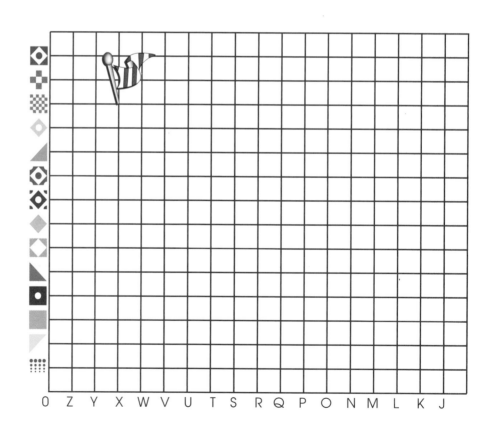

Across

1. Garment worn by a squire during his knighting ceremony.
4. Island country that was the home of King Arthur and the Knights of the Round Table.
8. War games played by knights on horseback in hand-to-hand combat.
11. Place where the king received visitors, performed ceremonies and held balls.
12. Name of the ceremony during which a squire became a knight.
14. What every knight swore to his king.
15. A noble who has trained and proven himself to be worthy of this title.

Down

2. Code of honor that all true knights followed.
3. The time in history also known as the Middle Ages.
5. To be kind and polite.
6. The first step to becoming a knight.
7. The second step to becoming a knight.
9. Name of the upper class during the Middle Ages.
10. Proving that you deserve an honor—you are _____.
13. To not eat in order to purify yourself.

	Language Skills	Spelling	Reading
Monday	Review the proper way to write quotations using commas, capital letters and quotation marks. *See* Language Skills, Week 32, number 1. Write ten sentences on the chalkboard, omitting quotation marks and other punctuation. Have your child add the correct punctuation. Also, make sure your child writes a thank you note for the field trip you took on Friday.	Pretest your child on these spelling words. biggest earlier prettier brighter firmer quietest clumsiest flattest simpler crazier greener tastiest cruelest noisiest widest Have your child correct the pretest, add personalized words and make two copies of this week's study list.	Read chapters 13 and 14 of *Goodbye, Vietnam*. Have your child imagine what life will be like for Mai's family in America. Have him/her write an epilogue for the book.
Tuesday	Have your child write dialogue for pictures that suggest conversation between two or more characters. *See* Language Skills, Week 32, number 2.	Have your child use each of this week's spelling words correctly in a sentence.	Read *The Velveteen Rabbit* by Margery Williams, taking turns reading aloud with your child. Make a list of the events that are real and a list of events that are fantasy (could not happen). Have your child name other books that involve fantasy. Are some books more fantastic than others? How so (unrealistic characters like dragons or unrealistic worlds)?
Wednesday	Choose a play to read with your child. Read the play aloud together, using lots of expression and omitting the words that tell who is speaking. Find other children in the neighborhood who would like to perform a play with your child. Allow time for the children to practice the play and make simple costumes and sets. Invite guests to a performance.	Have your child complete **Comparison Words** (p. 316).	Make a profile graph that shows the fortunes of the velveteen rabbit. Throughout the story there are times when things are going well for the rabbit and times when things are not going well. Brainstorm a list of events from the story. Have your child write the events on sticky notes and number them in the order they occurred. Make a graph. *See* Reading, Week 32, number 1.
Thursday	**Readers' Theater:** Find a picture book in which two characters interact. Help your child rewrite the story so it is only dialogue, removing all the "he said" and "she said"s. Also, remove any narrative passages. Save the rewritten piece for tomorrow's lesson.	Have your child write comparative sentences using words from this week's list and draw pictures to go along with the sentences.	Reread *The Velveteen Rabbit*. Have your child list the pros and cons of becoming real. Help your child practice distinguishing fact from fantasy. Give your child a topic such as a vacation. Ask him/her to write one statement of fact and one of fantasy on the topic. Repeat with other topics.
Friday	Practice the readers' theater dialogue together. Encourage your child to read with expression and minimal acting.	Give your child the final spelling test. Have your child record the pretest and final test words in his/her word bank.	Have your child write a fantasy making one of his/her toys real. Alternately, ask him/her to remove the fantasy from a familiar story. *See* Reading, Week 32, number 2 for an example.

Learn at Home, Grade 4

Math	Science	Social Studies
Probability Introduce the study of probability by asking your child to predict what color sock you will pull out of a bag of 2 red socks and 3 blue socks. Let him/her pull a sock out of the bag. Discuss the result. *See* Math, Week 32, number 1. Have your child build a spinner (*see* Math, Week 32, number 2) and have your child complete **Spinner Fun** (p. 317).	Discuss the purpose of an electric switch. A switch is a moveable conductor that, when moved, temporarily interrupts the flow of the current. Help your child make a circuit with a switch. You will need a scrap of wood as a base, large and small paper clips, two rubber bands, a battery, insulated wire, wire cutters, a flashlight bulb and socket, a pocket knife and two thumbtacks. Follow directions on **Switches and Circuits** (p. 319).	Discuss who lived in the castle and where in the castle they lived. *See* Social Studies, Week 32. Have your child choose one person who lived in the castle, then write a script for that person telling about his/her life in the castle. Have the character describe a typical day.
You will need two colors of small manipulatives (cubes, tiles or marbles). Place ten in a bag while your child is not looking. Put in a small number of one color and a large number of the other color (3 and 7 or 2 and 8). Have your child pull out three objects at once without looking. After your child looks at the objects, ask him/her to guess the total number of each color. *See* Math, Week 32, number 3.	Help your child explore several different ways of making a switch. Encourage him/her to try using other conductors as a switch. Tell your child to build a circuit with two switches.	Read about castle social life. At times, life in a castle was exciting. At times, life was dull. Have your child describe in writing the events at a medieval feast.
Listen to or read weather predictions. Talk about the meaning of words such as *chance, likelihood, mostly sunny* and *90%* (add these terms to this week's spelling list). Follow local weather forecasts for 1 week. Compare the predictions with the actual weather. Help your child determine the probability of an accurate weather prediction. Discuss why weather predictions are not always correct and why weather forecasters use probability language.	Read about the telegraph and Morse code in an encyclopedia. Use the circuit and switch as a telegraph and practice tapping messages or spelling words in Morse code. *See* Science, Week 32, number 1.	Jousting was a form of entertainment for knights and the castle inhabitants who observed the jousts. Teach your child a simplified form of jousting. *See* Social Studies, Week 32, number 1.
Read *Heads, I Win* by Patricia Hermes. Use a penny to make a probability prediction. *How many times will the penny show heads in 25 tosses?* Have your child make a guess and record it before tossing the penny. Keep a tally while he/she tosses the penny 25 times. Have your child make a second guess before tossing the penny another 25 times. Repeat several more times. Do your child's guesses improve?	Replace the bulb in the light bulb telegraph with a buzzer. Ask: *Who might benefit from a light signal? A noise signal? Which was easier to follow?*	Show your child how to make a stained glass window of a knight, lord, lady or priest. *See* Social Studies, Week 32, number 2.
After completing the activity sheet, your child may wish to build each of the spinners and see if the predicted outcome (probability) is close to the actual outcome. **Hint:** The more times your child spins, the closer his/her predictions will be to the actual. Have your child complete **More Spinner Fun** (p. 318).	Discuss the use of electricity in your home. Have your child count the number of switches in the house, both on the walls and on appliances, lamps and other electrically powered items. Observe the electric meter just outside your house. Note how the disk spins faster when more electricity is being used. Teach your child how to read the meter in kilowatt hours. Have your child read the meter every day for a week and figure the average daily usage.	Discuss the life of a peasant. Talk about the advantages and disadvantages of being a knight or a peasant. Have your child decide which one he/she would rather have been and explain why.

313

TEACHING SUGGESTIONS AND ACTIVITIES

LANGUAGE SKILLS (Readers' Theater)

▷ 1. Only the speaker's exact words are included inside quotation marks. Words such as *he said* are separated from the quotation by a comma. The comma is included inside the quotation marks when *he said* follows the quote. Ending punctuation is usually included within the quotation marks.

Examples: Alex asked, "What is in that box?"
"Come here," his father said. "I'll show you."
"It's a puppy!" Alex shrieked.
"He's a birthday present," said his father. "Your grandparents sent him."

▷ 2. Collect several pictures that suggest a conversation between characters. Brainstorm a list of words with your child that can replace the overused word *said*. Have your child choose a picture, think about what the characters might be saying to each other, then write a conversation. Insist that he/she use words other than *said* to convey the spirit of the conversation. See below for examples.

replied	hooted	shouted	yelled	related	explained
stated	responded	uttered	questioned	chortled	demanded
laughed	answered	chirped	exclaimed	commented	retorted
called	remarked	queried	argued	cried	asked

READING (Story Analysis)

▷ 1. To make a profile graph, draw a large box like the one shown below. The numbers along the bottom refer to the numbered events from the story. The scale along the left side ranges from things going very badly to things going wonderfully for the rabbit. Plot each event (place a sticky note) from the story along the scale, showing the relative fortunes of the velveteen rabbit.

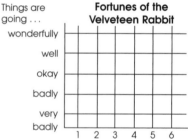

▷ 2. Have your child rewrite a fairy tale so that all the fantasy is removed.

Example: *James and the Beanstalk*

There once was a huge man that lived with his very petite wife in an old brick house on a bean farm. The man had a loud, booming voice, and the ground seemed to shake when he walked. The children in the neighborhood were afraid of the big man, but they were curious at the same time.

One evening, after it had grown dark, a group of three boys decided to look into the kitchen window of the large brick house. Because the window was so high, they had to stand on each other's shoulders. The heaviest boy stood at the bottom, then the next boy climbed onto his shoulders. The lightest boy, James, stood at the top and peeked into the window. He watched as the large man counted his earnings from the day at the farmers' market. When the weight became too much for the bottom boy, all three of the boys came tumbling down with a racket. When the man heard this, he sent his wife out to see what had made the noise.

The little woman saw the boys scrambling away in the night. She called out in a loud whisper that they should not cross her irritable husband. She went back inside and told her husband that it was only a cat knocking over the trash can. (Story may be continued.)

MATH (Probability)

▷ 1. Explain to your child that the probability of pulling out a red sock was 2 out of 5, and 3 out of 5 for pulling out a blue one. To determine probability or the chance that something will occur, count the number of times a given response is present and place it over the total number of responses. Two red socks out of five total socks looks like 2/5.

2. To build this spinner, cut out a circle from index card stock and draw the numbers as indicated in the picture at right. Put a paper fastener (brad) through the end of a large safety pin and through the center of the spinner base. The pin will act as a spinning arrow. Let your child use the spinner to complete **Spinner Fun** (p. 317).

	Colors	
	_____	_____
1		
2		
3		
4		
5		
6		

3. Make a chart like the one to the right. When your child takes three blocks out of the bag, have him/her record the number of each color. He/she should put the three blocks back in the bag before reaching in to take the next three. Have your child total the blocks of each color,

Total: _____ _____
Guess: _____ _____
Actual: _____ _____

then guess how many blocks there are of each color in the bag. By sampling, your child may be able to see that the probability is higher for one color than the other. After guessing, your child may look in the bag and get an actual count. Play this game several times using other number combinations.

SCIENCE (Electricity)

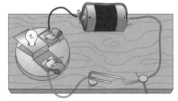 

1. Use the switch and circuit materials your child made to make a light bulb telegraph. Press the switch down and the bulb lights—the circuit is complete. Release the switch and the light goes out—the circuit is broken. Have your child use a reference book to find Morse code. A dot is made by quickly pressing down the switch. A dash is made by holding the switch down a little longer. Now, take turns sending messages. The receiver marks the dots and dashes on a sheet of paper, then decodes the message.

SOCIAL STUDIES (The Middle Ages)

BACKGROUND

The lord and his family lived in the castle, along with their servants and staff. Clergy and knights often lived in the castles as well. Animals also lived inside the castle walls. During times of fighting, the peasants sought shelter in the castle, but they did not live there regularly. Since the castle tower was often the strongest structure, many of the castle's residents lived within its walls. The servants and soldiers' quarters were on the first floor. The second level served as the secure sleeping quarters of the lord and his family. Since the basement held the wells and stored food, the tower was the best place for survival in a siege.

1. Ask your child if he/she has ever seen anyone fencing. Fencing is like jousting on foot. Teach your child to fence using the following simplified weapons and rules. Use two 3' x 1/4" sticks made of balsa wood as fencing weapons. The object will be to knock the stick out of the opponent's hand or to break the opponent's stick. Set rules such as no rough play, swing the stick only between the waist and the shoulders and no pointing or jabbing the stick at the opponent.

2. Give your child crayons and a 9" x 12" sheet of drawing paper. Tell him/her to draw and color a medieval figure (king, princess, knight or other) in the center of the paper. When the figure is complete, your child should trace around the outline with a black crayon, pressing hard. Draw curvy lines from the figure to the paper's edge with a black crayon. Divide some of the spaces between the lines into two or three spaces. Color the spaces different colors. Tell your child to put vegetable oil on a cotton ball and rub it over the entire **back** of the picture. Have him/her make a window frame from a sheet of black paper by cutting out a rectangle slightly larger than the colored picture. Glue the frame onto the picture and hang it on a window. When the sun shines through it, the picture will look like a stained glass window.

315

Comparison Words

biggest
brighter
clumsiest
crazier
cruelest
earlier
firmer
flattest
greener
noisiest
prettier
quietest
simpler
tastiest
widest

All the spelling words are adjectives that can be used to compare people, places or things. An **er** ending is used to compare two things; **est** is used to compare three or more. **Fill in** the chart below with spelling words and the other missing word that completes the comparison.

List Word	Adding **er**	Adding **est**
1. big	_____	_____
2. _____	_____	brightest
3. clumsy	_____	_____
4. _____	_____	craziest
5. _____	crueler	_____
6. _____	_____	earliest
7. firm	_____	_____
8. _____	flatter	_____
9. green	_____	_____
10. _____	noisier	_____
11. _____	_____	prettiest
12. quiet	_____	_____
13. _____	_____	simplest
14. _____	tastier	_____
15. _____	wider	_____

Spinner Fun

Using what you know about probability, try to predict how many times your spinner would land on the following numbers if you were to spin the spinner 20 times.

Predictions

	Number of Times
Spinning a 1	
Spinning a 2	
Spinning a 3	
Spinning a 4	

Now, actually spin the spinner 20 times and compare your predictions with what you actually spin. Use tally marks to record the number of spins.

Actual Spins

	Number of Times
Spinning a 1	
Spinning a 2	
Spinning a 3	
Spinning a 4	

1. Were your predictions close to the actual? _____

2. What did you notice about your predictions and the actual spinning?

_____

_____

3. Why do you think this is? _____

_____

More Spinner Fun

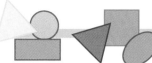

What is the probability that the arrow will land on . . .

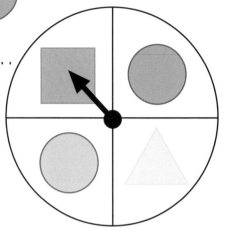

1. a circle? _____

2. a square? _____

3. a triangle? _____

Which shape has the greatest chance (probability) of having the arrow land

on it? _____

Why do you think that? _____

What is the probability that the arrow will land on . . .

1. a shape? _____

2. a number? _____

3. a number or shape? _____

4. a circle? _____

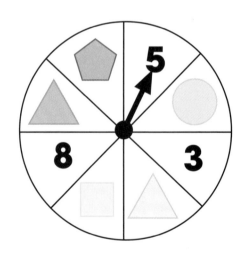

5. a triangle? _____

6. a pentagon? _____

7. a square? _____

8. a three? _____

9. an eight? _____

10. a five? _____

11. a five or eight? _____

318

Switches and Circuits

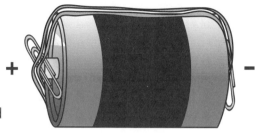

Making the Battery Holder

Wind two rubber bands very tightly around the positive and negative poles of the battery. Slip a small paper clip under the rubber band at each pole and bend the clips over. This is your battery holder. It should look like the one here.

Attaching the Socket

Screw the flashlight bulb into the socket.

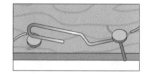

Making the Switch

Have an adult use a pocket knife to strip the insulation off the ends of three pieces of wire. Bend a large paper clip into the shape shown here. Wrap one bare end of a wire and one end of the paper clip around a large thumbtack and press the thumbtack into the wood as far as it will go. Wrap the bare end of a second wire around another large thumbtack. Line up the thumbtack under the other end of the paper clip and press the tack into the wood as far as it will go. This is what your switch should look like.

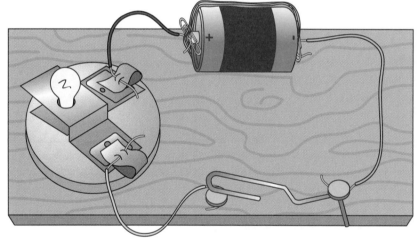

Building the Circuit

1. Attach the bare end of the wire extending from one thumbtack of your switch to the clip on one side of the socket.

2. Attach the bare end of the wire extending from the other thumbtack of your switch to the clip under one end of the battery holder.

3. Use the third wire to connect the other end of the battery holder to the other clip of the socket.

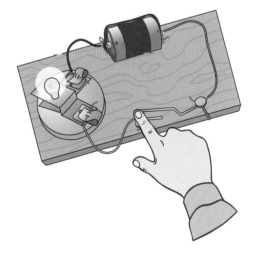

Using the Switch

Bend the paper clip switch up until it is about 1 inch from the top of the other thumbtack. Press the clip down to touch the thumbtack. The bulb should light. If it does not light, check all the connections to make sure they are tight.

Learn at Home, Grade 4

	Language Skills	Spelling	Reading
Monday	Discuss the different types of information that can be found in a dictionary. Using a dictionary, locate examples of the information described. *See* Language Skills, Week 33.	Pretest your child on these spelling words. bass file minute bowl flounder object close grave paddle cobbler hawk present does list sow Have your child correct the pretest, add personalized words and make two copies of this week's study list.	Read aloud one of the tales in *Just So Stories* by Rudyard Kipling. Have your child recall how the main character acquired its unusual characteristic or came to be. Rent or borrow a video of a *Just So* story after reading it (Rabbit Ears Productions videos are nicely done). View it with your child.
Tuesday	Guide words help narrow the search for a word. The guide words list the first and last entry word on a page. As you flip through the pages of a dictionary, watch the guide words at the top of each page. You know you are on the right page when your word fits in alphabetical order between the guide words. Provide your child with a list of words to look up. Ask him/her to look up the words and copy the guide words from the top of the page containing each word.	Have your child use each of this week's spelling words correctly in a sentence.	Have your child read aloud another tale from *Just So Stories,* reading with expression and using different voices. Have him/her outline the story with the following headings: *Setting, Characters, Problem, Events* and *Solution.*
Wednesday	Play a dictionary search game. Have your child look up words and find information at your request. **Examples:** What part of speech is the word *intelligent*? What is the meaning of the word *lagomorph*?	Have your child complete **Same Spelling But...** (p. 324).	Repeat yesterday's lesson with another tale from Kipling's *Just So Stories.*
Thursday	Explain to your child that many words in the dictionary have more than one meaning. Some might even have seven or eight! Have your child read the words below and look them up in the dictionary. Then, have your child write (in his/her own words) at least *three* different meanings for each word: *down, tip, last, bend, slip, part, pound, fly, title, note.*	Have your child choose five words from this week's list. Have him/her write out each word neatly on a separate sheet of paper, then illustrate two different meanings of each.	Have your child choose an animal with an unusual characteristic and imagine how the animal might have acquired that trait. Then, have your child write his/her own *Just So* story. Before writing, have your child outline the story using the following headings: *Setting, Characters, Problem, Events* and *Solution.*
Friday	Review alphabetical order to the third and fourth letter. Provide your child with a list of words to put in alphabetical order. *See* Language Skills, Week 33, number 1.	Give your child the final spelling test. Have your child record the pretest and final test words in his/her word bank.	Finish reading *Just So Stories* together for pleasure. Help your child create a puppet show to tell his/her *Just So* story. Build a simple stage with an old box and paint. Use stick, finger or sock puppets for the characters. Have your child perform for friends or family.

Learn at Home, Grade 4

Math	Science	Social Studies
Roman Numerals Gather some items that display Roman numerals (clocks, introductory pages of a book, copyright dates). Have your child name the symbols used. Identify the value of each symbol. Write the numerals on a chart as you explain the rules of writing Roman numerals. *See* Math, Week 33.	Electricity may produce heat or light. Ask for your child's help in making a list of electrically powered items in the house that produce heat, then a list of those that produce light. Are there some things that produce both heat and light?	Look at a map showing the feudal states of Europe during the Middle Ages. With your child, compare the map to a current map of Europe and discuss the changes.
Review the rules for writing Roman numerals. Guide your child as he/she writes Roman numerals to fifty. *See* Math, Week 33. Have your child do some research and find out five facts about ancient Rome. Ask him/her to write out the facts and number them with Roman numerals I–V.	Read about lightning and lightning safety. Find books with beautiful pictures of lightning. Teach your child about lightning so he/she respects lightening but knows it is not something to fear. Ask your child how he/she can avoid being a conductor for lightning.	Discuss how the strong feudal governments of France and England laid the foundation for a strong central government in these countries. Have your child explain how a strong government might have made people feel at peace in the Middle Ages. Does a strong government make people feel at peace today?
Write the Roman numeral symbols I, V, X and L on index cards. Write I on three separate cards, V on one, X on four and L on one. You will need nine cards in all. Say a number (from one to fifty) and have your child "build" it in Roman numerals, arranging the index cards in the correct order. Repeat several times to give your child plenty of practice.	For a culminating project, help your child make an electric lamp. After it is made, have your child explain how the lamp works. *See* Science, Week 33, numbers 1–13.	Provide research materials about the Crusades. Have your child complete **The Crusades** (p. 325).
Write random Roman numerals for your child to translate into Arabic (1, 2, 3…). Introduce C, D and M as your child seems ready. You may wish to spend more time on numbers below fifty until your child is comfortable with the pattern.	Continue working on the lamp.	*See* Social Studies, Week 33, numbers 1–3 for discussion topics and project ideas.
Using the index card numerals, help your child create a crossword puzzle with Roman numerals as the answers. Have your child copy the number of boxes necessary for each row and column, then number the boxes across and down. Ask him/her to write clues in Arabic numbers and give the crossword puzzle to someone else to solve.	Help your child finish the lamp. Then, ask him/her to explain to you how it works.	Discuss with your child what some of the positive results of the failed Crusades were.

TEACHING SUGGESTIONS AND ACTIVITIES

LANGUAGE SKILLS (Dictionary Skills)

BACKGROUND

A dictionary is a book that contains lists of words in alphabetical order. You can use a dictionary to look up the spelling of a word, the meaning of a word or the pronunciation of a word. You can also use the dictionary for . . .

illustrations —A dictionary sometimes uses illustrations to help clarify the meaning of a word.

parts of speech —A dictionary uses abbreviations to show the grammatical use of a word. Common abbreviations include *adj.* for adjective, *n.* for noun, *adv.* for adverb and *v.* for verb.

phrases/sentences —The word will also be used in sentences to help convey its meanings.

synonyms—A dictionary often provides synonyms. The synonyms follow the definition of a word

▶ 1. Have your child put the following words in alphabetical order:

smart	endangered	fearful	plan	raised	smile	flavor	rapid
ending	recreation	lean	leave	small	letter	recline	flatter

MATH (Roman Numerals)

BACKGROUND

Roman numerals and their Arabic equivalents:

$$I = 1 \quad V = 5 \quad X = 10 \quad L = 50 \quad C = 100 \quad D = 500 \quad M = 1,000$$

Roman numerals use these seven symbols in different combinations to form all the numbers. There are a few simple rules to apply. Follow the same pattern for all numbers.

Rules: a. Symbols are listed from largest to smallest.
b. If a smaller symbol precedes a larger, subtract its value. (IV or 5 – 1 = 4).
c. Do not write the same symbol four times in a row. (40 = XL, not XXXX)

Roman numerals to fifty:

I, II, III, IV, V, VI, VII, VIII, IX, X (1–10)
XI, XII, XIII, XIV, XV, XVI, XVII, XVIII, XIX, XX (11–20)
XXI, XXII, XXIII, XXIV, XXV, XXVI, XXVII, XXVIII, XXIX, XXX (21–30)
XXXI, XXXII, XXXIII, XXXIV, XXXV, XXXVI, XXXVII, XXXVIII, XXXIX, XL (31–40)
XLI, XLII, XLIII, XLIV, XLV, XLVI, XLVII, XLVIII, XLIX, L (41–50)

SCIENCE (Electricity)

Provide the following materials for making the electric lamp. Most can be found at a hardware store.

Wood pieces (soft pine):
7" x 7" x 1" square (base)
5" x 5" x 1" square (socket base)
two $1^1/_2$" x 10" x 1" (pillars)

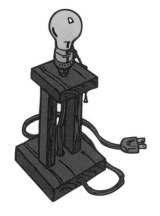

Lamp assembly:
$^1/_8$" LP threaded lamp nipple, 2–3" long
two $^1/_8$" LP hex-nuts
1 pull-chain lamp socket
at least 10' of lamp wire
lamp plug
40- or 60-watt bulb

Tools:
hammer
screwdriver
flat-head wood screws
drill
$^3/_4$" and $^3/_8$" drill bits
wire cutter
paintbrushes
varnish, paint or stain
sandpaper
wood glue
ruler
pencil

Before beginning, show your child a picture of the finished lamp or draw it on the chalkboard. This will help your child visualize it as he/she works. Work together on this project. The directions are written for your child, but **this project should be completed with adult supervision**. The adult may need to handle the drilling.

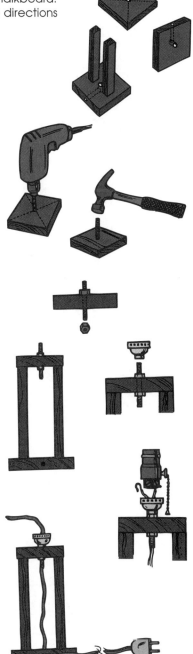

▶ 1. Sand all the wood pieces to create a smooth surface. Paint, varnish or stain all wood pieces.

▶ 2. Find the center of the 7" x 7" base and drill a $3/4$" diameter hole through the 1" thickness.

▶ 3. Turn the base on its edge. Mark the center of one side of the base. Very carefully drill a $3/8$" diameter hole halfway through the 7" thickness. This hole should meet the original hole to allow the cord to thread through. Turn the base so the $3/4$" hole faces up.

▶ 4. Position the long, narrow wood pieces like pillars on either side of the $3/4$" hole on the base. Attach each pillar using wood glue and screws. Be careful that neither pillar is attached to the base through the tunnel made by the $3/8$" drill bit.

▶ 5. Find the center of the 5" x 5" socket base and drill a $3/8$" hole through the 1" thickness.

▶ 6. Gently tap the lamp nipple into the hole of the socket base with a hammer. Leave an equal amount of the nipple exposed on either side of the socket base.

▶ 7. Fasten the hex-nuts to both ends of the extended nipple. Screw them all the way down the nipple to the socket base.

▶ 8. Use wood glue and screws to fasten the socket base to the pillars. The nipple should extend down between the pillars.

▶ 9. Screw the bottom portion of the lamp socket onto the nipple that extends up from the socket base.

▶ 10. Thread the lamp cord down through the lamp socket, socket base and inside the uprights. When you get to the base, run the lamp cord out the $3/8$" hole. Pull the cord all the way through, leaving about 1" of wire at the top in the lamp socket.

▶ 11. Remove an inch of insulation from the cord at both ends. Attach the exposed wires in the lamp socket at the top of the lamp. Snap the top portion of the lamp socket onto the bottom part.

▶ 12. Attach the exposed wires on the other end of the cord to the plug. Put a bulb in the socket. Plug the lamp into a wall socket and pull the chain.

▶ 13. Purchase an appropriate lamp shade.

SOCIAL STUDIES (The Middle Ages)

▶ 1. Have your child define each of the following words and use it in a sentence: *majority, pilgrimage, pilgrim and crusade.*

▶ 2. Ask: *Who fought in the Crusades? Why did people join the Crusades? Why didn't more peasants join? Some knights brought their entire families along on the Crusades. Why would they do that?*

▶ 3. Have your child imagine that he/she is traveling to the Holy Land. Have him/her write a letter home describing what he/she has seen and heard.

Learn at Home, Grade 4

Same Spelling But . . .

bass
bowl
close
cobbler
does
file
flounder
grave
hawk
list
minute
object
paddle
present
sow

Homophones are words that have the same spelling but are different in meaning and sometimes pronunciation. Use the spelling words to **fill in** the blanks. Indicate the part of speech in the parentheses. The same word is used twice in each sentence.

1. The secretary wanted to_____ ( ) her fingernails before she put all the papers in the _____ ( ).
2. Before my dad goes to_____ ( ), he eats a big_____ ( ) of cereal.
3. Our_____ ( ) broke, the boat overturned and we had to_____ ( ) quite a distance.
4. The_____ ( ) singer enjoys fishing for _____ ( ).
5. The ship's captain was reading the_____ ( ) of passengers when he suddenly felt the ship _____ ( ).
6. After the_____ ( ) has repaired shoes all day, he enjoys eating a fruit_____ ( ).
7. The _____ ( ) was hooked tightly, but I couldn't reel it in, so it began to _____ ( ) in the shallow water.
8. As the peddler was getting ready to_____ ( ) his vegetables, a hungry_____ ( ) was perched on a nearby tree branch.
9. The company hired to dig the_____ ( ) realized the cemetery needed _____ ( ) attention.

Circle the correct pronunciation and **write** the word on the line.
1. The president was so_____ I could shake his hand.   klōz   klōs
2. Three _____ were nibbling grass by the road.   dōz   dūz
3. After doing our research, we had to _____ a report.
   prĕz′ ent   prĭ zĕnt′
4. The gardener will_____ grass seed for a new lawn.   sō   sou

The Crusades

1099-1291

1. Identify the following on your map (refer to a world atlas to find a map of Europe):

- England
- France
- Spain
- Portugal
- Germany
- Italy
- Hungary
- Czech Republic

- Switzerland
- Austria
- Turkey
- Syria
- Israel
- Poland
- Bulgaria
- Slovakia

- Romania
- Egypt
- Jerusalem
- Jordan
- Mediterranean Sea
- Red Sea
- Black Sea

2. **Color** the water blue, the land tan, and the area known as the Holy Land purple.

3. Using an encyclopedia, **draw** the route that Christian knights traveled when going to the Holy Land during the Crusades.

4. Why did the Christians, Muslims and Jews call Jerusalem the Holy Land?

_____

5. If you were a Crusader from France, would you travel to the Holy Land by land or sea?_____Why?_____

_____

	Language Skills	Spelling	Reading
Monday	Teach your child to answer the phone properly, speaking clearly and directly into the phone. Tell your child to say "Hello," announce the family name, then identify him/herself. **Example:** "Hello, Moore residence. This is Jeff." Simulate a phone call and have your child practice answering the phone correctly.	Pretest your child on these spelling words. board council knot ring bored counsel not wring coarse creak lead who's course creek led whose Have your child correct the pretest, add personalized words and make two copies of this week's study list.	**Folktales** Introduce your child to folktales. *See* Reading, Week 34. What is a folktale? Discuss the definition with your child. What folktales does your child know or has he/she heard? Read *The Rough-Face Girl* by Rafe Martin. Have your child rewrite the story as if he/she were the Rough-Face Girl writing about the events in her journal.
Tuesday	Discuss important phone manners. Think about how your child should respond if someone is not available. Model the language that is polite and confident. **Examples:** "May I tell her who is calling?" "She is not available. May I take a message?" Also, discuss what information should never be given over the phone. Do not frighten your child, but explain why that information should not be given.	Have your child use each of this week's spelling words correctly in a sentence.	Read *Mufaro's Beautiful Daughters* by John Steptoe. Have your child compare this story to the tale of Cinderella, using a Venn diagram to chart the similarities and differences. Exercise your child's critical thinking skills. Have your child complete **What Probably Happened?** (p. 331).
Wednesday	Teach your child to make a phone call. Your child should identify him/herself and state the reason for calling. Then, he/she should either ask for a specific person or ask for the person who can help him/her. Teach your child to be polite and end the call with "Thank you." Practice different phone calls that your child may need to make. Show him/her where to find emergency numbers. Discuss when to call 911.	Have your child complete **Bizarre Bazaar!** (p. 330).	Read *Lon Po Po* by Ed Young. Have your child write about the lesson that the girls learned. What other story has a similar lesson? Has your child learned this same lesson through his/her own experience? Ask him/her to share the experience.
Thursday	Show your child examples of Uncial script, a type of script used during the time of knights and castles. Then, teach your child to write with Uncials. Have your child write a sentence or two about his/her favorite medieval topic. *See* Language Skills, Week 34, numbers 1 and 2.	Write sentences on the chalkboard using words from this week's list, then erase the spelling words in each sentence. Have your child read the sentences and write in the correct words.	Let your child choose another folktale from the library to read. Ask him/her to read the tale carefully two or three times. *See* Reading, Week 34, number 1 for follow-up activities.
Friday	Review the concept of alliteration. Have your child come up with several alliterative sentences about the Middle Ages.	Give your child the final spelling test. Have your child record the pretest and final test words in his/her word bank.	Relate folktales to the larger concept of folklore. Folklore not only includes folktales but arts and crafts, songs, dances and games as well. Explore folklore with your child. *See* Reading, Week 34, number 2.

Learn at Home, Grade 4

Math	Science	Social Studies
Uses of Numbers Numbers can be used to tell which one in the order of something. **Examples:** *My team came in* fourth *place. I would like the* fifth *book on the shelf.* Numbers such as *fourth* and *fifth* are called *ordinal* numbers. Have your child write the ordinal numbers from *first* to *twentieth*. If there are any words he/she spells incorrectly, add them to this week's spelling list.	**Health** Discuss reasons to exercise, including fitness, weight control and stress reduction. Have your child name ways in which he/she already gets exercise. Have your child think about how he/she feels before, during and after exercise. Make a heart rate chart. Have your child record his/her resting heart rate each day. Have your child record his/her heart rate during and after he/she exercises, too.	Read about the structure and arrangement of a castle. You can find information in an encyclopedia or one of the many books about castles. Have your child define the following castle terms: *keep, merlon, battlements, crenellation, portcullis, gatehouse, motte, palisade, bailey, moat* and *drawbridge*.
Practice pronunciation with dates. Point to a day on the calendar and have your child tell you the date—e.g., May sixteenth. Vary the activity by stating a date (June twentieth) and asking your child to point to it. Teach your child to write ordinal numbers as symbols (1st, 2nd, 3rd, 4th, 5th,…). Have your child draw twenty items in a row. Then, ask him/her to count the items from left to right and label each with its ordinal number.	Have your child write an imaginary story about a character who does not get enough exercise. Include an illustration.	Read about the other buildings that might be found around the castle in a fiefdom. Have your child draw a map of a fiefdom, including the farmland.
Problem for your child to explore: *Draw a large square. How many regions can you divide the square into using four straight lines? Try several different arrangements of the four lines, but the lines must always be straight. What is the smallest number of regions? What is the greatest number of regions?*	Stretching, weight lifting and aerobic activity are three types of exercise. Each is important for maintaining physical fitness. Stretching exercises lengthen muscles and prevent muscles from getting tight. You should always stretch before and after vigorous exercise. Teach your child some basic stretching exercises. *See* Science, Week 34, number 1.	Help your child build a model castle. Read all the directions before beginning. Follow the directions on **Creating a Castle** (pgs. 333–335) and use copies of the patterns found on **Outside Wall Patterns** and **Inside Wall Patterns** (pgs. 336 and 337).
Problem for your child to explore: *Choose your three favorite ice-cream flavors. How many different double-dip combinations can you make with those three flavors? (It helps to draw a picture.) How many different double-dip combinations can you make with 4 flavors? 5 flavors? 10 flavors? 31 flavors?*	Weight lifting develops muscle strength. There are different exercises for different muscle groups in the body. Most physicians recommend that children under 12 refrain from lifting weights. Instead, use resistance to build muscle tone. Teach your child some safe resistance exercises. *See* Science, Week 34, number 2.	Have your child continue building the model castle.
Have your child complete **Number Puzzles** (p. 332).	Aerobic exercise is extremely important for life-long good health and fitness. Aerobic exercise increases heart and breathing rates. It makes heart and lungs stronger. If you exercise regularly, you should notice your resting heart rate decreasing. That is because your heart is able to work more efficiently when it is healthier. Have your child analyze the data he/she has collected on the heart rate chart. What does he/she notice?	Have your child complete the castle. Let your child present the finished castle to an audience. Ask him/her to name the different parts of the castle and their functions.

TEACHING SUGGESTIONS AND ACTIVITIES

LANGUAGE SKILLS (Forms of Communication)

▶ 1. You will need calligraphy pens with ink and nibs or calligraphy markers to write Uncials. You will also need scratch paper for practice and watercolor paper for the final project. Give your child some scratch paper and a calligraphy pen or marker. Demonstrate how to hold the pen properly, with the nib at a 45° angle on the page. Let your child practice making different strokes with the pen—curves, vertical and horizontal lines, diagonals, and so on. When he/she feels comfortable with the pen, have your child try writing the Uncial alphabet (shown below). The Uncial alphabet was used in manuscripts from the fifth through eighth centuries. There is no distinction between lower- and upper-case letters, except that the upper-case letters are larger in size.

$$a B c D e f g h i j k l m n$$
$$o p Q R s t u v w x y z$$

▶ 2. Once your child has mastered the Uncial alphabet, ask him/her to write a sentence or two about a favorite medieval topic. Let him/her try once on scratch paper, then a second time on the watercolor paper. Have him/her illustrate the sentences with a watercolor painting.

READING (Folktales)

BACKGROUND
Folktales are stories that have been passed on orally since before written language existed. They probably began with a storyteller entertaining a group of people with a story that taught a lesson. Over the years and through retelling, folktales have grown into tales of fantasy and enchantment. Folktales come from countries all over the world. It is fascinating to find that stories from different countries and cultures can have the same themes. The folktales included this week are modern retellings. Go to the library for more traditional tales.

▶ 1. After reading a folktale, have your child choose one of the following activities:

   a. List the main characters and descriptive phrases for each one. Write one paragraph about each of the main figures in the story. Draw a picture of each character based on the descriptions.

   b. Change the actions of one of the characters in the story. Imagine how this change would affect the rest of the story. Rewrite the story incorporating the changes to the plot. Does the lesson of the story change as well? Formulate a new one if necessary.

   c. Imagine that the story takes place in a completely different setting. Choose a new setting (time and place) for the story, giving the characters different names, if appropriate. Keeping the lesson and basic plot the same, rewrite the story in the new setting. Give the story a new title as well.

▶ 2. Help your child choose a country or culture to explore. Have your child consider his/her own heritage in making a choice. Next, help him/her research the following:

   a. Research the arts and crafts of the chosen country or culture. Try to imitate the art if possible.

   b. Learn a folk song. Teach your child the lyrics and melody and sing together.

   c. Learn a folk dance. Teach your child the steps and dance together. Play appropriate music along with it.

   d. Have your child interpret a proverb. Is there a similar saying in your own culture?

SCIENCE (Health)

▶ 1. Stretching exercises:
  arm circles
  touch your toes
  bend sideways at the waist
  calf stretch
  lower back stretch
  hamstring stretch
  squats (knee bends)

▶ 2. Push-ups and crunches are excellent resistance exercises for building muscle in the arms and abdomen. To strengthen the legs, have your child lie on his/her back and push a heavy box with his/her feet.

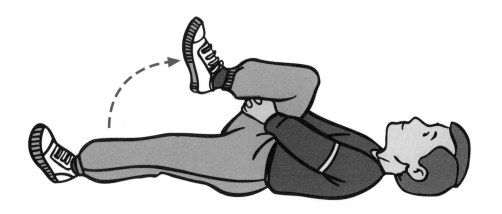

Bizarre Bazaar!

board
bored
coarse
council
counsel
course
creak
creek
knot
lead
led
not
ring
who's
whose
wring

Three pairs of homophones are not next to each other in the spelling list because of alphabetical order. **Write** those three pairs.

a. _____   a. _____   a. _____

b. _____   b. _____   b. _____

Fill in the blanks with spelling words. Not all words are used.

1. The pipe was made out of _ _ _ ☐.

2. She broke the _ _ ☐ _ _ with a karate chop.

3. In scouting, he learned to tie a _ _ _ ☐.

4. Students will elect class members to the student _ _ ☐ _ _ _ _ .

5. The umpire shouted, "_ ☐ _ _ _ bat is this?"

6. Grandpa gave me good _ _ _ ☐ _ _ _ whenever I had important decisions to make.

7. With nothing to do, I am ☐ _ _ _ _ .

8. It is _ ☐ _ nice to hit anyone.

9. The _ _ _ _ _ ☐ material made my arms itch.

10. The hikers followed a _ _ _ _ ☐ _ to the north.

11. The thief stole a diamond _ _ _ ☐.

12. We sailed paper boats in the _ _ _ _ ☐.

13. The old floor started to ☐ _ _ _ _ when I walked across it.

Match the boxed letter from each sentence to the numbered lines below to answer the riddle: *Why was the man happy to get a job at the bakery?*

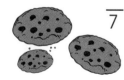

$\overline{7}\ \overline{9}\ \overline{13}\ \overline{2}\ \overline{4}\ \overline{10}\ \overline{9}$ $\overline{5}\ \overline{9}$ $\overline{12}\ \overline{6}\ \overline{9}\ \overline{2}\ \overline{1}\ \overline{9}\ \overline{1}$

$\overline{3}\ \overline{5}\ \overline{9}$ $\overline{1}\ \overline{8}\ \overline{4}\ \overline{11}\ \overline{5}$.

What Probably Happened?

Each sentence below tells of something which happened after something else happened first. Read each sentence. **Write** two different things which could have caused the second thing to happen.

1. The dog ran back with a bone in its mouth.

   What happened before?   1. _____

   2. _____

2. Paula said "Thank you" to her friend Kelly.

   What happened before?   1. _____

   2. _____

3. The pilot said that he was making an emergency landing.

   What happened before?   1. _____

   2. _____

4. The audience rose to its feet with thunderous applause.

   What happened before?   1. _____

   2. _____

5. Pete sat in total exhaustion at the edge of the lake.

   What happened before?   1. _____

   2. _____

6. The restaurant owner apologized to the Carr family.

   What happened before?   1. _____

   2. _____

Number Puzzles

Use the numbers in each box to make number sentences.
Use each number only once.

8	9	7
4	4	6
3	14	36

_____ + _____ = _____

_____ – _____ = _____

_____ x _____ = _____

3	7	5
4	28	9
8	3	12

_____ + _____ = _____

_____ – _____ = _____

_____ x _____ = _____

6	4	13
9	7	27
8	12	3

_____ + _____ = _____

_____ – _____ = _____

_____ x _____ = _____

10	6	13
7	4	5
9	5	42

_____ + _____ = _____

_____ – _____ = _____

_____ x _____ = _____

11	3	15
21	8	6
7	7	5

_____ + _____ = _____

_____ – _____ = _____

_____ x _____ = _____

7	9	12
20	5	16
3	9	4

_____ + _____ = _____

_____ – _____ = _____

_____ x _____ = _____

Creating a Castle

Make your own castle by following the directions below.

1. **Cut out** the two outside wall patterns (p. 336).
2. Place the two patterns on a piece of cardboard.
3. **Trace** around each pattern twice, making four walls.
4. **Cut out** the four walls using a knife or sharp scissors.

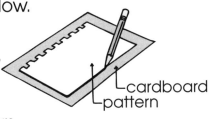

cardboard pattern

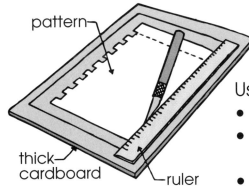

pattern

thick cardboard

ruler

If you use scissors, cut very slowly along the lines. If you use a knife, you will use a ruler and a thick piece of cardboard on which to cut.

Using a knife:
- Put the ruler along the line to be cut.
- Press down hard on the ruler so it won't slip, but keep your fingers away from the blade.
- Hold the knife with your other hand. Go over the line as many times as it takes to cut through.
- In order to bend cardboard, it has to be scored. To do this, follow the first three steps again but do not cut through. Go over the line only once or twice, making a very shallow groove.

5. **Score** all the dotted lines on the patterns.
6. **Fold** all scored lines.

score → ← fold

7. **Cut** windows and doors in the walls including a front door.

glue

8. **Glue** the four walls together on the folds. Make sure the battlements are on top.
9. To make the inside walls, walkway and rooms under it, **cut out** the inside wall patterns (p. 337).
10. Place the two inside wall patterns (p. 337) on a piece of cardboard and **trace** around each pattern twice, making four walls.

Creating a Castle (continued)

11. **Cut out** all four walls using a knife or sharp scissors. (Follow directions in step 4 on page 333.)
12. **Cut** two slits on either end as shown on the smaller inside wall pattern.
13. **Score** and **fold** along dotted lines as indicated on both patterns.

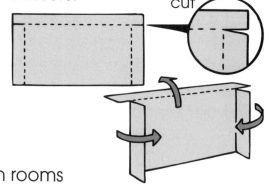

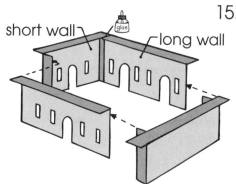

14. **Cut** windows and doors in rooms where you want them.

short wall   glue   long wall

15. **Glue** the two lower side tabs on the shorter walls (the ones folded forward) behind either end of the long walls. **Fold** the top back so its ends go over the ends of the long walls. **Glue** down under each corner. Let dry.

16. Set the walkway rooms inside the castle.

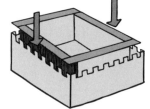

17. Measure $3\frac{1}{2}$" up from the bottom of four toilet tissue rolls. **Cut out** bottom half of rolls. **Cut** notches in tops of rolls as shown.
18. Run glue down each corner of the castle. Press each tower, one at a time, into position until it holds.

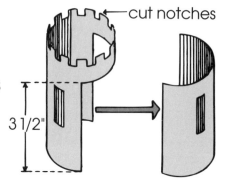

cut notches

3 1/2"

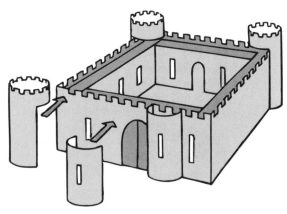

19. Use the other halves of toilet tissue rolls as gatehouse towers. **Cut** windows in all towers.
20. **Glue** the gatehouse towers on either side of the front door.

Creating a Castle (continued)

21. To make a hill for your castle, wet shredded pieces of newspaper in papier-mâché paste.

22. Wad them together on a 12" square of cardboard. Build them up to form a small flat-topped hill. (Make sure the hill is large enough for your castle.)

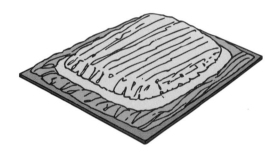

23. Put wet strips of paper across the hill to smooth it out and hold it in place.

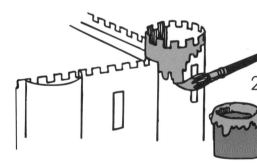

24. While the papier-mâché is still wet, make a dent around the outer edge of the hill to make a moat.

25. Paint your castle, hill and moat. Add a flag on a toothpick.

26. When all are dry, set the castle on the hill. Display your "kingdom."

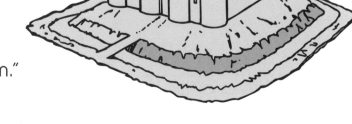

Outside Wall Patterns

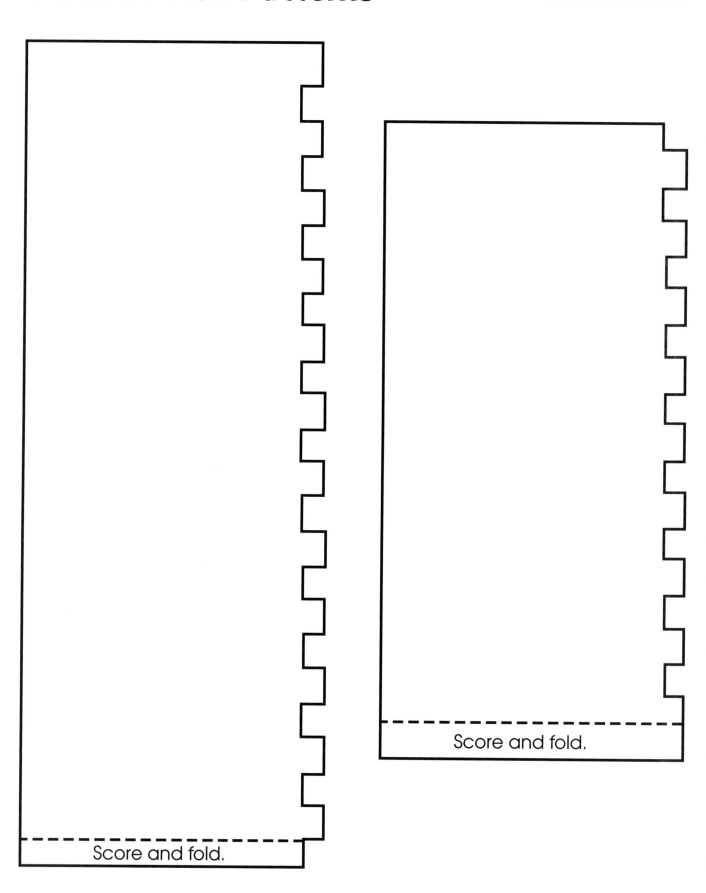

Score and fold.

Score and fold.

Inside Wall Patterns

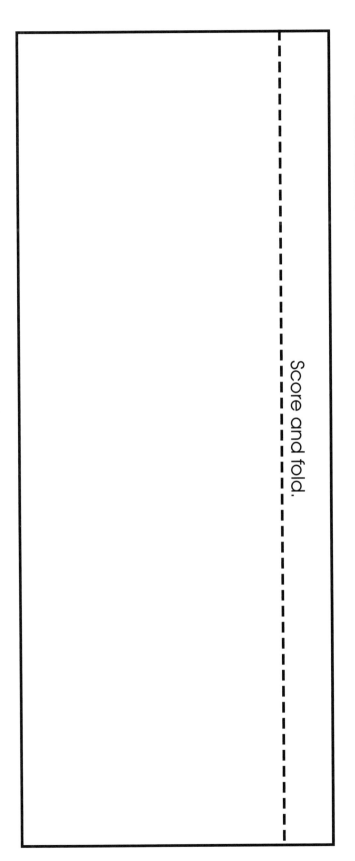

Score and fold.

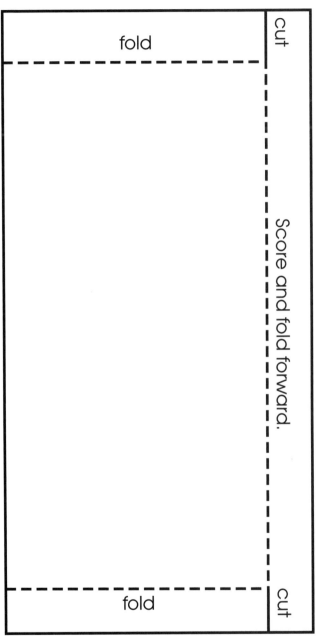

cut

fold

Score and fold forward.

fold

cut

Learn at Home, Grade 4

	Language Skills	Spelling	Reading
Monday	**Proofreading** Teach your child how to proofread his/her own writing. What should he/she look for? Show your child the basic proofreading marks. *See* Language Skills, Week 35, number 1.	Pretest your child on these spelling words. accepted dozed pledged admiring fanning practicing captured guarded proving choking hoping rearranged dining invited squeezing Have your child correct the pretest, add personalized words and make two copies of this week's study list.	Read the first chapter of *Sarah, Plain and Tall* by Patricia MacLachlan. Discuss the setting (time and place) and characters introduced so far. Questions for your child: *Do you think the family is happy? Explain your answer. What is Papa like?* Have your child draw Sarah's family and home.
Tuesday	Have your child write a descriptive paragraph about something he/she did this week. The paragraph should include a description using all the senses. Good topics include hiking in the woods, eating at a restaurant or visiting a new location. Using proofreading marks, have your child edit his/her story.	Have your child use each of this week's spelling words correctly in a sentence.	Read chapter 2 of *Sarah, Plain and Tall*. Have your child write the letter that he/she imagines either Caleb or Anna wrote to Sarah.
Wednesday	Have your child complete **Proofreading** (p. 342).	Have your child complete **Changing Tenses** (p. 341).	Read chapters 3–5 of *Sarah, Plain and Tall*. Have your child list the hints that make Anna and Caleb think Sarah is staying and the hints that she will want to go back to Maine.
Thursday	Provide your child with a story containing intentional mistakes. Have him/her correct the story using proofreading marks. *See* Language Skills, Week 35, number 2.	Have your child study this week's spelling words by using clap-tap spelling. *See* **Background Information and Supporting Activities** (p. 8).	Read chapters 6 and 7 of *Sarah, Plain and Tall*. Have your child draw a character web that shows how Sarah interacts with or feels about each character. *See* Reading, Week 35, number 1.
Friday	Again, provide your child with a story containing intentional mistakes. Have him/her correct the story using proofreading marks. *See* Language Skills, Week 35, number 3.	Give your child the final spelling test. Have your child record the pretest and final test words in his/her word bank.	Finish reading *Sarah, Plain and Tall*. With your child, choose from the reading response activities found in Reading, Week 35, numbers 2–4.

Math	Science	Social Studies
Teach your child to find the relevant information in a word problem. *See* Math, Week 35, number 1. Have your child read word problems, cross out any extra information and solve the problems. Then, have him/her write word problems using only relevant information. *See* Math, Week 35, number 2.	Brainstorm together a list of games, activities and exercises that make the heart beat faster and increase the breathing rate. Make a plan in which your child does an aerobic exercise at least three times a week all summer. Design a chart to help your child keep track of his/her exercise.	Read and discuss several children's books that take place in the Middle Ages. Books might include King Arthur tales, a version of *Saint George and the Dragon* or stories of people living in castles.
Mental math is a good exercise for visualization and thinking. Have your child solve a series of operations without using paper and pencil. Slowly dictate a problem, such as 4 + 6 – 7 or 4 x 3 – 2, for your child to solve mentally. **Note:** If your child has trouble with mental math, you will need to provide more experiences with hands-on manipulative practice.	Discuss the elements of a healthy diet. Refer to the food pyramid to learn what you and your child should eat each day. Have your child design a menu of nutritionally appropriate foods for one day. Your child should choose foods that he/she likes, but still make sure he/she has included the correct number of foods from each food group. Have your child complete a copy of **Pyramid Puzzler** (p. 345).	Read about some famous figures associated with the Middle Ages, including Charlemagne, William I, Kings Henry II of England and Louis IX of France, Thomas Aquinas and Eleanor of Aquitaine. Have your child choose a person and write about his/her accomplishments.
Test your child's mathematical understanding with math riddles. Give your child several clues about a number. Then, ask him/her to guess the number. *See* Math, Week 35, number 3.	The amount of food you eat should balance the amount of your daily activity. Discuss with your child clues for determining appropriate quantities. Discuss the consequences of eating too much or too little.	Read about the end of the Middle Ages. There were many events that caused the medieval civilization to fall back. Those events included the Hundred Years' War, civil wars, peasant revolts, disease and plague, famine and trouble in the church.
Teach your child order of operations. When there is more than one operation in an equation, have your child complete the operation in parentheses first. Then, multiply, divide, add, then subtract. *See* Math, Week 35, number 4.	Staying physically fit is a life-long job. Some days you will not feel like exercising or eating healthy. Discuss the reasons for working at good health. Have your child design a poster that promotes healthy living and make up a rhyme or slogan of encouragement and inspiration. Hang the poster at home.	Based on the information learned in this unit, have your child write a short puppet show script. The script should bring to life some aspect of the Middle Ages. Make sure the script is based on accurate information.
Have your child complete **Identifying Operations** (p. 344).	Help your child make a pie chart to show how he/she spends each day. Divide a large circle first into 24 pie-shaped wedges. Each represents an hour of the day. Color code different activities: yellow for sleep, red for watching TV, blue for eating, green for exercise, and so on. For each hour in the day, have your child color a wedge showing what he/she did. Keep like colors together on the circle. *See* Science, Week 35, number 1.	Help your child revise, edit and proofread the puppet show script. Save it for next week's lessons.

Learn at Home, Grade 4

TEACHING SUGGESTIONS AND ACTIVITIES

LANGUAGE SKILLS (Proofreading)

▷ 1. Introduce your child to the following proofreading marks:

Use a capital letter.	Insert quotation marks
Insert a period.	Insert an apostrophe
Insert a comma.	Indent
Insert	Start a new paragraph
Use a lowercase letter.	Delete

Write several sentences on the board containing errors. Have your child call out the errors he/she sees, then show him/her how to mark the errors with proofreading marks. Be sure to leave enough space for your child to make his/her corrections.

▷ 2. Copy the following paragraph for your child. Ask him/her to find the capitalization and punctuation errors and to divide the article into paragraphs using the paragraph symbol.

recently my dad took my two friends and me to the zoo we left early in the morning it was miles away the first exhibit we visited was the reptile house we saw many kinds of reptiles next we visited the aquarium where numerous species of fish lived they were very colorful after a good lunch we made our way to the wild cats section of the zoo my favorite was the bobcat the final exhibit we visited before heading home was the jungle bird sanctuary

▷ 3. Copy the following paragraphs for your child. Ask him/her to watch for subject/verb agreement, capitalization and apostrophes. Make marks as necessary.

george washington was born on February 22, 1732 in virginia. When he was three years old, his family move to an undeveloped plantation, later called mount vernon. They had no nearby neighbors.

george didnt receive many years of formal education. He wrote his lessons on sheets of paper that his mother then sewed into a notebook. His favorite subject were math. His father had plan to send him to school in england, but when george were just eleven years old, his father died. george was then needed by his mother on the farm. At a young age, george helped manage a plantation worked by twenty slaves. No one know for sure if he really chopped down his fathers cherry tree, but he were a quiet, patient, dependable and honest young man.

READING (Story Analysis)

▷ 1. Show your child how to make a character web. Draw a small circle in the center of a blank page and write Sarah's name in it. All around the circle, write the names of each of the other characters, including those in Maine. Connect each name to Sarah's circle and write a word or phrase that expresses how Sarah interacts with or feels about that person. For example, between Sarah and William, you could write the word *misses* because Sarah misses William. Add words between other characters to show their relationships.

▷ 2. What if Sarah had decided to buy a train ticket back to Maine? How would the story have ended? What would Anna, Caleb and their father have done? Have your child write a new ending to the story.

▷ 3. Have your child describe the wedding of Sarah and Jacob as he/she imagines it. Encourage your child to use descriptive language like the author's.

▷ 4. Have your child write a letter to William as if he/she were Sarah. In the letter, Sarah should tell William all the reasons why she is staying to marry Jacob.

Learn at Home, Grade 4

MATH (Uses of Numbers)

▶ 1. Teach your child to read word problems critically. Add unnecessary information to word problems and guide your child to choose only the information relevant to solving the problem. In the following word problem, the cost of the paper cups is not relevant information and can be crossed out: *Mrs. Miller needed to buy 6 packages of paper plates for a party. She found some plates for $2.50 per package. She also saw some paper cups for $3.00. How much did Mrs. Miller spend on paper plates?* Design problems similar to this one for your child to solve.

▶ 2. Provide your child with facts for creating word problems. Ask him/her to write a story problem for each set of facts, leaving out any unnecessary information. Here are two sample sets of facts:

5 ice-cream cones at $0.75 each	11 boys and 9 girls
12 candy bars at $0.65 each	tickets cost $1.50 each
total cost of ice cream	total cost of the boys' tickets

▶ 3. Describe a number in the form of a riddle and have your child try to guess it.

Example: I am an even number.
I have two digits.
The sum of my two digits is 13.
The difference between my two digits is one.
Answer: 76

Now, have your child make up several riddles for you to solve.

▶ 4. Write the problem below on the chalkboard. Have your child solve the problem from left to right.

6 + 3 x 10 – 3 x 7 + 5 =

Rewrite the problem as shown: 6 + (3 x 10) – (3 x 7) + 5 =

Have your child calculate the problem again by starting with the operations in parentheses. Challenge him/her to study the very different results and come up with an explanation. Make up more equations with multiple operations for your child to solve. Put parentheses around the multiplication and division operations.

SCIENCE (Health)

▶ 1. Have your child look at the finished pie chart. Have him/her calculate the approximate percentage of the day spent with each activity. Is your child pleased with how he/she spends a typical day?

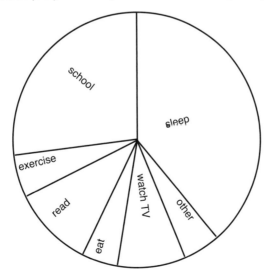

Proofreading

It is important to be able to proofread things that you write to correct any errors.

Read each paragraph. Proofread for these errors:
- indentation
- punctuation
- capitalization
- sentences which do not belong (mark out)
- spelling
- run-on sentences (rewrite as two sentences)

Rewrite each paragraph correctly on the lines.

1. my brother will graduate from high school this week everyone is so excited for him Many of our relatives are coming from out of town for his graduation our town has a university. mom and Dad have planed a big surprise party

_____

_____

_____

_____

2. riding in a hot air balloon is an incredible experience first, everyone climbs into the basket the pilot then starts the fuel which produces the hot air that makes the ballone rise. The road leads to an open field to lower the balloon, the pilot gradually releases air

_____

_____

_____

_____

3. a caterpiller is a young butterfly the caterpillar originally hatches from an egg and later, it develops a hard case around its body inside the case, the caterpillow becomes a butterfly after a short time, the case opens and a beautiful butterfly flies out the tree has hndreds of blossoms

Rewrite this paragraph on another sheet of paper.

Changing Tenses

accepted
admiring
captured
choking
dining
dozed
fanning
guarded
hoping
invited
pledged
practicing
proving
rearranged
squeezing

For each spelling word, **write** the present tense of the verb. Watch out for missing or extra letters.

1. _____   9. _____
2. _____   10. _____
3. _____   11. _____
4. _____   12. _____
5. _____   13. _____
6. _____   14. _____
7. _____   15. _____
8. _____

Complete the word search. The 30 words are written vertically, horizontally and diagonally.

```
R B E S Z C Q U H X O O G X C D K Y D G N
G H I Q H I V T K E E N O M R S E V O G U
U C A U O C X N C V I K I M T Z I L N T B
A C C E P T E D P N S D U N O C Z I A G H
R H C E I R R N Q E C Z D V U C H O K E
D O E Z N B A A C G U A R D I I G K P D P
E K P E G B F C D U G P O Q T N T W L U L
D I T P N M C E T M S T P C I Q I E E E S
R N D T A O L A L I I U A Z Z Y F N D G Y
T G T L I P J L P H C R E A R R A N G E O
K X A J W H V Y H T P E I A D M I R E J A
N N I Q S Q T S S A U A R N Y C E P O H O
L U M D Z H W Z P Q P R C C G N O G N N O
U Q V G A Z U P S R W R E W I H P S U B I
E V Y C A Y J X R E A A O D J D X F U T G
V B G S N F P U X O L N D V E G G I X Q O
I V W E Z M A T P V V G Q Z I J C N M Y C
F W D F L W I N V I T E O M J N B W C R C
E P M F Y P H M P O X D U Q R A G V M X G
```

Identifying Operations

Fill in the correct sign for each problem.

5 ◯ 5 = 10	14 ◯ 59 = 73	21 ◯ 9 = 30	36 ◯ 63 = 99
9 ◯ 9 = 81	56 ◯ 17 = 73	64 ◯ 8 = 8	6 ◯ 9 = 54
56 ◯ 8 = 48	40 ◯ 5 = 8	7 ◯ 8 = 56	33 ◯ 57 = 90
91 ◯ 16 = 75	9 ◯ 3 = 27	76 ◯ 19 = 57	27 ◯ 3 = 9
54 ◯ 6 = 9	29 ◯ 37 = 66	43 ◯ 7 = 50	63 ◯ 9 = 54
28 ◯ 17 = 11	6 ◯ 5 = 30	4 ◯ 9 = 36	8 ◯ 38 = 46
25 ◯ 5 = 5	36 ◯ 5 = 31	48 ◯ 8 = 6	2 ◯ 9 = 18
72 ◯ 9 = 63	56 ◯ 8 = 7	9 ◯ 1 = 9	55 ◯ 37 = 92
64 ◯ 8 = 56	7 ◯ 1 = 7	45 ◯ 5 = 9	81 ◯ 9 = 9
36 ◯ 4 = 9	57 ◯ 9 = 48	36 ◯ 27 = 63	80 ◯ 17 = 63
45 ◯ 5 = 40	7 ◯ 6 = 42	48 ◯ 6 = 42	32 ◯ 4 = 8
82 ◯ 9 = 91	8 ◯ 8 = 64	9 ◯ 8 = 72	71 ◯ 15 = 86
17 ◯ 77 = 94	40 ◯ 6 = 34	47 ◯ 38 = 9	56 ◯ 9 = 47
36 ◯ 6 = 30	15 ◯ 38 = 53	3 ◯ 6 = 18	5 ◯ 9 = 45
72 ◯ 8 = 9	43 ◯ 48 = 91	27 ◯ 18 = 45	6 ◯ 6 = 36
49 ◯ 7 = 7	7 ◯ 7 = 49	8 ◯ 3 = 24	16 ◯ 16 = 32

Pyramid Puzzler

In 2005, the United States Department of Agriculture introduced the new food pyramid shown below. Each of the colored bands within the pyramid represents a different food group. The width of bands in the food groups indicates the proportion of that food you should eat. The character walking up the side of the pyramid shows the importance of exercise. (The food pyramid is a guideline; your pyramid may be different than this one.)

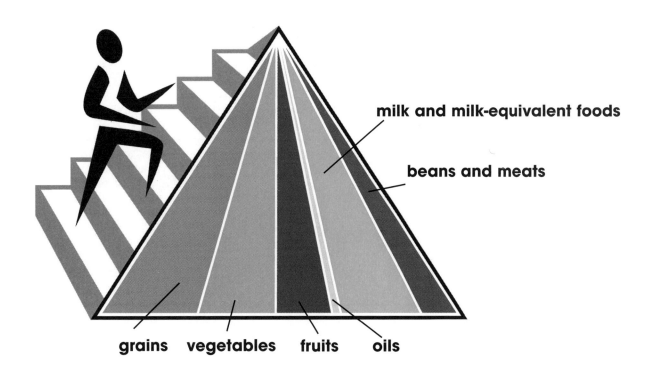

milk and milk-equivalent foods

beans and meats

grains   vegetables   fruits   oils

Discuss the importance of a healthy and varied diet, and reinforce this by selecting a variety of foods from the food groups to 'build a rainbow' for each meal throughout the day. Examine a variety of food labels and discuss which foods contain high amounts of carbohydrates, vitamins, minerals, fiber, and proteins. Make a list of sweet and calorie-heavy foods that the food pyramid suggests we should avoid, and discuss the importance of moderation in consuming such foods.

	Language Skills	Spelling	Reading
Monday	**Review Week** Have your child write three paragraphs based on an outline. *See* Language Skills, Week 36, number 1. Assess your child's paragraphs for organization and adherence to the outline. Reteach, if necessary.	**Review Week** Choose words from the past 8 weeks for the pretest. Pretest your child on these spelling words. Have your child correct the pretest. Make a study list of misspelled words, if any. Remind him/her to study the words each day this week.	**Review Week** Review a variety of poetry. Read rhyming couplets, silly poems, cinquains and acrostic poems. Can your child identify the different types of poems? Let your child choose any style of poem to write.
Tuesday	Review the story outline or plot outline. *See* Language Skills, Week 29, number 2. Assess your child's story. Does it contain all the elements of the outline? Have your child complete **What's the Story?** (p. 350).	Have your child categorize the spelling words from the past 8 weeks by parts of speech (verbs, nouns, adjectives, adverbs) or by number (singular or plural). You may want to have the words written individually on index cards for today's and tomorrow's activities.	Review tall tales. Read a tall tale with your child and discuss the exaggerated elements. Have your child write exaggerated sentences about something or someone. Sentence starters: *He is as boring as…. She is as tall as…. The book was as long as….*
Wednesday	Find or write a descriptive or persuasive paragraph. Have your child read the paragraph and identify the main topic and underline the supporting details.	Have your child sort the spelling words from the past 8 weeks by number of syllables.	Review main idea. On index cards, write the main idea for each of several books your child has read recently. Write the titles of the books on another set of cards. Have your child match each book title with the book's main idea.
Thursday	Review the use of quotation marks. Share some "knock-knock" jokes with your child. Have your child add quotation marks where needed. *See* Language Skills, Week 36, number 2. Then, let your child write his/her own "knock-knock" jokes.	Have your child make a crossword puzzle using spelling words from the past 8 weeks. Have him/her write definitions for the clues.	Review critical thinking. Have your child solve a logic problem. *See* Reading, Week 36, number 1.
Friday	Have your child write in his/her journal about what he/she has learned this year. Encourage him/her to use the grammar, writing and handwriting skills he/she has learned.	Give your child the final spelling test.	With your child, discuss his/her accomplishments this year. Help your child set goals for the summer and next year.

Math	Science	Social Studies
Review Week Review making change. Use real money. Pretend you are buying school supplies from your child at a store. Use sticky notes to put price tags on each item—pencil, notebook, etc. Conduct several transactions. Buy several items at a time. Let your child give you a total before handing him/her money. Then, have your child give you change. Reteach, if necessary.	**Review Week** Review the parts of a plant. Have your child draw a diagram and explain how flowers produce seeds. Reteach, if necessary. Review seed dispersal. Have your child write a story from the point of view of a seed. Have him/her tell where the seed has been and how it traveled from place to place.	**Review Week** Have your child make puppets for his/her original puppet show script.
Assess your child's ability to estimate money values. Give him/her a cash register receipt. Have your child round the amounts of the first five items and tell you an approximate cost. Then, have him/her calculate the exact amount on a calculator to determine whether he/she was within a close range. Repeat this exercise with different receipts.	Review photosynthesis. Have your child create a diagram of the process.	Allow your child time to practice, then perform the puppet show for an audience.
Assess your child's understanding of decimals. Shade a given number of boxes on a base-ten square (use a copy of **Base-Ten Squares**, page 295). Have your child name the shaded area as a fraction, then as a decimal. Repeat with other squares. Have your child order the completed squares from largest to smallest.	Discuss the consequences of using too much electricity, then brainstorm methods of conservation. Have your child design and create a poster that encourages people to conserve energy by turning off lights.	Read *A Proud Taste for Scarlet and Miniver* by E. L. Konigsburg. After reading it, have your child write his/her thoughts about women's rights in the Middle Ages. Then, have your child reverse roles and write a paragraph about what Eleanor of Aquitaine might say about women's rights in the world today.
Game: Play a game to assess decimal skills. *See* Math, Week 36, number 1. Have your child color a copy of the **Stepping Stones** gameboard (p. 351) as indicated, then cut out 40 game cards from construction paper—eight of each color indicated.	Quiz your child on electricity terms gathered in his/her Science Log (*see* Science, Week 30, Wednesday). Have your child define each term. Reteach, if necessary.	Write MIDDLE AGES down the left side of a sheet of writing paper. Have your child write a sentence or phrase beginning with each letter about something learned during this unit.
Review problem solving and putting it all together. *See* Math, Week 36, number 2 for problems. Have your child write and solve several problems on his/her own.	Read nutrition labels on products in your kitchen cupboard. Have your child assess the nutritional value of each product and determine which food groups the product represents.	Have your child complete **Siege the Castle Word Search** (p. 352).

Learn at Home, Grade 4

TEACHING SUGGESTIONS AND ACTIVITIES

LANGUAGE SKILLS

▷ 1. Write the following outline on the chalkboard for your child to follow.
The Amazon River

I. The second largest river in the world
   A. Four thousand miles long
   B. Drains 250,000 square miles of land
   C. Empties three billion gallons of water a minute into Atlantic Ocean
   D. Over 200 miles wide at the mouth

II. Amazing variety of life in and along river
   A. Contains flesh-eating piranha
   B. Contains largest fish in South America—the pirarucu
   C. Thousands of unusual insects
   D. Home for creatures such as alligators, anacondas and parrots

III. Many explorations of river
   A. 1541—first complete trip down Amazon
   B. 1637—first complete trip up Amazon
   C. Three centuries later, first scientific expedition
   D. Modern scientists study river and life

▷ 2. Write a "knock-knock" joke on the board without punctuation. Have your child write in the correct punctuation.

Example: Knock, knock said Orange
Who's there asked Squeezer
Orange replied Orange
Orange who Squeezer asked again
Orange you glad you get to squeeze me laughed Orange

READING

▷ 1. Four friends, Isaac, Steve, Andrea and Monica, all play on the school soccer team. Which position does each of them play? Use the chart below to help you find out.

   a. Isaac invited the goalie, halfback and defender to his house after practice.

   b. The goalie and Steve challenged the forward and the defender to a game of two-on-two.

   c. Andrea helped the team win when she caught an attempted goal kicked by the other team.

Use the chart below to help sort out the information. Draw an **x** in the box if the answer is no. Draw a • in the box if the answer is yes.

The goalie is _____. (Andrea)

The forward is _____. (Isaac)

The halfback is _____. (Steve)

The defender is _____. (Monica)

	goalie	forward	defender	halfback
Steve				
Andrea				
Monica				
Isaac				

Learn at Home, Grade 4

MATH

▶ 1. **Game:** The "Stepping Stones" game offers practice adding, subtracting, comparing and rounding decimals.

Preparation: On the gray cards, write addition problems. On the red cards, write subtraction problems. On the orange cards, write decimals to be rounded. (Underline the place to which each is to be rounded.) On the yellow cards, write two decimals to be compared. On the pink cards, write game directions that move the player ahead or back a given number of spaces. Examples are shown below. Make an answer key for the cards.

GRAY	RED	ORANGE	YELLOW	PINK
0.307 0.900 + 0.620	0.216 − 0.040	3.5$\underline{3}$5 Round to the underlined number	7.2 ◯ 7.5 > or <	Oops! Lost your balance. Move back 1 stone.

Directions: This game can be played with any number of players. Place the five colors of cards in separate piles. One player rolls the die and moves the number of spaces indicated. When he/she lands on a space, the player must take a card matching the color of that space and solve the problem on the card. If correct, the player may stay on the new stone. If incorrect, he/she goes back to his/her previously earned stone. If any player lands on a space with a bridge, he/she must cross the bridge (forward or back). A player wins the game when he/she reaches END.

▶ 2. Have your child solve the following realistic problems using the operations necessary.

a. You are having a party for your birthday and you have invited five other friends. Your parents gave you $15 to spend on food and party supplies. Look at the choices below. Decide how you will spend your money and write a plan and explanation to show your parents before you make the purchases.

$1.89 — cake mix	$2.59 — 6 cans of soda pop
$1.19 — frosting	$1.88 — 2 liters of soda pop
$1.99 — chips	89¢ — 6 paper cups
98¢ — chip dip	89¢ — 6 paper plates
79¢ — 6 apples	$1.39 — 12 plastic forks
45¢ — apple dip	$2.59 — 6 large balloons
$2.99 — candy	$1.09 — 24 small balloons
$8.95 — bakery cake (decorated)	99¢ — construction paper
$1.09 — 2 quarts of juice	$3.75 — wall decorations

b. You have three 10¢ stamps and two 8¢ stamps. How many different amounts of postage can you make with these stamps?

c. You make $3 per hour baby-sitting and $2.50 per hour mowing lawns. If you earned $53.50 this month, how many hours did you work each job? (There is more than one answer for this.)

What's the Story?

Create a story just for fun! Choose the kind of story you want to write. Now, brainstorm for ideas. **Write** your ideas on the correct lines below.

_____

Kind of Story (mystery, adventure, etc.)

I. Setting (where and when the story takes place)

A. Where _____ Description _____

_____

B. When _____

II. Plot (events of the story)
   List main events in order
   A. _____
   B. _____
   C. _____
   D. _____

III. Characters (people in the story)

   A. Name _____ Description _____

   B. Name_____ Description _____

   C. Name _____ Description _____

   D. Name _____ Description _____

Use your ideas to write a story. Remember to tell the story in the correct time order. Organize the events into a **beginning, middle** and **ending** section of the story.

_____

_____

_____

_____

_____

Finish your story on another sheet of paper

Stepping Stones

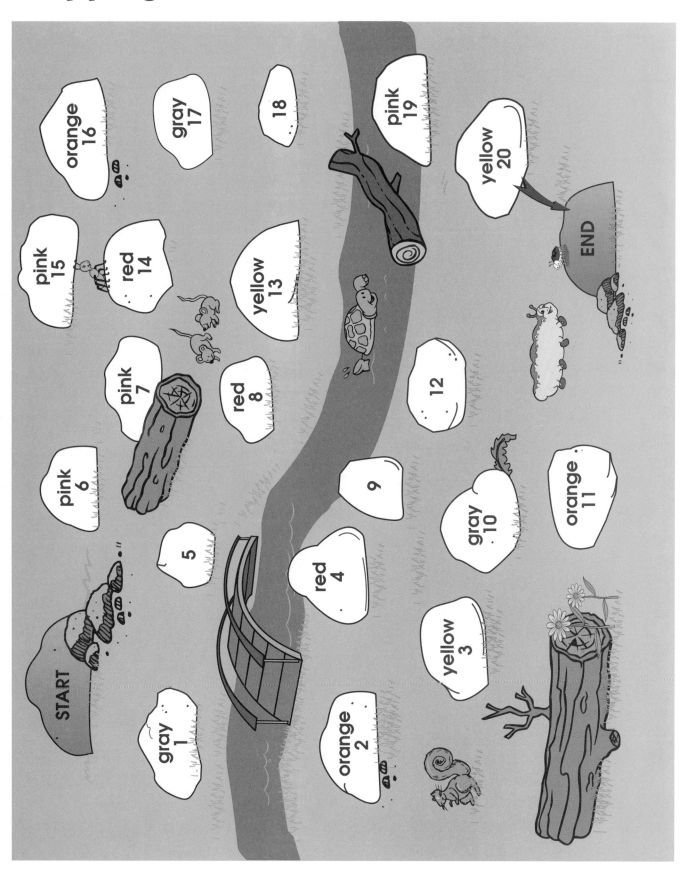

Siege the Castle

```
S O U Z T E V J V D E O D S P H Y
F C A T A P U L T C G N C A P F F
G F M F B A L L I S T A G C B E I
D V C Y K Z N P F Y E W S Y M V R
E B T M V Q E O X S F B K K C C E
V E Z D D U R R R F X N U U V O D
F H Q K J B A T T E R I N G R A M
R Z Z I I A B C R O S S B O W R B
U J J T U T L U I O H K F P Y T I
C H N O T T E L V S R U N O Z U V
V A S S A L H L A Z Q F B K A S B
J T K K E E P I L L Y D F D C N A
R A N S O M D S I U L L K E N G H
X A T I T E U L A Q N M J L I Y O
A Y T E Q N E J S E S U I J P V I
C O A G Q T B O C B D Z W D B N L
K Z P E L S T R K P X L L I R P V
```

Find these words:

BATTERING RAM	BATTLEMENTS	PORTCULLIS
VULNERABLE	BALLISTA	CATAPULT
CROSSBOW	RANSOM	VASSAL
RIVAL	SIEGE	KEEP

Learn at Home, Grade 4

Answer Key

Common and Proper Nouns

A **common noun** names any person, place or thing.
A **proper noun** names a specific person, place or thing.
A proper noun always begins with a capital letter.

Example: boy, state (common nouns)
Peter, Georgia (proper nouns)

Underline the nouns in the sentences.
1. <u>Bobby</u> was wondering what the <u>weather</u> would be on <u>Friday</u>.
2. The <u>boys</u> and <u>girls</u> from <u>Lang School</u> were planning a <u>picnic</u>.
3. <u>Bobby</u> asked his <u>teacher</u>, <u>Mr. Lewis</u>, how the <u>class</u> could find out.
4. The <u>teacher</u> suggested that the <u>children</u> call a local <u>newspaper</u>, <u>The Bugle</u>.
5. <u>Ms. Canyon</u>, the <u>editor</u>, read the <u>forecast</u> to <u>Eddie</u>.
6. <u>Rain</u> was predicted for the <u>day</u> of their <u>picnic</u>.
7. Their <u>town</u>, <u>Grand Forks</u>, also had a radio <u>station</u>.
8. When <u>Rick</u> called the <u>number</u>, he was disappointed.
9. The <u>weatherman</u>, <u>George Lee</u>, said that <u>rain</u> was possible.
10. The <u>children</u> were delighted when the <u>sun</u> came out on <u>Friday</u>.

Now, **write** each noun you have underlined in the correct category below.
Do not use any words more than once.

Common Nouns		Proper Nouns
1. weather	10. rain	1. Bobby
2. boys	11. day	2. Lang School
3. girls	12. town	3. Mr. Lewis
4. picnic	13. station	4. The Bugle
5. teacher	14. number	5. Ms. Canyon
6. children	15. weatherman	6. Eddie
7. newspaper	16. sun	7. Grand Forks
8. editor	17. class	8. Rick
9. forecast		9. George Lee
		10. Friday

page 21

Forming Plural Nouns

Most **singular nouns** can be made into **plural nouns** by following one of these rules.

Rules	Examples
1. Add **s** to most nouns.	elephant, elephant**s**
2. If the noun ends in **s**, **sh**, **ch** or **x**, add **es**.	box, box**es**
3. If the noun ends in **y** with a consonant before it, change the **y** to **i** and add **es**.	fly, fl**ies**
4. If the noun ends in **y** with a vowel before it, add **s**.	monkey, monkey**s**
5. To some nouns ending in **f**, add **s**.	chief, chief**s**
6. To some nouns ending in **f** or **fe**, change the **f** to **v** and add **es**.	knife, kni**ves** thief, thie**ves**
7. Some nouns stay the same for singular and plural.	sheep, **sheep**
8. Some nouns have an irregular plural.	goose, **geese**

Change each singular noun to plural. Write the number of the rule you used. Use a dictionary when needed.

Singular	Plural	Rule #	Singular	Plural	Rule #
1. chimney	chimneys	4	11. woman	women	8
2. class	classes	2	12. bus	buses	2
3. wolf	wolves	6	13. judge	judges	1
4. deer	deer	7	14. shelf	shelves	6
5. story	stories	3	15. chair	chairs	1
6. elf	elves	6	16. beach	beaches	2
7. tooth	teeth	8	17. tax	taxes	2
8. brush	brushes	2	18. lady	ladies	3
9. attorney	attorneys	4	19. roof	roofs	1
10. mouse	mice	8	20. penny	pennies	3

page 22

I, We; Me, Us

I and **we** are **subject pronouns**. **Me** and **us** are **object pronouns**.
Examples:
Mark and **I** are on our way to the park.
(subject pronoun)
We just love to launch rockets!
(subject pronoun)
Will Sara come with **me**?
(object pronoun)
Please feel welcome to join **us**.
(object pronoun)
Choose the correct pronoun for each sentence from those in parentheses.
Write it in the blank.

1. <u>We</u> plan to launch rockets at the park on Saturday.
(we, us)
2. Monica bought <u>me</u> a two-stage rocket.
(I, me)
3. Bill and <u>I</u> both brought fresh batteries for the rocket launcher.
(I, me)
4. Curt plans to build <u>us</u> a rocket.
(we, us)
5. Gwen wants <u>me</u> to attend the rocket safety course.
(I, me)
6. <u>I</u> always like to paint the fins a bright color.
(I, me)
7. Tom wants Michele and <u>me</u> to chase after his rocket when it lands.
(I, me)
8. Heather wants <u>us</u> to go to the launching site.
(we, us)
9. Carolyn and <u>I</u> just bought a model rocket with a payload section.
(I, me)
10. Jim will be showing <u>us</u> his model rocket.
(we, us)
11. David taught <u>me</u> all the same safety rules.
(I, me)

page 23

A Is for Apple

ache
admit
animal
April
bacon
bathroom
camera
flap
grateful
happiness
manage
navy
plane
radish
waste

Write the spelling words that contain a **short a** that sounds like the **a** in **apple**.

admit
animal
bathroom
camera

flap
happiness
manage
radish

List all the spelling words that contain a **long a** that sounds like the **a** in **cake**.

ache
April
bacon
grateful

navy
plane
waste

Use the spelling words to complete the word search. The words are written vertically, horizontally and diagonally.

```
T F I U H F C B K Q G H E N P N
M X G O A X J K I W G T I U R M
O C S B P J I P R E J T D P V R
C Q A I P M W L P H M F C F J Z
E E Y V I N U A H W T L L N A V
B C V Y N F Y D C E W L B X L
W A S T E L B O A T A D X S M H
N M C X I S S A B L K A V J J U X
I E A O S R T O A U B P U E M
G R T K N I H E P G O T E G U R
G A E A M U R R R M S A A C H E
D F K D U Y O B I D L N U U O A
G A B V M O X L R A D I S H N
G L N C U Z M X E M N Y E Z A H
H U V I Z K U K J U I S E L T E
K S Y K Q R H T Q W M N T V W L
M D T B H T C R F L A P T I F K
L C L N A V Q H R L U D Z Y A J
S B N T D J K M P C U I I E H A
```

page 24

Camp Rules

Donald, Arnold and Jack are at Camp Explore-It-All this week. They think camp is a lot of fun. They have also learned from their instructors that there are some very important rules all campers must obey so that everyone has a good time.

All campers must take swimming tests to see what depth of water they can swim in safely. Donald and Jack pass the advanced test and can swim in the deep water. Arnold, however, only passes the intermediate test. He is supposed to stay in the area where the water is waist deep. When it is time to swim, Arnold decides to sneak into advanced with Donald and Jack. After all, he has been swimming in deep water for three years. No way is he going to stay in the shallow water with the babies.

Donald and Jack don't think Arnold should come into the deep water, but they can't tell him anything. So the boys jump into the water and start swimming and playing. Fifteen minutes later, Arnold is yelling, "Help!" He swims out too far and is too tired to make it back in. The lifeguard jumps in and pulls him out. Everyone stops to see what is happening. Arnold feels very foolish.

Check:
The main idea of this story is
☐ Arnold ends up feeling foolish.   ☐ Camp is fun.
☐ All campers take swimming tests.   ☑ Rules are made for good reasons.
☐ You can learn a lot from instructors.   ☐ Rules are made to be broken.

Underline:
Arnold got himself into a(n) <u>dangerous</u> situation.
amusing   funny   <u>dangerous</u>   ambiguous

Circle:
Arnold thought the guys in the shallow area were (bullies/(babies)). However, he should have ((stayed with them)/gone to the advanced area).

Write:
What lesson do you think Arnold learned? <u>Answers will vary.</u>
<u>Example: Stay within your limits.</u>
What do you think the other campers learned? <u>Answers will vary.</u>
<u>Example: Don't disobey rules or you could get hurt.</u>

page 25

How Adjectives Compare

There are certain spelling rules to follow when **adjectives** are used to compare people, places or things.

1. To many adjectives, simply add **er** or **est** to the end.
fast fast**er** fast**est**

2. When an adjective ends with a consonant preceded by a single vowel, double the final consonant and add **er** or **est**.
fat fat**ter** fat**test**

3. When an adjective ends in an **e**, drop the final **e** and add **er** or **est**.
brave brav**er** brav**est**

4. If an adjective ends in a **y** preceded by a consonant, change the **y** to **i** and add **er** or **est**.
heavy heav**ier** heav**iest**

Complete the chart below using the spelling rules you have learned. **Write** the number of the rule you used.

Adjective	Add **er**	Add **est**	Rule
1. weak	weaker	weakest	1
2. kind	kinder	kindest	1
3. easy	easier	easiest	4
4. clear	clearer	clearest	1
5. close	closer	closest	3
6. noisy	noisier	noisiest	4
7. large	larger	largest	3
8. red	redder	reddest	2
9. pretty	prettier	prettiest	4
10. hungry	hungrier	hungriest	4
11. big	bigger	biggest	2
12. happy	happier	happiest	4
13. wet	wetter	wettest	2
14. cute	cuter	cutest	3
15. plain	plainer	plainest	1
16. busy	busier	busiest	4
17. loud	louder	loudest	1
18. strong	stronger	strongest	1
19. fresh	fresher	freshest	1
20. hot	hotter	hottest	2

page 30

Learn at Home, Grade 4

Easy Does It

Use spelling words containing the **short e** sound to **fill in** the blanks.

bedtime
being
beverage
cedar
decoy
elegant
female
jelly
lemon
medicine
meteor
rectangle
recycle
secret
skeleton

1. A __lemon__ is sour.

2. The new living room carpet was stained by grape __jelly__ and a spilled __beverage__

3. For your sore throat, you can take __medicine__ before __bedtime__.

4. The body's bony frame is called a __skeleton__.

5. A queen would probably be __elegant__

6. A __rectangle__ has four sides.

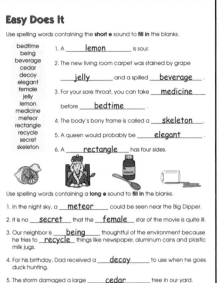

Use spelling words containing a **long e** sound to **fill in** the blanks.

1. In the night sky, a __meteor__ could be seen near the Big Dipper.

2. It is no __secret__ that the __female__ star of the movie is quite ill.

3. Our neighbor is __being__ thoughtful of the environment because he tries to __recycle__ things like newspaper, aluminum cans and plastic milk jugs.

4. For his birthday, Dad received a __decoy__ to use when he goes duck hunting.

5. The storm damaged a large __cedar__ tree in our yard.

page 31

Place Value

$$1,234,567$$

millions / hundred thousands / ten thousands / thousands / hundreds / tens / ones

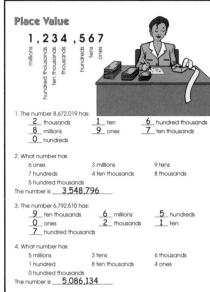

1. The number 8,672,019 has:

__2__ thousands   __1__ ten   __6__ hundred thousands

__8__ millions   __9__ ones   __7__ ten thousands

__0__ hundreds

2. What number has

6 ones   3 millions   9 tens

7 hundreds   4 ten thousands   8 thousands

5 hundred thousands

The number is __3,548,796__.

3. The number 6,792,510 has:

__9__ ten thousands   __6__ millions   __5__ hundreds

__0__ ones   __2__ thousands   __1__ ten

__7__ hundred thousands

4. What number has

5 millions   3 tens   6 thousands

1 hundred   8 ten thousands   4 ones

0 hundred thousands

The number is __5,086,134__.

page 32

The First State

What state is known as the first state? Follow the directions below to find out.

1. If 31,842 rounded to the nearest thousand is 31,000, put an A above number 2.
2. If 62 rounded to the nearest ten is 60, put an E above number 2 .
3. If 4,234 rounded to the nearest hundred is 4,200, put an R above number 7.
4. If 677 rounded to the nearest hundred is 600, put an L above number 3.
5. If 344 rounded to the nearest ten is 350, put an E above number 5.
6. If 5,599 rounded to the nearest thousand is 6,000, put an A above number 4.
7. If 1,549 rounded to the nearest hundred is 1,500, put an A above number 6.
8. If 885 rounded to the nearest hundred is 800, put a W above number 2.
9. If 521 rounded to the nearest ten is 520, put an E above number 8.
10. If 74 rounded to the nearest ten is 80, put an R above number 6.
11. If 3,291 rounded to the nearest thousand is 3,000, put an L above number 3.
12. If 248 rounded to the nearest hundred is 300, put an R above number 4.
13. If 615 rounded to the nearest ten is 620, put a D above number 1.
14. If 188 rounded to the nearest ten is 200, put a W above number 1.
15. If 6,817 rounded to the nearest thousand is 7,000, put a W above number 5.

Peach Blossom State Flower

Blue Hen Chicken State Bird

Fort Christina—site of the first state's first permanent settlement. Build by the Swedes and Finns.

__D E L A W A R E__
1 2 3 4 5 6 7 8

page 33

Helping Verbs

A **verb phrase** is a verb that has more than one word. It is made up of a **main verb** plus one or more **helping verbs**.
Example: verb phrase
Tim **has practiced** hard.

helping verb   main verb
These words are often used as helping verbs with the main verb.

am, is, are, was, were, have, has

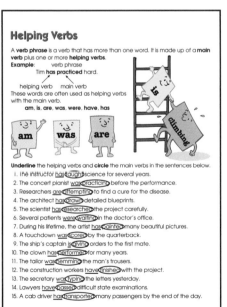

Underline the helping verbs and **circle** the main verbs in the sentences below.

1. The instructor _has_ (taught) science for several years.
2. The concert pianist _was_ (practicing) before the performance.
3. Researchers _are_ (attempting) to find a cure for the disease.
4. The architect _has_ (drawn) detailed blueprints.
5. The scientist _has_ (researched) the project carefully.
6. Several patients _were_ (waiting) in the doctor's office.
7. During his lifetime, the artist _has_ (painted) many beautiful pictures.
8. A touchdown _was_ (scored) by the quarterback.
9. The ship's captain _is_ (giving) orders to the first mate.
10. The clown _has_ (performed) for many years.
11. The tailor _was_ (hemming) the man's trousers.
12. The construction workers _have_ (finished) with the project.
13. The secretary _was_ (typing) the letters yesterday.
14. Lawyers _have_ (passed) difficult state examinations.
15. A cab driver _has_ (transported) many passengers by the end of the day.

page 38

Verb Tenses

A **present-tense** verb shows action that is happening now. A **past-tense** verb shows action that happened earlier. A **future-tense** verb shows action that will take place in the future.
Examples: The clockmaker **repairs** the clock.   (present)
The clockmaker **repaired** the clock.   (past)
The clockmaker **will repair** the clock.   (future)

Write these verbs using the tenses shown in parentheses.

	try	walk	work
(present)	Tom __tries__	Karen __walks__	They __work__
(past)	Tom __tried__	Karen __walked__	They __worked__
(future)	Tom __will try__	Karen __will walk__	They __will work__

Write the correct verb in each blank below.

1. time (future)   5. tell (present)   9. help (past)
2. chart (present)   6. reset (future)   10. invent (past)
3. trickle (past)   7. dine (present)   11. operate (future)
4. use (past)   8. move (future)

1. John __will time__ the runners in the race.
2. A calendar __charts__ the days of each month.
3. Sand __trickled__ through the hourglass.
4. People __used__ the hourglass before clocks were invented.
5. A pendulum __tells__ time by Earth's rotation.
6. John __will reset__ his watch when changing time zones.
7. He __dines__ at 8:00 every evening during the week.
8. Martha __will move__ the hands of the clock.
9. In the distant past, the Sun and the Moon __helped__ man tell time.
10. The Egyptians __invented__ the solar calendar.
11. Timepieces 100 years from now __will operate__ differently.

page 39

Irregular Verbs

Verbs that do not add **ed** to form the past tense are called **irregular verbs**. The spelling of these verbs changes.
Examples:
present	past	present	past
begin, begins	began	do, does	did
break, breaks	broke	eat, eats	ate

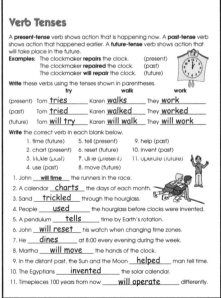

Write the past tense of each irregular verb below.

1. Samuel almost __fell__ (fall) when he kicked a rock in the path.
2. Diana made sure she __took__ (take) a canteen on her hike.
3. David __ran__ (run) over to a shady tree for a quick break.
4. Jimmy __broke__ (break) off a long piece of grass to put in his mouth while he was walking.
5. Eva __knew__ (know) the path along the river very well.
6. The clouds __began__ (begin) to sprinkle raindrops on the hikers.
7. Kathy __threw__ (throw) a small piece of bread to the birds.
8. Everyone __ate__ (eat) a very nutritious meal after a long adventure.
9. We all __slept__ (sleep) very well that night.

Many irregular verbs have a different past-tense ending when the helping verbs **have** and **has** are used.
Examples: Steven **has worn** special hiking shoes today.
Marlene and I **have known** about this trail for years.

Circle the correct irregular verb below.

1. Peter has (flew / (flown)) down to join us for the adventure.
2. Mark has (saw / (seen)) a lot of animals on the hike today.
3. Andy and Mike have (went / (gone)) on this trail before.
4. Bill has (took / (taken)) extra precautions to make sure no cacti prick his legs.
5. Heather has (ate / (eaten)) all the snacks her mom packed for her.

page 40

I Can Do This

Complete the crossword puzzle.

blindfold
cinnamon
dentist
giant
history
imagine
island
minus
pirate
principal
rifle
silence
skid
spinach
whine

Across
1. green, leafy vegetable
3. think about
6. covering for eyes
10. noiseless
12. land surrounded by water
13. robber on the seas
14. less

Down
1. slide
2. brown spice
4. head of a school
5. a study of the past
7. one who fixes teeth
8. gun
9. complain
11. very large person

Across/Down answers:
- ¹spinach
- ³imagine
- ⁵history / ⁶blindfold / ⁷dentist / rifle
- silence
- ¹³pirate / ¹²island / minus

page 41

Batter Up!

Complete each addition box.

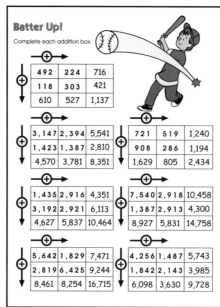

492	224	716
118	303	421
610	527	1,137

3,147	2,394	5,541
1,423	1,387	2,810
4,570	3,781	8,351

721	519	1,240
908	286	1,194
1,629	805	2,434

1,435	2,916	4,351
3,192	2,921	6,113
4,627	5,837	10,464

7,540	2,918	10,458
1,387	2,913	4,300
8,927	5,831	14,758

5,642	1,829	7,471
2,819	6,425	9,244
8,461	8,254	16,715

4,256	1,487	5,743
1,842	2,143	3,985
6,098	3,630	9,728

page 43

That's How It's Done

Adverbs answer the questions **when**, **where** and **how**. The adverbs in the sentences below answer **how**. **Underline** the adverbs in each sentence. Then, **circle** the verb it describes. The first one is done for you.

1. The two boys solemnly (shook) hands.
2. Chip (looked) down incredulously at the fallen shingle which (landed) softly at this feet.
3. "I don't salvage," (remarked) Rudy calmly when his counselor glared at him.
4. "Rudy," (whispered) Mike warningly. Chip was glaring in his direction.
5. The door opened and Mr. Warden emerged, smartly (dressed) in a white tennis outfit.
6. "Harold, you have no soul," (explained) Rudy pleasantly.
7. "Why do you immediately (assume) that I'm guilty?" asked Rudy in a hurt tone.
8. "I'd rather go back to arts and crafts," (nodded) Mike sheepishly.
9. "Tomorrow," Rudy (said) thoughtfully as they carefully (daubed) pale blue paint onto their creation, "we'll go earlier."
10. Arms (flailing) wildly, Chip (rushed) anxiously away from his cabin.
11. "Let's just (walk) directly away from the lake," declared Rudy.

Write four sentences of your own containing adverbs. **Underline** the adverbs and **circle** the verbs that are described.

1. _____
2. _____
3. _____
4. _____

Answers will vary.

page 48

Misused Words

Sometimes people have difficulty using **good**, **well**, **sure**, **surely**, **real** and **really** correctly. This chart may help you.

Adjectives	Adverbs
Good is an adjective when it describes a noun. That was a **good** dinner.	**Good** is never used as an adverb.
Well is an adjective when it means in good health or having a good appearance. She looks **well**.	**Well** is an adverb when it is used to tell that something is done capably or effectively. She writes **well**.
Sure is an adjective when it modifies a noun. A robin is a **sure** sign of spring.	**Surely** is an adverb. He **surely** wants a job.
Real is an adjective that means genuine or true. That was a **real** diamond.	**Really** is an adverb. Mary **really** played a good game.

Use the chart to help you choose the correct word from those in parentheses. **Write** it in the blank.

1. You did a very __good__ job of writing your book report. (good, well)
2. The detective in the story used his skills __well__. (good, well)
3. He __surely__ solved the case before anyone else did. (sure, surely)
4. I __really__ want to read that book now. (real, really)
5. Did it take you long to decide who the __real__ criminal was? (real, really)
6. Although the butler looked __well__ and healthy, he died. (well, good)
7. Detective Rains read the clues __well__ as he worked on the case. (good, well)
8. You will __surely__ get a good grade on that report. (surely, sure)
9. You had to __really__ work hard to get those good grades. (real, really)

page 49

Often-Used O's

auto, bobbin, bony, closet, cobra, doctor, elbow, frozen, hotel, knot, object, poetry, solemn, solve, total

Put a check to the left of the words in the list that have a **short o** sound as in **hot**. Put a star to the right of the words in the list that have a **long o** sound as in **open**.

Write a spelling word to answer each question.

1. What's another word for "sum"? __t o t a l__
2. Which word names a snake? __c o b r a__
3. Which word describes ice cream? __f r o z e n__
4. Where might you stay on a vacation? __h o t e l__
5. Where is thread kept? __b o b b i n__
6. What can be tied in a rope? __k n o t__
7. What happens when you find a solution? __s o l v e__
8. What word means serious? __s o l e m n__
9. What's between the wrist and the shoulder? __e l b o w__
10. Which word describes rhyming verse? __p o e t r y__
11. Where do clothes hang? __c l o s e t__
12. Who helps those who are sick? __d o c t o r__
13. Which word means "car"? __a u t o__
14. Which word describes a skeleton? __b o n y__

Match the boxed letter from each line to the numbered lines below to answer the riddle. *Where can you always find a lost object?*

__I n   t h e   l a s t__
 5 8   12 4 3   7 1 11 12

__p l a c e   y o u   l o o k !__
10 7 1 2 3   14 9 13   7 9 9 6

page 50

Break It Up!

For each word given below, **write** the root word and the prefix and/or suffix. Remember, some root words' spellings have been changed before adding suffixes. Not all words will have a prefix and a suffix.

Word	Prefix	Root Word	Suffix
resourceful	re	source	ful
accomplishment		accomplish	ment
numbness		numb	ness
convincing		convince	ing
merciless		mercy	less
sturdiest		sturdy	est
disobeying	dis	obey	ing
unmistakable	un	mistake	able
disinfecting	dis	infect	ing
disclaimed	dis	claim	ed
reopening	re	open	ing
inventive		invent	ive
restless		rest	less
precaution	pre	cautious	ion
imitating		imitate	ing

page 51

Learn at Home, Grade 4

Keeping the Order

Nine planets orbit the Sun. These planets are arranged in order according to their distance from the Sun.

Number the planets below in order with number one being the planet closest to the Sun. Use the mean (average) distances in miles to help you.

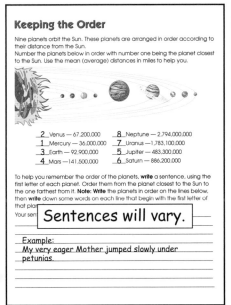

_2_ Venus — 67,200,000   _8_ Neptune — 2,794,000,000
_1_ Mercury — 36,000,000   _7_ Uranus — 1,783,100,000
_3_ Earth — 92,900,000   _5_ Jupiter — 483,300,000
_4_ Mars — 141,500,000   _6_ Saturn — 886,200,000

To help you remember the order of the planets, **write** a sentence, using the first letter of each planet. Order them from the planet closest to the Sun to the one farthest from it. **Note: Write** the planets in order on the lines below, then **write** down some words on each line that begin with the first letter of that plan...

Your sen... **Sentences will vary.**

Example:
My very eager Mother jumped slowly under petunias.

page 52

Tennis Anyone?

Jack and Ron are playing | **Some answers will vary.**

Example: 19

Examples: football basketball baseball

Examples: ten net set

1. It is a very hot day. **Draw** a yellow sun in the sky above the shortest tree.
2. Use red to mark the thermometer up to **93** degrees.
3. Jack is on the right side of the net. **Color** his shirt yellow and his shorts blue with a green stripe.
4. **Color** Ron's shorts the color of Jack's stripe. **Color** his shirt the color of Jack's shorts.
5. Ron has just hit the ball. It is in the air, but it has not gone over the net yet. Use yellow to **draw** the ball.
6. Jack dropped his racket. Use brown to **draw** the racket.
7. **Count** all the balls on the ground. **Add** your age to that number. **Write** the total in the top of the tallest tree.
8. On the trunk of the middle tree, **write** the names of three other sports which use balls.
9. Between the shortest tree and the middle tree, **write** three words that you can make from the letters in the word *tennis*.

page 58

You Can Spell Us

Circle the spelling words that contain the **short u** sound as in **cup**. Use your calculator to find the point value of each word that contains the **long u** sound as in **use**.

Assign a number to each letter in the alphabet.

(A = 1, B = 2, C = 3, and so forth)

a	1
b	2
c	3
d	4
e	5
f	6
g	7
h	8
i	9
j	10
k	11
l	12
m	13
n	14
o	15
p	16
q	17
r	18
s	19
t	20
u	21
v	22
w	23
x	24
y	25
z	26

amuse
(bubble)
(budding)
(budge)
computer
(customer)
duty
humor
(hungry)
(husky)
Jupiter
(number)
(sundown)
(summer)
usual

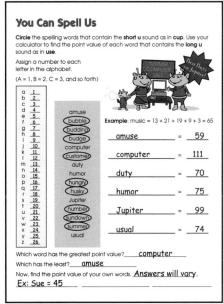

Example: music = 13 + 21 + 19 + 9 + 3 = 65

amuse = _59_
computer = _111_
duty = _70_
humor = _75_
Jupiter = _99_
usual = _74_

Which word has the greatest point value? _computer_
Which has the least? _amuse_
Now, find the point value of your own words. **Answers will vary.**
Ex: Sue = 45 _____

page 59

Watch for Grandpa's Watch

Each "watch" in the title of this activity sheet has a different meaning. One means "to look for," and the other means "a timepiece." **Write** two meanings for the words below.

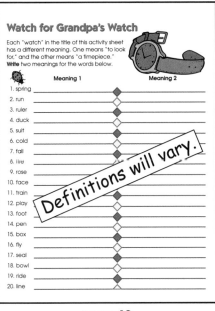

	Meaning 1	Meaning 2
1. spring		
2. run		
3. ruler		
4. duck		
5. suit		
6. cold		
7. fall		
8. line		
9. rose		
10. face		
11. train		
12. play		
13. foot		
14. pen		
15. box		
16. fly		
17. seal		
18. bowl		
19. ride		
20. line		

Definitions will vary.

page 60

The Imperial Alphabet

Number each group of words to show alphabetical order.

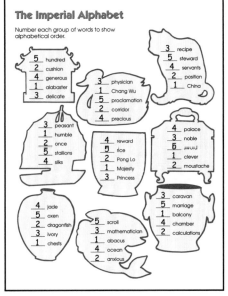

_5_ hundred
_2_ cushion
_4_ generous
_1_ alabaster
_3_ delicate

_3_ physician
_1_ Chang Wu
_5_ proclamation
_2_ corridor
_4_ precious

_3_ recipe
_5_ steward
_4_ servants
_2_ position
_1_ China

_3_ peasant
_1_ humble
_2_ once
_5_ stallions
_4_ silks

_4_ reward
_5_ rice
_1_ Pong Lo
_2_ Majesty
_3_ Princess

_4_ palace
_3_ noble
_5_ sword
_1_ clever
_2_ moustache

_4_ jade
_2_ oxen
_5_ dragonfish
_3_ ivory
_1_ chests

_5_ scroll
_3_ mathematician
_1_ abacus
_4_ ocean
_2_ anxious

_3_ caravan
_5_ marriage
_1_ balcony
_4_ chamber
_2_ calculations

page 61

A Clever Crossword

MAJESTY / PEASANT / ALABASTER / PROCLAMATION / REWARD / CHINA / MATHEMATICIAN / NOBLE / MARRIAGE / EMPEROR / DRAGONFISH / MELANCHOLY / MOUSTACHE / SERVANTS / RICE / PITTMAN / CHANGWU / ABACUS / CLEVER

Across
2. A poor Chinese countryman
4. The swan was made of it
6. An Imperial declaration
9. A prize
12. Wedding
13. The ruler of China
14. Sadness
16. The emperor's facial hair
17. Palace workers
19. The author's last name
20. The princess's name

Down
1. To address the emperor: "Your____."
2. Wanted to marry the princess
3. Counting beads on rods
7. He calculated on an abacus
8. They were called to the palace in hopes of finding a husband for the princess
10. 32 grains arrived in the mouth of a carved ____
11. Chang Wu's country
15. A long line of one hundred elephants
18. A grain of ____.

page 62

Jungle Math

Across

2. 517 − 228 = **289**

3. 428 − 249 = **179**

4. 562 − 274 = **288**

5. 924 − 348 = **576**

6. 923 − 346 = **577**

7. 535 − 248 = **287**

8. 857 − 389 = **468**

9. 561 − 247 = **314**

11. 845 − 599 = **246**

13. 325 − 186 = **139**

14. 356 − 168 = **188**

6. 921 − 346 = **575**

Down

1. 421 − 342 = **79**

2. 627 − 348 = **279**

3. 362 − 194 = **168**

4. 582 − 346 = **236**

5. 824 − 247 = **577**

7. 926 − 718 = **208**

8. 721 − 240 = **481**

10. 768 − 292 = **476**

12. 826 − 337 = **489**

13. 247 − 129 = **128**

page 63

Our Solar System

	MERCURY	VENUS	EARTH	MARS
DIAMETER	3,031 mi.	7,521 mi.	7,926 mi.	4,217 mi.
AVERAGE DISTANCE FROM SUN	36,000,000 mi.	67,200,000 mi.	92,900,000 mi.	141,500,000 mi.
REVOLUTION	88 days	225 days	365 days	687 days
ROTATION	59 days	243 days	23 hrs. 56 min.	24 hrs. 37 min.
KNOWN SATELLITES	0	0	1	2

JUPITER	SATURN	URANUS	NEPTUNE
88,730 mi.	74,900 mi.	31,763 mi.	30,775 mi.
483,300,000 mi.	886,200,000 mi.	1,783,100,000 mi.	2,794,000,000 mi.
4,329 days	10,753 days	30,664 days	61,608 days
9 hrs. 50 min.	10 hrs. 39 min.	17 hrs. 54 min.	19 hrs. 12 min.
16	18	15	8

page 64

Who Am I in the Solar System?

The solar system contains many different objects that travel around the Sun. Use the information from **Our Solar System** (p. 64) and other sources to explore the solar system and solve the following "Who Am I?" riddles.

1. I am the largest planet. **Jupiter**
2. I am the planet best known for my rings. **Saturn**
3. I am the planet known for my "Great Red Spot." **Jupiter**
4. I am the smallest planet. **Pluto**
5. I am the planet closest to the Sun. **Mercury**
6. I am known as the "Red Planet." **Mars**
7. Voyager 2 discovered new moons and rings around me. **Uranus**
8. Until 1999, I was the farthest planet from the Sun. **Pluto**
9. I am the planet closest in size to the Earth. **Venus**
10. I am the planet with the shortest rotation time. **Jupiter**
11. My moon, Titan, is larger than the planet Mercury. **Saturn**
12. My rotation time is the most similar to Earth's. **Mars**
13. I am the planet with the most natural satellites. **Jupiter**
14. My buddies and I form a belt between Mars and Jupiter. **asteroids**
15. I am the largest object in the solar system. **Sun**
16. I am the brightest planet in the sky. **Venus**
17. I am the only planet known to support life. **Earth**
18. I am the planet that orbits the Sun "on my side." **Uranus**
19. I am known as "Earth's Twin." **Venus**
20. I am the brightest object in the sky. **Sun**
21. I am the most distant planet that can be seen with the unaided eye. **Saturn**

page 65

Friendly Letter

A friendly letter is a casual letter between family or friends. A friendly letter can express your own personality. It can be written for a special reason or just for fun.

Write a friendly letter to a "friend" in another city. Invite the friend to visit you sometime during the summer. Follow these guidelines:

A. Write your address and the date.
B. Write a greeting (**Example**: Dear _____).
C. Write three paragraphs.
   First: pleasant greeting and invitation
   Second: details about the visit
   Third: summarize your excitement about the visit
D. Closing (**Example**: Your friend.).
E. Your signature

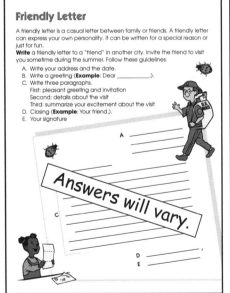

Answers will vary.

page 70

The Y's Have It

Put a check to the left of each spelling word that has a y sound like the **long e** in **bee**.
Put a star to the right of each word that has a y sound like the **long i** in **ice**.
Write the two words that do not have a mark.
hymn   _syllable_
What vowel sound do they have? _short i_

- ✓ already
- ✓ balcony
- ✓ country
- deny ★
- ✓ early
- ✓ envy
- ✓ February
- ✓ greedy
- hydrant ★
- hymn
- ✓ library
- reply ★
- satisfy ★
- skyline ★
- syllable

Answer each question.
1. Which word has the most syllables? **February**
2. Which word has only one syllable? **hymn**
3. Which word is a compound word? **skyline**
4. Which word is an antonym for "late"? **early**
5. Which word is a synonym for "jealousy"? **envy**
6. Which word is a geographic region? **country**
7. Which word is a home for books? **library**
8. Which word is capitalized? **February**
9. Which word denotes life-saving equipment? **hydrant**
10. Which word rhymes with "needy"? **greedy**

page 71

Homophone Hype

For each word given below, list the homophones in the spaces provided. Find and circle the homophone in the word search. Hint: You will only use one spelling of each homophone.

Sentences will vary.

Example:
1. Here **hear**
   Sentence: _I did not hear her say, "Come here!"_
2. Bridle **bridal**
   Sentence: _____
3. I'll **aisle**   **isle**
   Sentence: _____
4. Graze (Hint: plural form of a color) **greys**   **grays**
   Sentence: _____
5. Main **mane**   **Maine**
   Sentence: _____
6. Whey **way**   **weigh**
   Sentence: _____
7. Dew **do**   **due**
   Sentence: _____
8. Scent **sent**   **cent**
   Sentence: _____

page 72

Answer Key

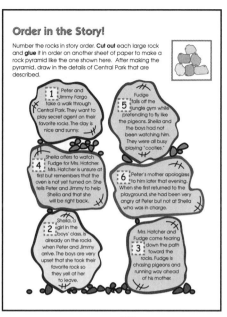

Order in the Story!

Number the rocks in story order. **Cut out** each large rock and **glue** it in order on another sheet of paper to make a rock pyramid like the one shown here. After making the pyramid, draw in the details of Central Park that are described.

1 Peter and Jimmy Fargo take a walk through Central Park. They want to play secret agent on their favorite rocks. The day is nice and sunny.

5 Fudge falls off the jungle gym while pretending to fly like the pigeons. Sheila and the boys had not been watching him. They were all busy playing "cooties."

4 Sheila offers to watch Fudge for Mrs. Hatcher. Mrs. Hatcher is unsure at first but remembers that the oven is not yet turned on. She tells Peter and Jimmy to help Sheila and that she will be right back.

6 Peter's mother apologizes to him later that evening. When she first returned to the playground, she had been very angry at Peter but not at Sheila who was in charge.

2 Sheila, a girl in the boys' class, is already on the rocks when Peter and Jimmy arrive. The boys are very upset that she took their favorite rock so they yell at her to leave.

3 Mrs. Hatcher and Fudge come tearing down the path toward the rocks. Fudge is chasing pigeons and running way ahead of his mother.

page 73

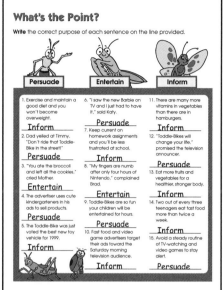

What's the Point?

Write the correct purpose of each sentence on the line provided.

Persuade	Entertain	Inform

1. Exercise and maintain a good diet and you won't become overweight. **Inform**

2. Dad yelled at Timmy, "Don't ride that Toddle-Bike in the street!" **Persuade**

3. "You ate the broccoli and left all the cookies," cried Mother. **Entertain**

4. The advertiser uses cute kindergarteners in his ads to sell products. **Persuade**

5. The Toddle-Bike was just voted the best new toy vehicle for 1999. **Inform**

6. "I saw the new Barbie on TV and I just had to have it," said Katy. **Persuade**

7. Keep current on homework assignments and you'll be less frustrated at school. **Inform**

8. "My fingers are numb after only four hours of Nintendo," complained Brad. **Entertain**

9. Toddle-Bikes are so fun your children will be entertained for hours. **Persuade**

10. Fast food and video game advertisers target their ads toward the Saturday morning television audience. **Inform**

11. There are many more vitamins in vegetables than there are in hamburgers. **Inform**

12. "Toddle-Bikes will change your life," promised the television announcer. **Inform**

13. Eat more fruits and vegetables for a healthier, stronger body. **Persuade**

14. Two out of every three teenagers eat fast food more than twice a week. **Inform**

15. Avoid a steady routine of TV-watching and video games to stay alert. **Persuade**

page 74

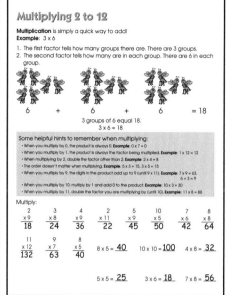

Multiplying 2 to 12

Multiplication is simply a quick way to add!
Example: 3 x 6

1. The first factor tells how many groups there are. There are 3 groups.
2. The second factor tells how many are in each group. There are 6 in each group.

6 + 6 + 6 = 18

3 groups of 6 equal 18.
3 x 6 = 18

Some helpful hints to remember when multiplying:
- When you multiply by 0, the product is always 0. **Example:** 0 x 7 = 0
- When you multiply by 1, the product is always the factor being multiplied. **Example:** 1 x 12 = 12
- When multiplying by 2, double the factor other than 2. **Example:** 2 x 4 = 8
- The order doesn't matter when multiplying. **Example:** 5 x 3 = 15, 3 x 5 = 15
- When you multiply by 9, the digits in the product add up to 9 (until 9 x 11). **Example:** 7 x 9 = 63, 6 + 3 = 9
- When you multiply by 10, multiply by 1 and add 0 to the product. **Example:** 10 x 3 = 30
- When you multiply by 11, double the factor you are multiplying by (until 10). **Example:** 11 x 8 = 88

Multiply:

2 x9	3 x8	4 x9	2 x11	5 x9	10 x5	7 x6	8 x8
18	**24**	**36**	**22**	**45**	**50**	**42**	**64**

11 x12	9 x7	8 x5
132	**63**	**40**

8 x 5 = **40** 10 x 10 = **100** 4 x 8 = **32**

5 x 5 = **25** 3 x 6 = **18** 7 x 8 = **56**

page 75

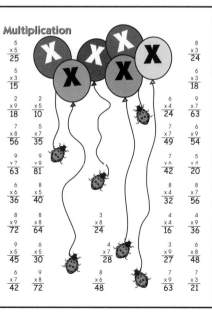

Multiplication

5 x5 **25**	8 x3 **24**
5 x3 **15**	6 x3 **18**
2 x9 **18**	2 x5 **10**	6 x4 **24**	9 x7 **63**
7 x8 **56**	5 x7 **35**	7 x7 **49**	6 x9 **54**
9 x7 **63**	9 x9 **81**	7 x6 **42**	5 x4 **20**
6 x6 **36**	8 x5 **40**	8 x4 **32**	8 x7 **56**
8 x9 **72**	8 x8 **64**	3 x8 **24**	4 x4 **16**	4 x9 **36**
9 x5 **45**	6 x5 **30**	4 x7 **28**	3 x9 **27**	6 x8 **48**
6 x7 **42**	9 x8 **72**	8 x6 **48**	9 x7 **63**	7 x3 **21**

page 76

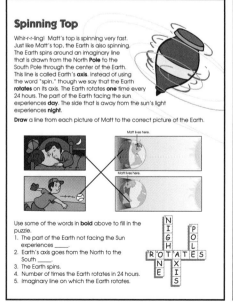

Spinning Top

Whir-r-r-ling! Matt's top is spinning very fast. Just like Matt's top, the Earth is also spinning. The Earth spins around an imaginary line that is drawn from the North **Pole** to the South Pole through the center of the Earth. This line is called Earth's **axis**. Instead of using the word "spin," though we say that the Earth **rotates** on its axis. The Earth rotates **one** time every 24 hours. The part of the Earth facing the sun experiences **day**. The side that is away from the sun's light experiences **night**.

Draw a line from each picture of Matt to the correct picture of the Earth.

Matt lives here.

Matt lives here.

Use some of the words in **bold** above to fill in the puzzle.
1. The part of the Earth not facing the Sun experiences _____.
2. Earth's axis goes from the North to the South _____.
3. The Earth spins.
4. Number of times the Earth rotates in 24 hours.
5. Imaginary line on which the Earth rotates.

Crossword answers: NIGHT, POLE, ROTATES, ONE, AXIS

page 77

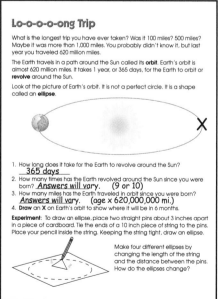

Lo-o-o-o-ong Trip

What is the longest trip you have ever taken? Was it 100 miles? 500 miles? Maybe it was more than 1,000 miles. You probably didn't know it, but last year you traveled 620 million miles.

The Earth travels in a path around the Sun called its **orbit**. Earth's orbit is almost 620 million miles. It takes 1 year, or 365 days, for the Earth to orbit or **revolve** around the Sun.

Look at the picture of Earth's orbit. It is not a perfect circle. It is a shape called an **ellipse**.

1. How long does it take for the Earth to revolve around the Sun?
   365 days
2. How many times has the Earth revolved around the Sun since you were born? **Answers will vary.** (9 or 10)
3. How many miles has the Earth traveled in orbit since you were born? **Answers will vary.** (age x 620,000,000 mi.)
4. **Draw** an **X** on Earth's orbit to show where it will be in 6 months.

Experiment: To draw an ellipse, place two straight pins about 3 inches apart in a piece of cardboard. Tie the ends of a 10 inch piece of string to the pins. Place your pencil inside the string. Keeping the string tight, draw an ellipse.

Make four different ellipses by changing the length of the string and the distance between the pins. How do the ellipses change?

page 78

359

Learn at Home, Grade 4

Leaning Into Summer

Why isn't it summer all year long?

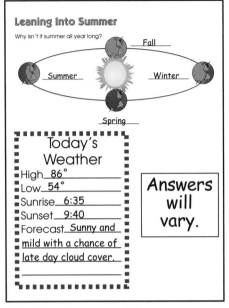

Fall / Summer / Winter / Spring

Today's Weather
- High _86°_
- Low _54°_
- Sunrise _6:35_
- Sunset _9:40_
- Forecast _Sunny and mild with a chance of late day cloud cover._

Answers will vary.

page 79

Autobiography

An **autobiography** is a written account of your life. Use the outline to fill in information about your life.

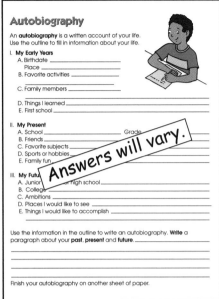

I. **My Early Years**
  A. Birthdate
    Place
  B. Favorite activities
  C. Family members
  D. Things I learned
  E. First school
II. **My Present**
  A. School _____ Grade
  B. Friends
  C. Favorite subjects
  D. Sports or hobbies
  E. Family fun
III. **My Future**
  A. Junior or high school
  B. College
  C. Ambitions
  D. Places I would like to see
  E. Things I would like to accomplish

Use the information in the outline to write an autobiography. **Write** a paragraph about your **past**, **present** and **future**.

Finish your autobiography on another sheet of paper.

Answers will vary.

page 84

Figures of Speech

A **figure of speech** can make a sentence more interesting. Here are four popular kinds of figures of speech:

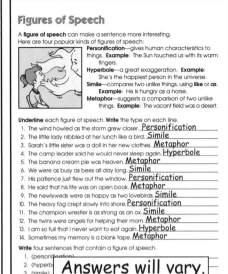

Personification—gives human characteristics to things. **Example:** The Sun touched us with its warm fingers.
Hyperbole—a great exaggeration. **Example:** She's the happiest person in the universe.
Simile—compares two unlike things, using **like** or **as**. **Example:** He is hungry as a horse.
Metaphor—suggests a comparison of two unlike things. **Example:** The vacant field was a desert.

Underline each figure of speech. **Write** the type on each line.
1. The wind howled as the storm grew closer. **Personification**
2. The little lady nibbled at her lunch like a bird. **Simile**
3. Sarah's little sister was a doll in her new clothes. **Metaphor**
4. The camp leader said he would never sleep again. **Hyperbole**
5. The banana cream pie was heaven. **Metaphor**
6. We were as busy as bees all day long. **Simile**
7. His patience just flew out the window. **Personification**
8. He said that his life was an open book. **Metaphor**
9. The newlyweds were as happy as two lovebirds. **Simile**
10. The heavy fog crept slowly into shore. **Personification**
11. The champion wrestler is as strong as an ox. **Simile**
12. The twins were angels for helping their mom. **Metaphor**
13. I am so full that I never want to eat again. **Hyperbole**
14. Sometimes my memory is a blank tape. **Metaphor**

Write four sentences that contain a figure of speech.
1. (personification)
2. (hyperbole)
3. (simile)
4. (metaphor)

Answers will vary.

page 85

A's Are Back

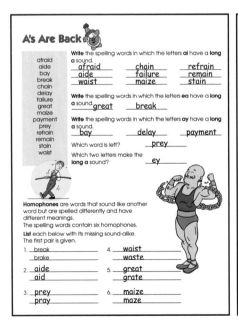

afraid, aide, bay, break, chain, delay, failure, great, maize, payment, prey, refrain, remain, stain, waist

Write the spelling words in which the letters **ai** have a long **a** sound.
afraid / chain / refrain
aide / failure / remain
waist / maize / stain

Write the spelling words in which the letters **ea** have a long **a** sound.
great / break

Write the spelling words in which the letters **ay** have a long **a** sound.
bay / delay / payment

Which word is left? prey

Which two letters make the **long a** sound? ey

Homophones are words that sound like another word but are spelled differently and have different meanings. The spelling words contain six homophones.
List each below with its missing sound-alike. The first pair is given.
1. break / brake
2. aide / aid
3. prey / pray
4. waist / waste
5. great / grate
6. maize / maze

page 86

It's Major

Main ideas can be anywhere in a paragraph. **Write** the main idea for each paragraph on the blank line. Choose from the main ideas listed below.

They had to get Fudge to the hospital.
Peter had to sit and wait alone.
Someone did care that he had lost Dribble.
Fudge had eaten Dribble.
They waited for news about Fudge.
After spending all day in the hospital waiting room, Peter was hungry.

1. Peter walked home from school. It was a spring day, and he was thinking about Dribble. Something was wrong when he got to his room. The bowl was there but not Dribble. When he asked Fudge where he was, Fudge just smiled and pointed to his tummy. **Fudge had eaten Dribble.**
2. Peter grabbed blankets while his mother called the ambulance. Henry made no other elevator stops on the way down. **They had to get Fudge to the hospital.** Two men in white were waiting with a stretcher and the ambulance.
3. **Peter had to sit and wait alone.** There were no magazines or books. He watched the clock. He read all the wall signs. He found out he was in the Emergency Room.
4. **After spending all day in the hospital waiting room, Peter was hungry.** Mother joined him in the hospital coffee shop for a hamburger. He didn't eat much after he found out that Fudge might need an operation if the castor oil, milk of magnesia and prune juice didn't work soon.
5. The next day was Saturday. Peter's grandmother came to stay with him. **They waited for news about Fudge.** Every hour the telephone rang with a report about Fudge. The good news came late at night.
6. Fudge came home with many presents. He was having fun and getting lots of attention. When Mr. Hatcher arrived home from work, he gave the biggest present to Peter. **Someone did care that he had lost Dribble.**

page 87

Synonyms and Antonyms

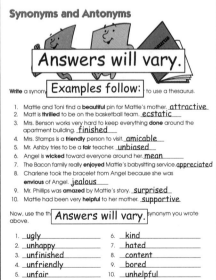

Answers will vary. Examples follow:

Write a synonym ... to use a thesaurus.
1. Mattie and Toni find a **beautiful** pin for Mattie's mother. attractive
2. Matt is **thrilled** to be on the basketball team. ecstatic
3. Mrs. Benson works very hard to keep everything **done** around the apartment building. finished
4. Mrs. Stamps is a **friendly** person to visit. amicable
5. Mr. Ashby tries to be a **fair** teacher. unbiased
6. Angel is **wicked** toward everyone around her. mean
7. The Bacon family really **enjoyed** Mattie's babysitting service. appreciated
8. Charlene took the bracelet from Angel because she was **envious** of Angel. jealous
9. Mr. Phillips was **amazed** by Mattie's story. surprised
10. Mattie had been very **helpful** to her mother. supportive

Now, use the th... synonym you wrote above.
Answers will vary.
1. ugly
2. unhappy
3. unfinished
4. unfriendly
5. unfair
6. kind
7. hated
8. content
9. bored
10. unhelpful

page 88

Learn at Home, Grade 4

Multiplication

Come on, this is easy!

1. 32 × 3 = 96	2. 21 × 4 = 84	
3. 43 × 3 = 129	4. 20 × 3 = 60	5. 11 × 3 = 33
6. 34 × 3 = 102	7. 21 × 3 = 63	
8. 33 × 3 = 99	9. 24 × 2 = 48	10. 22 × 4 = 88
11. 40 × 2 = 80	12. 32 × 2 = 64	
13. 13 × 3 = 39	14. 22 × 2 = 44	15. 20 × 4 = 80
16. 23 × 2 = 46	17. 11 × 3 = 33	
18. 41 × 2 = 82	19. 31 × 3 = 93	20. 44 × 2 = 88
21. 23 × 3 = 69	22. 12 × 4 = 48	
23. 33 × 2 = 66	24. 30 × 3 = 90	25. 21 × 2 = 42
26. 13 × 2 = 26		
27. 42 × 2 = 84	28. 12 × 3 = 36	29. 14 × 2 = 28
30. 22 × 3 = 66		

page 89

Regrouping

1. Multiply the ones column. Ask: Do I need to regroup?

```
  2
 38
 x 3
```
24 ones = 2 tens and 4 ones

2. Multiply the tens column. Ask: Do I need to regroup?

```
  2
 38
 x 3
 114
```
11 tens = 1 hundred and 1 ten

```
 38
 x 3
```
is the same as

```
  38
  38
+ 38
```

Multiply.

1. 29 × 3 = 87	2. 62 × 4 = 248	3. 39 × 4 = 156	4. 86 × 7 = 602	5. 43 × 6 = 258
6. 28 × 6 = 168	7. 48 × 2 = 96	8. 31 × 9 = 279	9. 25 × 5 = 125	10. 55 × 5 = 275

page 90

Space Math

Blast off into multiplication.

406 × 3 = 1,218	326 × 5 = 1,630	281 × 4 = 1,124	923 × 2 = 1,846	817 × 6 = 4,902
231 × 6 = 1,386	214 × 2 = 428	262 × 7 = 1,834	218 × 5 = 1,090	126 × 9 = 1,134
241 × 8 = 1,928	329 × 6 = 1,974	310 × 5 = 1,550	204 × 8 = 1,632	431 × 3 = 1,293
231 × 4 = 924	624 × 7 = 4,368			421 × 6 = 2,526
896 × 1 = 896				742 × 8 = 5,936
606 × 7 = 4,242				525 × 4 = 2,100
				814 × 9 = 7,326

page 91

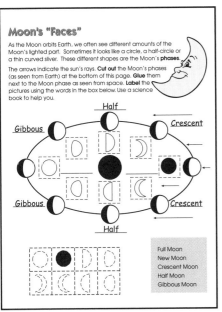

Moon's "Faces"

As the Moon orbits Earth, we often see different amounts of the Moon's lighted part. Sometimes it looks like a circle, a half-circle or a thin curved sliver. These different shapes are the Moon's **phases**.

The arrows indicate the sun's rays. **Cut out** the Moon's phases (as seen from Earth) at the bottom of this page. **Glue** them next to the Moon phase as seen from space. **Label** the pictures using the words in the box below. Use a science book to help you.

Half — Gibbous — Crescent — Gibbous — Crescent — Half

Full Moon
New Moon
Crescent Moon
Half Moon
Gibbous Moon

page 92

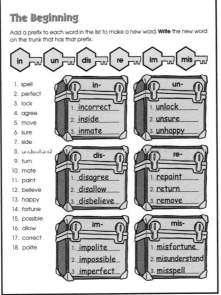

The Beginning

Add a prefix to each word in the list to make a new word. **Write** the new word on the trunk that has that prefix.

in — un — dis — re — im — mis

1. spell
2. perfect
3. lock
4. agree
5. move
6. sure
7. side
8. understand
9. turn
10. mate
11. paint
12. believe
13. happy
14. fortune
15. possible
16. allow
17. correct
18. polite

in-
1. incorrect
2. inside
3. inmate

un-
1. unlock
2. unsure
3. unhappy

dis-
1. disagree
2. disallow
3. disbelieve

re-
1. repaint
2. return
3. remove

im-
1. impolite
2. impossible
3. imperfect

mis-
1. misfortune
2. misunderstand
3. misspell

page 98

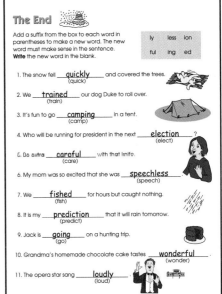

The End

Add a suffix from the box to each word in parentheses to make a new word. The new word must make sense in the sentence. **Write** the new word in the blank.

ly — less — ion — ful — ing — ed

1. The snow fell __quickly__ and covered the trees. (quick)
2. We __trained__ our dog Duke to roll over. (train)
3. It's fun to go __camping__ in a tent. (camp)
4. Who will be running for president in the next __election__? (elect)
5. Be extra __careful__ with that knife. (care)
6. My mom was so excited that she was __speechless__. (speech)
7. We __fished__ for hours but caught nothing. (fish)
8. It is my __prediction__ that it will rain tomorrow. (predict)
9. Jack is __going__ on a hunting trip. (go)
10. Grandma's homemade chocolate cake tastes __wonderful__. (wonder)
11. The opera star sang __loudly__. (loud)

page 99

361

Still Easy

Put a check to the left of the spelling words in which the letters **ea** make the **long e** sound.

Put a star to the right of the spelling words in which the letters **ee** make the **long e** sound.

Which word uses the letters **eo** for the **long e** sound? __people__

agree	easel	preach
between	greenery	season
breathe	greetings	wheat
disease	meek	wheel
eagle	people	yeast

Fill in the blanks.

1. During the holiday __season__, our family sends lots of __greetings__.

2. The Reverend Smith will __agree__ to __preach__ a shorter time because of extra musical selections.

3. In earlier times, __wheat__ was ground into flour with a large stone __wheel__.

4. The soaring __eagle__ is a proud creature, not __meek__ or timid.

5. In the park surrounded by __greenery__ stood the artist painting at his __easel__.

6. The swimming coach taught the swimmers to __breathe__ evenly __between__ strokes.

7. Two topics or terms studied in life science are __disease__ and __people__.

page 100

Story Organizer

Date _____ Title _____

Vocabulary	Definitions

Setting: _____

Characters: _____

Answers will vary.

Problem: _____

Events: _____

Solution: _____

Did you enjoy this story? 1 2 3 4 5 6
Not at all   Very much!

page 101

Like . . . a Simile

In the sentences below, underline the two things or persons being compared. In the blank, **write** simile or metaphor. Remember, a simile uses **like** or **as**; metaphors do not.

1. Angel was as mean as a wild bull. __simile__

2. Toni and Mattie were like toast and jam. __simile__

3. Mr. Ashby expected the students to be as busy as beavers. __simile__

4. The pin was a masterpiece in Mattie's mind. __metaphor__

5. The park's peacefulness was a friend to Mattie. __metaphor__

6. The words came as slow as molasses into Mattie's mind. __simile__

7. Mrs. Stamp's apartment was like a museum. __simile__

8. Mrs. Benson was as happy as a lark when Mattie won the contest. __simile__

9. Mr. Phillip's smile was a glowing beam to Mattie and Mrs. Benson. __metaphor__

10. Mattie ran as fast as the wind to get her money. __simile__

11. Angel's mean words cut through Charlene like glass. __simile__

12. Mr. Bacon was a fairy godmother to Mattie. __metaphor__

13. The gingko tree's leaves were shaped like fans. __simile__

Complete the following sentences using similes.

1. Matt was as artistic as __Example: Picasso__

2. Hannibal's teeth were like _____

3. Toni's mi[...] _____

4. Mattie w[...] **Answers will vary.**

5. Mrs. Stamp was like _____

page 102

Amazing Arms

What will happen to a starfish that loses an arm? To find out, **solve** the following problems and **write** the corresponding letter above the answer at the bottom of the page.

O. 2,893 × 4 = 11,572	W. 1,763 × 3 = 5,289	W. 7,665 × 5 = 38,325

A. 1,935 × 6 = 11,610	W. 3,097 × 3 = 9,291	E. 2,929 × 4 = 11,716

G. 6,366 × 5 = 31,830	T. 7,821 × 8 = 62,568	L. 6,283 × 7 = 43,981	I. 5,257 × 3 = 15,771	R. 3,019 × 6 = 18,114

N. 2,908 × 7 = 20,356	I. 6,507 × 8 = 52,056	N. 5,527 × 2 = 11,054

L. 6,626 × 3 = 19,878	O. 7,219 × 9 = 64,971	E. 3,406 × 6 = 20,436

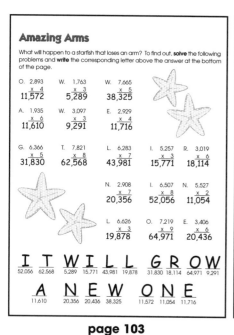

I T W I L L G R O W
52,056 62,568 5,289 15,771 43,981 19,878 31,830 18,114 64,971 9,291

A N E W O N E
11,610 20,356 20,436 38,325 11,572 11,054 11,716

page 103

Elephant Escapades

56 × 43 = 2,408	13 × 24 = 312	24 × 56 = 1,344	20 × 93 = 1,860

23 × 54 = 1,242	28 × 43 = 1,204	13 × 82 = 1,066	21 × 64 = 1,344

25 × 34 = 850	13 × 64 = 832	34 × 21 = 714	32 × 55 = 1,760

42 × 23 = 966	62 × 31 = 1,922	51 × 43 = 2,193	21 × 64 = 1,344

10 × 84 = 840	35 × 24 = 840	24 × 30 = 720	24 × 53 = 1,272

81 × 46 = 3,726	32 × 27 = 864

page 104

Star Light, Star Bright

Lie on your back. Gaze up into the night sky. Which star is the brightest? On a clear night you can see hundreds of stars, some are bright and others are dim. Why are some stars brighter than others? Let's try to find out by looking at the picture on this page.

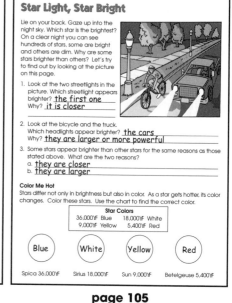

1. Look at the two streetlights in the picture. Which streetlight appears brighter? __the first one__ Why? __it is closer__

2. Look at the bicycle and the truck. Which headlights appear brighter? __the cars__ Why? __they are larger or more powerful__

3. Some stars appear brighter than other stars for the same reasons as those stated above. What are the two reasons?
   a. __they are closer__
   b. __they are larger__

Color Me Hot

Stars differ not only in brightness but also in color. As a star gets hotter, its color changes. Color these stars. Use the chart to find the correct color.

Star Colors	
36,000°F Blue	18,000°F White
9,000°F Yellow	5,400°F Red

Blue   White   Yellow   Red

Spica 36,000°F   Sirius 18,000°F   Sun 9,000°F   Betelgeuse 5,400°F

page 105

Learn at Home, Grade 4

Space Snowballs

Planets and moons are not the only objects in our solar system that travel in orbits. Comets also orbit the Sun.

A **comet** is like a giant dirty snowball that is $\frac{1}{2}$ to 3 miles wide. It is made of frozen gases, dust, ice and rocks.

As the comet gets closer to the Sun, the frozen gases melt and evaporate. The dust particles floating in the air form a cloud called a **coma**. The "wind" from the Sun blows the coma away from the Sun. The coma forms the comet's tail.

There are more than 800 known comets. Halley's comet is the most famous. It appears about every 76 years. The last scheduled appearance in this century was in 1985. When will it appear next?

Find the words from the box in the word search. (They are horizontal or vertical.) When you are finished, **write** down the letters that are not circled. Start at the top left of the puzzle.

```
S P M E L I L A N H E
O T S S H A C O M A V
L E N O R D B I T L S
R C W L E S S C O E M
S E B T S T H A V V E
Y O A R O R B I T B I
S T L S S H A P E D L
T I U K T A I L E A F
E O O T I C E B A L L
M S K Y S H I N I N G
```

dust	Halley
coma	snowball
melt	orbit
tail	ice
sky	shining
solar	system

PLANETS HAVE ORBITS
LIKE CIRCLES. COMETS
HAVE ORBITS SHAPED
LIKE A FOOTBALL.

page 108

A Black Hole

Have you ever heard of a mysterious black hole? Some scientists believe that a black hole is an invisible object somewhere in space. Scientists believe that it has such a strong pull toward it, called gravity, that nothing can escape from it!

These scientists believe that a black hole is a star that has collapsed. The collapse made its pull even stronger. It seems invisible because even its own starlight cannot escape! It is believed that anything in space that comes near the black hole will be pulled into it forever. Some scientists believe there are many black holes in our galaxy.

Check: Some scientists believe that:
- ☑ a black hole is an invisible object in space.
- ☑ a black hole is a collapsed star.
- ☑ a black hole will not let its own light escape.

Write:

A - gravity	**B**	To fall or cave in
B - collapse	**A**	A strong pull toward an object in space

Draw what you think the inside of a black hole would be like.

page 109

Action and Linking Verbs

An **action verb** is a word that shows action.
Examples: We **play** basketball. I **think** about my pet.

Underline the action verb in each sentence below.
1. Have you ever <u>wished</u> for a dog of your very own?
2. <u>Choose</u> the breed of your dog very carefully.
3. Puppies may <u>grow</u> to be very large or very small.
4. Your dog must <u>receive</u> good care, attention and exercise.
5. The right dog will <u>give</u> you years of pleasure and enjoyment.
6. Can you <u>imagine</u> yourself as a dog owner?

A **linking verb** does not show action. Instead, it links the subject with a noun or adjective in the predicate of the sentence. Forms of the verb **be** are common linking verbs.
Example: Puppies **are** cute.

Underline the linking verb in each sentence. Then, **fill in** the chart.
1. Tom's new puppy <u>is</u> playful and mischievous.
2. His dad's socks <u>are</u> a temptation to that puppy.
3. Mom and Dad <u>were</u> angry when the puppy chewed up a shoe.
4. They <u>were</u> surprised when the puppy got into Mom's flowers.
5. He <u>was</u> so happy rolling around in the dirt.
6. The puppy <u>will be</u> less trouble when he grows up.

Subject	Linking Verb	Noun or Adjective(s)	Subject	Linking Verb	Noun or Adjective(s)
1. puppy	is	playful and mischievous	4. They	were	surprised
2. socks	are	temptation	5. He	was	happy
3. Mom and Dad	were	angry	6. puppy	will be	trouble

page 114

Fore and Aft

Fill in the blanks with the appropriate affixes. Some will be used more than once.

Prefixes: dis im re un mis   Suffixes: ful ish ist less ly ness ward

	Meaning	Root Word + Affix	New Word
1.	having no fear	fear **l e s s**	fearless
2.	to vanish	**d i s** appear	disappear
3.	toward a lower level	down **w a r d**	downward
4.	having no friends	friend **l e s s**	friendless
5.	an error in action	**m i s** take	mistake
6.	to enter again	**r e** enter	reenter
7.	too many to count	count **l e s s**	countless
8.	not happy	**u n** happy	unhappy
9.	perfection seeker	perfection **i s t**	perfectionist
10.	quality of being dark	dark **n e s s**	darkness
11.	not possible	**i m** possible	impossible
12.	having doubts	doubt **f u l**	doubtful
13.	without a care	care **l e s s**	careless
14.	sad from being alone	lone **l y**	lonely
15.	not thinking	**u n** thinking	unthinking
16.	without shoes	shoe **l e s s**	shoeless
17.	in a mysterious way	mysterious **l y**	mysteriously
18.	appear again	**r e** appear	reappear
19.	in a quiet manner	quiet **l y**	quietly
20.	call by wrong name	**m i s** call	miscall
21.	somewhat yellow	yellow **i s h**	yellowish
22.	cautious	care **f u l**	careful
23.	to release	**d i s** engage	disengage

page 116

Double Trouble

Fill in the blanks with the correct definition number for each **underlined** word.
Example: __3__ I was covered with **pitch** after climbing the pine tree.

winding	1. having bends or curves
	2. the act of turning something around a central core
wolf	1. to gulp down
	2. a large carnivorous member of the dog family
pitch	1. to sell or persuade
	2. to throw a ball from the mound to the batter
	3. a resin that comes from the sap of pine trees

__1__ 1. Do the children's clubs **pitch** cookies?
__2__ 2. We are **winding** the top's string tightly.
__2__ 3. The adult **wolf** returned to her lair.
__2__ 4. Red didn't **pitch** after the fourth inning.
__1__ 5. The Mother family had a **winding** driveway.
__1__ 6. The young ball player **wolfed** down his lunch.

choke	1. to strangle
	2. to bring the hands up on the bat
hitch	1. obstacle
	2. to fasten or tie temporarily
wind-up	1. the swing of the pitcher's arm just before the pitch
	2. to close or conclude

__2__ 1. We **hitched** the mule to the cart.
__2__ 2. Skip would not **choke** up on his bat.
__1__ 3. Paul wished to play, but there was just one **hitch**.
__2__ 4. We wish to **wind-up** our program with more music.
__1__ 5. Mom was afraid the dog would **choke** itself on its leash.
__1__ 6. He has a great **wind-up** and curve ball.

page 117

Wheels of Wonder

Solve the following problems by multiplying each number by the power of 10 in the center.

31,000	52,000		3,210	910
7,000	6,000		80	70
	820,000			3,310
900	76,100		2,710	90
700	2,200		110	620
	80,100			2,080
3,000	621,000		300	9,300
92,000	15,000		5,200	700
	608,000			80,600

page 119

Learn at Home, Grade 4

Series Commas

Commas are used to separate words or groups of words in a series of three or more.

Example: Martha had fried chicken, baked potatoes, green beans and a tossed salad for dinner.

Use commas to separate the items in a series in the sentences below.

1. John bought buttered popcorn, diet soda, peanuts and a hot dog at the game.
2. The vending machine contained candy bars, crackers, bags of popcorn, peanuts and jelly beans.
3. The package of jelly beans held assorted flavors such as banana, licorice, strawberry, watermelon and grape.
4. Sam put ketchup, mustard, onions, lettuce and pickles on his hamburger.
5. Barbara, Carol and John each ordered sweet and sour pork, fried rice and wonton soup.
6. The picnic basket was filled with sandwiches, pickles, potato chips, oranges, apples and brownies.

Rewrite the sentences below. Place the commas so that the number of food items listed is the same as the number in parentheses.

1. Susan had chocolate ice cream peanut butter cookies and strawberry licorice. (3) **Susan had chocolate ice cream, peanut butter cookies and strawberry licorice.**
2. Megan had an orange juice cinnamon toast bacon and eggs for breakfast. (5) **Megan had an orange, juice, cinnamon toast, bacon and eggs for breakfast.**
3. Mrs. Clark put tuna fish soda crackers and salad dressing into the grocery cart.(5) **Mrs. Clark put tuna, fish, soda, crackers and salad dressing into the grocery cart.**

page 124

Direct Quotations

Use **quotation marks** to enclose the exact words of the speaker. The speaker's first word must begin with a capital letter. Also follow these rules:

1. When the speaker is named **before** the direct quotation, separate the speaker from the quotation with a comma.
2. When the speaker is named **after** the direct quotation, use a comma or the proper end mark inside the last quotation.

Examples: 1. Mother said, "You must clean your room."
2. "Sara is cleaning her room," said Mother.
3. "Have you found your shoes?" asked Tina.
4. "Hurry up!" yelled John.

Punctuate these sentences correctly.

1. Father asked, "John, will you be home for dinner?"
2. "No, I will be at football practice," said John.
3. "When will you have time to eat?" asked Dad.
4. "I'll have to eat after practice," grumbled John.
5. "Hurry up!" yelled Pete.
6. Pete commented, "We'll be late for practice if you don't move faster."

Rewrite these sentences. Punctuate and capitalize them correctly.

1. will you take out the garbage asked Mother
"Will you take out the garbage?" asked Mother.
2. Mary answered I don't have time now
Mary answered, "I don't have time now."
3. is it alright if I do it later she added
"Is it alright if I do it later?" she added.
4. please do that job as soon as you get home Mother said
"Please do that job as soon as you get home," Mother said.

page 125

Ouch Words

Fill in the blanks. Each spelling word is used only once.

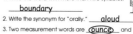

1. Write the word with more than two syllables. **boundary**
2. Write the synonym for "orally." **aloud**
3. Two measurement words are (ounce) and **pound**. Circle the lighter weight.
4. A synonym for "sofa" is **couch**.
5. The opposite of north is **south**.
6. The name of a person, place or thing is called a **noun**.
7. Which word could describe a violation of the rules in a sport? **foul**
8. Which word names a geographic landform? **mountain**
9. Which word names an item often found in classrooms or hallways? **fountain**
10. If you make a deposit at the bank, the teller will add that **amount** of money to your savings **account**.
11. Three spelling words have not been used. Use those three in one sentence.
use: **hound doubt county**

Answers will vary.

Word list: account, aloud, amount, boundary, couch, county, doubt, foul, fountain, hound, mountain, noun, ounce, pound, south

page 126

Division

1. $\frac{6}{5\overline{)30}}$ 2. $\frac{3}{7\overline{)21}}$
3. $\frac{7}{4\overline{)28}}$ 4. $\frac{7}{9\overline{)63}}$ 5. $\frac{7}{5\overline{)35}}$
6. $\frac{9}{1\overline{)9}}$ 7. $\frac{6}{4\overline{)24}}$ 8. $\frac{4}{8\overline{)32}}$ 9. $\frac{6}{6\overline{)36}}$ 10. $\frac{7}{2\overline{)14}}$ 11. $\frac{8}{7\overline{)56}}$ 12. $\frac{9}{4\overline{)36}}$
13. $\frac{3}{9\overline{)27}}$ 14. $\frac{7}{6\overline{)42}}$ 15. $\frac{1}{8\overline{)8}}$ 16. $\frac{8}{3\overline{)24}}$ 17. $\frac{9}{7\overline{)63}}$ 18. $\frac{6}{9\overline{)54}}$ 19. $\frac{9}{3\overline{)27}}$
20. $\frac{7}{1\overline{)7}}$ 21. $\frac{3}{8\overline{)24}}$ 22. $\frac{8}{2\overline{)16}}$ 23. $\frac{6}{7\overline{)42}}$ 24. $\frac{9}{6\overline{)54}}$ 25. $\frac{7}{8\overline{)56}}$ 26. $\frac{8}{4\overline{)32}}$
27. $\frac{8}{9\overline{)72}}$ 28. $\frac{9}{5\overline{)45}}$ 29. $\frac{7}{3\overline{)21}}$ 30. $\frac{8}{8\overline{)64}}$ 31. $\frac{9}{5\overline{)45}}$ 32. $\frac{7}{7\overline{)49}}$ 33. $\frac{6}{9\overline{)54}}$
34. $\frac{12}{3\overline{)36}}$ 35. $\frac{9}{8\overline{)72}}$ 36. $\frac{4}{7\overline{)28}}$ 37. $\frac{8}{5\overline{)40}}$ 38. $\frac{5}{6\overline{)30}}$

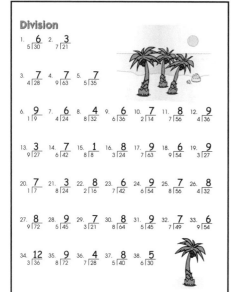

page 127

Snowball Bash

Help Pete climb down this mound of giant snowballs.

$\frac{12}{7\overline{)84}}$ $\frac{15}{5\overline{)75}}$

$\frac{15}{3\overline{)45}}$ $\frac{11}{9\overline{)99}}$ $\frac{22}{4\overline{)88}}$ $\frac{16}{5\overline{)80}}$

$\frac{16}{4\overline{)64}}$ $\frac{19}{3\overline{)57}}$ $\frac{26}{3\overline{)78}}$ $\frac{24}{3\overline{)72}}$ $\frac{12}{8\overline{)96}}$

$\frac{43}{2\overline{)86}}$ $\frac{19}{2\overline{)38}}$ $\frac{11}{6\overline{)66}}$ $\frac{13}{5\overline{)65}}$ $\frac{13}{4\overline{)52}}$

$\frac{17}{4\overline{)68}}$ $\frac{13}{6\overline{)78}}$ $\frac{13}{7\overline{)91}}$ $\frac{21}{2\overline{)42}}$ $\frac{12}{6\overline{)72}}$

page 128

Majestic Mountains

The word **mountain** means different things to different people. Some people who live on vast, level plains, consider a small hill a mountain. While others, who live in the mountains, would not consider a region mountainous unless it was very high and rugged.

Listed below are eight famous mountains of the world along with their heights. Graph each mountain's height. On the bottom of the graph, **write** the mountain's name and, on the side of the graph, **chart** the height. When you have finished graphing, use the results to answer the questions below.

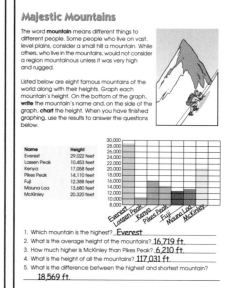

Name	Height
Everest	29,022 feet
Lassen Peak	10,453 feet
Kenya	17,058 feet
Pikes Peak	14,110 feet
Fuji	12,388 feet
Mauna Loa	13,680 feet
McKinley	20,320 feet

1. Which mountain is the highest? **Everest**
2. What is the average height of the mountains? **16,719 ft.**
3. How much higher is McKinley than Pikes Peak? **6,210 ft.**
4. What is the height of all the mountains? **117,031 ft.**
5. What is the difference between the highest and shortest mountain? **18,569 ft.**

page 131

Learn at Home, Grade 4

Book Words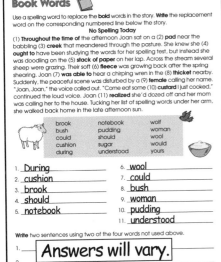

Use a spelling word to replace the **bold** words in the story. **Write** the replacement word on the corresponding numbered line below the story.

No Spelling Today

(1) **Throughout the time of** the afternoon Joan sat on a (2) **pad** near the babbling (3) **creek** that meandered through the pasture. She knew she (4) **ought to** have been studying the words for her spelling test, but instead she was doodling on the (5) **stack of paper** on her lap. Across the stream several sheep were grazing. Their soft (6) **fleece** was growing back after the spring shearing. Joan (7) **was able to** hear a chirping wren in the (8) **thicket** nearby. Suddenly, the peaceful scene was disturbed by a (9) **female** calling her name. "Joan, Joan," the voice called out. "Come eat some (10) **custard** I just cooked," continued the loud voice. Joan (11) **realized** she'd dozed off and her mom was calling her to the house. Tucking her list of spelling words under her arm, she walked back home in the late afternoon sun.

brook	notebook	wolf
bush	pudding	woman
could	should	wool
cushion	sugar	would
during	understood	yours

1. During
2. cushion
3. brook
4. should
5. notebook
6. wool
7. could
8. bush
9. woman
10. pudding
11. understood

Write two sentences using two of the four words not used above.

1. Answers will vary.
2.

page 136

Looking to the Stars

Solve the problems. To find the path to the top, **color** the spaces where the answers match the problem number.

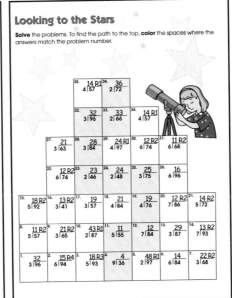

35. $4\overline{)57}$ = 14 R1	36. $2\overline{)72}$ = 36	
32. $3\overline{)96}$ = 32	33. $2\overline{)66}$ = 33	34. $4\overline{)57}$ = 14 R1
27. $3\overline{)63}$ = 21	28. $3\overline{)84}$ = 28	29. $4\overline{)97}$ = 24 R1	30. $6\overline{)74}$ = 12 R2	31. $6\overline{)74}$ = 11 R2
22. $6\overline{)74}$ = 12 R2	23. $2\overline{)46}$ = 23	24. $2\overline{)48}$ = 24	25. $3\overline{)75}$ = 25	26. $6\overline{)96}$ = 16
15. $5\overline{)92}$ = 18 R2	16. $3\overline{)41}$ = 13 R2	17. $3\overline{)57}$ = 19	18. $4\overline{)84}$ = 21	19. $4\overline{)76}$ = 19	20. $7\overline{)86}$ = 12 R2	21. $5\overline{)72}$ = 14 R2
8. $5\overline{)57}$ = 11 R2	9. $3\overline{)65}$ = 21 R2	10. $2\overline{)87}$ = 43 R1	11. $5\overline{)55}$ = 11	12. $7\overline{)84}$ = 12	13. $3\overline{)87}$ = 29	14. $7\overline{)93}$ = 13 R2
1. $3\overline{)96}$ = 32	2. $6\overline{)94}$ = 15 R4	3. $5\overline{)93}$ = 18 R3	4. $7\overline{)36}$ = 4	5. $2\overline{)97}$ = 48 R1	6. $6\overline{)84}$ = 14	7. $3\overline{)68}$ = 22 R2

page 137

A Funnel Cloud–Danger!

Did you know that a tornado is the most violent windstorm on Earth? A **tornado** is a whirling, twisting storm that is shaped like a funnel.

A tornado usually occurs in the spring on a hot day. It begins with thunderclouds and thunder. A cloud becomes very dark. The bottom of the cloud begins to twist and form a funnel. Rain and lightning begin. The funnel cloud drops from the dark storm clouds. It moves down toward the ground.

A tornado is very dangerous. It can destroy almost everything in its path.

Circle:
A (thunder, (tornado)) is the most vicious windstorm on Earth.

Check:
Which words describe a tornado?
☑ whirling ☑ twisting ☐ icy ☑ funnel-shaped ☑ dangerous

Underline:
A funnel shape is: ○ ☐ ⬭ ▽ ⋊

Write and Circle:
A tornado usually occurs in the ____spring____ on a ((hot) cool) day.

Write 1 - 2 - 3 below and in the picture above.
(3) The funnel cloud drops down to the ground.
(1) A tornado begins with dark thunder clouds.
(2) The dark clouds begin to twist and form a funnel.

page 138

Native American Alphabet Book

Copy the following outline to help your student organize information on different tribes. (See Week 10, Social Studies, number 2.)

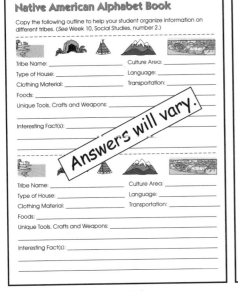

Tribe Name: _____ Culture Area: _____
Type of House: _____ Language: _____
Clothing Material: _____ Transportation: _____
Foods: _____
Unique Tools, Crafts and Weapons: _____

Interesting Fact(s): _____

Answers will vary.

Tribe Name: _____ Culture Area: _____
Type of House: _____ Language: _____
Clothing Material: _____ Transportation: _____
Foods: _____
Unique Tools, Crafts and Weapons: _____

Interesting Fact(s): _____

page 139

Subject/Verb Agreement

The **subject** and **verb** in a sentence must *agree*. If the subject is **singular**, add **s** to the verb. If the subject is **plural**, do not add an ending to the verb.

Examples:
Lava only **flows** when it is very hot. (singular)
Cinders **shoot** out of an active volcano. (plural)

Complete each sentence below using a form of the verb in parentheses.

1. Some volcanoes __erupt__ quietly. (erupt)
2. The ground __swells__ around a volcano just before an eruption. (swell)
3. Volcanoes __explode__ with great fury. (explode)
4. Tremors __increase__ as magma works its way to the surface. (increase)
5. Magma __escapes__ to the Earth's surface. (escape)
6. A volcano __erupts__ so violently that the mountain can be blown apart. (erupt)
7. Obsidian __forms__ when flying volcanic debris cools quickly in the air. (form)
8. Volcanoes __spew__ hot lava high into the air. (spew)
9. The sky __darkens__ from the ash and dust that explode out of a volcano. (darken)
10. Ash __covers__ the ground for many miles around a volcanic explosion. (cover)
11. Molten lava __glows__ bright red and yellow as it escapes from underneath the Earth's surface. (glow)
12. Steam __forms__ when molten lava comes in contact with water. (form)

page 144

Pronoun/Verb Agreement

The **subject pronoun** and the **verb** in a sentence must agree. If the subject pronoun is **singular**, add **s** to the verb. If the subject pronoun is **plural**, do not add an ending to the verb.

Examples:
He **wears** a helmet every time he rides his bike. (singular)
They **wear** helmets whenever they go roller-blading. (plural)

Circle the verb in parentheses that agrees with the subject pronoun.

1. She (ride (rides)) her bike to band practice on Tuesdays.
2. They ((zoom) zooms) down the hill to help them get up the steep incline on the other side.
3. He (glide (glides)) nicely on his skateboard when he's going around the corners on the skating path.
4. We ((travel) travels) as a family every Saturday to the park on our bikes.
5. It (rain (rains)) sometimes while we're riding our bikes to school.
6. He (love (loves)) to climb the hills on bikes with his mom and dad.
7. She (wear (wears)) a helmet and kneepads whenever she goes roller-blading with her friends.

Write the subject pronoun that agrees with the verb.

1. __He__ (They, We, He) tries very hard to skate backwards at the skating rink.
2. __She__ (I, She, You) tells everyone about all the fun things there are to do at the park.
3. __He__ (We, You, He) invites a friend every time he goes to the bicycle acrobatic demonstrations.
4. __They__ (She, They, He) look both ways very carefully before crossing the street on their roller-blades.
5. __We__ (It, We, He) send invitations to all our friends whenever there is a safety seminar at our school.

page 145

Soup in a Canoe

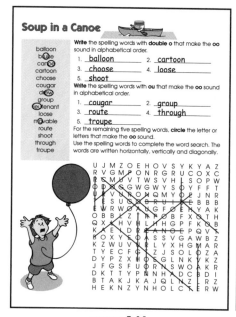

balloon
bou~~t~~e
canoe
cartoon
choose
cougar
d~~rew~~
group
le~~u~~tenant
loose
m~~o~~vable
route
shoot
through
troupe

Write the spelling words with **double o** that make the **oo** sound in alphabetical order.

1. __balloon__
2. __cartoon__
3. __choose__
4. __loose__
5. __shoot__

Write the spelling words with **ou** that make the oo sound in alphabetical order.

1. __cougar__
2. __group__
3. __route__
4. __through__
5. __troupe__

For the remaining five spelling words, **circle** the letter or letters that make the **oo** sound.
Use the spelling words to complete the word search. The words are written horizontally, vertically, and diagonally.

```
U J M Z O E H O V S Y K Y A Z
R V G M P O N R G R U C O X C
R M U V T W S V H L Q N H L L
R O X S G W G W Y S O Y F F A
E W Q Q M Q M Y O F E H B B B
R O M O N N L B R U I E E E L
O B B L Z T R P O B F X O L L
K A E I L D R E A N O E P Q V
B O X V W V U P S J O K H O V
K Z W U V I R L Y X H G M A Z
T Y E P Z X H O G L N K V M A
D Y F V J U O R H S O W B B A
J F G S T P N N H A D C B Z E
D K T T F Y P N N H A D C B Z
B T A K J J K A J Q L N Z W
H E K N Z Y N H O L C X R W
```

page 146

If . . . Then

Match the sentence parts that go together best. **Write** the number of the first sentence part on the line in front of the last sentence part for each one.

1. If you baby-sit for me Saturday night
2. If you are nice
3. If we leave work by 4:30
4. If you leave a note on your door
5. If you don't have enough money for the movie
6. If my father isn't too tired
7. If the wind keeps up
8. If you want to get a seat at the concert
9. If our neighbor cuts the grass early Sunday morning
10. If the plant doesn't feel damp
11. If my house were painted white
12. If everyone talked at the same time
13. If you don't get a haircut
14. If the tea kettle whistles
15. If no one answers the door
16. If the little boy crosses the street
17. If the horse is tired
18. If you have a long stick
19. If you don't want any dessert
20. If a king comes into a room
21. If it snows a lot tomorrow

__4__ the delivery man will leave the package.
__10__ It needs to be watered.
__18__ you could roast marshmallows.
__15__ probably no one is at home.
__20__ everyone will rise.
__1__ I'll pay you double.
__14__ the water is boiling.
__7__ tomorrow will be a great kite-flying day.
__17__ let him rest.
__12__ no one could hear directions.
__3__ we will avoid rush hour.
__19__ say "No, thank you."
__9__ the noise will wake me up.
__21__ we can build an igloo.
__6__ he said he would show me how to shoot baskets.
__11__ it would look like a miniature White House.
__5__ I'll loan you the rest.
__16__ he must hold onto his mother's hand.
__2__ you will have many friends.
__8__ you will have to be at the auditorium early.
__13__ you will have long hair.

page 147

Case Rests

Select the correct main idea from the book for each paragraph below by circling A, B or C.

1. In "The Case of the Scattered Cards," Encyclopedia noticed that cards on the floor of the tent were dry, not wet or muddy. It had been raining for two days.
   A. Encyclopedia had brought his own dry playing cards.
   (B) The tent had been put up before it started raining.
   C. Bugs had fixed all the holes to keep the floor dry.

2. In "The Case of the Civil War Sword," Encyclopedia could tell the sword was a fake by writing on the blade. He knew there had been two battles at Bull Run. He claimed that this sword belonged to General Stonewall Jackson.
   A. Bugs had found a valuable war memento.
   (B) The writing used the Yankee name for the battle instead of the Confederate.
   C. Bugs was as smart as Encyclopedia.

3. In "The Case of Merko's Grandson," Encyclopedia realized that Fred Gibson was the real heir. The tall woman really was a relative, too, but not Fred's grandchild. The woman insisted that the Great Merko was not Fred's grandfather.
   A. Merko died in a circus accident.
   B. The tall woman was lying.
   (C) The Great Merko was a woman—Fred's grandmother.

4. In "The Case of the Bank Robber," Encyclopedia figured out why the robber and Blind Tom had rolled on the ground. When they found the robber, he did not have the money. When Encyclopedia visited Blind Tom, the lights were on and a newspaper was on the bed.
   (A) Blind Tom and the robber were working together and traded yellow bags.
   B. Encyclopedia buys bread in yellow bags.
   C. Blind people can see if the lights are on.

page 148

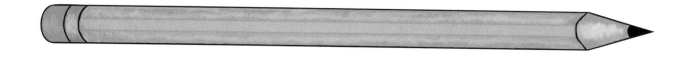

To Catch a Butterfly

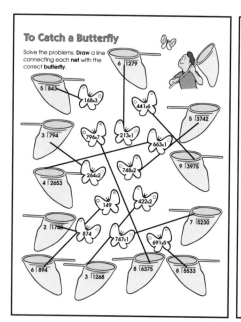

Solve the problems. **Draw** a line connecting each **net** with the correct **butterfly**.

page 149

A Visit to Space Camp

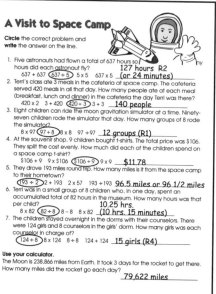

Circle the correct problem and **write** the answer on the line.

1. Five astronauts had flown a total of 637 hours so hours did each astronaut fly?
   637 + 637   (637 ÷ 5)   5 x 5   637 x 5   __127 hours R2__ __(or 24 minutes)__
2. Terri's class ate 3 meals in the cafeteria at space camp. The cafeteria served 420 meals in all that day. How many people ate at each meal (breakfast, lunch and dinner) in the cafeteria the day Terri was there?
   420 x 2   3 ÷ 420   (420 ÷ 3)   3 + 3   __140 people__
3. Eight children can ride the moon gravitation simulator at a time. Ninety-seven children rode the simulator that day. How many groups of 8 rode the simulator?
   8 x 97   (97 ÷ 8)   8 x 8   97 ÷ 97   __12 groups (R1)__
4. At the souvenir shop, 9 children bought t-shirts. The total price was $106. They split the cost evenly. How much did each of the children spend on a space camp t-shirt?
   $106 ÷ 9   9 x $106   ($106 ÷ 9)   9 x 9   __$11.78__
5. They drove 193 miles round trip. How many miles is it from the space camp to their hometown?
   (193 ÷ 2)   2 + 193   2 x 57   193 ÷ 193   __96.5 miles or 96 1/2 miles__
6. Terri was in a small group of 8 children who, in one day, spent an accumulated total of 82 hours in the museum. How many hours was that per child?
   8 x 82   (82 ÷ 8)   8 – 8   8 x 82   __10.25 hrs.__ __(10 hrs. 15 minutes)__
7. The children stayed overnight in the dorms with their counselors. There were 124 girls and 8 counselors in the girls' dorm. How many girls was each counselor in charge of?
   (124 ÷ 8)   8 x 124   8 + 8   124 + 124   __15 girls (R4)__

Use your calculator.
The Moon is 238,866 miles from Earth. It took 3 days for the rocket to get there. How many miles did the rocket go each day?
__79,622 miles__

page 150

Volcanoes

Using the **Fire Mountains** activity sheet (p. 151) and the box below, label the parts of the volcano.

crater
ash and dust
lava
vent
side vent
conduit
Earth's crust
Earth's mantle
magma chamber

Earth's crust	lava	side vent
Earth's mantle	crater	vent
magma chamber	ash and dust	conduit

page 152

The Hunters

Although they farmed and ate other foods besides meat, hunting was very important to most Woodland Native Americans, especially during the winter.

The information below shows the game that was caught by two Eastern Woodland tribes. Use the information to complete a double bar graph comparing the successes of the two tribes. Be sure to use a different color for each tribe.

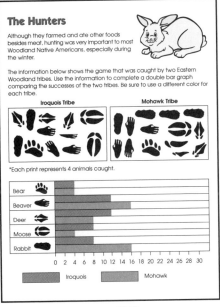

*Each print represents 4 animals caught.

page 153

Simple Subjects and Predicates

The **simple subject** is the most important word in the complete subject. It is a **noun** or **pronoun** that tells who or what the sentence is about.
The **simple predicate** is the most important word in the complete predicate. It is a **verb** that tells what the subject is or does.

Example:

simple subject   simple predicate
Handmade pottery can be very beautiful.
complete subject   complete predicate

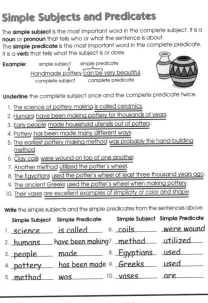

Underline the complete subject once and the complete predicate twice.

1. The science of pottery making is called ceramics.
2. Humans have been making pottery for thousands of years.
3. Early people made household utensils out of pottery.
4. Pottery has been made many different ways.
5. The earliest pottery making method was probably the hand-building method.
6. Clay coils were wound on top of one another.
7. Another method utilized the potter's wheel.
8. The Egyptians used the potter's wheel at least three thousand years ago.
9. The ancient Greeks used the potter's wheel when making pottery.
10. Their vases are excellent examples of simplicity of color and shape.

Write the simple subjects and the simple predicates from the sentences above.

	Simple Subject	Simple Predicate		Simple Subject	Simple Predicate
1.	science	is called	6.	coils	were wound
2.	humans	have been making	7.	method	utilized
3.	people	made	8.	Egyptians	used
4.	pottery	has been made	9.	Greeks	used
5.	method	was	10.	vases	are

page 158

What's That Noise?

Use the word list to complete the crossword puzzle.

Across
5. trip at sea
6. harmful substance
7. to express joy
9. to take pleasure from
11. an agreement to meet
13. faithfulness
15. sound produced by speaking

Down
1. to bring together
2. to stay away from
3. to ruin
4. farm crop
8. one who pays wages
10. dampness
12. selection
14. regal

appointment   moisture
avoid   poison
choice   rejoice
destroy   royal
employer   soybean
enjoy   voice
join   voyage
loyalty

page 159

Yum-Yum!

What edible fungus is occasionally found on pizzas or in omelets? To find out, solve the problems. Then, **write** the corresponding letter above the answer at the bottom of the page.

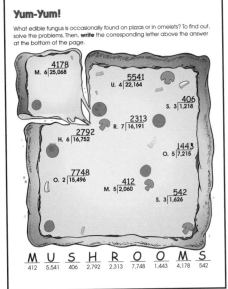

M U S H R O O M S
412 5,541 406 2,792 2,313 7,748 1,443 4,178 542

page 160

Puzzling Numbers

factor	factor	product
45	4	180
16	8	128
55	5	275
4	26	104

factor	factor	product
3	41	123
2	5	10
6	53	318
47	3	141

factor	factor	product
5	25	125
44	7	308
30	3	90
42	20	840

factor	factor	product
114	2	228
6	33	198
3	40	120
2	66	132

Shade in your answers below to reveal a picture.

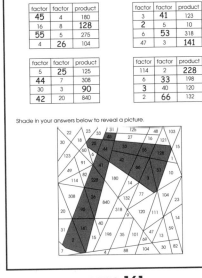

page 161

The Buffalo Hunters

The Plains Indians' survival depended on the buffalo. They killed only as many as they needed and wasted none of the animal. As a matter of fact, they had over 500 uses for the buffalo.

Answers may vary.

Your Logical Guess	
clothing, tepees, drums •	• teeth
decorations •	• brain
bowls for cooking •	• tongue
cups, spoons •	• hide
jewelry •	• large intestine
strings on bows •	• horns
bags for storage •	• muscles
ropes, belts •	• stomach
food •	• hair
tanning mixture for leather •	• tail

Name another buffalo part and its function. Example: Hooves may have been used in making weapons.

page 163

I Before E or Not?

Write the **ei** spelling words in alphabetical order.

1. beige
2. conceited
3. eight
4. freight
5. height
6. leisure
7. neighbor
8. receive
9. sleigh
10. weigh

beige
believe
conceited
eight
fiend
freight
friend
height
leisure
neighbor
receive
sleigh
thief
weigh

How many **ei** words have a **long a** sound? __6__

How many **ei** words have a **long e** sound? __3__

Which of the **ei** words is left? __height__

What sound does it have? __long i__

Write the **ie** spelling words in alphabetical order.

1. believe
2. field
3. fiend
4. friend
5. thief

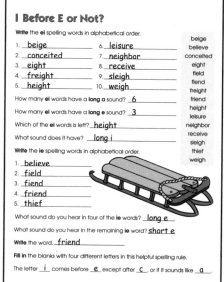

What sound do you hear in four of the **ie** words? __long e__

What sound do you hear in the remaining **ie** word? __short e__

Write the word. __friend__

Fill in the blanks with four different letters in this helpful spelling rule.

The letter __i__ comes before __e__ except after __c__, or if it sounds like __a__.

page 168

China's Dragon Kite

Solve the problems in this incredible dragon kite!

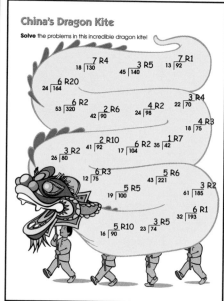

7 R4
18 ⟌130

3 R5
45 ⟌140

7 R1
13 ⟌92

6 R20
24 ⟌164

6 R2
53 ⟌320

2 R6
42 ⟌90

4 R2
24 ⟌98

3 R4
22 ⟌70

4 R3
18 ⟌75

3 R2
26 ⟌80

2 R10
41 ⟌92

6 R2
17 ⟌104

2 R5
35 ⟌42

1 R7

6 R3
12 ⟌75

5 R6
43 ⟌221

5 R5
19 ⟌100

3 R2
61 ⟌185

6 R1
32 ⟌193

5 R10
16 ⟌90

3 R5
23 ⟌74

page 169

Combining Sentences

Two sentences can be written as one sentence by using **connecting words**.

Choose one of the words in the box to combine the two sentences into one sentence.

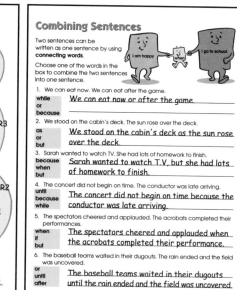

1. We can eat now. We can eat after the game.

while
or
because

We can eat now or after the game.

2. We stood on the cabin's deck. The sun rose over the deck.

as
or
but

We stood on the cabin's deck as the sun rose over the deck.

3. Sarah wanted to watch TV. She had lots of homework to finish.

because
when
but

Sarah wanted to watch T.V. but she had lots of homework to finish.

4. The concert did not begin on time. The conductor was late arriving.

until
because
while

The concert did not begin on time because the conductor was late arriving.

5. The spectators cheered and applauded. The acrobats completed their performance.

when
if
but

The spectators cheered and applauded when the acrobats completed their performance.

6. The baseball teams waited in their dugouts. The rain ended and the field was uncovered.

or
until
after

The baseball teams waited in their dugouts until the rain ended and the field was uncovered.

page 176

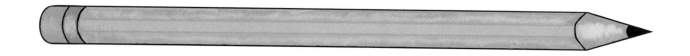

Cause and Effect Sentences

A **cause and effect sentence** has two parts: a **cause**, which tells why, and an **effect**, which tells what happened. It can be written two ways.

Example: Today is Saturday, so I don't have to go to school.
　　　　　　　cause　　　　　　　　effect

I don't have to go to school because today is Saturday.
　　　effect　　　　　　　　　　　cause

Combine the two sentences into a cause and effect sentence.
Write the sentence two ways: A. cause-effect. B. effect-cause.

1. I could not eat my dessert. I was full from dinner.

A. I was full from dinner, so I could not eat my dessert.

B. I could not eat my dessert because I was full from dinner.

2. I forgot to take my umbrella. I got wet in the rain.

A. I forgot to take my umbrella, so I got wet in the rain.

B. I got wet in the rain because I forgot my umbrella.

3. The astronomer could not see clearly. The night was cloudy.

A. The night was cloudy, so the astronomer could not see clearly.

B. The astronomer could not see clearly because the night was cloudy.

4. I love animals. I want to be a veterinarian someday.

A. I love animals, so I want to be a veterinarian someday.

B. I want to be a veterinarian someday because I love animals.

Write two sets of cause and effect sentences about any subject.

A. _____

B. _____

A. _____

B. _____

Sentences will vary.

page 177

Prize Words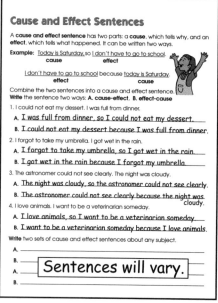

Fill in the blanks. Each spelling word is used only once.

1. **One** is to **once** as **two** is to __twice__
2. **Reverse** is to **forward** as **sit** is to __arise__
3. **Book** is to **library** as **typewriter** is to __office__
4. **Shiny** is to **dull** as **foolish** is to __wise__
5. **Teacher** is to **education** as **judge** is to __justice__
6. **Illness** is to **doctor** as **crime** is to __police officer__
7. **Tag** is to **label** as **cost** is to __price__
8. **1, 2, 3** is to **count** as **A, B, C** is to __alphabetize__
9. **Imagine** is to **think** as **guess** is to __surmise__
10. **Wordy** is to **long-winded** as **brief** is to __concise__

alphabetize	memorize	service
arise	office	surmise
concise	police	surprise
enterprise	price	twice
justice	prize	wise

Use the remaining words from the list to **answer** each question.

1. What do you usually get when you win a contest?

__prize__.

2. What do actors do with their lines? __memorize__.

3. What is a risky or important project? __enterprise__.

4. What is a synonym for "helpfulness"? __service__.

5. What is a synonym for "astonish"? __surprise__.

page 178

Guide-Worthy Words

Use a pencil to **write** ten vocabulary words from the box under each of the guide words. Remember to put them in alphabetical order.

Reflection	Syllable		Abrupt	Authority
reindeer	scowl		accidently	ammunition
resolute	stance		accustom	ancient
retort	stealth		additional	appoint
salute	subside		allow	ashamed
schoolmaster	surpass		almanac	assign

Babyhood	Crest		Defense	Exult
barometer	commerce		defiant	earthenware
barracks	commotion		demoralize	enormous
beneficial	consternation		discard	entirely
burrow	cordial		disposition	epidemic
calamity	corporal		disturbance	explosive

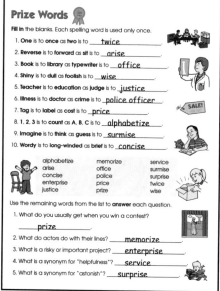

burrow	commerce	cordial	corporal	accustom
accidently	barracks	barometer	explosive	schoolmaster
stealth	allow	calamity	stance	defiant
epidemic	ancient	scowl	discard	ammunition
disturbance	subside	salute	reindeer	consternation
assign	demoralize	disposition	appoint	beneficial
resolute	enormous	ashamed	retort	entirely
earthenware	additional	commotion	almanac	surpass

page 179

Learn at Home, Grade 4

Weird Words

Use a dictionary to help you **answer** the questions using complete sentences.

1. Which would you use to treat a sore throat: a **gargoyle** or a **gargle**?
   I would use a gargle to treat a sore throat.

2. Which might be used on a gravestone: an **epiphyte** or an **epitaph**?
   An epitaph might be used on a gravestone.

3. Which is an instrument: **calligraphy** or a **calliope**?
   A calliope is an instrument.

4. Would a building have a **gargoyle** or an **argyle** on it?
   A building would have a gargoyle.

5. If you trick someone, do you **bamboozle** him or **barcarole** him?
   If you trick someone you bamboozle him.

6. If you studied handwriting, would you learn **calligraphy** or **cajolery**?
   If you studied handwriting, you would learn calligraphy.

7. What would a gondolier sing: a **barcarole** or an **argyle**?
   A gondolier would sing a barcarole.

8. If you tried to coax someone, would you be using **cajolery** or **calamity**?
   If you tried to coax someone, you might use cajolery.

9. Which might you wear: **argyles** or **calliopes**?
   You might wear argyles.

10. In Venice, Italy, would you travel in a **gondola** or a **calamity**?
    In Venice, Italy, you would travel in a gondola.

page 180

Figure Finding

Find Figure 1 in Design 1 and shade it. Do this for each shape. The figure may be turned, and it may not be the same size.

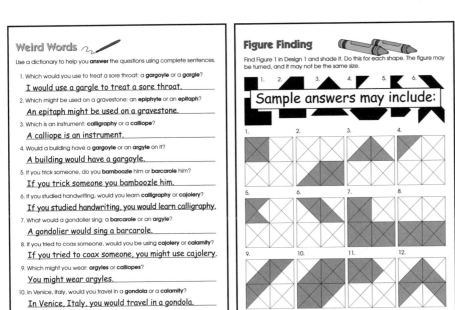

Sample answers may include:

page 181

Connect the Dots

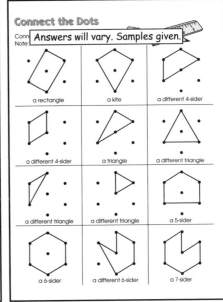

Answers will vary. Samples given.

a rectangle	a kite	a different 4-sider
a different 4-sider	a triangle	a different triangle
a different triangle	a different triangle	a 5-sider
a 6-sider	a different 6-sider	a 7-sider

page 182

The Rocket Puzzle

The rocket has four parts. **Cut** them apart.
The rocket can change itself into many shapes.
Use all 4 pieces to make each shape below.

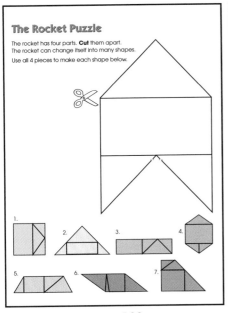

page 183

Run-On Sentences

A **sentence** expresses a clear thought. But if two or more sentences are written together without punctuation, their meaning is confusing. This is called a **run-on sentence**.
Example: The artist has painted twenty portraits the paintings will be displayed in the new museum.
   The artist has painted twenty portraits.
   The paintings will be displayed in the new museum.

Read each diary entry below. **Rewrite** each run-on sentence as two or more good sentences.

Dear Diary,
   After lunch we went to the animal shelter the cages were full of adorable pets to adopt we chose a frisky two-year-old brown dog.
   After lunch we went to the animal shelter. The cages were full of adorable pets to adopt. We chose a frisky two-year-old brown dog.

Dear Diary,
   While we were on our field trip my friend, Joe, found an animal fossil Mrs. Roberts is taking it to the university tomorrow.
   While we were on a field trip, my friend, Joe, found an animal fossil. Mrs. Roberts is taking it to the university tomorrow.

page 188

Elf on an Elephant

Use the spelling words to **fill in** the blanks.
Look for a cause/effect relationship in each situation.

1. **cause:** cutting in __half__
   effect: sharing a candy bar

2. **cause:** having a __cough__
   effect: covering your mouth

3. **cause:** hearing the __telephone__
   effect: answering "hello"

4. **cause:** reading about an __elf__
   effect: enjoying a fairy tale

5. **cause:** telling a joke
   effect: hearing __laughter__

6. **cause:** having a __sniffle__
   effect: blowing your nose

Complete these statements by **filling in** the blanks.

1. An antonym for "alike" is __different__
2. An antonym for "fragile" is __tough__
3. An antonym for "smooth" is __rough__
4. A kind of beverage is __coffee__
5. The word that is a pronoun is __oneself__

Four words have not been used. Use two of them in one sentence and the other two in a separate sentence. Underline the words.

Answers will vary.

coffee
cough
different
elephant
elf
enough
graph
half
laughter
oneself
photo
rough
sniffle
telephone
tough

page 189

Learn at Home, Grade 4

Double Negatives

Only use one negative word in a sentence.
Not, **no**, **never** and **none** are negative words.

Examples:

Incorrect: No one nowhere was sad when it started to snow.
Correct: No one anywhere was sad when it started to snow.

Incorrect: There weren't no icicles hanging from the roof.
Correct: There weren't any icicles hanging from the roof.

Underline the word in parentheses to say no correctly.

1. There wasn't (no, <u>any</u>) snow on our grass this morning.
2. I couldn't find anyone (nowhere, <u>anywhere</u>) who wanted to build a snowman.
3. We couldn't believe that (<u>no one</u>, anyone) wanted to stay inside today with all the beautiful snow outside to play in.
4. We shouldn't ask (<u>anyone</u>, no one) to go ice skating with us.
5. None of the students could think of (nothing, <u>anything</u>) to do at recess except play in the newly fallen snow!
6. No one (never, <u>ever</u>) thought it was a waste of time to go ice skating on the pond.
7. Not a single student skiing (nowhere, <u>anywhere</u>) was unhappy yesterday!

Replace the negative in parentheses correctly.

1. You shouldn't (never) **ever** play catch with a snowball unless you like to be covered with snow.
2. Isn't (no one) **anyone** going to join me outside to eat icicles?
3. There wasn't (nothing) **anything** wrong with using the clean, fresh snow to make our fruit drinks.
4. The snowman outside isn't (nowhere) **nearly** as large as the statue in front of our school.
5. Falling isn't (no) **any** fun if you can't go out and play in it.

page 194

You Are Beautiful

argue
beautiful
beauty
cue
feud
few
hue
mew
newt
pew
queue
review
view
you
yule

Write the spelling words that contain the letters **ew** or **iew** (as the **yoo** sound) in alphabetical order.

1. few
2. mew
3. newt
4. pew
5. review
6. view

Use the spelling words to **fill in** the blanks. Not all words are used; one is used twice.

1. TV announcers read from c u e cards.
2. It's good manners to say "Thank y o u" when someone gives you something.
3. A cat says m e w.
4. A church seat is called a p e w.
5. Christmas is sometimes called y u l e.
6. Roses are b e a u t i f u l flowers.
7. A hungry kitten says m e w.
8. Look at the v i e w out the window.
9. A salamander is related to a n e w t.
10. B e a u t y is only skin-deep.

Read the letters in the box to **answer** the question: What have you received if someone says, "You are beautiful"? **compliment**

What three spelling words have not been used?
argue   feud   hue

page 195

Circles and Squares

Shade the correct shapes to keep each pattern going.

Make your own patterns using two colors.

Answers will vary.

page 196

The Weird Worm Puzzle

- **Cut out** the Weird Worm.
- **Fold** on the dashed lines.
- **Trace** the fold lines on the back.
- **Fold** flat to make each shape below.

Parent check shapes against pictures.

page 197

Capitalize I, Names and Initials

The pronoun **I** is always capitalized. Each part of a person's or pet's name begins with a capital letter.

Examples: I, Mary Ann Smith, Lassie

An initial (the first letter of a name) is always capitalized and is followed by a period.

Example: M. A. Smith

Rewrite each sentence using capital letters correctly.

1. Where did molly parsons get her dog, laddie?
   Where did Molly Parsons get her dog, Laddie?
2. Her grandmother, louella cane, bought it for the family.
   Her grandmother, Louella Cane, bought it for the family.
3. The most unusual pet is tom simpson's parrot named showboat.
   The most unusual pet is Tom Simpson's parrot named Showboat.
4. I have heard showboat say words quite clearly.
   I have heard Showboat say words quite clearly.
5. Tom says his parrot's full name is a. h. showboat.
   Tom says his parrot's full name is A. H. Showboat.
6. What do the initials a. h. stand for?
   What do the initials A. H. stand for?
7. tom told me that his parrot's first name is always and his middle name is hungry. Tom told me that his parrot's first name is Always and his middle name is Hungry.
8. i call my dog "m. m." instead of megan mae.
   I call my dog "M. M." instead of Megan Mae.

Follow each direction carefully.

1. Write your full name. **Answers will vary.**
2. Write the full name and initials of one of your parents.
   Answers will vary.
3. Use the pronoun "I" to tell what you like to eat best.
   Answers will vary.

page 202

Commas With Compound Sentences

A **compound sentence** contains two simple sentences joined by a comma and a connecting word such as "and." The simple sentences must be about the same topic.

Example: Jane helps prepare dinner, and Pat sets the table.

Write compound on the line if it is a compound sentence and add the needed comma. **Write no** on the line if it is not a compound sentence.

1. The porpoise looks very much like a fish. — no
2. It is a mammal, and it bears its young alive. — compound
3. The porpoise resembles and is closely related to the dolphin. — no
4. The top of a porpoise is mostly black, and its underside is white. — compound
5. It searches out and eats small fish and shellfish. — no
6. A mother porpoise has just one baby, and that baby is large. — compound
7. The mother nurses the baby while swimming through the water. — no
8. Porpoises seem to like humans, and they have saved people who were drowning. — compound
9. Porpoises are social animals and swim in large groups. — no
10. Porpoises often travel with tuna, and they are sometimes caught in the tuna nets. — compound

Use a comma and the word and to combine each pair of sentences.

1. Most species of dolphins live only in salt water. They can be found in almost all the oceans. **Most species of dolphins live only in salt water, and they can be found in almost all the oceans.**
2. The word "dolphin" also refers to a big game fish. This fish is good to eat.
   The word "dolphin" also refers to a big game fish, and this fish is good to eat.

page 203

Learn at Home, Grade 4

What a Day!

Read the story that goes with each picture. **Write** the word which best describes each day on the line.

special   unlucky   hectic   relaxing   energetic

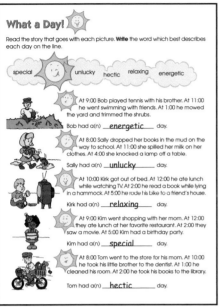

At 9:00 Bob played tennis with his brother. At 11:00 he went swimming with friends. At 1:00 he mowed the yard and trimmed the shrubs.

Bob had a(n) __energetic__ day.

At 8:00 Sally dropped her books in the mud on the way to school. At 11:00 she spilled her milk on her clothes. At 4:00 she knocked a lamp off a table.

Sally had a(n) __unlucky__ day.

At 10:00 Kirk got out of bed. At 12:00 he ate lunch while watching TV. At 2:00 he read a book while lying in a hammock. At 5:00 he rode his bike to a friend's house.

Kirk had a(n) __relaxing__ day.

At 9:00 Kim went shopping with her mom. At 12:00 they ate lunch at her favorite restaurant. At 2:00 they saw a movie. At 5:00 Kim had a birthday party.

Kim had a(n) __special__ day.

At 8:00 Tom went to the store for his mom. At 10:00 he took his little brother to the dentist. At 1:00 he cleaned his room. At 2:00 he took his books to the library.

Tom had a(n) __hectic__ day.

page 204

Lucky Beth or Lucky Kim?

Kim thinks Beth is so lucky. Almost every day, Beth comes to school with something new. One day, she might be wearing a new outfit her mom bought her at the department store where her mom works. The next day, Beth may have something really unique from her father, like a watch that has the days of the week in a foreign language. He brings her gifts when he comes home from traveling on business.

Beth, however, does not think she is so lucky. Beth's mom works until 7 p.m. every night and also has to work every Saturday. Her father travels so much with his job, that Beth is lucky if she gets to see him one week a month. Beth loves her parents, but she wishes they were both home every night and every weekend like Kim's parents so they could do special things together. She also wishes she had a little brother like Kim does so she wouldn't be so lonely.

Check:
Kim thinks Beth is lucky because Beth . . .
- [x] gets lots of neat gifts.
- [ ] doesn't have a brother or sister.
- [ ] has a father who travels a lot.

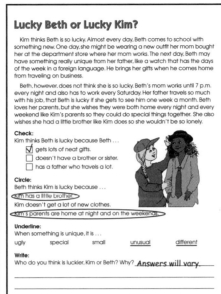

Circle:
Beth thinks Kim is lucky because . . .
(Kim has a little brother.)
Kim doesn't get a lot of new clothes.
(Kim's parents are home at night and on the weekends.)

Underline:
When something is unique, it is . . .
ugly   special   small   __unusual__   __different__

Write:
Who do you think is luckier, Kim or Beth? Why? __Answers will vary.__

page 205

Shootin' Hoops

Shoot some hoops but make sure that you shoot them alphabetically into the correct basket. **Write** the words from the basketballs into the correct hoop.

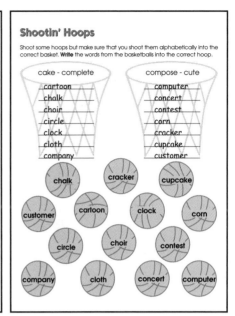

cake - complete
- cartoon
- chalk
- choir
- circle
- clock
- cloth
- company

compose - cute
- computer
- concert
- contest
- corn
- cracker
- cupcake
- customer

chalk   cracker   cupcake
customer   cartoon   clock   corn
circle   choir   contest
company   cloth   concert   computer

page 206

Work It Out

The **average** is the result of dividing the **sum** of addends by the **number** of addends. **Match** the problem with its answer.

$$\begin{array}{r} 62 \\ 79 \\ +87 \\ \hline 228 \end{array} \longrightarrow \begin{array}{r} 76 \\ 3)\overline{228} \end{array}$$

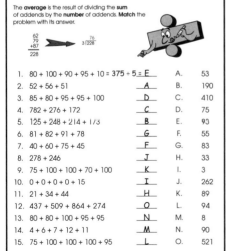

1. 80 + 100 + 90 + 95 + 10 = 375 ÷ 5 = __E__   A. 53
2. 52 + 56 + 51   __A__   B. 190
3. 85 + 80 + 95 + 100   __D__   C. 410
4. 782 + 276 + 172   __C__   D. 75
5. 125 + 248 + 214 + 173   __B__   E. 93
6. 81 + 82 + 91 + 78   __G__   F. 55
7. 40 + 60 + 75 + 45   __F__   G. 83
8. 278 + 246   __J__   H. 33
9. 75 + 100 + 100 + 70 + 100   __K__   I. 3
10. 0 + 0 + 0 + 15   __I__   J. 262
11. 21 + 34 + 44   __H__   K. 89
12. 437 + 509 + 864 + 274   __O__   L. 94
13. 80 + 80 + 100 + 95 + 95   __N__   M. 8
14. 4 + 6 + 7 + 12 + 11   __M__   N. 90
15. 75 + 100 + 100 + 100 + 95   __L__   O. 521

page 207

Number Puzzles

Answers will vary.

Examples:

1
Write your age.   __10__
Multiply it by 3.   __30__
Add 18.   __48__
Multiply by 2.   __96__
Subtract 36.   __60__
Divide by 6. (your age) __10__

2
Write any number.   __20__
Double that number.   __40__
Add 15.   __55__
Double again.   __110__
Subtract 30.   __80__
Divide by 2.   __40__
Divide by 2 again.   __20__

3
Write any 2-digit number. __11__
Double that number.   __22__
Add 43.   __65__
Subtract 18.   __47__
Add 11.   __58__
Divide by 2.   __29__
Subtract 18.   __11__

4
Write the number of children in your neighborhood. __15__
Double that number.   __30__
Add 15.   __45__
Double it again.   __90__
Subtract 30.   __60__
Divide by 4.   __15__

page 208

"State"istics

Numbers are approximate.

State Name	Approximate Miles L - W	Approximate Miles N - S	Area in Square Miles
Alabama			50,000
Alaska			587,000
Arizona			115,000
Arkansas			53,000
California			158,000
Colorado			104,000
Connecticut			5,000
Delaware			2,000
Florida			59,000
Georgia			59,000
Hawaii			6,000
Idaho			84,000
Illinois			56,000
Indiana			36,000
Iowa			56,000
Kansas			82,000
Kentucky			40,000
Louisiana			48,000
Maine			33,000
Maryland			10,000
Massachusetts			8,000
Michigan			59,000
Minnesota			84,000
Mississippi			48,000
Missouri			70,000

State Name	Approximate Miles L - W	Approximate Miles N - S	Area in Square Miles
Montana			147,000
Nebraska			77,000
Nevada			110,000
New Hampshire			9,000
New Jersey			8,000
New Mexico			122,000
New York			49,000
North Carolina			53,000
North Dakota			70,000
Ohio			41,000
Oklahoma			70,000
Oregon			97,000
Pennsylvania			45,000
Rhode Island			1,000
South Carolina			31,000
South Dakota			77,000
Tennessee			42,000
Texas			267,000
Utah			85,000
Vermont			10,000
Virginia			41,000
Washington			68,000
West Virginia			24,000
Wisconsin			56,000
Wyoming			98,000

page 209

End Punctuation

A **statement** ends with a period. (.)
A **question** ...
A **comma** ...
An **excl**...

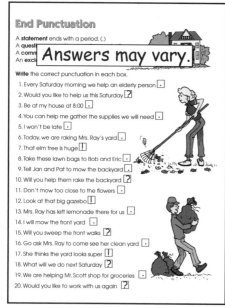
Answers may vary.

Write the correct punctuation in each box.

1. Every Saturday morning we help an elderly person [.]
2. Would you like to help us this Saturday [?]
3. Be at my house at 8:00 [.]
4. You can help me gather the supplies we will need [.]
5. I won't be late [.]
6. Today, we are raking Mrs. Ray's yard [.]
7. That elm tree is huge [!]
8. Take these lawn bags to Bob and Eric [.]
9. Tell Jan and Pat to mow the backyard [.]
10. Will you help them rake the backyard [?]
11. Don't mow too close to the flowers [.]
12. Look at that big gazebo [!]
13. Mrs. Ray has left lemonade there for us [.]
14. I will mow the front yard [.]
15. Will you sweep the front walks [?]
16. Go ask Mrs. Ray to come see her clean yard [.]
17. She thinks the yard looks super [.]
18. What will we do next Saturday [?]
19. We are helping Mr. Scott shop for groceries [.]
20. Would you like to work with us again [?]

page 214

"X"citing Words

anxious
ax
boxes
coax
example
except
excuse
exercise
Mexico
saxophone
sixteen
sixth
taxes
Texas
toxic

Fill in the blanks.

1. Write the two proper nouns and circle the country.

   Texas   (Mexico)

2. A synonym for "eager" is **anxious**.
3. One **example** of a reed instrument is a **saxophone**.
4. A synonym for "persuade" is **coax**.
5. Another word for "hatchet" is **ax**.
6. Which word is a preposition? **except**
7. Which word refers to poison? **toxic**
8. Which word refers to money collected by the government? **taxes**
9. There were **sixteen** **boxes** of toys for the children in the flooded town.
10. Jogging is a type of **exercise**.
11. He celebrated his **sixth** birthday on the last day of kindergarten.
12. Jane's father did not believe her **excuse**.

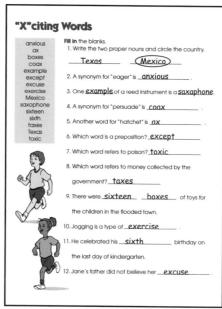

page 215

Recalling Details

Read *Jackie Robinson*. Then **write** the answer to each question on the lines.

1. Where is the Baseball Hall of Fame located? **C**ooperstown, New York
2. Who was the first African American to play professional baseball? **B**(u)d Fowler
3. What is it called when baseball teams travel the countryside playing games? **B**arnstorming
4. What did Rube Foster start in 1920? **N**egro N(a)tional League
5. What baseball team made history on April 15, 1947, by having Jackie Robinson in the lineup? **B**rooklyn Dodgers
6. Who was called the "Black Babe Ruth" because he hit so many home runs? **J**osh **G**ibson
7. What position did Satchel Paige play? **P**itcher
8. Who was the president and general manager of the team that hired Jackie Robinson? **B**ranch Rickey
9. Who was the first African American elected to to the Baseball Hall of Fame? **J**ackie Robinso(n)
10. For what team did Judy Johnson, Oscar Charleston, and Cool Pappa Bell play? **P**i(t)tsburgh Crawfords
11. In 1948, Satchel Paige helped what American League team win the World Series? **C**leveland Indian(s)

Write the circled letters in order on the lines to find out the name of the first all-black baseball team. **Cuban Giants**

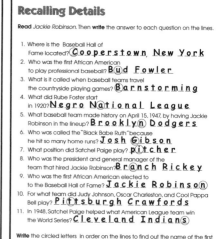

page 216

Is It Fiction Or Nonfiction?

Write on the blank **fiction** or **nonfiction**.

1. *The Chicken and the Dragon* by Arthur C. Feather. This is the story of a dragon who helps a chicken remember his way home.
   Fiction
2. *The Planets* by Peter Starlight. This book describes the planets in our solar system. Descriptions and pictures of each planet are included.
   Nonfiction
3. *Explorers Go to America* by James Boat. This book gives the routes the explorers took to America. Maps and illustrations are given.
   Nonfiction
4. *Pinky, the French Poodle* by James Poof-Poof. This is the story of a French poodle with pink fur.
   Fiction
5. *Dinosaurs of Long Ago* by Peter Tail. This book tells the types of dinosaurs that lived long ago.
   Nonfiction
6. *Dogs and Their Owners* by Roger Leash. This book describes the types of ways to train your dog.
   Nonfiction
7. *How To Start Your Aquarium* by Peter Fish. This book tells what to buy and how to put it together.
   Nonfiction
8. *Sports Legends* by Alvin Bat. This book describes the lives of famous sports stars.
   Nonfiction
9. *Flower Designs* by Hilda Vase. This book tells how to arrange flowers for special occasions.
   Nonfiction
10. *Hamsters! Hamsters! Hamsters!* by Roger Pellet. This book tells how to train and care for your hamster.
    Nonfiction

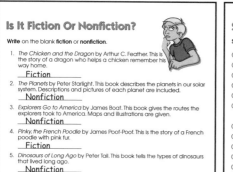

page 217

Skill Search

Answers may vary.

Search throu...

(p. 5) 1. Four proper nouns: **Ebbet's Field, Jackie Robinson**
(p. 6) 2. The words before each question mark: **player, special**
(p. 7) 3. Three number words: **twenty-seven, first, twentieth**
(p. 9) 4. Two contractions: **doesn't, he's**
(p. 10) 5. The name of a train: **Jackie Robinson Special**
(p. 11) 6. Five words with three syllables: **beginning, seventy, Robinson, history, forgotten**
(p. 12) 7. The name of a war: **Civil War**
(p. 14) 8. Four Giant teams: **Cuban, Leland, Columbia, Cuban X**
(p. 15) 9. Two hyphenated words: **all-white, out-of-the-way**
(p. 18) 10. Two color words: **black, white**
(p. 19) 11. Five words with **ed** suffixes: **wanted, respected, started, called, turned**
(p. 20) 12. Three compound words: **powerhouse, baseball, spitball**
(p. 21) 13. A three-syllable word: **important**
(p. 22) 14. Five **long a** words: **players, made, games, way, bases**
(p. 23) 15. Words beginning with these consonant blends:
   bl **ack**   pl **ayers**   st **adiums**   cr **owds**
(p. 24) 16. Four different years: **1920, 1926, 1930, 1940**
(p. 26) 17. Three adjectives to describe Satchel Paige: **tall, thin, skinny**
(p. 36) 18. The name of a state: **Indiana**
(p. 39) 19. Seven words with double consonants: **college, football, basketball, baseball, officers, all, arrest**

page 218

What Fraction Am I?

Identify the fraction for each shaded section.

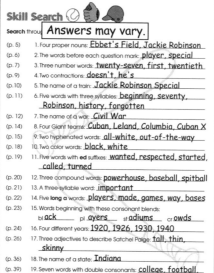

A. $\frac{4}{12} = \frac{1}{3}$
B. $\frac{3}{6} = \frac{1}{2}$
C. $\frac{2}{7}$
D. $\frac{1}{3}$
E. $\frac{4}{8} = \frac{1}{2}$
F. $\frac{1}{2}$
G. $\frac{1}{5}$
H. $\frac{2}{5}$
I. $\frac{2}{4} = \frac{1}{4}$
J. $\frac{2}{8} = \frac{1}{4}$
K. $\frac{5}{16}$
L. $\frac{1}{4}$
M. $\frac{7}{27}$

page 219

No Troubles With Doubles

across
afford
battle
goddess
copper
difference
difficult
gallon
message
official
recess
success
suppose
terrible
traffic

Fill in the blanks. One spelling word is used twice.

1. Write the three-syllable words and divide them into syllables. _difference_ _difficult_ _terrible_ _official_

2. Our secretary wrote down the telephone _message_ for our boss.

3. Which word names a metal? _copper_

4. Which word refers to a lot of vehicles? _traffic_

5. The in-line skates were so expensive that Jill had to save money before she could _afford_ them.

6. Write the four words which do not have syllable divisions between some of their double letters. _across_ _recess_ _success_ _goddess_

7. Of the three words that have not been used, which one is always a verb? _suppose_

8. Which word names a measurement? _gallon_ Name an item sold in this quantity. _milk_ Answers will vary.

9. Use the remaining spelling word in a sentence. _Sentence will vary. (battle)_

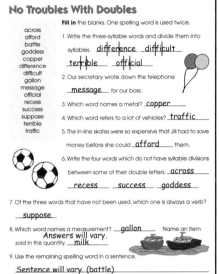

page 224

Descriptive Sentences

Turn a good sentence into a great sentence by using more descriptive words.

Example: The dog chased the boy. The big brown dog playfully chased the little boy.

Add descriptive words to make each a great sentence. **Write** the improved sentence on each line.

1. The man climbed the mountain.
Example: The old man climbed slowly up the steep mountain.

2. The group found a buried tomb.
Example: The archaeological group found an ancient buried tomb.

3. The girls painted a sign.

4. The sunlight came through the window.

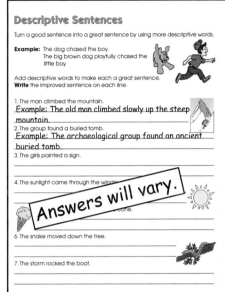

Answers will vary.

6. The snake moved down the tree.

7. The storm rocked the boat.

page 230

Is the Bear Bare?

bare
bear
berry
bury
groan
grown
hall
haul
pain
pane
raise
rays
stair
stare
wait
weight

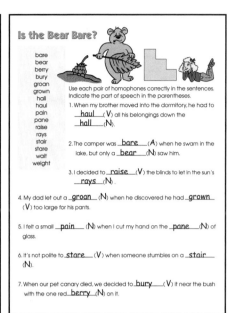

Use each pair of homophones correctly in the sentences. Indicate the part of speech in the parentheses.

1. When my brother moved into the dormitory, he had to _haul_ (V) all his belongings down the _hall_ (N).

2. The camper was _bare_ (A) when he swam in the lake, but only a _bear_ (N) saw him.

3. I decided to _raise_ (V) the blinds to let in the sun's _rays_ (N).

4. My dad let out a _groan_ (N) when he discovered he had _grown_ (V) too large for his pants.

5. I felt a small _pain_ (N) when I cut my hand on the _pane_ (N) of glass.

6. It's not polite to _stare_ (V) when someone stumbles on a _stair_ (N).

7. When our pet canary died, we decided to _bury_ (V) it near the bush with the one red _berry_ (N) on it.

page 231

Bubble Math

Reduce each sum to a whole number or a mixed number in lowest terms.

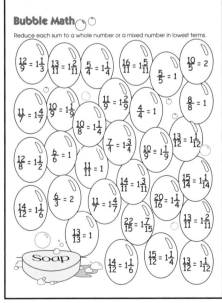

$\frac{12}{9} = 1\frac{1}{3}$ $\frac{13}{11} = 1\frac{2}{11}$ $\frac{5}{4} = 1\frac{1}{4}$ $\frac{16}{11} = 1\frac{5}{11}$ $\frac{10}{5} = 2$

$\frac{5}{5} = 1$

$\frac{11}{7} = 1\frac{4}{7}$ $\frac{10}{9} = 1\frac{1}{9}$ $\frac{11}{9} = 1\frac{2}{9}$ $\frac{4}{4} = 1$ $\frac{8}{8} = 1$

$\frac{10}{8} = 1\frac{1}{4}$

$\frac{7}{4} = 1\frac{3}{4}$ $\frac{10}{9} = 1\frac{1}{9}$ $\frac{13}{12} = 1\frac{1}{12}$

$\frac{12}{8} = 1\frac{1}{2}$ $\frac{6}{6} = 1$

$\frac{11}{11} = 1$

$\frac{14}{11} = 1\frac{3}{11}$ $\frac{15}{14} = 1\frac{1}{14}$

$\frac{14}{12} = 1\frac{1}{6}$ $\frac{11}{7} = 1\frac{4}{7}$ $\frac{20}{16} = 1\frac{1}{4}$

$\frac{6}{3} = 2$

$\frac{13}{13} = 1$ $\frac{22}{15} = 1\frac{7}{15}$ $\frac{13}{11} = 1\frac{2}{11}$

$\frac{14}{12} = 1\frac{1}{6}$ $\frac{15}{12} = 1\frac{1}{4}$ $\frac{13}{12} = 1\frac{1}{12}$

page 232

Crazy Quilts

Toni and her mother made a crazy quilt. It doesn't have a set pattern; the pieces are many colors and sizes. Read each story problem. **Circle** the correct problem, and **write** the answer on the line.

1. Toni had $\frac{4}{8}$ of a yard of yellow gingham. She used $\frac{3}{8}$ of a yard to make two triangles for the quilt. How much yellow gingham did she have left?
$\frac{3}{8} - \frac{2}{8}$ ($\frac{6}{8} - \frac{3}{8}$) $\frac{6}{8} + \frac{2}{8}$ _$\frac{3}{8}$ yd._

2. Toni's mother found $\frac{5}{10}$ of a yard of red velvet material. She made a rectangle from $\frac{2}{10}$ of a yard. How much red velvet did she have left?
($\frac{5}{10} - \frac{2}{10}$) $\frac{5}{10} + \frac{2}{10}$ $\frac{5}{10} \times \frac{5}{10}$ _$\frac{3}{10}$ yd._

3. Mother and Toni liked to sew black satin between the red and yellow pieces. They had $\frac{3}{4}$ of a yard of black satin. They used $\frac{1}{4}$ of a yard to place between the red and yellow pieces. How much black satin did they have left?
($\frac{3}{4} - \frac{1}{4}$) $\frac{3}{4} - \frac{3}{4}$ $\frac{2}{4} + \frac{3}{4}$ _$\frac{2}{4}$ yd. ($\frac{1}{2}$ yd.)_

4. Toni had $\frac{2}{3}$ of an hour before her piano lesson. She wanted to make one more blue piece. It took her $\frac{1}{3}$ of an hour to make the blue piece. What fraction of an hour did she have left to get ready for her piano lesson?
$\frac{1}{3} + \frac{1}{3}$ ($\frac{2}{3} - \frac{1}{3}$) $\frac{2}{4} + \frac{1}{4}$ _$\frac{1}{3}$ hr._

5. Mother and Toni finished $\frac{4}{8}$ of the quilt. Toni did $\frac{1}{8}$ of it herself. How much did Mother do?
$\frac{1}{8} + \frac{4}{8}$ $\frac{3}{8} + \frac{4}{8}$ ($\frac{4}{8} - \frac{1}{8}$)   _$\frac{3}{8}$_

6. Toni and her mother wanted to give the quilt to Grandmother for her birthday. They used purple cotton to make the edging. They had $\frac{6}{8}$ of a yard of the purple cloth. They used $\frac{5}{8}$ of a yard to make the edging. How much purple cloth did they have left?
$\frac{6}{8} \times \frac{5}{8}$ ($\frac{6}{8} - \frac{5}{9}$) $\frac{6}{8} - \frac{5}{8}$ _$\frac{1}{8}$ yd._

page 233

Expanding Sentences

You can s-t-r-e-t-c-h a sentence by adding more information. Stretch these sentences by adding words to **answer** each question.

Example: The plane landed. When? The plane landed at 1:30 p.m.

Example:
1. We are all going to the airport. How?
We are going to the airport on a bus.

2. I am taking three pieces of luggage. Why?

3. The passengers are lined up. Why?

4. The baggage was stacked. Where?

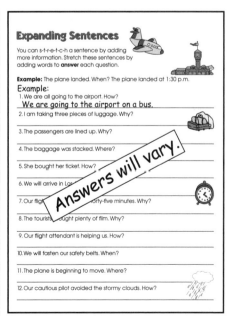
Answers will vary.

6. We will arrive in Los Angeles. When?

7. Our flight will last forty-five minutes. Why?

8. The tourists bought plenty of film. Why?

9. Our flight attendant is helping us. How?

10. We will fasten our safety belts. When?

11. The plane is beginning to move. Where?

12. Our cautious pilot avoided the stormy clouds. How?

page 238

Twice the Fun

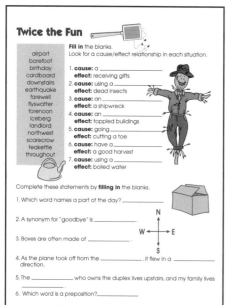

airport
barefoot
birthday
cardboard
downstairs
earthquake
farewell
flyswatter
forenoon
iceberg
landlord
northwest
scarecrow
teakettle
throughout

Fill in the blanks.
Look for a cause/effect relationship in each situation.

1. **cause:** a
   effect: receiving gifts
2. **cause:** using a
   effect: dead insects
3. **cause:** an
   effect: a shipwreck
4. **cause:** an
   effect: toppled buildings
5. **cause:** going
   effect: cutting a toe
6. **cause:** have a
   effect: a good harvest
7. **cause:** using a
   effect: boiled water

Complete these statements by **filling in** the blanks.

1. Which word names a part of the day? _____

2. A synonym for "goodbye" is _____

3. Boxes are often made of _____

4. As the plane took off from the _____, it flew in a _____ direction.

5. The _____ who owns the duplex lives upstairs, and my family lives _____

6. Which word is a preposition? _____

page 239

Picture the Problem

Use the picture to solve the problem.

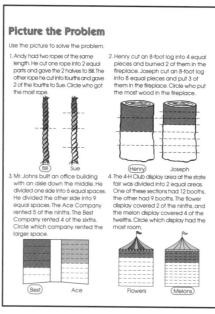

1. Andy had two ropes of the same length. He cut one rope into 2 equal parts and gave the 2 halves to Bill. The other rope he cut into fourths and gave 2 of the fourths to Sue. Circle who got the most rope.

2. Henry cut an 8-foot log into 4 equal pieces and burned 2 of them in the fireplace. Joseph cut an 8-foot log into 8 equal pieces and put 3 of them in the fireplace. Circle who put the most wood in the fireplace.

3. Mr. Johns built an office building with an aisle down the middle. He divided one side into 6 equal spaces. He divided the other side into 9 equal spaces. The Ace Company rented 5 of the ninths. The Best Company rented 4 of the sixths. Circle which company rented the larger space.

4. The 4-H Club display area at the state fair was divided into 2 equal areas. One of these sections had 12 booths, the other had 9 booths. The flower display covered 2 of the ninths, and the melon display covered 4 of the twelfths. Circle which display had the most room.

page 240

Dare To Compare

Compare the fractions below. Use >, < and =.

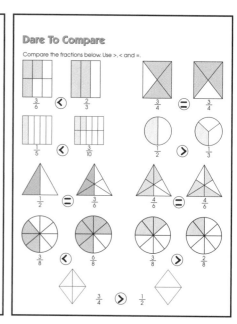

$\frac{3}{6}$ < $\frac{2}{3}$ $\frac{3}{4}$ = $\frac{3}{4}$

$\frac{1}{5}$ < $\frac{3}{10}$ $\frac{1}{2}$ > $\frac{1}{3}$

$\frac{1}{2}$ = $\frac{3}{6}$ $\frac{4}{6}$ = $\frac{4}{6}$

$\frac{3}{8}$ < $\frac{6}{8}$ $\frac{3}{8}$ > $\frac{2}{8}$

$\frac{3}{4}$ > $\frac{1}{2}$

page 241

Tricky Y

batteries
cowboys
delays
donkeys
gravies
ivies
ladies
Mondays
pennies
ponies
stories
trays
Tuesdays
valleys
Wednesday

Write the singular (S) form of each spelling word. Then, **write** its plural (P) form below it. The first one is done for you.

1. (S) battery
   (P) batteries
2. (S) cowboy
   (P) cowboys
3. (S) delay
   (P) delays
4. (S) donkey
   (P) donkeys
5. (S) gravy
   (P) gravies
6. (S) ivy
   (P) ivies
7. (S) lady
   (P) ladies
8. (S) Monday
   (P) Mondays
9. (S) penny
   (P) pennies
10. (S) pony
    (P) ponies
11. (S) story
    (P) stories
12. (S) tray
    (P) trays
13. (S) Tuesday
    (P) Tuesdays
14. (S) valley
    (P) valleys
15. (S) Wednesday
    (P) Wednesdays

What part of speech is each of these words? **noun**

Which word can also be used as a verb? **delay**

How do you know when to change the y to an i before adding **es**?
If the letter before the y is a consonant, you need to change the y to i before adding es.

page 246

Match the Fractions

Above each bar, **write** a fraction for the shaded part. Then, **match** each fraction on the left with its equivalent fraction on the right.

1. $\frac{2}{6}$ — d   a. $\frac{4}{5}$
2. $\frac{2}{3}$ — f   b. $\frac{3}{5}$
3. $\frac{6}{10}$ — b   c. $\frac{2}{10}$
4. $\frac{2}{8}$ — g   d. $\frac{1}{3}$
5. $\frac{3}{6}$ — e   e. $\frac{1}{2}$
6. $\frac{8}{10}$ — a   f. $\frac{4}{6}$
7. $\frac{1}{5}$ — c   g. $\frac{1}{4}$

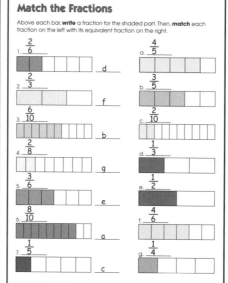

page 247

Paragraph Form

A **paragraph** is a group of sentences about one main idea. When writing a paragraph:
1. **Indent** the first line.
2. **Capitalize** the first word of each sentence.
3. **Punctuate** each sentence.
Example: There are many reasons to write a paragraph. A paragraph can describe something or tell a story. It can tell how something is made or give an opinion. Do you know other reasons to write a paragraph?

Read the _____ paragraphs correctly. _____

1. Inde

Answers may vary.

the number of teeth you have depends on your age a baby has no teeth at all gradually, milk teeth, or baby teeth, begin to grow later, these teeth fall out and permanent teeth appear by the age of twenty-five, you should have thirty-two permanent teeth

   The number of teeth you have depends on your age. A baby had no teeth at all. Gradually, milk teeth, or baby teeth begin to grow. Later, these teeth fall out and permanent teeth appear. By the age of twenty-five, you should have thirty-two permanent teeth.

my family is going to Disneyland tomorrow we plan to arrive early my dad will take my little sister to Fantasyland first meanwhile, my brother and I will visit Frontierland and Adventureland after lunch we will all meet to go to Tomorrowland

   My family is going to Disneyland tomorrow. We plan to arrive early. My dad will take my little sister to Fantasyland first. Meanwhile, my brother and I will visit Frontierland and Adventureland. After lunch we will all meet to go to Tomorrowland.

page 252

Learn at Home, Grade 4

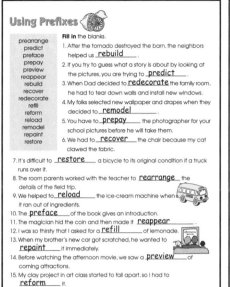

Using Prefixes

prearrange
predict
preface
prepay
preview
reappear
rebuild
recover
redecorate
refill
reform
reload
remodel
repaint
restore

Fill in the blanks.

1. After the tornado destroyed the barn, the neighbors helped us __rebuild__.
2. If you try to guess what a story is about by looking at the pictures, you are trying to __predict__.
3. When Dad decided to __redecorate__ the family room, he had to tear down walls and install new windows.
4. My folks selected new wallpaper and drapes when they decided to __remodel__.
5. You have to __prepay__ the photographer for your school pictures before he will take them.
6. We had to __recover__ the chair because my cat clawed the fabric.
7. It's difficult to __restore__ a bicycle to its original condition if a truck runs over it.
8. The room parents worked with the teacher to __rearrange__ the details of the field trip.
9. We helped to __reload__ the ice-cream machine when it ran out of ingredients.
10. The __preface__ of the book gives an introduction.
11. The magician hid the coin and then made it __reappear__.
12. I was so thirsty that I asked for a __refill__ of lemonade.
13. When my brother's new car got scratched, he wanted to __repaint__ it immediately.
14. Before watching the afternoon movie, we saw a __preview__ of coming attractions.
15. My clay project in art class started to fall apart, so I had to __reform__ it.

page 253

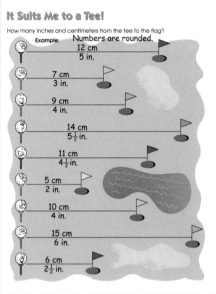

It Suits Me to a Tee!

How many inches and centimeters from the tee to the flag?

Example: Numbers are rounded.

12 cm
5 in.

7 cm
3 in.

9 cm
4 in.

14 cm
5½ in.

11 cm
4½ in.

5 cm
2 in.

10 cm
4 in.

15 cm
6 in.

6 cm
2½ in.

page 254

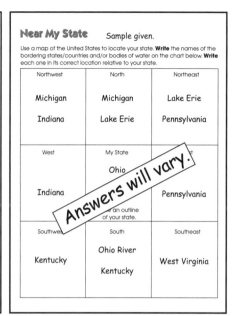

Near My State   Sample given.

Use a map of the United States to locate your state. **Write** the names of the bordering states/countries and/or bodies of water on the chart below. **Write** each one in its correct location relative to your state.

Northwest	North	Northeast
Michigan	Michigan	Lake Erie
Indiana	Lake Erie	Pennsylvania
West	My State	
Indiana	Ohio *Answers will vary.* an outline of your state.	Pennsylvania
Southwest	South	Southeast
Kentucky	Ohio River Kentucky	West Virginia

page 255

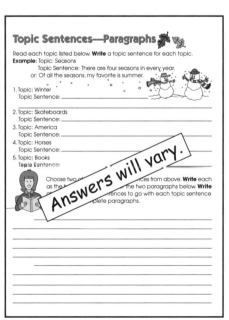

Topic Sentences—Paragraphs

Read each topic listed below. **Write** a topic sentence for each topic.
Example: Topic: Seasons
   Topic Sentence: There are four seasons in every year.
   or: Of all the seasons, my favorite is summer.

1. Topic: Winter
   Topic Sentence: _____

2. Topic: Skateboards
   Topic Sentence: _____

3. Topic: America
   Topic Sentence: _____

4. Topic: Horses
   Topic Sentence: _____

5. Topic: Books
   Topic Sentence: _____

Answers will vary.

Choose two ___ sentences from above. **Write** each
as the ___ two paragraphs below. **Write**
___ sentences to go with each topic sentence
___ plete paragraphs.

page 260

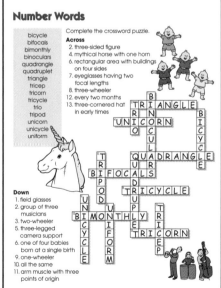

Number Words

bicycle
bifocals
bimonthly
binoculars
quadrangle
quadruplet
triangle
tricep
tricorn
tricycle
trio
tripod
unicorn
unicycle
uniform

Complete the crossword puzzle.

Across
2. three-sided figure
4. mythical horse with one horn
6. rectangular area with buildings on four sides
7. eyeglasses having two focal lengths
8. three-wheeler
12. every two months
13. three-cornered hat in early times

Down
1. field glasses
2. group of three musicians
3. two-wheeler
5. three-legged camera support
6. one of four babies born at a single birth
9. one-wheeler
10. all the same
11. arm muscle with three points of origin

Crossword answers:
TRIANGLE, UNICORN, BICYCLE, QUADRANGLE, BIFOCALS, TRIPOD, TRICYCLE, BIMONTHLY, TRICORN, UNICYCLE, UNIFORM, TRICEP

page 261

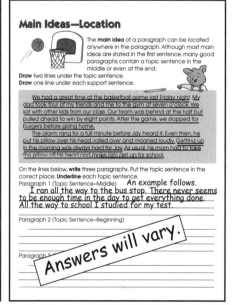

Main Ideas—Location

The **main idea** of a paragraph can be located anywhere in the paragraph. Although most main ideas are stated in the first sentence, many good paragraphs contain a topic sentence in the middle or even at the end.

Draw two lines under the topic sentence.
Draw one line under each support sentence.

We had a great time at the basketball game last Friday night. My dad took four of my friends and me to the gym at seven o'clock. We sat with other kids from our class. Our team was behind at the half but pulled ahead to win by eight points. After the game, we stopped for burgers before going home.

The alarm rang for a full minute before Jay heard it. Even then, he put his pillow over his head, rolled over and moaned loudly. Getting up in the morning was always hard for Jay. As usual, his mom had to take the pillow off his head and make him get up for school.

On the lines below, **write** three paragraphs. Put the topic sentence in the correct place. **Underline** each topic sentence.

Paragraph 1 (Topic Sentence–Middle)   An example follows.
I ran all the way to the bus stop. There never seems to be enough time in the day to get everything done. All the way to school I studied for my test.

Paragraph 2 (Topic Sentence–Beginning)

Paragraph 3   *Answers will vary.*

page 266

Support Sentences

The **topic sentence** gives the main idea of a paragraph. The **support sentences** give the details about the main idea. Each sentence must relate to the main idea.

Read the paragraph below. **Underline** the topic sentence. **Cross out** the sentence that is not a support sentence. On the line, **write** a support sentence to go in its place.

Giving a surprise birthday party can be exciting but tricky. The honored person must not hear a word about the party. On the day of the party, everyone should arrive early. A snack may ruin your appetite.

Example: *When the birthday person comes in, everyone will yell, "Surprise!"*

Write three support sentences to go with each topic sentence.

Giving a dog a bath can be a real challenge! Example:
1. First, you must make sure that you have supplies.
2. Then, you must convince your dog to stand still.
3. Finally, you must make sure that your dog is dried completely.
I can still remember how embarrassed I was that day!
1. _____
2. _____
3. _____

Sometimes I like to imagine what our ~~prob~~

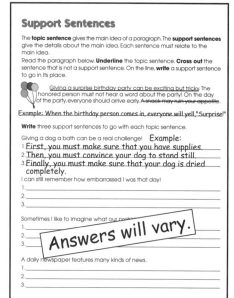
Answers will vary.

A daily newspaper features many kinds of news.
1. _____
2. _____
3. _____

page 267

Don't Be So Negative

discolor
dislike
disobey
distrust
nondairy
nonfat
nonsense
unbreakable
uncertain
unfair
unfold
unfriendly
unhappiness
unlucky
unselfish

Write the spelling word that closely matches each definition.

1. unjust	unfair
2. foolishness	nonsense
3. stain	discolor
4. unfortunate	unlucky
5. open; spread out	unfold
6. aversion to	dislike
7. suspicion; no confidence	distrust
8. sadness	unhappiness
9. cannot be easily broken	unbreakable
10. misbehave	disobey
11. lacking grease	nonfat
12. generous	unselfish
13. doubtful; questionable	uncertain
14. lacking milk	nondairy
15. hostile	unfriendly

What do all three prefixes mean? **not**

page 268

Who Is It?

Write the correct descriptions below each character's name.

- a very thorough planner
- knew the weather was in for a change
- risked his life to save a life
- always seems to get everything right
- was daring enough to throw a snowball
- daring as any boy
- destroyed the snowman
- became a very good leader
- wanted a chance for freedom in America
- loved the *Cleng Peerson*
- helped the children learn to load the gold
- wanted a shoe polisher

Uncle Victor
a very thorough planner
loved the *Cleng Peerson*

Peter Lundstrom
was daring enough to throw a snowball
became a very good leader

Per Garson
knew the weather was in for a change
helped the children learn to load the gold

Jan Lasek
risked his life to save a life
wanted a chance for freedom in America

Helga Thomsen
always seems to get everything right
daring as any boy

The Commandant
destroyed the snowman
wanted a shoe polisher

page 269

What Made It Happen?

Each set of sentences includes a cause and an effect. Remember: The cause is what makes something happen, and the effect is the result.
Write the cause on the line and **circle** the effect.

1. The snow came down harder than anyone could ever remember. (For days the people of the village were housebound.)
   The snow came down harder than anyone could ever remember.

2. Many of the soldiers decided to learn to ski. (The children called one soldier "Lieutenant Sit-Down," because he fell down more than he stood.)
   ...he fell down more than he stood.

3. The Commandant kept kicking the snowman covering the gold. (Peter threw a snowball to distract the Commandant from discovering the gold.)
   The Commandant kept kicking the snowman covering the gold.

4. (Per Garson was skiing in crazy patterns around and around the Lundstrom's house.) Uncle Victor had been there earlier on his skis.
   Uncle Victor had been there earlier on his skis.

5. Peter was sailing down the slope at high speed. In his path, he could see approaching soldiers. Peter was going so fast he could not stop his sled. (The soldiers scattered to let Peter through.)
   Peter was going so fast he could not stop his sled.

6. (Mrs. Holms seemed very excited to see the Lundstroms coming to her home. She acted as though she could not wait to speak.) Earlier in the day a German soldier had been in the Holms's barn.
   a German soldier had been in the Holms's barn.

page 270

Creative Endings

Many events occurred in the story because of well thought-out plans. Now it is your turn to do the thinking. Each of the following events have been given a new twist. **Write** what happens.

1. Uncle Victor was really a German Spy. With all of the gold he ...
   _____

2. Peter Lundstrom was unable to escape from the camp. The Commandant has called for him ...
   _____

3. Per Garson was wrong about ~~the~~ ...dren then decided to take ...

Answers will vary.

4. Jan Lasek accidentally led the troops to the hiding place of the Cleng Peerson ...
   _____

5. The Commandant ordered his doctor to examine the patients ...
   _____
   _____

page 271

Minute Monsters

The Minute Monsters have their pairs of shoes mixed-up. **Cut out** the shoes. **Glue** the matching pairs onto another paper.

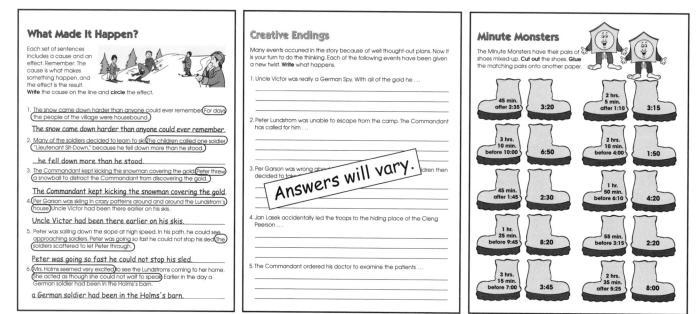

45 min. after 2:35	3:20
2 hrs. 5 min. after 1:10	3:15
3 hrs. 10 min. before 10:00	6:50
2 hrs. 10 min. before 4:00	1:50
45 min. after 1:45	2:30
1 hr. 50 min. before 6:10	4:20
1 hr. 25 min. before 9:45	8:20
55 min. before 3:15	2:20
3 hrs. 15 min. before 7:00	3:45
2 hrs. 35 min. after 5:25	8:00

page 272

Learn at Home, Grade 4

How Far Is It?

Use your ruler to measure each distance on the map. Then, use the letters on the tires and your answers to solve the message at the bottom of the page.

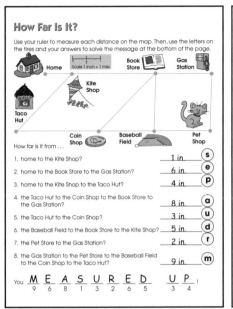

Scale 1 inch = 1 mile

How far is it from . . .

1. home to the Kite Shop? — 1 in. (s)
2. home to the Book Store to the Gas Station? — 6 in. (e)
3. home to the Kite Shop to the Taco Hut? — 4 in. (p)
4. the Taco Hut to the Coin Shop to the Book Store to the Gas Station? — 8 in. (a)
5. the Taco Hut to the Coin Shop? — 3 in. (u)
6. the Baseball Field to the Book Store to the Kite Shop? — 5 in. (d)
7. the Pet Store to the Gas Station? — 2 in. (r)
8. the Gas Station to the Pet Store to the Baseball Field to the Coin Shop to the Taco Hut? — 9 in. (m)

You M E A S U R E D   U P !
     9 6 8 1 3 2 6 5   3 4

page 273

Dudley's Doing It Again!

Dudley is up to his old tricks again. He just finished dog school six weeks ago, and he had really been doing so well. He heeled when Donald said, "heel." He sat when he was supposed to sit. He would even do tricks like roll over, play dead and speak to impress Donald's friends, if Donald gave him a doggy treat. But lately, Dudley hasn't been doing any of the things he was taught.

For the past several days, Dudley has been digging in the yard. This makes Donald's dad really mad. Dudley has also been chewing up the newspapers instead of bringing them to Donald's mom. One day, he chewed up all her grocery coupons. Boy, was she angry! And, Dudley won't sit or heel when Donald tells him to. Two days ago, Dudley knocked down Donald's friend Lee. Something has to be done about Dudley!

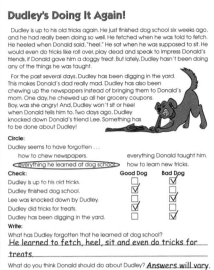

Circle:
Dudley seems to have forgotten . . .
   how to chew newspapers.   everything Donald taught him.
   (everything he learned at dog school)   how to learn new tricks.

Check:

	Good Dog	Bad Dog
Dudley is up to his old tricks.		☑
Dudley finished dog school.	☑	
Lee was knocked down by Dudley.		☑
Dudley did tricks for treats.	☑	
Dudley has been digging in the yard.		☑

Write:
What has Dudley forgotten that he learned at dog school?
He learned to fetch, heel, sit and even do tricks for treats.

What do you think Donald should do about Dudley? __Answers will vary.__
Example: Practice his dog school activities every day.

page 278

The Mystery of the Missing Sweets

Some mysterious person is sneaking away with pieces of desserts from Sam Sillicook's Diner. Help him figure out how much is missing.

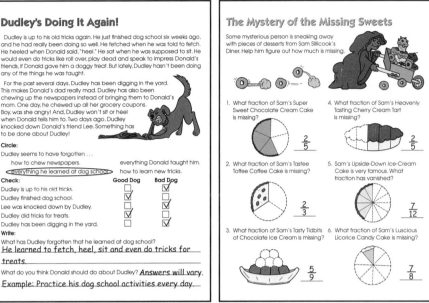

1. What fraction of Sam's Super Sweet Chocolate Cream Cake is missing? — $\frac{2}{5}$

2. What fraction of Sam's Tastee Toffee Coffee Cake is missing? — $\frac{2}{3}$

3. What fraction of Sam's Tasty Tidbits of Chocolate Ice Cream is missing? — $\frac{5}{9}$

4. What fraction of Sam's Heavenly Tasting Cherry Cream Tart is missing? — $\frac{2}{5}$

5. Sam's Upside-Down Ice-Cream Cake is very famous. What fraction has vanished? — $\frac{7}{12}$

6. What fraction of Sam's Luscious Licorice Candy Cake is missing? — $\frac{7}{8}$

page 279

Your State

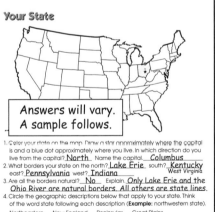

Answers will vary. A sample follows.

1. Color your state on the map. Draw a star approximately where the capital is and a blue dot approximately where you live. In which direction do you live from the capital? __North__ Name the capital. __Columbus__
2. What borders your state on the north? __Lake Erie__ south? __Kentucky__ east? __Pennsylvania__ west? __Indiana__   West Virginia
3. Are all the borders natural? __No__ Explain. __Only Lake Erie and the Ohio River are natural borders. All others are state lines.__
4. Circle the geographic descriptions below that apply to your state. Think of the word state following each description (**Example:** northwestern state).
   Northeastern   New England   Peninsular   Great Plains
   Border   Southwestern   (Midwestern)   Rocky Mountain
   (Inland)   Northwestern   Gulf Coast   Middle Atlantic   Southeastern
5. Write the names of several points of interest in your state. __Cedar Point, Lake Erie, Football Hall of Fame, Rock & Roll Hall of Fame__
6. Select one of the points of interest you would like to visit. Write a sentence or two about it. On the map, put a red dot approximately where it is located __I would love to visit Lake Erie. There are many interesting islands to visit and beautiful beaches for swimming.__

page 280

State Fact Sheet

My state is _____
The date my state entered the Union. _____
It was the _____ state to join the Union.
How many years has it been one of the United States? _____
How many states were already part of the Union when my state entered it? _____
How many states joined the Union after my state? _____
Total area in square miles _____
Rank in size among states _____
How many states are smaller than my state? _____
How many states are larger than my state? _____
Population _____
Rank in population among states _____
How many other states have more people living in them? _____
How many other states have fewer people living in them? _____
What are the names of my state's _____

Answers will vary.

Is the state capital one of the five largest cities? _____
How many people live in these five cities altogether? _____
How many people live in the rest of the state? _____
What are the names of several famous people from my state? _____

Select one of these people about whom to write a few sentences.
_____
_____
_____

page 281

Book Review

A **book review** is a good way to share a favorite book with others. Most good book reviews give facts about the book as well as the writer's opinions. There are many ways to write about a book, but it may be helpful to follow a basic plan.

1. Organize facts about the book.
2. Make notes of your opinions.
3. Write several paragraphs—combining facts and opinions.
4. End with a paragraph which tells why others should read the book.

Choose a favorite book. Use the plan to **write** a short book review.

FACTS   Title: _____
Author: _____   Kind of Book: _____
Setting: _____
Main Characters: _____
Basic Plot: _____
Special Features: _____

Answers will vary.

____ did I like best and why? _____
Was the plot interesting? _____
What was my favorite part? _____
Did the author use interesting language? _____
How would I change the book? _____
Other things I liked best about the book: _____

Some things I did not like: _____

WRITE REVIEW   **SUMMARY**
Use the information above to **write** a review of your book.
I have just read a fascinating book, _____
_____, by _____
Finish writing your review on another sheet of paper.

page 286

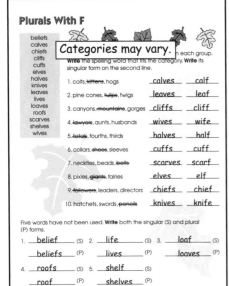

Plurals With F

beliefs
calves
chiefs
cliffs
cuffs
elves
halves
knives
leaves
lives
loaves
roofs
scarves
shelves
wives

Categories may vary. n each group.

Write the spelling word that fits the category. **Write** its singular form on the second line.

1. colts, ~~kittens~~, hogs — **calves** — **calf**
2. pine cones, ~~tulips~~, twigs — **leaves** — **leaf**
3. canyons, ~~mountains~~, gorges — **cliffs** — **cliff**
4. ~~lawyers~~, aunts, husbands — **wives** — **wife**
5. ~~totals~~, fourths, thirds — **halves** — **half**
6. collars, ~~shoes~~, sleeves — **cuffs** — **cuff**
7. neckties, beads, ~~belts~~ — **scarves** — **scarf**
8. pixies, ~~giants~~, fairies — **elves** — **elf**
9. ~~followers~~, leaders, directors — **chiefs** — **chief**
10. hatchets, swords, ~~pencils~~ — **knives** — **knife**

Five words have not been used. **Write** both the singular (S) and plural (P) forms.

1. **belief** (S) 2. **life** (S) 3. **loaf** (S)
   beliefs (P)   **lives** (P)   **loaves** (P)

4. **roofs** (S) 5. **shelf** (S)
   roof (P)   **shelves** (P)

page 287

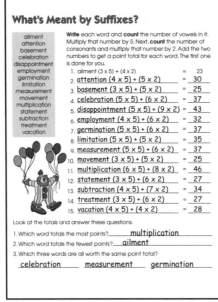

What's Meant by Suffixes?

ailment
attention
basement
celebration
disappointment
employment
germination
limitation
measurement
movement
multiplication
statement
subtraction
treatment
vacation

Write each word and **count** the number of vowels in it. Multiply that number by 5. Next, **count** the number of consonants and multiply that number by 2. Add the two numbers to get a point total for each word. The first one is done for you.

1. ailment (3 x 5) + (4 x 2) = 23
2. attention (4 x 5) + (5 x 2) = **30**
3. basement (3 x 5) + (5 x 2) = **25**
4. celebration (5 x 5) + (6 x 2) = **37**
5. disappointment (5 x 5) + (9 x 2) = **43**
6. employment (4 x 5) + (6 x 2) = **32**
7. germination (5 x 5) + (6 x 2) = **37**
8. limitation (5 x 5) + (5 x 2) = **35**
9. measurement (5 x 5) + (6 x 2) = **37**
10. movement (3 x 5) + (5 x 2) = **25**
11. multiplication (6 x 5) + (8 x 2) = **46**
12. statement (3 x 5) + (6 x 2) = **27**
13. subtraction (4 x 5) + (7 x 2) = **34**
14. treatment (3 x 5) + (6 x 2) = **27**
15. vacation (4 x 5) + (4 x 2) = **28**

Look at the totals and answer these questions.

1. Which word totals the most points? **multiplication**
2. Which word totals the fewest points? **ailment**
3. Which three words are all worth the same point total?

celebration **measurement** **germination**

page 292

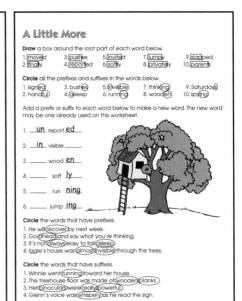

A Little More

Draw a box around the root part of each word below.
1. moved 3. pushes 5. invited 7. jumpy 9. slapped
2. finally 4. reported 6. softly 8. privately 10. parents

Circle all the prefixes and suffixes in the words below.
1. signed 3. bushes 5. invisible 7. thinking 9. Saturdays
2. handful 4. asleep 6. running 8. wooden 10. spying

Add a prefix or suffix to each word below to make a new word. The new word may be one already used on this worksheet.

1. **un** report ed
2. **in** visible
3. _____ wood en
4. _____ soft ly
5. _____ run ning
6. _____ jump ing

Circle the words that have prefixes.
1. He will recover by next week.
2. Go ahead and say what you're thinking.
3. It's not always easy to fall asleep.
4. Iggie's house was almost invisible through the trees.

Circle the words that have suffixes.
1. Winnie went running toward her house.
2. The treehouse floor was made of wooden planks.
3. Her binoculars were really powerful.
4. Glenn's voice was whispery as he read the sign.

page 293

Who Says?

Write fact or **opinion** in the blanks to show which each sentence is.

Some answers will vary.

1. "Peanut butter ... thirsty." — **opinion**
2. Because ... ate all the sandwiches, Glenn paid ... pops. — **fact**
3. The blue lake looked sparkling and pretty to Winnie. — **opinion**
4. Glen rowed to the middle of the lake. — **fact**
5. Winnie needed new shoes for school. — **fact**
6. Winnie thought that Wednesday would be a good day to play. — **opinion**
7. Mrs. Barringer thinks that moving is too much trouble. — **opinion**
8. Mr. Barringer was snoring after reading the Sunday papers. — **fact**
9. Winnie thought her parents didn't care about the Garbers. — **opinion**
10. The letter to Iggie said that Winnie missed her. — **fact**
11. Winnie liked how her hair looked. — **opinion**
12. Winnie's family went to pick up her brother. — **fact**

page 294

Shortening Words

aren't
couldn't
doesn't
hasn't
he'd
I'd
she's
should've
they'll
wasn't
weren't
what's
who'd
won't
you've

Write each contraction and the two words that form it.
1. **aren't** — **are** — **not**
2. **couldn't** — **could** — **not**
3. **doesn't** — **does** — **not**
4. **hasn't** — **has** — **not**
5. **he'd** — **he** — **would**
6. **I'd** — **I** — **would**
7. **she's** — **she** — **is**
8. **should've** — **should** — **have**
9. **they'll** — **they** — **will**
10. **wasn't** — **was** — **not**
11. **weren't** — **were** — **not**
12. **what's** — **what** — **is**
13. **who'd** — **who** — **would**
14. **won't** — **will** — **not**
15. **you've** — **you** — **have**

Sometimes a contraction can represent different words. **Circle** the correct answer in each of the following.
1. In the sentence, "He'd had a cold," the **'d** stands for ...
   a. would b. had c. did
2. In the sentence, "He'd like to go," the **'d** stands for ...
   a. would b. had c. did
3. In the question "Who'd volunteer?" the **'d** stands for ...
   a. would b. had c. did
4. In the question "Who'd you say it was?" the **'d** stands for ...
   a. would b. had c. did

page 300

A Picture Is Worth . . .

Look at the first picture. Put a check in the box by each sentence which seems sensible. Look at the second picture. **Write** six sentences that tell your conclusions about the picture.

☑ It is a very hot day.
☑ The beach is a popular place to go.
☐ The beach is a quiet place to study.
☑ Some people picnic at the beach.
☑ A lifeguard helps protect swimmers.
☐ It is hard to nap at a noisy beach.
☐ Sailing is just for kids.
☑ Sailing and swimming are fun water sports.
☐ Every town has a beach.

Answers will vary. own conclusions. Examples:
1. **It is fall**
2. **The yard needs to be raked.**
3. _____
4. _____
5. _____
6. _____

page 301

Learn at Home, Grade 4

Animal Trivia

1. An earthworm is 14.9 cm long. A grasshopper is 8.7 cm long. What is the difference?

   6.2 cm

2. A pocket gopher has a hind foot 3.5 cm long. A ground squirrel's hind foot is 6.4 cm long. How much longer is the ground squirrel's hind foot?

   2.9 cm

5. A cottontail rabbit has ears which are 6.8 cm long. A jackrabbit has ears 12.9 cm long. How much shorter is the cottontail's ear?

   6.1 cm

3. A porcupine has a tail 30.0 cm long. An opossum has a tail 53.5 cm long. How much longer is the opossum's tail?

   23.5 cm

6. The hind foot of a river otter is 14.6 cm long. The hind foot of a hog-nosed skunk is 9.0 cm long. What is the difference?

   5.6 cm

4. A wood rat has a tail which is 23.6 cm long. A deer mouse has a tail 12.2 cm long. What is the difference between the two?

   11.4 cm

7. A rock mouse is 26.1 cm long. His tail adds another 14.4 cm. What is his total length from his nose to the tip of his tail?

   40.5 cm

page 302

Grouping Letters

scheme
scholar
school
schooner
scratch
scream
screw
scrimmage
scrub
straight
strainer
strength
string
stripe
struggle

Cross out the word that does not belong in each group. **Write** the spelling word that fits the category.

1. filter, mixture, sieve __strainer__
2. pinch, claw, rip __scratch__
3. rope, leather, cord __string__
4. college, academy, apartment __school__
5. soil, wash, clean __scrub__
6. power, weakness, force __strength__
7. tramp, pupil, learner __scholar__
8. fight, conflict, agreement __struggle__
9. laugh, yell, cry __scream__
10. plan, vacation, plot __scheme__
11. nail, bolt, hammer __screw__
12. ship, locomotive, vessel __schooner__
13. band, line, cable __straight__

Which two words were not used? __stripe__ __scrimmage__

Write one sentence using both words. __Sentence will vary.__

page 308

From Whose Point of View?

Read each sentence below. Decide if it is the first or third person's point of view. If it is a first person's point of view, **rewrite** the sentence to make it a third person's point of view. If it is a third person's point of view, **rewrite** it to make it a first person's point of view.

Answers may include:

1. I wanted to tell Anh and Thant the secret of our leaving, but I had given my word.

Cindy wanted to tell Anh and Thant the secret of their leaving, but she had given her word.

2. The grandmother did not want to go aboard the boat.

I did not want to go aboard the boat.

3. The people on shore were pushing to get on the deck of the boat.

We were pushing to get on the deck of the boat.

4. Though I had worked many days in the rice paddies watching planes fly over, I never thought I'd be on one.

Though Loi had worked many days in the rice paddies watching planes fly over, he never thought he'd be on one.

5. Loi made a net from pieces of string and caught a turtle with his new device.

I made a net from pieces of string and caught a turtle with it.

6. I know of a place where we can wash our clothes.

Anh knows of a place where everyone can wash their clothes.

7. The officer looked at them with great interest.

The officer looked at us with great interest.

8. When I looked into the harbor, I could see the shape of the sampan boats.

When she looked into the harbor she could see the shape of the sampan boats.

9. This is my duck and I choose to share it with everyone for the celebration of Tet.

This is their duck and they choose to share it with everyone for the celebration of Tet.

page 309

Gliding Graphics

Draw the lines as directed from point to point for each graph.

Draw a line from:
F,7 to D,1
D,1 to I,6
I,6 to N,8
N,8 to M,3
M,3 to F,1
F,1 to G,4
G,4 to E,4
E,4 to B,1
B,1 to A,8
A,8 to D,11
D,11 to F,9
F,9 to F,7
F,7 to I,9
I,9 t6 I,6
I,6 to F,7

Draw a line from:
J, ◼ to N, ◣
N, ◣ to U, ◣
U, ◣ to Z, ◼
Z, ◼ to X, ❖
X, ❖ to U, ◣
U, ◣ to S, ◙
S, ◙ to N, ◣
N, ◣ to N, ◙
N, ◙ to J, ◙
J, ◼ to L, ▥
L, ▥ to Y, ▥
Y, ▥ to Z, ◼
Z, ◼ to L, ◼
L, ◼ to J, ◼

page 310

Steps to Knighthood Crossword

Across
1. Garment worn by a squire during his knighting ceremony.
4. Island country that was the home of King Arthur and the Knights of the Round Table.
8. War games played by knights on horseback in hand-to-hand combat.
11. Place where the king received visitors, performed ceremonies and held balls.
12. Name of the ceremony during which a squire became a knight.
14. What every knight swore to his king.
15. A noble who has trained and proven himself to be worthy of this title.

Down
2. Code of honor that all true knights followed.
3. The time in history also known as the Middle Ages.
5. To be kind and polite.
6. The first step to becoming a knight.
7. The second step to becoming a knight.
9. Name of the upper class during the Middle Ages.
10. Proving that you deserve an honor—you are _____.
13. To not eat in order to purify yourself.

page 311

Comparison Words

biggest
brighter
clumsiest
crazier
cruelest
earlier
firmer
flattest
greener
noisiest
prettier
quietest
simpler
tastiest
widest

All the spelling words are adjectives that can be used to compare people, places or things. An **er** ending is used to compare two things; **est** is used to compare three or more. **Fill in** the chart below with spelling words and the other missing word that completes the comparison.

List Word	Adding er	Adding est
1. big	**bigger**	**biggest**
2. **bright**	**brighter**	brightest
3. clumsy	**clumsier**	**clumsiest**
4. **crazy**	**crazier**	craziest
5. **cruel**	crueler	**cruelest**
6. **early**	**earlier**	earliest
7. firm	**firmer**	**firmest**
8. **flat**	flatter	**flattest**
9. green	**greener**	**greenest**
10. **noise**	noisier	**noisiest**
11. **pretty**	**prettier**	prettiest
12. quiet	**quieter**	**quietest**
13. **simple**	**simpler**	simplest
14. **tasty**	tastier	**tastiest**
15. **wide**	wider	**widest**

page 316

Spinner Fun

Using what you know about probability, try to predict how many times your spinner would land on the following numbers if you were to spin the spinner 20 times.

Predictions

	Number of Times
Spinning a 1	
Spinning a 2	
Spinning a 3	
Spinning a 4	

Now, actually spin the spinner 20 times... ...s with what you actually s... ...er spins.

Answers will vary.

	Number of Times
Spinning a 1	
Spinning a 2	
Spinning a 3	
Spinning a 4	

Examples:
1. Were your predictions close to the actual? __yes__

2. What did you notice about your predictions and the actual spinning? __Some were less and some were more.__

3. Why do you think this is? __Probability is not certain.__

page 317

More Spinner Fun

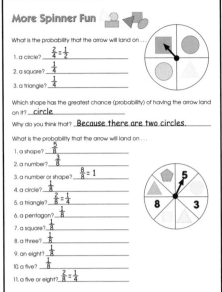

What is the probability that the arrow will land on . . .
1. a circle? $\frac{2}{4} = \frac{1}{2}$
2. a square? $\frac{1}{4}$
3. a triangle? $\frac{1}{4}$

Which shape has the greatest chance (probability) of having the arrow land on it? __circle__

Why do you think that? __Because there are two circles.__

What is the probability that the arrow will land on . . .
1. a shape? $\frac{5}{8}$
2. a number? $\frac{3}{8}$
3. a number or shape? $\frac{8}{8} = 1$
4. a circle? $\frac{1}{8}$
5. a triangle? $\frac{2}{8} = \frac{1}{4}$
6. a pentagon? $\frac{1}{8}$
7. a square? $\frac{1}{8}$
8. a three? $\frac{1}{8}$
9. an eight? $\frac{1}{8}$
10. a five? $\frac{1}{8}$
11. a five or eight? $\frac{2}{8} = \frac{1}{4}$

page 318

Same Spelling But . . .

bass
bowl
close
cobbler
does
file
flounder
grave
hawk
list
minute
object
paddle
present
sow

Homophones are words that have the same spelling but are different in meaning and sometimes pronunciation. Use the spelling words to **fill in** the blanks. Indicate the part of speech in the parentheses. The same word is used twice in each sentence.

1. The secretary wanted to __file__ (V) her fingernails before she put all the papers in the __file__ (N).
2. Before my dad goes to __bowl__ (V), he eats a big __bowl__ (N) of cereal.
3. Our __paddle__ (N) broke, the boat overturned and we had to __paddle__ (V) quite a distance.
4. The __bass__ (A) singer enjoys fishing for __bass__ (V).
5. The ship's captain was reading the __list__ (N) of passengers when he suddenly felt the ship __list__ (V).
6. After the __cobbler__ (N) has repaired shoes all day, he enjoys eating a fruit __cobbler__ (N).
7. The __flounder__ (N) was hooked tightly, but I couldn't reel it in, so it began to __flounder__ (V) in the shallow water.
8. As the peddler was getting ready to __hawk__ (V) his vegetables, a hungry __hawk__ (N) was perched on a nearby tree branch.
9. The company hired to dig the __grave__ (N) realized the cemetery needed __grave__ (A) attention.

Circle the correct pronunciation and **write** the word on the line.
1. The president was so __close__ I could shake his hand. klōz (klōs)
2. Three __does__ were nibbling grass by the road. (dōz) dŭz
3. After doing our research, we had to __present__ a report. prĕz' ent (prĭ zĕnt')
4. The gardener will __sow__ grass seed for a new lawn. (sō) sou

page 324

The Crusades

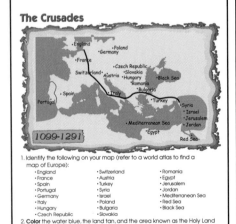

1099-1291

1. Identify the following on your map (refer to a world atlas to find a map of Europe):
   - England
   - France
   - Spain
   - Portugal
   - Germany
   - Italy
   - Hungary
   - Czech Republic
   - Switzerland
   - Austria
   - Turkey
   - Syria
   - Israel
   - Poland
   - Bulgaria
   - Slovakia
   - Romania
   - Egypt
   - Jerusalem
   - Jordan
   - Mediterranean Sea
   - Red Sea
   - Black Sea
2. **Color** the water blue, the land tan, and the area known as the Holy Land purple.
3. Using an encyclopedia, **draw** the route that Christian knights traveled when going to the Holy Land during the Crusades.
4. Why did the Christians, Muslims and Jews call Jerusalem the Holy Land? __It was the region where Jesus Christ lived.__
5. If you were a Crusader from France, would you travel to the Holy Land by land or sea? __Mainly land__ Why? __You can see the most direct route by the path of the crusades.__

page 325

Bizarre Bazaar!

board
bored
coarse
council
counsel
course
creak
creek
knot
lead
led
not
ring
who's
whose
wring

Three pairs of homophones are not next to each other in the spelling list because of alphabetical order. **Write** those three pairs.
a. __coarse__ a. __knot__ a. __ring__
b. __course__ b. __not__ b. __wring__

Fill in the blanks with spelling words. Not all words are used.
1. The pipe was made out of l e a d.
2. She broke the b o a r d with a karate chop.
3. In scouting, he learned to tie a k n o t.
4. Students will elect class members to the student c o u n c i l.
5. The umpire shouted, "W h o s e bat is this?"
6. Grandpa gave me good c o u n s e l whenever I had important decisions to make.
7. With nothing to do, I am b o r e d.
8. It is n o t nice to hit anyone.
9. The c o a r s e material made my arms itch.
10. The hikers followed a c o u r s e to the north.
11. The thief stole a diamond r i n g.
12. We sailed paper boats in the c r e e k.
13. The old floor started to c r e a k when I walked across it.

Match the boxed letter from each sentence to the numbered lines below to answer the riddle: Why was the man happy to get a job at the bakery?

B e c a u s e   h e   k n e a d e d
7 9 13 2 4 10 9   5 9   12 6 9 2 1 9 1
t h e   d o u g h.
3 5 9   1 8 4 11 5

page 330

What Probably Happened?

Each sentence below tells of something which happened after something else happened first. Read each sentence. **Write** two different things which could have caused the second thing to happen.

1. The dog ran back with a bone in its mouth.
   What happened before? Examples: 1. __The dog deserved a treat.__
   2. __The dog found the bone.__
2. Paula said "Thank you" to her friend Kelly.
   What happened before? 1. __Kelly gave her a gift.__
   2. __Kelly opened the door for her.__
3. The pilot said that he was making an emergency landing.
   What happened before? 1. _____
   2. _____

Answers will vary.

4. The audi... ...pause.
   What hap...
5. Pete sat in total exhaustion at the edge of the lake.
   What happened before? 1. _____
   2. _____
6. The restaurant owner apologized to the Carr family.
   What happened before? 1. _____

page 331

Number Puzzles

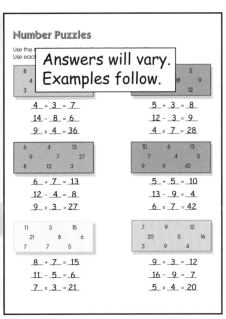

Answers will vary. Examples follow.

4 + 3 = 7
14 - 8 = 6
9 x 4 = 36

5 + 3 = 8
12 - 3 = 9
4 x 7 = 28

6 + 7 = 13
12 - 4 = 8
9 x 3 = 27

5 + 5 = 10
13 - 9 = 4
6 x 7 = 42

8 + 7 = 15
11 - 5 = 6
7 x 3 = 21

9 + 3 = 12
16 - 9 = 7
5 x 4 = 20

page 332

Proofreading

It is important to be able to proofread things that you write to correct any errors.

Read each paragraph. Proofread for these errors:
• indentation
• punctuation
• capitalization
• sentence
• spelling
• run-on

Answers may vary.

Rewrite each paragraph correctly on the lines.

1. my brother will graduate from high school this week everyone is so excited for him Many of our relatives are coming from out of town for his graduation our town has a university. mom and Dad have planed a big surprise party

My brother will graduate from high school this week. Everyone is so excited for him. Many of our relatives are coming from out of town for his graduation. Mom and Dad have planned a big surprise party.

2. riding in a hot air balloon is an incredible experience first, everyone climbs into the basket the pilot then starts the fuel which produces the hot air that makes the ballone rise. The road leads to an open field to lower the balloon, the pilot gradually releases air

Riding in a hot air balloon is an incredible experience. First, everyone climbs into the basket. The pilot then starts the fuel which produces the hot air that makes the balloon rise. To lower the balloon, the pilot gradualtly releases air.

3. A caterpillar is a young butterfly. The caterpillar originally hatches from an egg. Later, it develops a hard case around its body. Inside the case, the caterpillar becomes a butterfly. After a short time, the case opens and a beautiful butterfly flies out.

page 342

Changing Tenses

accepted
admiring
captured
choking
dining
dozed
fanning
guarded
hoping
invited
pledged
practicing
proving
rearranged
squeezing

For each spelling word, **write** the present tense of the verb. Watch out for missing or extra letters.

1. accept
2. admire
3. capture
4. choke
5. dine
6. doze
7. fan
8. guard
9. hope
10. invite
11. pledge
12. practice
13. prove
14. rearrange
15. squeeze

Complete the word search. The 30 words are written vertically, horizontally, and diagonally.

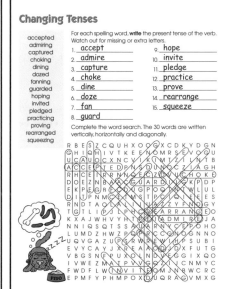

page 343

Identifying Operations

Fill in the correct sign for each problem.

5 (+) 5 = 10 · 14 (+) 59 = 73 · 21 (+) 9 = 30 · 36 (+) 63 = 99
9 (×) 9 = 81 · 56 (+) 17 = 73 · 64 (+) 8 = 8 · 6 (×) 9 = 54
56 (−) 8 = 48 · 40 (+) 5 = 8 · 7 (×) 8 = 56 · 33 (+) 57 = 90
91 (−) 16 = 75 · 9 (×) 3 = 27 · 76 (−) 19 = 57 · 27 (+) 3 = 9
54 (+) 6 = 9 · 29 (+) 37 = 66 · 43 (+) 7 = 50 · 63 (−) 9 = 54
28 (−) 17 = 11 · 6 (×) 5 = 30 · 4 (×) 9 = 36 · 8 (+) 38 = 46
25 (+) 5 = 5 · 36 (−) 5 = 31 · 48 (+) 8 = 6 · 2 (×) 9 = 18
72 (+) 9 = 63 · 56 (+) 8 = 7 · 9 (×) 1 = 9 · 55 (+) 37 = 92
64 (+) 8 = 56 · 7 (×) 1 = 7 · 45 (+) 5 = 9 · 81 (+) 9 = 9
36 (+) 4 = 9 · 57 (−) 9 = 48 · 36 (+) 27 = 63 · 80 (−) 17 = 63
45 (+) 5 = 40 · 7 (×) 6 = 42 · 48 (−) 6 = 42 · 32 (+) 4 = 8
82 (+) 9 = 91 · 8 (×) 8 = 64 · 9 (×) 8 = 72 · 71 (+) 15 = 86
17 (+) 77 = 94 · 40 (−) 6 = 34 · 47 (−) 38 = 9 · 56 (−) 9 = 47
36 (−) 6 = 30 · 15 (+) 38 = 53 · 3 (×) 6 = 18 · 5 (×) 9 = 45
72 (+) 8 = 9 · 43 (+) 48 = 91 · 27 (+) 18 = 45 · 6 (×) 6 = 36
49 (+) 7 = 7 · 7 (×) 7 = 49 · 8 (×) 3 = 24 · 16 (+) 16 = 32

page 344

What's the Story?

Create a story just for fun! Choose the kind of story you want to write. Now, brainstorm for ideas. **Write** your ideas on the correct lines below.

Kind of Story (mystery, adventure, etc.)

I. Setting (where and when the story takes place)
A. Where ___ Description ___
B. When ___

II. Plot (events of the story)
List main events in order
A. ___
B. ___
C. ___
D. ___

III. Characters (who is in the story)
A. Name ___ Description ___
B. Name ___ Description ___
C. Name ___ Description ___
D. Name ___ Description ___

Answers will vary.

Use your ideas to write a story. Remember to tell the story in the correct time order. Organize the events into a **beginning**, **middle** and **ending** section of the story.

Finish your story on another sheet of paper

page 350

Siege the Castle

Find these words:

BATTERING RAM · BATTLEMENTS · PORTCULLIS
VULNERABLE · BALLISTA · CATAPULT
CROSSBOW · RANSOM · VASSAL
RIVAL · SIEGE · KEEP

page 352

Write Government Officials

The government needs to hear from kids just like you! Our nation's leaders and the leaders of other countries need to hear our concerns. Most government officials welcome letters and want to know your thoughts.

Write letters that clearly state what you are concerned about and why you are concerned. Using the information that you have learned will help influence the people who make decisions about the laws and funding that govern the safety of our planet.

NO MATTER HOW YOUNG YOU ARE
YOU CAN MAKE A DIFFERENCE.

Here are some addresses of where to write to our government officials.

Representative _____
US House of Representatives
Washington DC 20515

Senator _____
US Senate
Washington DC 20510

(You will need to know the names of your state's Senators and Representatives.)

President _____
The White House
1600 Pennsylvania Ave.
Washington DC 20500
(Begin your letter, "Dear Mr. President.")

If you wish to write to the leaders of other foreign countries, request the proper address from:

(Country's Name) Embassy
The United Nations,
United Nations Plaza
New York, NY 10017

Organizations to Contact

The Acid Rain Foundation
1630 Blackhawk Hills
St. Paul, MN 55122

Acid Rain Information
Clearinghouse Library
Center for Environmental Information, Inc.
33 S. Washington St.
Rochester, NY 14608

Adopt-A-Stream Foundation
P.O. Box 5558
Everett, WA 98201

Air Pollution Control
Bureau of National Affairs Inc.
1231 25th St. NW
Washington DC 20037

Alliance To Save Energy
1925 K St. NW
Suite 206
Washington DC 20036

American Association of Zoological Parks and Aquariums
Oglebay Park
Wheeling, WV 26003

American Wind Energy Association
1730 N Lynn St.
Suite 610
Arlington, VA 22209

Canadian Coalition On Acid Rain
112 St. Clair Ave. West
Suite 504
Toronto, Ontario, Canada
M4V 2Y3

Center for Marine Conservation
1725 DeSales St. NW
Suite 500
Washington DC 20036

Friends of the Earth
530 Seventh St. SE
Washington DC 20003

Global Releaf, c/o the American Forestry Association
P.O. Box 2000
Washington DC 20013

Greenpeace
1436 U Street NW
Washington DC 20009

Household Hazardous Waste Project
901 S. National Ave.
Box 108
Springfield, MO 65804

National Association of Recycling Industries
330 Madison Ave.
New York, NY 10017

National Clean Air Coalition
530 7th St. SE
Washington DC 20003

National Wildlife Federation
1412 16th St. NW
Washington DC 20036

Public Affairs Office
US Environmental Protection Agency
Washington DC 20036

Renew America
1400 16th St. NW
Suite 710
Washington DC 20036

Save the Manatee Club
500 N. Maitland Ave.
Suite 200
Maitland, FL 32751

U.S. Environmental Protection Agency
401 M St. SW
Washington DC 20460

United Nations Environment Programme
North American Office
Room DC2-0803, United Nations
New York, NY 10017